The Hebrew-Christian Messiah

The Hebrew-Christian Messiah

Or The Presentation of the Messiah to the Jews in the Gospel according to St. Matthew

Being Twelve Lectures delivered before the Honourable Society of Lincoln's Inn on the Foundation of Bishop Warburton in the years 1911-1915

By

A. LUKYN WILLIAMS, D.D.

Vicar of Guilden Morden & Hon. Canon of Ely Cathedral, formerly Tyrwhitt Hebrew Scholar in the University of Cambridge

With an Introductory Note by
THE BISHOP OF ELY

PUBLISHERS
Eugene, Oregon

"And I beleue also and professe, that Jesu Christe is not only Jesus, and lorde to all menne that beleue in him, but also that he is my Jesus, my god, and my lorde."

The Institution of a Christian man, 1537, *p.* 2 § 2.

Wipf and Stock Publishers
199 West 8th Avenue, Suite 3
Eugene, Oregon 97401

The Hebrew-Christian Messiah
or the Presentation of the Messiah to the Jews in the Gospel according to St. Matthew
By Williams, A. Lukyn
ISBN: 1-59244-705-8
Publication date 5/19/2004
Previously published by SPCK, 1916

Introductory Note

By the Bishop of Ely

DR. LUKYN WILLIAMS has asked me to write a few words of preface to the Lectures contained in this volume. Such a preface, I confess, seems to me unnecessary; for the Lectures themselves make their sufficient appeal to any one who has a genuine interest in the great problems with which they deal. I cannot, however, refuse the request of a friendship which is 'hastening to fulfil' its fortieth year.

There is no subject within the whole range of Christian theology which in so high a degree demands for its treatment reverence, honesty, sobriety, knowledge, scholarship, as the early history of the doctrine of our Lord's Person. Moreover, in the scientific prosecution of this study it seems to be essential that the careful investigation of each small section of the whole field should prepare the way for the work of generalisation. For many reasons the Gospel according to St. Matthew holds a position of singular significance. And this Gospel is the one which Dr. Lukyn Williams has chosen as his subject.

Many years ago he allowed me to read the proofs of a work of his dealing with part of this same Gospel. I was then able to give a good deal of time to what he had written. And I at once saw that he possessed those qualifications which I have indicated above. In particular I learned much from his wide acquaintance with Jewish literature and thought both ancient and

INTRODUCTORY NOTE

modern; and since then he has been continually adding to his store.

Though now with but little leisure at my disposal I have read with some care what I believe to be the most characteristic parts of these Lectures. And of this I am sure, that the arguments and the conclusions set forth in the following pages are the outcome of first-hand knowledge and of long-continued thought, and are a contribution of real importance to the study of a group of momentous problems.

F. H. ELY.

St. Matthew's Day, 1916.

Preface

THE following Lectures are, in the first place, an attempt to understand the motives with which the author of the First Gospel composed his book, and to interpret his words in the sense in which he desired the contemporary believers of his own race to apprehend them. This is not easy for us who live in the twentieth century, and have been brought up in Christian and non-Jewish surroundings. But the attempt must be made.

Secondly, they desire to be more than only academic, and, as occasion offers, to expound the teaching of St. Matthew in its relation to ourselves. In this there is nothing new. Almost every commentator on the Gospel, perhaps every single one before the nineteenth century, has tried to draw out some of its moral and spiritual lessons for the men of his own day. The only direction in which the present writer can hope to have anything fresh to bring forward is to be found in the light which the First Gospel sheds when it is studied, so far as may be possible, in the spirit, and from the point of view, of its Hebrew-Christian author.

Thirdly, the writer hopes that incidentally his work may be of service in the cause of presenting Christ to the Jews of to-day, whether by a more exact statement to them of the nature of portions of Christian truth than is generally offered, or by a clearer elucidation to Christians of the difficulties felt by many Jews in accepting the Lord Jesus.

PREFACE

It may be that to those whose studies have not been directed towards Jewish thought and literature a few of the details of the exposition will seem strange. This is perhaps even inevitable, for that growth in our knowledge of the Lord Jesus Christ, our blessed Saviour and Redeemer, which the Holy Spirit has been commissioned to unfold to us, implies that earlier conceptions must be replaced by new, and we are all well aware that the adjustment of old to new, of past to present, which is the unfailing mark of vitality in every part of creation, may bring surface scars, while it developes and perfects the life.

But the writer prays that every word he has uttered may tend to ' the light of the knowledge of the glory of God in the face of Christ.'

P.S.—The author regrets that his Lectures were completed and delivered before the publication of books which would otherwise have been of much assistance to him, in particular Dr. McNeile's *Commentary on the Gospel according to St. Matthew*, Dr. Headlam's *The Miracles of the New Testament*, Dr. Illingworth's *The Gospel Miracles*, and the recent volume of his friend Canon Box, *The Virgin Birth of Jesus : a critical examination of the Gospel-narratives of the Nativity, and other New Testament and early Christian evidence, and the alleged influence of heathen ideas.*

Contents

	PAGE
INTRODUCTORY NOTE by the Bishop of Ely	v
PREFACE	vii

LECTURE ONE

INTRODUCTORY — THE GENEALOGY — THE BIRTH TO THE MANIFESTATION IN GALILEE — THE EVANGELIST'S USE OF SCRIPTURE

INTRODUCTION

Hebrew-Christians after the Fall of Jerusalem needed encouragement 3
They already possessed St. Mark and 'Q' . . 4
Why the author wrote in Greek 6
The duty of modern Christians to present Christ to modern Jews 8
Plan of the Lectures stated 10
Materials for learning the representation of the Messiah current among Jews c. 25 A.D. . . ,,
The new facts compelled a modification of such a representation, the result being Christianity . . 12
I. THE GENEALOGY—its form and meaning . . 14
II. THE VIRGIN-BIRTH. Isa. vii. 14 considered. How far St. Matthew regarded it as a 'proof' . . 20
III. THE PLACE—BETHLEHEM. Micah v. 2 considered 26
   The visit of the Magi 28
IV. THE FLIGHT TO EGYPT. Hosea xi. 1 . . . 30
V. THE MASSACRE OF THE INNOCENTS. Jer. xxxi. (xxxviii.) 15 31
VI. NAZARETH 33
VII. THE MESSIAH AND JOHN THE BAPTIST, the true Elijah 34

CONTENTS

		PAGE
VIII.	THE BAPTISM AND THE VOICE	39
IX.	THE TEMPTATION	41
X.	THE MANIFESTATION IN GALILEE	46

LECTURE TWO

THE JEWISH PARTIES IN THE TIME OF THE MESSIAH, ESPECIALLY THE PHARISEES

I. THE ESSENES	51
II. THE SADDUCEES	53
The name from the Zadok in David's time, and its application connected with the claim of the High Priests to be 'sons of Zadok'	,,
But including nobles as well as members of the High Priestly family	54
Pro-Roman in politics, and both conservative and worldly in religion	55
Described in the *Assumption of Moses*	57
Passages in this Gospel dealing with them	59
III. THE PHARISEES	62
1. The Scribes	,,
Oral law a necessity when there is a code	63
Their origin and history	64
Passages in this Gospel implying that some became Christians	67
But most were opposed to Christ	68
2. The Pharisees as such	72
i. Their connexion with the Assidæans	,,
ii. The ordinary members of the party, of which the leaders were scribes	,,
iii. The name and their history	,,

CONTENTS

	PAGE
iv. Two points of extreme importance . . .	74
They had little authority in the time of our Lord	,,
They themselves were divided into two parties, the harsher having the greater power . .	,,
3. Passages in this Gospel dealing with them . .	76
i. Our Lord's indictment	,,
ii. The favourable opinion of them expressed by many modern scholars	80
iii. Suggested explanations of the severity of the Gospels	83
The probable solution	89
The verdicts of St. Paul and the Messiah hold good to-day	92

LECTURE THREE

MESSIAH, THE HEALER OF DISEASE

Twenty years ago apologists believed in miracles because they first believed in Christ: now they are reverting to the earlier order, and the place of miracles in the evidence to Christ is being recognised	97
I. THE POSITION OF MIRACLES IN ST. MATTHEW'S PRESENTATION OF THE MESSIAH TO THE JEWS .	98
1. The impossibility of severing the miracles from the history	,,
2. The Jews did not deny the fact of Christ's miracles, but attributed them to demonic power . .	99
3. Miracles at heathen temples, and down to our own time	103
4. How far St. Matthew regarded the miracles as evidence for the Messiahship	105

CONTENTS

	PAGE
II. THE POSITION OF MIRACLES IN THE EVIDENCES FOR CHRISTIANITY TO-DAY	113
1. The classification of our Lord's miracles . .	,,
2. The explanation of them	114
i. 'Functional diseases'	,,
ii. 'Organic'	116
iii. The raising of the dead	119
iv. On inanimate nature	120
3. The relation of our Lord to His miracles . .	,,
i. Non-Biblical cures examined	121
ii. In the case of our Lord	122
a. No evidence that He claimed to perform His miracles by His own power as God . .	123
b. He the Ideal, or Archetypal, Man doubtless combined in Himself all powers which are intrinsically human	,,
c. The explanation suggested by the Evangelist is that they are the result of His bearing on Himself sickness and its cause . . .	125
d. Christ's own explanation of miracles wrought by His disciples is that they were performed by God in answer to prayer . . .	126
iii. We thus have left to us three possible methods by which our Lord performed His miracles, and probably all three were combined . .	,,
The use of His human powers, Utter self-sacrifice for men, Faith on His Father in heaven . . .	,,
4. His miracles are evidence to Him on the predictive side and the moral	128
APPENDIX. A few examples of non-Biblical miracles of healing	131

CONTENTS

LECTURE FOUR

THE MESSIAH AS TEACHER—HIS ORIGINALITY

	PAGE
I. CURRENTS OF THOUGHT LIKELY TO INFLUENCE HIM	143
1. Not Buddhist	144
Nor Persian (belonging to His time), nor Greek directly	145
2. But Hellenism as seen in the Apocrypha	146
and the Pseudepigraphic books, in proportion as these were akin to the Old Testament	,,
Influence of Apocalyptic teaching in the home-life of our Lord	147
3. The Oral Law was necessary if the Law was treated as a code	148
But the contents of the Oral Law in our Lord's day cannot be defined, and it is uncritical to illustrate Jewish life and thought in His time by statements in later books	149
It is very improbable that sayings common to the New Testament and the Rabbis were borrowed by the latter	151
II. HOW FAR HE WAS AFFECTED BY THESE CURRENTS	152
St. Matthew says so much of Him as Teacher that he may contrast Him with Jewish teachers	,,
1. The form of His teaching had much in common with theirs, especially externally:	154
Parables. Hyperbole. Pithy sayings	,,
The Discourses, were they spoken as they stand?	157
Quotations from the Old Testament	,,
2. His independence, and the originality of His treatment	158

CONTENTS

	PAGE
A fundamental difference; He does not appeal to authority	158
No sign of eclecticism, or of systematisation	159
He raises every question to a higher plane through His character and personality	160
We have thus seen both the influence of current thought upon Him, and His originality	161
This shown from the Lord's Prayer	,,
and His great Commandment of Love	167

LECTURE FIVE

THE MESSIAH AS TEACHER—THE PERMANENCE OF THE LAW

The Messiah states that the Law is permanent	181
I. WHAT DID HE MEAN BY THE 'LAW'?	182
II. WHAT KIND OF PERMANENCE DID HE ATTRIBUTE TO IT?	183
Not the literal observance of its details, as the Orthodox Jews insist	,,
Nor the observance only of its more important parts, as the Reform Jews teach	184
Nor the observance of the written in contrast to the oral Law	186
But the principles and truths lying at the base of the details	187
Such a kind of permanence is not wholly contradictory to Rabbinic teaching, though an attempt is made to combine with it the literal observance	190
III. DID HE MAKE ANY DISTINCTION BETWEEN HIS JEWISH AND HIS GENTILE FOLLOWERS?	191
No, for during His life on earth He had, we may say, no Gentile followers	192

CONTENTS

IV. ARE JEWISH CHRISTIANS AT LIBERTY TO OBSERVE THE JEWISH LAW LITERALLY, EITHER IN ITS DETAILS OR IN ITS MORE IMPORTANT PARTS? . 193

    This appears to be contrary to the kind of permanence attributed to the Law by Christ . . . ,,

    And in any case is not possible in the present landless condition of the Jewish nation. (*See* Appendix.) ,,

V. WHAT RELATION DOES THE MESSIAH'S STATEMENT OF THE PERMANENCE OF THE LAW HOLD TO ST. PAUL'S VERDICT THAT IT WAS OF A TEMPORARY CHARACTER? 194

    The true meaning of the word *Torah* . . . ,,

    St. Paul did not misinterpret it, and in any case he was not writing to theologians 199

    He regarded its external observance, the Messiah its inner depths 200

VI. WHAT RELATION DOES CHRIST'S TEACHING AS A WHOLE, THE GOSPEL, HOLD TO THE LAW? . . 201

    It is not a second Law, although the word has been used of it, with a lack of exactness . . . ,,

    The legal spirit has too often invaded Christianity . 202

    But the subject of the New Testament is not a system but a Person 204

APPENDIX. A Hebrew-Christian Church . . . 205

LECTURE SIX

THE MESSIAH AS TEACHER—THE ETHICAL DEMANDS IN THE SERMON ON THE MOUNT

I. MUCH WAS ALREADY WELL KNOWN . . . 217

    Examples. Purity, Oaths, Charity, Love of money ,,
Our Lord endeavoured to impress on His hearers all the best in what they had learned . . . 222

CONTENTS

	PAGE
II. Yet Parts, it is said, seemed Impracticable and Undesirable	223
Examples. Marriage and Divorce, Oaths, Charity, Wealth	,,
Is the Sermon on the Mount suited only for visionaries, or at best for a very small community? .	229
III. Certain Considerations	230
1. Jewish-Christians less likely than we to misunderstand hyperbolic statements, or to underrate the burden of the Law	,,
2. We must not isolate single demands from the Sermon as a whole	231
i. Though the Sermon as a whole has been attacked, *e.g.* for its omissions. It, however, never pretends to be a code	232
i. Its demands are said to be too high for the average man	233
But they are addressed only to sincere believers, up to the highest stage of spiritual progress .	234
Dependence of the heart on God is presupposed	235
The importance of such humility before God is indeed recognised in Jewish writings, but has always been too much forgotten . . .	237
Our Lord's words *are* contrary to the conventional religion of the 'average man' . .	240
iii. Christ expects no blind performance of His demands	,,
The believer draws on his fellowship with God for knowledge to know how to act in details .	242
3. The demands said to be subversive of society and the nation	243
Christ rightly makes no distinction between individual and national ethics	245
But the application depends on the spiritual state of individuals and of nations	,,

xvi

CONTENTS

LECTURE SEVEN

THE MESSIAH—THE SON OF DAVID

	PAGE
INTRODUCTORY	249
I. THE BELIEF IN A COMING NATIONAL KING	250
In the Old Testament	251
the Apocrypha	252
the Pseudepigraphic Writings	,,
and Rabbinic works	256
The nature of it illustrated also by the false Messiahs	258
Yet St. Matthew dares to claim the meek and gentle Jesus as the true Son of David!	259
II. PASSAGES IN THE GOSPEL WHERE THE TITLE IS USED	260
The reality of the Jewish origin of Jesus	261
The inheritance through Joseph	262
Mary also of the Davidic line	264
Other passages, in particular xxii. 41–45	266
The current view of the Messiah as the Son of David was insufficient. Jesus moved on a higher plane	273

LECTURE EIGHT

THE MESSIAH—THE SON OF MAN

I. PRE-CHRISTIAN PASSAGES WHERE THE PHRASE OCCURS. Ezekiel, Daniel, Enoch; *cf.* 2 (4) Esdras	277
II. PRELIMINARY QUESTIONS WITH REGARD TO ITS EMPLOYMENT BY OUR LORD	285
1. Why did not His hearers understand Him to refer to the Messiah?	,,
Was it that the Book of Enoch was generally unknown?	,,

CONTENTS

	PAGE
Or that the contrast between the future Son of man in glory and Himself seemed too great to suggest identity?	286
2. Did our Lord Himself really employ the term?	287
3. What did He mean by it?	288
Especially in Aramaic?	289
Probably the stress lies not on 'Son' but on 'man'	290
III. THE THREEFOLD USE OF THE PHRASE IN THE GOSPEL	291
1. The Son of man suffering and dying	,,
2. The Son of man exercising power	293
3. The Son of man coming in the future to judge	297
IV. IMPRESSIONS PRODUCED BY THE CONSIDERATION OF THESE PASSAGES	301
1. What was the source from which our Lord derived the phrase?	,,
2. Why was it His favourite title?	304
3. Why did our Lord use it, and not the first person?	306
4. He would also teach by it a wider meaning of Messiahship than Jews had acknowledged	307
5. It has a permanent significance for ourselves	,,

LECTURE NINE

THE MESSIAH—THE SON OF GOD

I. THE SIGNIFICANCE OF THE PHRASE IN ST. MATTHEW	311
1. Its earlier history	312
2. Its usage in St. Matthew	315
II. REASONS FOR BELIEF IN THE FULL DIVINITY OF JESUS	326
1. In the case of St. Matthew	,,
2. In our own case	328
i. We believe	,,
a. Not because St. Matthew did	,,
b. Nor because of the authority of the Church	,,

CONTENTS

		PAGE
c. But because of the pressure of the facts related in the Gospel		329
The irreducible minimum . . .		331
Unsatisfactory explanations of them		332
The reasons that weigh with us . .		,,
ii. Objections		333
a. Spirit clothe itself with matter ! . . .		,,
Answer. The objection antiquated. We only know matter in connexion with spirit		,,
b. Is it consonant with the dignity of God that the Godhead should be in Jesus ? . .		335
If we think in terms of space, regardless of man's nature and man's sin . . .		,,
But Love and Holiness are greater than space.		337
Other attributes would be impossible in a man if he is to be man		338
iii. Wherein lies Jesus' personality ? Is it human or Divine ?		,,
What *is* personality ?		,,
Jesus' personality Divine, but not non-human, this being the necessary self-limitation of God		339
iv. The self-limitation of God Himself so far as He is in contact with nature—*i.e.* Jesus is very God of very God		342

LECTURE TEN

THE MESSIAH AND THE APOCALYPTISTS

INTRODUCTION
  Catastrophe, Development, Catastrophe are the law of life 347
I. THE APOCALYPTISTS 348
  Their teaching not esoteric, but popular . . . 349

CONTENTS

	PAGE
It was rejected by the Pharisaic leaders of Judaism, partly because it tended to draw men's minds away from the Oral Law	350
Partly because Christianity had so much in common with it	351
Its main subject the approaching change, which was often connected by them with the Messiah . .	352
Illustrations	,,
II. OUR LORD'S ATTITUDE TO THIS TEACHING . .	358
While He clearly accepted it as a whole we find difficulty in perceiving whether He expected the kingdom to come in its fulness at once . .	359
The sources used by St. Matthew	,,
Sometimes our Lord implies that the kingdom has come already	,,
Sometimes that it has not come, but is near at hand.	360
Sometimes that many years will pass before its full manifestation	361
Results—while Q and St. Matthew's 'Sondergut' (Mt) presuppose that the kingdom has already come, and Q and Mk expect it immediately, Mt also lays special stress on the length of time that will elapse	362
Explanations of the threefold utterances of our Lord	,,
III. THE REAL NATURE OF THE FINAL CONSUMMATION	368
APPENDIX on Matt. xxiv.	369

LECTURE ELEVEN

THE MESSIAH AND THE CROSS

Why does the Evangelist lay so much stress on the Passion ?	373
I. A PRELIMINARY QUESTION : UPON WHOM DOES HE LAY THE RESPONSIBILITY FOR THE DEATH OF CHRIST ?	,,
The Romans ?	374
The Sadducees ?	375

CONTENTS

	PAGE
The Pharisees?	387
The People?	380
The Passion suggests that there is something radically wrong with the human race	381
II. THE VALUE AND EFFECT OF THE DEATH IN THE LIGHT OF THE FIRST GOSPEL	,,
Jesus expected suffering from the very first. His horror of the cup at Calvary	383
The reasons for the self-sacrifice	384
To 'save His people from their sins'	386
The ransom	387
The blood of the covenant	388
'Bearing'	390
Even in His death there was hope	392

LECTURE TWELVE

THE MESSIAH—THE VICTOR

I. ST. MATTHEW'S REPLY TO JEWISH OPPONENTS	397
The Jews have never denied that the tomb was empty, but assert that human hands removed the Body	,,
St. Matthew's reply, and objections to it considered	398
II. THE NATURE OF THE RESURRECTION OF THE LORD'S BODY	401
The mere survival of His personality insufficient	402
St. Paul and the empty tomb	404
Events in our Lord's life preparatory to His Resurrection	406
Science and the Resurrection	407

CONTENTS

	PAGE
III. THE LORD'S INTERPRETATION OF HIS VICTORY OVER DEATH	408
Why in Galilee?	,,
The Messiah supreme	409
The admission of Gentiles to the faith	,,
The everlasting Presence	410
SUMMARY OF THE LECTURES AND CONCLUSION	,,

INDICES—

I. Names and Subjects	415
II. Holy Scripture and other Early Literature	423

Lecture One

INTRODUCTORY—THE GENEALOGY—THE BIRTH TO THE MANIFESTATION IN GALILEE—THE EVANGELIST'S USE OF SCRIPTURE

'The book of the generation of Jesus Christ, the son of David, the son of Abraham.'
—MATT. i. 1.

Lecture One

INTRODUCTORY—THE GENEALOGY—THE BIRTH TO THE MANIFESTATION IN GALILEE—THE EVANGELIST'S USE OF SCRIPTURE

JERUSALEM had fallen.[1] The long strain of war was over. The ceaseless march of soldiers, and the straggling parties of frightened fugitives, ever bringing fresh news of disaster, were things of the past. The few remaining religious leaders of the Jews, notably Jochanan ben Zakkai, who had escaped from Jerusalem only by allowing himself to be carried out as though he were a corpse,[2] were gathered at Jamnia, and at Lydda,[3] and were beginning to discuss the best means of preserving Judaism in new surroundings, in which there were neither Temple nor sacrifices. For the revolt against the tyranny of the heathen had failed; the Romans had triumphed.

But to one body of men, gathered for the most part at Pella across the Jordan, though now beginning to return, even to the Holy City, the awful history of the last few years had brought no surprise. They were well aware that the real crisis of the nation had taken place some forty years earlier, and that recent events had been but the result of that. They had indeed themselves lost much. Relations, friends,

---

[1] On the whole it is probable that the Gospel was written 'immediately after' the capture of Jerusalem, 70 A.D.—Harnack (*Neue Untersuchungen*, 1911, p. 93).

[2] *T. B. Gittin*, 56 a.b.; *Lam. R.* on i. 5; *Aboth d' R. Nathan*, vi. (Schechter's edition, p. 10).

[3] See Büchler, *Die Priester und der Cultus im letzten Jahrzehnt des Jerusalemischen Tempels*, 1895, p. 26.

possessions, had, in large measure, passed away from them in this terrible Day of the LORD's judgment. But their trust in Him, and in His Messiah, remained unshaken. They, like their great teacher, who had laid down his life in Rome some five or six years earlier, knew Whom they had believed, and in steady confidence braced themselves up for their new work, under the fresh conditions brought about by the fall of Jerusalem.

Was then this to be the chief result of the appearance of Messiah, that the beloved city should be destroyed, its people, the peculiar treasure of the LORD, be scattered and enslaved ? How did the faith of those who believed in Jesus of Nazareth consort with their position as Jews, to whom by race and education they belonged ? Where could they turn for comfort and encouragement ? Had they no writings to guide them ? Nothing in their hands to strengthen their faith and explain their present difficulties ? They had indeed, like other Jews, the revelation of God enshrined for them in the Law, the Prophets, and the Holy Writings; and they had also some written memoirs of the life and teaching of the Lord Jesus. Of these, the one which was most in use is known to us to-day by the name of the Gospel according to St. Mark,[1] a summary of the life and actions of the Lord, from the time of His official entry upon His work until His resurrection. The outline contained in it had been used as far back as the days of the very earliest preachers of the Gospel,[2] and it had embodied the substance

---

[1] After the investigations of Sir J. C. Hawkins and others the priority of this may be said to be established.

[2] St. Peter (Acts x. 37–41), St. Paul (Acts xiii. 24–31).

INTRODUCTORY

of the message which St. Peter was accustomed to deliver until the end of his life.[1] But, notwithstanding, it was insufficient for the requirements, especially the new requirements, of Jewish Christians. These, for the most part, Jews observant of Jewish practices, and worshippers at the Temple services while they were held,[2] desired more light upon the relation of the Lord Jesus to the thoughts and hopes of those to whom He appeared and among whom He taught. They themselves had had experience of the difficulties of their position. They had been compelled to listen to many a bitter gibe at their beloved Master, for His birth, for details of His life and words, for, above all, His shameful death; they had borne ridicule at their poverty, blame for disobeying the traditional law of their nation, and, as they were but human, they required to be strengthened in their Christian faith.

True that they had heard from their teachers, nay, even possessed already in some written form,[3] a collection of Sayings by the Lord Jesus, which served to explain both His and their attitude towards current Judaism, yet there was room, or, rather, an earnest demand, for a permanent record, which should enshrine in one short document the more important parts of the history of the Lord in His relation to the Jews, and present a picture—complete as far as it went—of Jesus as the Messiah expected by their nation, the Messiah who in reality was the completion of the Divine purpose, foretold of old.

---

[1] So the Elder as quoted by Papias in Eusebius, *Church History*, iii. 39.

[2] St. Paul, Acts xxi. 28 (56 A.D.), St. James the Lord's brother; Eusebius, *Church History*, ii. 23 (about 60 A.D.).

[3] Designated now by Q, which, speaking in very general terms, corresponds roughly to the non-Marcan matter common to Matthew and Luke.

It is perhaps going too far to assert that that Apostle was still alive, who, as it seems, had already made an attempt to satisfy this demand. If he were, he would be like Josephus, who, but a few years later, having first written his 'War' in Aramaic, as he tells us, in order that his work might be read by the people of the East, 'the Parthians, and the Babylonians, and the remotest Arabians and those Jews beyond Euphrates, with the Adiabeni,'[1] then wrote them over again in Greek, that his book might be of use to the whole Roman Empire. But, in any case, even if St. Matthew was not alive, there was one who belonged to the same group of believers as he, and had inherited his traditions, and held the same attitude towards the Jews, and in particular the Jewish leaders, as we can suppose the former tax-gatherer once held. Whatever the Aramaic form of the First Gospel contained, and at present we are almost entirely ignorant of this, it was not sufficient for the pressing needs of those who lived immediately after the fall of Jerusalem.[2]

The author wrote in Greek, because he desired to reach a wide audience. Aramaic would have satisfied a part, perhaps the greater part, of those Jewish Christians who lived in Palestine, but he wished to help those many other believers belonging to his own race, who had either settled there from foreign countries, or were still abroad. It is probable,

---

[1] *War*, Preface, §§ 1, 2.

[2] It will be convenient, however, for the purposes of these lectures, to speak of the author of the First Gospel briefly by the name of St. Matthew; but it must be understood that in doing so no claim is made that St. Matthew himself was the actual writer of its present form. Tradition has invariably assigned it to him, and it is hard to see why tradition should have assigned it to so unimportant a member of the Apostolic band unless he had some direct connexion with it. But we cannot say more.

1] THE NEED OF THE HEBREW-CHRISTIANS

however, that we greatly underrate the number of Greek-speaking Jews who before the war had made their homes in Palestine, and also the influence that the presence of many foreigners, Gentile as well as Jewish, must have had upon the upper strata of the people in all parts, and upon all classes in the north.[1] We can understand, therefore, that now, when a fresh record of the Lord's life was required, one which should present it from a different point of view from that hitherto chosen, and set it forth in connexion with the more pressing difficulties of the time, the Greek language was chosen as the medium likely to reach most hearts.

It is evident, from what has been said, that this Gospel according to St. Matthew was written for the use of Jewish Christians, to build them up in the fear and love of the Lord, and to lead them to understand more accurately the relation, both of Himself and of His teaching, to the Old Testament on the one hand, and to the actual religion of the Jews on the other. Hence the author would find it necessary to consider not only the days of the Lord's sojourn in the flesh, but also those in which he himself was writing. Further, although the book was addressed strictly to Christian, not to non-Christian, members of his race, yet seeing that Jewish Christians would find in it innumerable arguments enabling them to meet objections adduced by their non-Christian neighbours, we are justified in regarding it also as a presentation of Messiah to the Jews.

Now to us, in our own day, this is a subject of increasing importance. There was a time when,

[1] This is well brought out in the works of M. Friedländer, e.g., *Die religiösen Bewegungen*, u.s.w., p. 16.

largely owing to our unworthy treatment of the sons of Abraham, very few, if any, of them could be found in our land. This is not the case now. They are with us, and are deservedly taking a high place in the State, and are gaining our esteem and confidence. The qualities into which they have been trained by centuries of persecution, and by their faithful adherence, as a whole, to the traditional form of their religion, and the study of the strange, but singularly attractive, books in which it is enshrined, have made them what they are—extraordinarily acute, and also trustworthy. But, at the same time, Jews do not shrink from criticising our Christian religion, and from endeavouring, directly or indirectly, to show that its fundamental doctrines are mistaken. On the other hand, our own people are for the most part extremely ignorant of Judaism, both past and present, and, as they grow jealous of the Jew's success in business, are inclined to vent their envy by employing methods quite unworthy of professing Christians. Hence, whether we consider the defence of our own faith, or the instruction of our own people, or, lastly, the paramount duty resting upon us as believers in the Lord Jesus, it is but right that we should try to present Christ to the Jews afresh. Further, in order to prepare ourselves for this task, it is well that we should make the attempt to see how an early Christian writer, himself of Jewish birth, and living in daily intercourse with non-Christian Jews, regarded Jesus of Nazareth, and so framed his description of Him as to help the other Jewish-Christians of his time to meet arguments with which they were continually assailed.

It may be urged as an objection, that if this is the

1]   THE TRUST DEED OF THESE LECTURES

object of these Lectures, they will be controversial. Yes, and No. No, for I trust that they will not be controversial in any unworthy sense. Thoughtful Christians of to-day do not desire to imitate the methods, or entertain the feelings, of controversialists of past generations. But controversial in the better sense they must be, if they are to be faithful to the words of the Trust Deed which governs their delivery. For, according to this, the lectures are to be ' in the form of a Sermon to prove the Truth of Revealed Religion in General, and of the Christian in particular, from the completion of those prophecies in the Old and New Testament which relate to the Christian Church, especially to the Apostasy of Papal Rome.' I shall make no attempt to carry out the last clause, nor indeed the first. The second and central clause will be sufficient to occupy us throughout the course. One book of the New Testament alone, continually referring as it does to the Old Testament, will be considered.

One other matter I must mention. These are days in which attempts, and, on the whole, successful attempts, are made to go behind the Gospels in their present form, with a view to discover the sources, documentary or oral, out of which they were composed. I do not intend taking much notice of the many important questions which these investigations suggest. For, in the first place, it is agreed by most critics that these sources themselves were earlier than 70 A.D., the approximate date at which we put the original composition of this Gospel; and, secondly, I myself feel sure that as it stands it represents the truth about both the Person and the Teaching of the Messiah.

The general plan of the Lectures is as follows.

The first, after making certain preliminary remarks, will consider the presentation of the Messiah to the Jews, from His birth to the commencement of His work, as contained in the first four chapters of the Gospel. The second lecture will consider Him in relation to the Jewish sects and parties of His day, particularly the Pharisees. The third will deal with St. Matthew's presentation of Him as the Healer of disease. The fourth, fifth, and sixth Lectures will be taken up with the presentation of Messiah as Teacher, in particular His relation to the Law of Moses and the traditional teaching of the Jewish religion. Lectures seven, eight, and nine will treat of the three titles which the Lord Jesus Himself accepted—'The Son of David,' 'The Son of Man,' and 'The Son of God,' each bringing out one side of the complex character and position of the Messiah. To these will be added a lecture on the Messiah in His relation to the apocalyptic teaching current at the time. Then will follow one on Messiah the Sufferer, and, finally, one on Messiah the Victor over death, Him who is 'Immanuel,' 'God with us.' In this way we shall have gone—cursorily no doubt, but, I trust, sufficiently for our immediate purpose—over the whole of this First Gospel, and shall have learned, I hope, something more of Him Who is here depicted for us by one who either himself had actually lived with Him in the flesh, or, at the least, had received his knowledge from one who had.

Before, however, we come to our subject proper, we can hardly avoid asking ourselves what was the representation of Messiah which was current among

1] THE JEWISH REPRESENTATION OF MESSIAH

the Jews, in the time immediately preceding the public appearance of the Lord Jesus ? What were to be the nature, character, position, work of the Messiah according to the belief of the Jews, more particularly the Jews of Palestine, in, say, the year 25 A.D. ? It might have been thought that it would be fairly easy to answer these questions. In reality it is not so. For, in the first place, it is evident that we cannot take the canonical books of the Old Testament and affirm that their description of the Messiah is so plain that the Jews of 25 A.D. must have accepted it, for the nature of the description, if any, contained in the Old Testament, both was and is a principal matter of dispute between Jews and Christians. Neither, in our inquiry for information, can we turn to a single non-canonical book, and say for certain that it was acknowledged as authoritative, or even as accurate, by the majority of Palestinian Jews at that time, much less that it was composed at or about that date. Neither, again, although we possess voluminous writings by Philo the Alexandrian, composed from about 10 to 50 A.D.,[1] and preserved to us solely through the means of the Christian Church, can we affirm that they correspond in any detail with the opinions of Palestinian Jews contemporary with him. The same difficulty, but increased in measure, meets us when we attempt to use the works of Josephus, composed after the fall of Jerusalem, and designed to meet different needs from those existing in 25 A.D. To be sure, there are the sayings of the Palestinian teachers themselves in the Mishna, but the remains of those who lived at this time are extraordinarily

[1] Philo was born about 20 B.C., and visited Rome in 39 or 40 A.D., but appears to have lived for some years longer.

scanty, and I am not aware that a single sentence about the Messiah has survived which was uttered by a Palestinian Rabbi as early as 25 A.D. No saying by Hillel on this subject has come down to us,[1] no saying by Shammai, not even one by Gamaliel, the teacher of St. Paul. No doubt there are sayings, to which reference will be made as occasion serves, by Rabbis who were, in fact, alive at or about that date. But they were not spoken until later, and we cannot be sure, to say the least, that they were not the result, conscious or unconscious, of opposition to Christian teaching. The evidence as to the nature of the belief of the Jews in the Messiah before the public appearance of our Lord is at best indirect, and far from assured.[2]

One thing must be borne in mind. It is the merit of a recent Jewish writer upon the belief in Messiah held by Jews during the first two centuries of our era,[3] to have pointed out more plainly and emphatically than has been done before, that the development of Messianic beliefs has always been profoundly modified

---

[1] 'R. Hillel' is a different person altogether. He was the son of Gamaliel III, and lived in the third century A.D.

[2] Much information will be found scattered throughout this volume, particularly in Lectures VII–IX. Canon Charles' brief summary in his *Religious Development between the Old and the New Testaments*, 1914, pp. 64–96, may be consulted with advantage. Volz, *Jüdische Eschatologie von Daniel bis Akiba*, 1903, pp. 197–237, is very full.

[3] Klausner, *Die Messianischen Vorstellungen des jüdisches Volkes im Zeitalter der Tannaim*, 1904, p. 88:

'In der Regel (selbstredend hat auch diese Regel Ausnahmen) nicht der Bibelvers (wenn er nicht klar und deutlich auf irgend welche Thatsache hinweist) den neuen Gedanken hervorruft, sondern der schon aufgetauchte neue Gedanke wird durch einen Bibelvers belegt und unterstützt.'

Besides, it must not be forgotten that the aim of the Gospel, and indeed of all the historical books of the Bible, is not to prove by logic, but to attract by presentation. It adduces facts rather than elaborate arguments.

I] THE N.T. WRITTEN FOR BELIEVERS

by events; that men did not take the Old Testament, and by a study of it come to the conclusion that the expected Messiah was to be of such and such a kind; but, on the contrary, they felt the burden of facts and incidents in their own experience, and being sure that the Messiah would correspond to these, turned to the Old Testament to see if the confirmation of their hopes was contained in it. We shall, no doubt, have occasion to refer later on to this Jewish method of discovering doctrines in the Old Testament.

Here it must suffice to say that the nature of the Jewish belief in the expected Messiah about the year 25 A.D. was such, and, with possible exceptions in detail, no more than such, as could be derived from events known to them which had already taken place. It remained for the new facts—the new great facts— of the next few years to produce such a modification and development in that belief that the result was Christianity.

The experience of facts brought Christian truths home to the consciousness of the devout. 'Of the devout.' For they alone could be expected to understand the revelation of the LORD, the fulness of the Divine love in the Lord Jesus. No book in the New Testament, it must be remembered, was written with the aim of convincing unbelievers, whether Jewish or heathen. Each had for its object the building up of those who were already convinced. For the believer in the Lord Jesus, and for him alone, was the Gospel according to St. Matthew written, that he might understand more fully how Jesus of Nazareth answered to the expectations of the Jews of His time, and far more than answered to them. His life, teaching, death, and resurrection showed that, while

He was truly man, He was much more than man, even very God, and also that everything He said, or did, or bore, was strictly in accordance with the true teaching of the revelation of God, contained in the written word of God.

Let us now turn to the Gospel itself, and examine its presentation of the Messiah until the commencement of His public work, considering very cursorily the Genealogy, the Virgin-birth (with its place and time and the Visit of the Magi), the Flight to Egypt, the Massacre of the Innocents, the home at Nazareth, the position of John the Baptist, the Baptism (with the Voice from heaven), the Temptation, and the manifestation in Galilee, bearing in mind that the narrative in every case was written for Jewish Christians, who were trying to live out their Christian life among non-Christian Jews.

I. 'The book of the generation of Jesus Christ, the son of David, the son of Abraham.'

It is a characteristic opening, likely to catch the attention of every one of Jewish origin, especially every one who was acquainted with the current Greek translation of the Book of Genesis. For the phrase 'the book of the generation' is identical with the Septuagint form in Genesis ii. 4 : 'The book of the generation of heaven and earth,' and in v. 1 : 'The book of the generation of men.' It is as though the writer would carry back his readers to the beginning of the creation of all things, and suggest to them that here in the Lord Jesus Christ they would find One with whom begins afresh the history of humanity. Whether indeed the writer really had this intention in mind is not certain. We can but say that the

THE SON OF ABRAHAM

thought of the Second Adam was known in Christian circles long before the composition of this Gospel.[1]

Yet St. Matthew does not dwell upon this. He is concerned with other aspects of the Lord Jesus Christ, who is entitled ' the son of David ' and ' the son of Abraham.' To the former appellation we must return in a later lecture. Here we need only remember that it suggests to every Jew the fulfilment of the glorious promises made to David, and of the glad expectation that one of his race should come to rule in his spirit, and subdue the nations, bringing them under the yoke of the kingdom of Jehovah, both in politics and in religion.

Why, however, does the author add ' the son of Abraham ' ? Is it merely a chance selection from the multitude of David's ancestors ? Every Jew knows better. It is nothing less than a claim, that while to Abraham and his seed were the promises made, the true seed was not so much the nation of Israel, as He who was its finest product, its flower and its fruit, Jesus Christ. But there was more even than this in the expression. To the Christian, as to the thoughtful Jew, Abraham was not only the ancestor of the Jews, and the parent of their creed. He was the first missionary to the heathen, and he received from God the promise of becoming a blessing to all the nations. It is not therefore by accident that that very Gospel which shows the most plainly of any of the four that the Lord Jesus was the Messiah of the Jews, should also state more explicitly than any the fact that He came also to call all nations to the true knowledge of God. If the phrase ' the son of David ' summoned every loyal Jew to range him-

[1] On the doctrine *cf.* Lecture III, pp. 123 *sq.*

self under the banner of the King, the words 'the son of Abraham' bade him not be surprised that the Gentiles were flocking in to worship Jesus the Christ. If the Gentiles were being admitted in large numbers to the Christian fold, this was only the carrying out of the promise made to Abraham, and the completion of the work which he began. The union of the two phrases 'the son of David, the son of Abraham,' proclaims Jesus as the Messiah of the Jews, and the Light to lighten the Gentiles.

Then St. Matthew gives us a summary of Jewish history (i. 2–17).[1] It is in the form of a genealogy, and as a genealogy it has for his purpose a special value. But this must not make us overlook its substance. The genealogy is, of course, thoroughly Jewish in plan and method. St. Matthew has arranged his matter by the Hebrew letters of the word David.[2] As David in Hebrew has three letters, so in the genealogy there are three divisions. As these three letters make up fourteen by numerical value (for in Hebrew there are no separate numerals, but to every letter a numerical value is attached), so the writer arranges his matter in fourteens. Thus at the end of the passage he is able to write (*v.* 17) : 'So all the generations from Abraham unto David are fourteen generations; and from the carrying away to Babylon unto the Christ fourteen generations.'

To a Jew the record of the names, for it is little more, would be sufficient. 'Abraham' would recall the summons from Ur of the Chaldees and the courageous venture of faith, which bade him, the first

[1] *Cf.* Zahn, *Das Evangelium des Matthäus*, 1910, pp. 44, 50.
[2] Gfrörer, *Die heilige Sage*, 1838, ii. p. 9. See also Canon Box, *The Virgin Birth of Jesus*, 1916, pp. 12 *sqq*.

patriarch of the nation, set forth, trusting solely on God's promise, not knowing whither he went. ' Isaac ' would recall the obedient son, offering himself up to death, and restored, as it were, to life ; ' Jacob ' the faults, the exile, then the change of heart and character, with the promises attached to the Israel of God ; ' Judah and his brethren ' would hint at the opposition of the typical Jew to his innocent brother, and the consequent misery in Egypt. Then come names suggestive of the wild times, and the low religious life, of the Judges. Only after these, and that from a line not untainted with sin, and even with heathenism, was born David the king.

Here there is a pause. The first fourteen generations are completed. The author next brings before us the events of the kingdom. David himself was not sinless, and it was Bathsheba's second son who became the famous Solomon. Rehoboam recalls pusillanimity and the division of the kingdom ; the names Abijah to Josiah various vicissitudes, now good, now evil, in the rule of the kings, some of whom were very bad, others good and adherents of the worship of Jehovah, but all imperfect. The list ends with Jechoniah (by which name, as it seems, Jehoiakim is intended) and his brothers, with whom the list of kings closes, for the nation is carried off into a deserved captivity. Gone are the glories of David, the kingdom has perished.

Is there then no hope ? Shall the LORD's promises prove to be of no effect ? The last fourteen generations supply the answer. God leaves not Himself without successors to David, though they be no longer in high estate. Jechoniah, Jehoiakim's son, lived long in the captivity, but he had no son who became king. His successor, whether by natural or only legal succession we cannot say, but probably the latter, was Shealtiel. To Shealtiel succeeded Zerubbabel, who, as Jews would remember, received the promise that he should be as a seal upon the LORD's arm. With him the Biblical evidence for the succession came to an end, and in consequence the remaining names until that of Joseph are of quite unknown persons. Yet David's line did not die out. It was maintained, in all probability, in many families.[1] But, as it seems, the direct line of heirship was continued in that family of humble circumstances, into which the Christ was born. God had not been unfaithful to His promises. He had been preparing the nation through the early years of its development. He had raised up David, and allowed the nation to feel both the good and the evil of earthly rulers. He had brought down the nation in captivity, and then had permitted a long season of humiliation to follow—that thus, in spite of the political unimportance of the family of David, yes, perhaps even because of this, it might be raised up to become the recipient of the final gift of God.[2]

Through many changes, by much affliction and even through obscurity and neglect, God had been carrying out His purpose and preparing the family of David to receive the Christ. 'And Jacob begat Joseph the husband of Mary, of whom was born Jesus, who is called Christ.'[3]

[1] Down to the end of the second century of our era at least, and perhaps much later. See Dalman, *The Words of Jesus*, 1902, pp. 321 *sqq.*

[2] On the Davidic origin of our Lord see also Lecture VII, pp. 261 *sqq.*

[3] It does not seem to be necessary to discuss the text of this verse (i. 16) here.

JEWISH SLANDERS REBUTTED

Before leaving this portion of the first chapter of the Gospel, it is necessary to speak rather more plainly about a subject to which allusion has already been made—St. Matthew's reference to the four other women besides the Virgin Mary.

It was indeed reserved for Jews of the early middle ages to write out at length the filthy stories of the birth and life of the Lord Jesus which are to be found in the *Toledoth Jeshu*.[1] But we are not justified in supposing that these accusations had so late an origin.[2] On the contrary, it may be assumed that unbelieving Jews made the Virgin-birth the subject of ribald tales almost immediately after the fact was divulged to Christians. If so, we can readily perceive a reason for the strange way in which St. Matthew draws attention to four of the mothers of persons mentioned in the genealogy. There would not appear to have been any necessity for him to have mentioned Tamar, or Rahab, or even Ruth, or ' her that had been the wife of Uriah,' at all, unless he had desired to meet difficulties raised by Jews. In all probability his reason for doing so was to bring forward a demurrer against all such objections. For they would come with a bad grace from Jews, whose greatest kings—kings through whose line the Messiah was confessedly to come—were themselves descended from women, three of whom were of more than doubtful reputation, and one of whom was even of non-Jewish birth. The silent contrast of the purity of Mary, and the irreproachableness of her religion, would be felt by every Hebrew-Christian,

---

[1] The standard edition of its different forms is in Krauss' *Das Leben Jesu nach jüdischen Quellen*, 1902.

[2] *Cf.* Zahn, *op. cit.* p. 66*n*; Box, *op. cit.* p. 14.

and would form a valuable weapon against the shameless insinuations of the Jews.

II. In the next portion of the Gospel (i. 18–25) St. Matthew deals specifically with the birth of Christ.[1] He says that this was far otherwise than Jewish slanders pretended. For the mother of Jesus was absolutely pure, and Jesus was conceived of the Holy Ghost, without the intervention of any human fatherhood at all. Observe, first, the writer is above all careful to point out that before, apparently long before, the birth of Jesus His mother was legally the wife of Joseph, who had already been shown to be the heir to the kingdom. Secondly, stress is laid on the character of Joseph, in order perhaps to suggest the religious tone of the home in which Jesus was brought up. But, as it seems, it is also said that the character of Joseph was very different from that of the mere legalist who exalted the letter of the law above its spirit. For it is probable that we must read the nineteenth verse in the sense that because Joseph was a man who entered into the true meaning of the law, and therefore was of a kindly heart as well as strictly just, he did not wish to put his wife away with greater publicity than was necessary. The kindness of his heart bade him put her away as privately as he could.

His judgment, however, natural though it was, was mistaken. She was guiltless of any wrongdoing. He was convinced of this by a dream, in which an angel appeared to him, and told him she was innocent.

---

[1] See Lecture VII, pp. 263 *sqq.* Harnack remarks: 'Die Verlobung gab dem Manne die Rechte des Ehemanns' (*Neue Untersuchungen*, 1911, p. 104). See further Krauss, *Talmudische Archäologie*, 1911, ii. 36; Box, *op. cit.* pp. 209–214. After betrothal no further ceremony was necessary.

THE 'VIRGIN' OF ISA. VII. 14

Further, the angel himself, as it seems,[1] confirms this statement by an appeal to the prophet Isaiah: 'Behold, the virgin shall be with child, and shall bring forth a son, and they shall call his name Immanuel.' The justice of this appeal has been disputed by many Christians, and, much more strangely, by Jews. For we as Christians sometimes find it rather difficult to defend St. Matthew's use of the prophet's words. Yet something may be said for him even judging by the standard of modern exegesis.

We can certainly defend the use of the word 'virgin,' and affirm that the Jewish translator of the Septuagint made no mistake when he translated the Hebrew word '*Almah* by παρθένος. It is true indeed that if we enquire only into the etymology of '*Almah* we find that it does not express virginity but only sexual maturity, and therefore in itself the word may be used for a young woman who is either single or married. But in the actual usage of the Bible it is limited to virgins. See, for example, Cant. vi. 8, where virgins, '*alamoth*, are contrasted with queens and concubines. It is strange that in Hebrew there is no word (I am speaking of Biblical usage only, not of technical terms employed in later forms of the language) which is used necessarily and exclusively of a virgin, with the exception of '*almah*. Seeing that the word *bethulim* is used strictly of 'virginity,' we should have expected that *bethulah* would, as a matter of course, and by itself, have meant 'virgin,' as indeed it generally does. But

---

[1] A comparison of xxvi. 56 (and perhaps also xxi. 4) suggests that this is the utterance of the angel, although the exact mode of recording it is the Evangelist's. See Ephraem's comment on the passage in Tatian's *Diatessaron*: 'Quod si dubitas. Isaiam audi.'

this is not always the case. In Gen. xxiv. 16 a further definition is required in order to ensure this meaning, and in Joel i. 8 is found the simile of a *bethulah* lamenting for the husband of her youth. So far as usage is concerned—I do not say etymology—'*almah* is the only word in Hebrew that is consistently employed to designate a virgin.

Isaiah then said, and intended to say, that the Child was to be born of a virgin. But what child, and what virgin ? Was it to be Isaiah's own child by the virgin who was to become his wife ? Hardly, for in viii. 8 Immanuel, the name given to the child in the verse we are considering (vii. 14), is said to own the land of Palestine : ' Thy land, O Immanuel.' Further, we can hardly distinguish the child of chapters vii. and viii. from that of chapter ix., of whom such glorious terms are predicated as ' Wonderful Counsellor, Mighty God, Everlasting Father, Prince of Peace.' Was then the child to be the son of king Ahaz (to whom the prophet was speaking) by, of course, a mother as yet unmarried ? Ahaz, an unspiritual person, unworthy to have divine truth revealed to him, may have so understood the words; but, in any case, the child could not have been Hezekiah, as some Jews have thought,[1] for Hezekiah was already nine years old when his father Ahaz came to the throne.[2] There is another explanation, if we can trust the verdict of Pastor Jeremias, who, writing out of the fulness of his knowledge, in his book on the influence of Babylon on the New Testament, says : ' If people had known the circle

---

[1] So Trypho in Justin Martyr's *Dialogue*, § 67. See also Klausner, *Die Messianischen Vorstellungen*, p. 69.
[2] See Kimchi on Isa. vii. 15.

of ideas current in the ancient East, they would never have doubted that a son of a virgin was certainly in the mind of the author of Isaiah vii.'[1] If this be true, then we may suppose that Isaiah accepted the belief of the East, and was commissioned to tell Ahaz, the Deliverer shall be born of a virgin. Ahaz himself, no doubt, may have been satisfied with seeing in the words a promise of deliverance within a year. But to Isaiah the words meant far more, the fulfilment of God's promise in due course of the birth of a Deliverer, the Messiah, from a virgin. If this be the true explanation of the passage, St. Matthew was, of course, fully justified in quoting it as he did, even when judged by modern Christian rules of quotation.

It must, however, be granted that we possess, so far as I am aware, no pre-Christian evidence for such an interpretation of the prophet's language by Jewish writers, and that there is room for doubt whether St. Matthew himself would have been aware of this belief of Isaiah in the Virgin-birth of the Messiah, if he did believe it.[2] But, as a Jew of the first century of our era, he would not feel compelled to quote a passage of the Old Testament only in its original sense. It would be sufficient for him if he found a truth which he desired to affirm expressed in so many words in the sacred scriptures independently of the question whether these words properly meant this truth or not. St. Matthew would be satisfied if he found written: 'A virgin shall conceive and bear a son.'

He accepted the fact of the Virgin-birth of our Lord, and gave the angel's assurance to Joseph in

---

[1] *Babylonisches im Neuen Testament*, 1905, p. 47.
[2] See further Box, *op. cit.* pp. 162–170.

words taken from Scripture. The language of the prophet was accepted by every Jew of the first century as itself inspired, and for St. Matthew it was now fulfilled by the marvellous fact recorded, the birth of Messiah from a virgin. By ancient Jewish methods of quotation at all events, if not by our methods, the Evangelist was fully justified in quoting the passage from Isaiah.

Passing from the question of the accuracy of St Matthew's quotation, we ask : What did the fact of the Virgin-birth mean to him ? What truth did it seem to him to teach ? This—that now God was with man, in a sense different from all human experience before. To him the Virgin-birth was, as we should say, a proof of the divinity of Jesus.[1] Let us not misunderstand his position. He did not, so far as we can see, accept the belief that Jesus was divine because He was born of a virgin. But, accepting the divinity of Jesus on other grounds, then, when he heard long afterwards from private information due ultimately to Mary or Joseph, that Jesus was born of no human father, he found this fully in accordance with his previous faith in His divinity. The Virgin-birth agreed with his belief that Jesus was divine ; it played no part at all in producing that belief.

But now, when he was presenting Jesus, the true Messiah, to his fellow-Christians of Jewish race, and through them to the many unbelieving Jews among whom they lived, he laid stress on the fact that Jesus was born of a pure Virgin, and called attention to the prophecy of Isaiah, which stated this in so many words. The statement of the

[1] *Cf. v.* 23, end.

THE VIRGIN-BIRTH ACCEPTED

fact, and the quotation of the scripture, together formed a convenient summary, from which might readily be deduced the argument that Jesus was divine.

It is probable, indeed, that for ourselves we should not be inclined to lay so much stress on the Virgin-birth, if the doctrine had not been commended to us by antiquity. We could not have affirmed, on *a priori* grounds, that it was necessary for Jesus to be born of a virgin if He was to be divine. At most, I suppose, we could have said, I know not with how much right, that it was easier for a Being to be born free from Original Sin without than with human fatherhood.[1] But knowing what we know of the Lord Jesus from other information concerning Him, and accepting the truth of His divinity on quite other grounds, we can see that it was fitting that even in His birth He should be superior to all of us. We ourselves do not, in logic and reason, believe in His divinity because of His birth from a Virgin. But we do see that the doctrine of His birth from a Virgin fits in admirably with His life and teaching, and therefore with His divinity.[2]

We are not surprised, therefore, that the Virgin-birth of our Lord has always been an integral part of the Church's belief, and is to be found as early as the creed preserved in the *Apology* of Aristides, written about the years 140–145 A.D. If we were to give it up now we should be acting not only against the evidence of the New Testament (if this be judged with a due regard for the privacy of such a communication in the

---

[1] *Cf.* Bishop F. Weston, *The One Christ*, 1914, pp. 239 *sq.*; Illingworth, *The Gospel Miracles*, 1915, p. 78.

[2] *Cf.* H. R. Mackintosh, *The Doctrine of the Person of Jesus Christ*, 1913, p. 532 *sq.*

earliest days of the Church); and not only against an article in the Creed which has always been held sacred, but also in such a way as to forward the denial of our Lord's divinity.

III. Having spoken of the birth of our Lord, St. Matthew calls attention to the place where it occurred, and to its date. Messiah was born in the reign of Herod the King, the last ' king ' of any independence. For there was no possibility that St. Matthew's contemporaries would confuse him with the later holders of the title.[1] Herod the King could mean none other than Herod the Great. His true successor, St. Matthew seems to hint, was Jesus, the Messiah.

The locality, however, looms larger in the Evangelist's mind than the date. Four times does he mention Bethlehem in the first eight verses of the second chapter. But in fact the whole passage lays stress on geography, bidding the reader notice the various places in which the Lord Jesus spent His infancy and youth. Why the writer lays so much emphasis on this, and in particular on the town of His birth, is not hard to guess. The sect of the Nazarenes, as their enemies called the Christians, owed allegiance to Jesus of Nazareth. But if He were only Jesus of Nazareth how could He be the Messiah? What good thing could come out of Nazareth? Nay, says St. Matthew, He came from Bethlehem. It was at Bethlehem that He was born. He did fulfil prophecy

---

[1] Herod Antipas the Tetrach was called king by courtesy, Matt. xiv. 9; Herod Agrippa I received the legal title of king from Caligula, 41 A.D., and held it till he died in 44 A.D., Acts xii. 1; Herod Agrippa II also legally enjoyed the title (Acts xxv. 13) from 53 A.D. till his death about 100 A.D.

in this particular also. For Micah said, and it so happened that the official body of Jewish leaders stated this to Herod, that the Messiah was to come from Bethlehem.

It is not necessary for us to-day to enter into the many questions raised by the variant form in which St. Matthew quotes the passage from Micah. It is enough to say that it is sufficiently near to the original to justify his use of it.

What, however, did the prophet mean by his apostrophe of Bethlehem ? 'But thou, Beth-lehem Ephrathah, which art little to be among the thousands of Judah, out of thee shall one come forth unto me that is to be ruler in Israel ; whose goings forth are from of old, from everlasting.' No doubt he was speaking of Messiah, but whether he intended to say more than that Messiah should spring from the stock of David, whose home was at Bethlehem, is not certain. On the other hand, the fact that in the next verse he speaks of the mother of the Messiah [1] suggests that here also he expects to find something strange about His birth. It should be observed, further, that the terms by which Micah describes the Messiah are such as to overpass the description of an ordinary man. For his ' goings forth are from of old, from everlasting.' Only a very jejune system of interpretation can refer these words to the short period of three hundred years from Micah to David, and it is little better to explain them of the time from the future birth of Messiah back to David, or to suppose that His long existence was only in the thought and purpose of God. It is not easy to get

---

[1] Micah v. 3: 'Therefore will he give them up, until the time that she which travaileth hath brought forth.'

over the impression that Micah's language implies the expectation of the coming of a Divine Person who has existed from eternity.

St. Matthew himself, however, does not touch on this. He is content to quote the passage more generally, combining with it, strictly in accordance with Jewish methods of quotation, the words 'who shall be shepherd of my people Israel,' based upon God's promise to David in 2 Sam. v. 2 : 'Thou shalt feed my people Israel.'

In using this prophecy as I said, St. Matthew states the occasion on which the leaders of the Jews formally referred to it. They were giving an answer to the enquiry of Herod. It was he who desired to know where the Christ should be born.

For a strange thing had happened. Herod the King knew not; the chief priests and learned men of the people of Israel, the Lord's own people, knew not; yet in Bethlehem of Judæa, the very place foretold, there was already born One who was King of the Jews, and Gentiles from distant lands had come to worship Him. Among the Jews the political head (the king), the religious leaders (the High Priests), and the foremost in learning (the Scribes), all alike were ignorant of the presence of their true King, and yet Gentiles had come from the far East expressly to worship Him! Every Jewish reader of St. Matthew's narrative could see the lesson that he intended to convey. Further, a star had taught these strangers, and a star now guided them along the road to Bethlehem, and seemed, as it lay low on the horizon, to be over the very house where at last they found the young Child.

The Magi saw, and worshipped, and gave. The

THE MAGI

sight of Jesus brought submission, and full consecration of the most precious things they had.

It is not necessary for our purpose to discuss the reality of the incident here described by St. Matthew, but it is too improbable an event in itself to have easily been invented. Certainly we hear that in 66 A.D. the Parthian king Tiridates came to visit Nero at Rome, and, being a wise man, a Magus, together with other Magi who were with him, worshipped Nero as the sun-god Mithra, and afterwards returned to his own land by a different way from that by which he had come.[1] But we may doubt whether St. Matthew had heard of this visit. If so, it may have suggested to him that he should incorporate in his Gospel this earlier incident of similar import.

Some writers would have us suppose that St. Matthew invented it, on the ground that it was unfitting that Nero, the Antichrist, should have received such homage, and Christ have received none. But this is very improbable. St. Matthew would have made more of the incident, and not have brought it in only by the way, in order to explain the reason why an official declaration was given that the Christ was to be born in Bethlehem. Hence he does not care to illustrate from the Old Testament either the appearance of the star, though he might have done so from Num. xxiv. 17, or the worship of the wise men, though he might have quoted Isa. lx. 3, 6; xlix. 12; Ps. lxxii. 9-15.

[1] *Dio Cassius*, lxiii. 7. Harnack thinks it quite unnecessary to think of embassies from the East to the Emperor's Court at Rome, though he can only say that the idea of 'the Star of Jacob,' and the presence of Chaldean astrologers in Jerusalem, might have been sufficient to produce 'the legend' (*Neue Untersuchungen*, 1911, p. 106). See also Dudden, *D.C.G.* ii. 99.

The place of Jesus' birth was the fact of primary importance to the Evangelist. The Son of David was born at David's home—in accordance with Scripture.[1]

IV. Let us pass on to ii. 13. The Jews affirmed that Jesus had been in Egypt, and they asked: What had Messiah to do with Egypt? Yes, answers St. Matthew, it is true that He was in Egypt, and it was but fitting that He should be. His going there indeed was directly due to the hatred of Herod, who endeavoured to kill the Messiah when he knew where He was to be born. Joseph, however, was warned beforehand in a dream by the angel of the Lord, and 'took the young Child and His mother by night and departed into Egypt.' Does this seem strange? Nay, to every thoughtful member of our race, the Evangelist implies, it seems but right. For was not Messiah to be the great representative of Israel, and was it not proper that He should go through the same kind of experience that our nation has endured? Is not (must we not confess it?) Messiah the true son of Jehovah, and when God says of the nation in the book of Hosea: 'Out of Egypt did I call my son,' should we not expect to find these words true also of the Messiah? This, at any rate, is what took place. We as devout Israelites cannot but see the hand of God overruling the wrath of princes, and cannot but admire His words, which suit first the nation, and then the Christ.[2]

---

[1] 'Die Geschichte ist Darstellung einer Idee. Soll sie darum nicht Geschichte sein?'—Zahn, *Matthäus*, p. 105.

[2] Whether this exhausts the meaning read into the quotation by the Evangelist is another matter. See Lecture IX, p. 320.

THE MASSACRE OF THE INNOCENTS

V. The Evangelist, however, tells his fellow-countrymen more about Herod. In his fury against the Messiah he did not scruple to put to death 'all the male children that were in Bethlehem, and in all the borders thereof, from two years old and under,' in order to ensure, as he thought, the death of Him who was born King of the Jews. Why did St. Matthew tell us this? I suppose because every Jew would at once recall the circumstances of the birth of Moses. Jews were ready—nay, are ready—to compare Jesus with Moses, greatly to the disadvantage of the former, and we shall see in the course of our studies that not once nor twice does the writer bear this contention in mind, and show its injustice. Here therefore it fits in admirably with the general purpose of his narrative to point out that even at His birth Jesus, like Moses, escaped the murderous intention of the ungodly king, while many of His fellow-babes perished.[1]

But St. Matthew finds in the incident more than this. The lamentation of the mothers in Bethlehem, as they saw their infants snatched from them and slain, recalls to his mind the words of Jeremiah,[2] describing the calamity that befell Israel when the Northern tribes were conquered by the bloodthirsty Assyrians, and were either slain or carried into captivity. Rachel, he says therefore, the ancestress of Ephraim and Manasseh, as well as the mother of Benjamin, is now shrieking in distress at her loss: ' A voice is heard in Ramah, lamentation, and bitter weeping, Rachel weeping for her children; she refuseth to be comforted for her children, because they are not.' The illustration was the more apt

---

[1] *Cf.* Box, *op. cit.* pp. 20 *sqq.*   [2] xxxi. (xxxviii.) 15.

because Rachel had died near Bethlehem (Gen. xxxv. 19, 20; xlviii. 7), and might be regarded as its patron-saint.

Perhaps there was another reason for making the quotation. Every reader of Talmudic and Rabbinic literature is aware that if he is to understand the point with which scriptural references are introduced, he must consider not only the actual words quoted, but also those which precede and follow them. So here. What are the next words of Jeremiah after he has described the wailing? 'Thus saith the LORD: Refrain thy voice from weeping, and thine eyes from tears: for thy work shall be rewarded, saith the LORD.' The sorrow is but the prelude to the deliverance. The grief is not the end, it introduces the joy. Again, what is foretold in the verses immediately preceding? What but the full restoration of the LORD's people, with their gladness and happiness? 'I will turn their mourning into joy, and will comfort them and make them rejoice from their sorrow. And I will satiate the soul of the priests with fatness, and my people shall be satisfied with my goodness, saith the LORD.' So closely in Jeremiah's mind is the thought of the lamentation of Rachel connected with happiness and blessing. It is not unreasonable to suppose that the same thought was in the mind of the Evangelist. The massacre of Rachel's children at Bethlehem was bound up with the coming time of blessing. The suffering connected with the infancy of the Christ was the prelude to His appearance as the Deliverer.

VI. The Christ had been born at Bethlehem, and there acknowledged by men of Gentile stock, but had

A NAZARENE

been driven out by the then ruler of the Jews, to go down to Egypt.[1]

He was not, however, to stay there long. After the death of those that sought the young Child's life (were there then others joined with Herod whose names are not recorded ?), Joseph was bid return into the land of Israel. At first the intention was to go to Judæa, the rightful home of the Messiah, but in consequence of the fact that Archelaus was now ruler there, and his character was well known, God warned Joseph to withdraw into the parts of Galilee. For in accordance with prophecy the Messiah was not to grow up recognised as such, but to be in a state of humiliation, with those round Him ignorant of His destiny. Hence it was but fitting that He whom the prophets called the *Netzer*, the scion of the roots of Jesse (Isa. xi. 1), should dwell at Nazareth. He 'came and dwelt in a city called Nazareth : that it might be fulfilled which was spoken by the prophets, that he should be called a Nazarene.'

Verbally indeed, as I have already implied, there is no such utterance in the prophets. The word *Netzer* is there, that is all. It may be that, like the Talmud, the Evangelist is making a play between *Netzer* and Nazarene,[2] or perhaps that he is taking the general sense of some of the prophetic utterances, which speak of Messiah growing up in obscurity.[3]

[1] St. Stephen appears to have seen in this the fulfilment of the typical history of Joseph the son of the Patriarch; *cf.* Acts vii. 9.

[2] T.B., *Sanhedrin*, 43a, in the uncensored text.

[3] *E.g.* Isa. liii. 2. See further Box, *op. cit.* pp. 28–33. Prof. Burkitt's identification of 'Nazareth' with Chorazin is more ingenious than convincing. He connects the word with 'Nazirite' (*The Syriac Forms of N.T. Proper Names*, 1912, pp. 15–18). Or the plural ('by the prophets') may be due to the employment by Jeremiah of a synonym, *tsemach*, Branch, in a Messianic sense (xxiii. 5).

In either case he was writing as a Hebrew-Christian for other Hebrew-Christians, who would have no difficulty in seeing the force of his allusion.

VII. With the third chapter of the Gospel we find ourselves in a different atmosphere. The writer, that is to say, has finished his prologue, derived in part from private information handed down from the Blessed Virgin or her husband, and partly from matter which had been found useful for hortatory exposition among Jewish Christians. For it is not likely that St. Matthew, or rather the writer of the First Gospel, was the actual originator of much of these two chapters. We may rather suppose that he edited materials which he already possessed either in documentary or in oral form.

He now leaves these sources and takes up a new one. Here, however, the source is known to us. We possess it almost, if not quite, in its entirety, and call it the Gospel according to St. Mark. The third and fourth chapters of the First Gospel are, speaking generally and neglecting details, derived directly, as it seems, from the Second.

Why then did St. Matthew trouble to write it over again? Because he felt that the Gospel according to St. Mark, however good it was for Christians in general, did not sufficiently present that view of the Messiah which he desired to bring before his fellow Hebrew-Christians. He knew that he could improve St. Mark's portraiture of the Lord Jesus, not only by slight touches which would bring out his own picture more plainly, but also by making many additions to it from other quarters. It is not, however, my duty to bring before you the various ways in which

JOHN THE BAPTIST

St. Matthew differs from St. Mark, but rather to draw out the presentation of Messiah contained in the First Gospel as it lies before us, written as it was for Hebrew-Christians living among unbelieving Jews.

The public proclamation of the Good News by the Apostles began with their mention of the appearance of John the Baptist.[1]

There was a reason for this, apart from mere historical order. The Jews expected Elijah to come before Messiah. Elijah was to prepare the way, and then Messiah would appear.[2]

This belief in the coming of Elijah was based upon the words of the prophet whom we know by the name of Malachi (iv. 5, 6) : ' Behold, I will send you Elijah the prophet before the great and terrible day of the LORD come. And he shall turn the heart of the fathers to the children, and the heart of the children to their fathers; lest I come and smite the earth with a curse.' We find this accepted by so early a writer as the son of Sirach, who, according to the most probable interpretation of the verse, addresses Elijah with the words : ' Thou of whom it is written, Prepared for a (future) time, to pacify anger, before it breaketh forth into wrath ' (Ecclus. xlviii. 10, Heb.).

St. Matthew falls in with this belief, as indeed he must have done in view of the general expectation of his time, but shows, indirectly here, and directly in later passages (xi. 14; xvii. 12), that the true Elijah was John the Baptist. Not of course that John was Elijah himself (John i. 21), but that he came in the spirit and power of Elijah. The Evangelist, however, is careful to indicate that the fulfilment is different

---

[1] See St. Peter's message in Acts x. 37, and St. Paul's in Acts xiii. 24.
[2] See 2 (4) Esdras vi. 26, with Canon Box's note.

from the expectation. For according to this (I refer only to traits described by teachers of the first and second centuries, and therefore reasonably near the time when this Gospel was written [1]) Elijah was to come in order to settle questions of ritual difficulty, or to determine whether or not certain families had legal rights. Nay, St. Matthew seems to say, the coming of Elijah was emphatically to prepare the way of the Lord—as Isaiah says : ' The voice of one crying in the wilderness, Make ye ready the way of the Lord, make his paths straight '—by preaching the need of repentance. It was thus that he would ' pacify (God's) anger, before it brake forth into wrath.'

And plainly John the Baptist was faithful to his task. Like the prophets of olden time in appearance and austerity of life, he fearlessly reproved all comers, in particular those who were Pharisees or Sadducees. But the general message of the forerunner of the Messiah is evident. The kingdom of heaven is at hand, therefore repent. The claim, he says, to be descendants of Abraham after the flesh can be of no avail. Abraham's true children may be formed of Gentiles, who seem to you to be like the stones that lie around me. Repent! for one is at hand, to whom I am unworthy to act as the meanest slave. I baptize with water, the mere symbol of penitence ; He has power to baptize with the Holy Ghost, and to burn up the ungodly with unquenchable fire, Gentiles and Jews alike.[2] St. Matthew, like every faithful evangelist, warns his readers that before the Messiah

---

[1] See in particular Klausner, *Messianische Vorstellungen* u.s.w., p. 58 *sqq.*

[2] The Jews were expecting the Messiah to bring judgment on the Gentiles. Yea, says the Baptist, and upon the Jews also. *Cf.* H. J. Holtzmann, *N.T. Theologie*, 1911, i. p. 172.

1] ELIJAH, PROPHET AND HIGH PRIEST

can be received there must be repentance, and a change of heart.

Again, an early form of the traditional teaching about Elijah tells us that he was to act as High Priest, in one particular. In the wilderness of the wandering of the children of Israel there was a small flask of holy oil, from which were anointed the tabernacle and its vessels, Aaron and his sons, and the whole line of high-priests and kings during the time of the first temple. Yet still the flask of oil remained undiminished in quantity for use in the future, when the Messiah was to be anointed with it, by the prophet and high-priest Elijah.[1]

That St. Matthew had this tradition in mind we cannot affirm for certain, but if we may suppose so we gain light upon the sequel to the preaching of John the Baptist. For in fact when Jesus comes from Galilee to the rightful place of His kingdom, Judæa, unto the Jordan to John, He is anointed by means of him, not indeed with oil, but with the reality for which the oil stood, the outpouring of the Holy Spirit. Thus the traditional teaching about Elijah was more than satisfied in John the Baptist.

We now expect St. Matthew to narrate the story of the Baptism. But there is still a delay. He has to take into account some persons with whom the Hebrew-Christians of his time came into contact. These were certain Jews who had been baptized by John in expectation of the coming of the kingdom, and had not made any further progress. Perhaps in the first instance these had been baptized, and had not waited to hear the preacher's later

[1] Klausner, *op. cit.* p. 62.

utterances respecting Jesus. Or perhaps they, unlike their master, had been altogether overcome by the difficulties which even John felt with regard to Jesus, when He did not work such miracles of deliverance from political oppression as they had expected Him to perform. At any rate, from one cause or another, and at present we have not the means of fully solving the riddle, many of those who professed to be John's disciples refused to acknowledge Jesus. They considered the austere teacher, by whose instrumentality they had been brought to repent of their former ways, to be superior to Jesus of Nazareth.

Hence St. Matthew is careful to point out that it was in no mere blindness, ignorant of what he was doing, much less in any assumption of superiority, that John the Baptist baptized Jesus. He did not wish to do so. *Prima facie* the less is baptized by the greater, and John felt that when Jesus presented Himself One was before him whose shoes' latchet he was not worthy to unloose. 'I have need,' he says, ' to be baptized of thee, and comest thou to me ? '

The answer of Jesus is remarkable, and the meaning of it not likely to escape a Jew trained in the religion of his fathers. ' Suffer it now : for thus it becometh us to fulfil all righteousness.' Jesus, that is to say, accepts the homage of John. He acknowledges that He is superior to the Baptist. Yet He bids him yield and baptize Him, for it was fitting, morally beautiful, that He and John should fulfil every demand of the will of God as made in rules and ordinances, this being exhibited for the occasion in the ceremony of baptism.

THE MESSIAH'S ACCEPTANCE OF HIS TASK

VIII. Observe that although Jesus is superior to John, He yet claims that they both ought to perform the will of God as affecting them for the moment. Jesus shows no sign of professing repentance, though He does thus place Himself on the level of the people, but He desires to make a public acceptance of the fact that the kingdom of heaven is at hand, and that He welcomes it.

We should be carried too far from our subject if we were to endeavour to investigate the nature of the feeling with which Jesus came to the Baptism. Sufficient now to say that, judging by the light of His after-life, He must have known that it meant for Him public entry into the work which He had come to perform, the commencement of a life of trial and opposition and even death, which, notwithstanding, should prove to be the means by which not only the will of God should be accomplished, but also the world should be saved.

So the Messiah was baptized, and He came up from the water, not indeed to enjoy fuller life with God, for that was impossible, but to receive in more conscious measure (we may say) the Holy Spirit, and to be assured afresh of His position and of the acceptance of His self-sacrifice.

We meet next, as it seems, with the first trace of that glorification of the human body of the Lord Jesus of which we are told later in the Gospel. At the Baptism His bodily powers were so far quickened beyond the power of men in general that He saw the heavens opened and God's Spirit descending, as it were a dove coming upon Him. How far before this our Lord was conscious of His high nature and calling we cannot tell. But we cannot easily overestimate the effect of such a vision. He would not be human if He had not felt Himself braced up by it, besides, of course, receiving in Himself all the imparted grace that the presence of the Holy Spirit implies. Heretofore He had lived the life of an ordinary man, but sinless, and in full communion with God. Now He sees that He has received special assistance for the special task before Him, and He can enter on it with courage.

His eyes were opened, but also His ears. For ' Lo, a voice out of the heavens, saying, This is my Son, the Beloved, in whom I am well pleased.' Here are three statements: Jesus is the Son of God; He is the Beloved; and God was well pleased with Him. The meaning of the first expression will come before us in a later lecture. Sufficient here to say that it sets Jesus forth in a wholly unique relation to God, as more truly His ' Son ' than any other person has ever been.

The second term describes Him, apparently, as that Person who was designated of old as the Chosen One (Isa. xlii. 1; see Matt. xii. 18), to whom in popular language was given the title once reserved for the nation of Israel (see Deut. xxxii. 15, xxxiii. 5, 26, in the LXX, where it represents the Hebrew Jeshurun). If this be so the word ' Beloved ' is here used to mark Jesus as the Messiah.[1]

The third phrase, ' in whom I am well pleased,' states that God is well pleased with the present act of Jesus. He has, that is to say, lived worthily of His nature, and His action in coming to Baptism,

---

[1] See J. A. Robinson, *Ephesians*, pp. 229 *sqq*. The sentence thus identifies the Messiah with the Servant, see Lecture XI, p. 381.

1]   THE DIVINE APPROVAL

and thus openly enrolling Himself among those who were expecting the coming of the kingdom, involving as this did His submission to the known will of God, won for Him the approval of His Father in heaven.[1]

Such was the voice, not, as Jewish fancy sometimes tells us, to decide in a dispute between learned doctors of the Law, but to assure Messiah Himself of the relation in which He stood to God by nature, by office, and by His own act. Vision and word alike warranted His belief that He was entering upon His public ministry in the full favour of God and His promised power.

IX. In iv. 1–11 St. Matthew describes an event which for his purpose is the crucial part of his whole narrative. For in the Temptation may be seen the methods deliberately adopted by the true Messiah, which form a complete contrast to the methods of all false Messiahs, as well as to those of the true Messiah according to Jewish expectation.[2]

St. Mark indeed mentions the Temptation as though it were a comparatively unimportant incident, either because the author did not perceive the significance of it, or because he was not acquainted with its details. Therefore he only tells us : ' And straightway the Spirit driveth him forth into the wilderness. And he was in the wilderness forty days tempted of Satan ; and he was with the wild beasts ; and the angels ministered unto him.' To St. Matthew,

---

[1] Perhaps this is the force of the aorist.

[2] ' Die alte Gemeinde hatte einen sehr unglaubwürdigen Satz zu verfechten, wenn sie behauptete, Jesus von Nazareth sei der Messias—denn gemessen an den vulgären Messias-Begriffen fehlte ihm zum König-Messias nicht weniger als alles' (J. Weiss, *Das Urchristentum*, 1914, p. 95).

on the other hand, the Temptation expressed, perhaps more clearly than any other part of the life of Jesus, the manner of His victory, and the true character of His Messiahship. Probably also the Evangelist perceived in it a description of the best and most fruitful method in Christian work for all time.

Now we all know that there have been few, if any, religious heroes who did not pass through a time of extreme loneliness, and spiritual trial, before they were enabled to carry out their work. Such a time of testing appears to be a necessary prelude to success. The Messiah was no exception. For, according to the presentation of Him recorded in this Gospel, He was not one of those imaginary persons who in the spiritual world, and with great issues at stake, come and see and conquer. He, being very man as well as very God, had to endure a severe test of His character. His work was the greatest that could be imagined, His trial corresponded to it, not only in severity, but also in nature.

Observe that the Evangelist is careful to tell us the moment when Jesus the Messiah met with this strange and awful experience. It was not before, but after, the Baptism, when He had received a special outpouring of the Holy Spirit. He had consecrated Himself without stint to the service of God, and His offering had been accepted. He had been granted the vision of the descent of the Spirit of God, and had heard the sweet words of assurance that He was God's Son, and His Servant, and the object of God's delight. He is now therefore ready for the crucial test of His ability to stand firm in the awful contest which He came to wage.

THE TEMPTATION

'Then was Jesus led up of the Spirit into the wilderness to be tempted of the devil.' St. Matthew relates a conflict higher in moral worth than the great war with which Jewish thinkers credited the Messiah. That was warfare between men, this between One who lived and fought as man, using weapons available to every man, and him who was at the head of the evil angels.

Observe further that the bodily frame of the Messiah, and therefore, if we may trust physiologists, His whole personality, was at its weakest. He was to derive no advantage from merely physical wellbeing. The devil was given every advantage. We may also suppose that the weakness of the body, after so long a fast, made our Lord the more susceptible to such sensuous sensations as His apparent removal in space to the temple's precincts, and the vivid panorama of 'all the kingdoms of the world and the glory of them.'

Be that as it may, for the Evangelist it was all important that the Messiah displayed the character of His work, and the nature of His methods in carrying it out, by the way He endured the three tests.

First, for His own needs He would trust His Father in heaven implicitly, and not exercise as God any power for Himself. It was necessary for St. Matthew to bring this out. For again and again Jews have said, and doubtless they said as much in St. Matthew's time, that if Jesus had been divine, as Christians affirm, He would not have experienced human weakness. For example, He would not have been hungry when He came to the barren fig-tree; again, He would have known by His divine power that there were no figs on it; also He would not have endured suffering at all, much less death; lastly, on the cross He would not have passed through the awful pain of conscious separation from His Father. All such arguments are met in the record that when He was bid satisfy His hunger by the exercise of power contrary to the will of God, He was content to reply : ' Man shall not live by bread alone [that is to say, by the means in front of him, if he chooses to take them], but by every word that proceedeth out of the mouth of God.' It is God's will, He says, which I have come to perform, not My own. I will wait His time, I will not be impatient and take My own way. My Father knows, and He will provide.

The second temptation represents the negative side of the same truth. Jesus the Messiah was subject to the ordinary laws of human nature, and had no right to expect miraculous intervention. The Jews perhaps had enthusiastic expectations of a Messiah who should disregard natural laws, and when He was breaking them be upheld by the hands of ministering angels. Not so with the true Messiah. He would not tempt His Father in heaven. He would claim God's preservation only when taking all possible care to ensure success, so far as human knowledge could ensure this beforehand. The presentation of Messiah is that of an eminently sane and sensible Person.[1]

The third temptation, on the other hand, is for St. Matthew the culminating point. Messiah is

---

[1] In T. J. Peah, viii. 9 [8] (21b), the devil quotes Scripture, and is answered by another text. Canon Streeter suggests that this temptation was to teach that Christ's work was slow, and that He was not to appear dramatically by throwing Himself from the pinnacle 'in sight of all Jerusalem' like an apocalyptic Christ (*Foundations*, p. 101). But this assumes that 'all Jerusalem' was present, of which there is no hint.

THE METHODS OF THE TRUE MESSIAH

offered immediate success, the submission of all the world, the gratification of His highest desires in the obedience of the peoples, on the condition, the trivial condition, as some might say, of acknowledging that He receives them at the hand of him who is in some sense the ruler of this world. Providing that He gives homage to Satan, the rulership of the world is offered to Jesus.

It is easy for us to perceive the general meaning of this temptation, but difficult to understand it altogether. Its sense, however, seems to be that in contrast to the means to be employed by the Messiah according to the common expectations of the Jews, the true Messiah used those that had no savour of the world. Bloodthirsty wars were far from Him. Political revolution He would have none of. Worldly measures He dismissed from His thoughts. The plane upon which He moved and carried out His purposes was far other than the ordinary grounds of men's actions. He made the service of God His one and only method. 'Get thee hence, Satan,' thou opponent of all that is good, 'for it is written, Thou shalt worship the Lord thy God, and him only shalt thou serve.'

The devil's attempt has failed. The messengers of God come and minister to Him who has not hesitated to prefer God's ways to others, however specious they may be.

Thus the character and methods of Messiah are presented to us as widely different from those of the Messiah of Judaism. He works no miracles for Himself. He expects no intervention contrary to nature. He uses no means unworthy of His high and holy cause.

X. In five more verses (iv. 12-16) St. Matthew will have completed his Introduction, before he describes the actual work of Jesus the Messiah. It was to be expected that the Messiah, when He had been consecrated for His work, and had proved His fitness to undertake it by the way in which He showed Himself superior to all forms of temptation by the professed ruler of this world, would begin His Messianic activity in Judæa, the seat of typical Judaism. It seems that He did not.

The reasons St. Matthew gives us are twofold— the accidental, if we may say so, and the real. The former consisted of the imprisonment of John the Baptist by Herod Antipas.[1] How did this affect our Lord? Was He afraid that if He began to preach in Judæa Herod would seize Him? Even if so it is likely that He was afraid not for Himself, but for the success of His plan. It is probable that if He had appeared in the centre of Judaism, as a Prophet whose connexion with the Baptist must have become known, the object of His coming would have been frustrated by the greatness of the political commotion He would have caused. If this prompted the withdrawal of Jesus to Galilee, it was entirely in accordance with His usual methods.

There was, however, a deeper and more vital reason. It was in agreement with the teaching of the prophets, not only that the Messiah should grow up in the obscurity of Galilee,[2] but also that Galilee should have the privilege of being the focus

---

[1] 'Now when he heard that John was delivered up, he withdrew into Galilee' (iv. 12).

[2] Not that Galilee was far removed from the influences of the world, for it was closely in touch with Roman and Greek movements, but it was distant from the centre of Jewish life.

THE DAWN IN GALILEE

from which His light should radiate. Jesus therefore visited His home at Nazareth, and then moved, permanently as it seems, to Capernaum, on the borders of the Sea of Galilee, and in the districts of Zebulun and Naphtali. Not indeed that Capernaum itself was in Zebulun, though Nazareth was, but it was situated, generally speaking, in the territory covered by the two names.

This reminds the Evangelist that the prophet Isaiah had described such a fact.[1] In Talmudic times Galilee was proverbial among the Jews for its spiritual darkness and ignorance of true religion, and possibly as early as this.[2] Yet there, amongst the darkness, the light was to arise! In the West towards the Great Sea, the Mediterranean, and in the East, on the farther side of Jordan, and in the northern circle largely inhabited by heathen, the people of the Lord which dwelt in darkness saw a great light; they were dwelling in the region of the shadow of death, yet to them the Dawn arose! Hebrew-Christians and unbelieving Jews alike could not but acknowledge that the fact of the public work of the Messiah having begun in Galilee was in agreement with the words of the prophet.

Thus far we have seen that St. Matthew has dealt with great preliminary questions raised by the men of his time against the Messiahship of Jesus. He has not indeed answered their objections in so many words. If he had done so it is improbable that his book would have come down to us. For it would have lacked many of the qualities that

[1] Isa. ix. 1, 2.
[2] See Neubauer, *La Géographie du Talmud*, 1868, p. 183.

have ensured its permanence. He has, on the contrary, put his strength into writing a devotional treatise for the use of his fellow Jewish believers. His narrative is very short, little more than notes from which preachers could have spoken, giving by word of mouth fuller explanations of the meaning of his sentences. But his work is unique. No other record of the life and teaching of the Messiah has been preserved which lays before believers of the Jewish race so vivid a description of Messiah as seen by Jewish eyes. May that Holy Spirit who guided the author in its composition Himself be with us, as, little by little, we endeavour to grasp the significance of the presentation of the Messiah to the Jews in the Gospel according to St. Matthew, while the Evangelist portrays the Hebrew-Christian Messiah, his Lord and ours.

Lecture Two

THE JEWISH PARTIES IN THE TIME
OF THE MESSIAH, ESPECIALLY THE
PHARISEES

'*Woe unto you, scribes and Pharisees, hypocrites!*'—
MATT. xxiii. 13.

Lecture Two

THE JEWISH PARTIES IN THE TIME OF THE MESSIAH, ESPECIALLY THE PHARISEES

'THE Jews,' writes Josephus, ' had for a great while three sects of philosophy peculiar to themselves : the sect of the Essenes, and the sect of the Sadducees, and the third sort of opinions was that of those called Pharisees.' [1]

In the present Lecture it is proposed to examine the relation in which the Messiah stood towards these three bodies, according to the presentation of Him contained in the Gospel according to St. Matthew.

I. The first will not give us much trouble, for, strictly speaking, it does not fall within our subject at all, and is included only for the sake of completeness.[2] For not only is the name of the Essenes not mentioned in either this or any other of the four gospels, but apparently there is not the slightest allusion to any of their customs or tenets, either directly or indirectly, by way of comparison or of contrast.[3]

It is true that some leading scholars of fifty years

---

[1] *Antt.* XVIII. i. 2. The threefold division recurs in *Antt.* XIII. v. 9 ; *War*, II. viii. 2 ; *Life*, § 2.

[2] The fullest account of the Essenes given by Josephus is in *War*, II. viii. 2-13, but see also *Antt.* XVIII. i. 5. The fullest modern discussions seem to be those of Lightfoot (*Colossians*, 1875, pp. 114-179), Kohler (*Jewish Encyclopedia*, v. 224-232), Schürer, (*G[eschichte des] j[üdischen] V[olkes]*, 4th ed. 1907, ii. 556-584), and J. Moffatt (*E.R.E. s.v.* Essenes).

[3] *E.g.* their ' tremendous oaths ' of obedience to the rules ; their celibacy.

THE HEBREW-CHRISTIAN MESSIAH [LECT.

ago [1] asserted that the Essenes had a close connexion with Christianity, and supposed that if Jesus of Nazareth Himself was not originally an Essene, certainly John the Baptist was. But it is rare to find any one of note holding this strange opinion now.[2] What has John the hermit, if even we may call him that, to do with the Essenes, who lived together in communities ? What connexion has his baptism, which was administered once for all, with the daily ceremonial washings practised by them ? What evidence is there that they insisted on repentance, even though they made much of a holy life ? Much less is there any reason for supposing that the Christian practice of kindliness to fellow-Christians on their travels is connected with the similar duty inculcated by the Essenes ; or that the Christian disregard of this world's goods was derived from the Essene custom of renouncing all private possessions and handing them over to the community. Every society of ethically earnest persons will have some traits in common, but it is quite unscholarly to attempt to derive one from another upon such slight evidence. It is not too much to say that, judging by the information at our disposal, those Jews who had been so far influenced by Greek (in particular Pythagorean), and possibly also by Buddhist, customs, as to form a semi-monastic community, the headquarters of which were near the Dead Sea, had no influence at all, or only the very slightest, upon John the Baptist, or the

---

[1] See note 1 on the next page.
[2] Even Prof. H. S. Nash, who derives Essenism essentially from anti-Hellenistic Judaism, virtually gives this up (Hastings-Selbie *s.v.* Essenes). Dr. Kohler still maintains it of John the Baptist, and partly of our Lord and His disciples (*Jewish Encyclopedia*, v. 231 ; *Grundriss*, 1910, pp. 318 *sq.*).

THE SADDUCEES

Lord Jesus Christ, or even the early Christians. The Essenes therefore may be left out of our consideration.[1]

II. We turn now to the Sadducees.[2] Curiously the very meaning of their name is uncertain. It can have no direct connexion with *Tsaddiq*, ' righteous,' a singularly unfortunate description of the Sadducees, but probably it has with Zadok. As the Boethusians took their name from Boethus, and the Epicureans from Epicurus, so the Sadducees may have taken theirs from Zadok.[3] If so, there is not much room for doubt as to who this Zadok was. He may indeed have been a person about whom no information has come down to us, a teacher perhaps of the first century B.C. or earlier. But such an hypothesis is unnecessary in view of him whose descendants were called the ' sons of Zadok ' by Ezekiel (xl. 46, and elsewhere), the line of priests and High Priests who traced their lineage back to the Zadok who filled the office of High Priest

---

[1] In spite of Grätz's self-satisfied dictum: 'Essäische Elemente im Urchristenthum sind nicht blos *erweislich*, sondern *erwiesen*, nur die Schönfärberei will sie nicht sehen' (*Geschichte der Juden*, 3rd edition, 1877, iii. 304). See H. J. Holtzmann, *N.T. Theologie*, 1911, i. 167 *sq*. Bousset in his lucid account of the Essenes in the *Religion des Judenthums*, 1906, p. 535, does not speak very decidedly, but in his *Jesus*, 1907, pp. 16 *sq*., writes: ' Jesus hat rein gar nichts mit der Sekte der Essener zu schaffen.' Similarly, but at greater length, M. Friedländer, *Die religiösen Bewegungen innerhalb des Judentums im Zeitalter Jesu*, 1905, pp. 163–168.

[2] I leave this as written, but the section should be supplemented by Dr. Oesterley's *The Books of the Apocrypha*, 1914, pp. 132–159. I cannot, however, but think he has been rather hasty in accepting the conclusions of Leszynsky (*vide infra*, pp. 57 *sq*. notes) and Lauterbach, and also the early date of the Zadokite Fragments.

[3] Geiger, *Urschrift*, 1857, pp. 20 *sqq*.; Hölscher, *Der Sadduzäismus*, 1906, p. 102; Schürer, *G.J.V.* ii. 408 *sq*. For the double 'd' compare the frequent form Σαδδούκ for Zadok in the LXX, and the name of the companion of Judas of Galilee in Josephus, *Antt.* XVIII, i. 1, §§ 4, 9; *cf.* also Burkitt, *Jewish and Christian Apocalypses*, 1914, p. 72.

in the time of David, and was 'put in the room of Abiathar' by king Solomon (1 Kings ii. 35).

The derivation of the name may be accepted without hesitation.[1] The doubt lies in the application of the name in New Testament times. We know indeed that the Sadducees were recruited only from the leading classes in Jerusalem,[2] and it has been argued that as the High Priests and their immediate relations belonged to these, the Sadducees were, to all intents and purposes, identical with them. The High Priests, using the term in its New Testament sense of the priestly families out of which alone the acting High Priest could be appointed,[3] claimed, it is said, to be the sons of Zadok, and thus they, and they only, were the Zadokites, or Sadducees.

This theory, however, assumes that the High Priests after the time of the Maccabæans were known by the name of Zadokites, and not, as seems to have been the case, by the name of Hasmonæans,[4] and also that the High Priestly families alone formed the wealthy class in Jerusalem, whereas many other families of distinction were settled there by Herod the Great. It has therefore been proposed rather to consider the Sadducees as containing within their ranks not the High Priestly families only but also others of high rank, and to regard the name Sadducee as referring not so much to lineal descent as to opinions.

For in the time of Antiochus Epiphanes the

---

[1] Dr. Cowley (*Enc. Bibl.* col. 4236) proposes a rather fantastic derivation from the Persian *Zindik*, used of one who rejected the sacred Avesta and followed only the commentary, and afterwards of an infidel generally. But the evidence is too late.

[2] Josephus, *Antt.* XIII, x. 6, § 298; *ibid.* XVIII, i. 4, § 17.

[3] Schürer, *G.J.V.* ii. pp. 222-224.   [4] Hölscher, *op. cit.* p. 103.

THE SADDUCEES PRO-ROMAN

High Priestly family favoured Hellenism—Jason, the successor of the godly Onias, and also his successor Menelaus, helping the king to overthrow the Law of Moses, and introducing heathen customs. Hence, it is urged, when in Roman times the leading classes in Jerusalem advocated nearly the same policy with respect to Rome, or at any rate did not show themselves the same staunch defenders of Hebrew customs as the Pharisees, they were given by their opponents the name Zadokites, Sadducees, as a term of abuse. The word implied that they were as bad as those pre-Maccabæan High Priests of old, who preferred heathenism to the Law of God.[1]

Whichever of these two theories is right the result, for our purpose, is very nearly the same. The difference is this: with the former, Sadduceeism, properly so called, is limited to the High Priests and the High Priestly families, with the second it is a tendency, exhibiting itself, coming to a head if you will, in the High Priests, but found among the wealthier class of Jerusalem generally. For us it makes but little difference. Sadduceeism was the peculiar form of belief fashionable among the upper classes of Jerusalem. It represented the opinion and the mode of life of the well-to-do, among whom the High Priests took a leading place.

Thus the Sadducees politically sided with the Romans, and dreaded anything which should endanger their security. It is evident, therefore, that they would not be likely to be in favour of any Messianic movement.[2] The saying of the worldly-wise Frenchman, 'Above all, no enthusiasm,' might well have been spoken by a typical Sadducee.

[1] Hölscher, *op. cit.* pp. 104 *sq.*   [2] *Ibid., op. cit.* pp. 34, 97 *sqq.*, 110 *sq.*

Their theological platform, if such an expression may be allowed, corresponded to the political. They were on the safe side. Not for them any new-fangled conceptions of the nature of the Law and their religious duties! What had been was good enough for them. It is true that we cannot defend the statement of Origen, Jerome, the author of the Philosopheumena, and Pseudo-Tertullian,[1] that they rejected the Prophets and other scriptures, receiving only the Law of Moses, if it means that they did not regard the Prophets and Holy Writings as canonical. But it may be so far true, that, like most other Jews, the Sadducees attributed to the Pentateuch so great a degree of inspiration as to far outweigh in value the other portions of Scripture. These in comparison with that were merely tradition.[2]

Somewhat similarly, it would be wrong to imagine that they altogether rejected the Oral Law. They did not accept it as it was explained by the Pharisees, but that is another matter. The Sadducees had been accustomed to certain traditional teaching, and raised no question against it. But as this became worked out, as we shall see, by the majority of the Scribes and their adherents the Pharisees, it gradually overpassed the limits to which the Sadducees had been accustomed, and they rejected both its rules and its doctrines.[3]

Further, they appear to have become very materialistic, if we may judge from the accounts of their opponents, and we have at present no other sources

---

[1] These are collected in Schürer, *G.J.V.* ii. 411, note 26.
[2] *E.g.* Talm. Bab. *Rosh ha-Shanah*, 7a, 19a.
[3] Josephus, *Antt.* XIII, x. 6, § 297.

THE ASSUMPTION OF MOSES

from which to derive our information.[1] The Sadducees are closely connected both in Josephus and in the Rabbinic writings with the 'Epicureans,' the typical unbelievers and materialists.[2]

Listen also to the description of them in the *Assumption of Moses*[3] (§ vii.), a Pharisaic work, written, according to Dr. Charles, between 3 B.C. and 30 A.D.: 'Scornful and impious men will rule, saying that they are just. And these will conceal the wrath of their minds, being treacherous men, self-pleasers, dissemblers in all their own affairs and lovers of banquets at every hour of the day, gluttons, gourmands. . . . Devourers of the goods of the poor, saying that they do so on the ground of their justice, but (in reality) to destroy them, complainers, deceitful, concealing themselves lest they should be recognised, impious, filled with lawlessness and iniquity from sunrise to sunset; saying, "We shall have feastings and luxury, eating and drinking, yea, we shall drink our fill, we shall be as princes." And though their hands and their minds touch unclean things, yet their mouths will speak great things, and they will say furthermore: "Do not touch me lest thou shouldst pollute me in the place where I stand."' It is not a pleasing picture that

---

[1] The *provenance* of the 'Zadokite' documents published by Dr. Schechter in 1910 is still too uncertain to afford an argument to the contrary. Leszynsky attributes to the Sadducees also the Book of Jubilees, the Testaments of the Twelve Patriarchs, the Book of Enoch, and the Ascension of Moses! See his *Die Sadduzäer*, 1912. On the 'Sadducean' origin of Ecclesiasticus, see Oesterley, *op. cit.* pp. 333-340.

[2] Such at least is the probable meaning of Josephus, *Antt.* X. xi. 7, §§ 277-281; see Hölscher, who also quotes the *Seder Olam*, c. 3.

[3] Dr. Büchler refers this passage to the leading members of the priesthood, which comes in effect to nearly the same thing (*Die Priester und der Cultus im letzen Jahrzehnt des Jerusalemischen Tempels*, 1895, pp. 77 sq.).

For quotations from the *Psalms of Solomon*, see below, p. 61.

the Pharisaic writer gives of his opponents. They claimed by right of their position to be everything that was good; in reality their lives and characters were worldly and sinful. If so, we can understand how it was that they paid little heed to the doctrine of reward and punishment in a future life, and disbelieved in a bodily resurrection. Neither did they accept the doctrine of angels, for this implied the continual care of God for them by the ministry of His unseen servants. It is quite consistent with such traits of character and faults in doctrine that their decisions in matters of the Law were harder and less sympathetic than those of the Pharisees,[1] and that they seem to have endeavoured to apply sometimes Roman law rather than Mosaic.[2] No wonder that they were not liked by the people generally.[3]

What was the attitude of the Lord Jesus towards them, according to this Gospel? We have not a great deal of information, if we strictly limit it to those passages where the word Sadducee actually occurs, and do not take into account those other verses where the chief priests are mentioned, tempting though it is to do so.

[1] Josephus, *War*, II, viii. 14, § 166. They seem to have insisted on the literalness of the precept 'eye for an eye,' &c., but the passage adduced in evidence of this (*Megillath Taanith*, iv.) is said to be of late origin (see D. W. Amram, *Jewish Quarterly Review*, Oct. 1911, p. 210; Geiger, *Urschrift*, 1857, pp. 120, 148).

[2] Hölscher, *op. cit.* pp. 30–32.

[3] See p. 54, note 2. Leszynsky (*op. cit.*), chiefly on the strength of very difficult and disputed sayings in the Mishna, argues that, after all, the Sadducees clung solely to the written Law, and were in fact the Karaites of antiquity. They succeeded so far (according to him) that they at last got the upholders of tradition to refuse everything that could not be proved, somehow or other, from Scripture. Experts have not said the last word on the subject yet, but it is hardly likely that Leszynsky will prove to be right. See also Miss Dampier's very interesting study in *Church and Synagogue*, Oct. 1913, pp. 151–168.

II] SADDUCEES AND THE RESURRECTION

They are mentioned by name in this Gospel only in four passages; three times in connexion with Pharisees, and once alone. The last is the famous section (xxii. 23–33), where they ask our Lord about the resurrection, and try to show its absurdity. Christ's answer, as we all know, was twofold. He reminded them that the absurdity lay with them, in presupposing that if there were a resurrection the conditions of earthly life would continue. We can indeed sympathise with the Sadducees if they were accustomed to have such representations of the future life brought before them as we find described by some mediæval Jewish teachers, who said that if a man had two wives on earth he would probably have only the wife of his youth in the resurrection-life.[1] Even though the Rabbi thought that the second life would be spent in a glorified earth, his statement remains grossly materialistic. We can understand that those Jews who had a tinge of Greek philosophy in them, as we may assume the Sadducees to have had, would shrink from the doctrine of the resurrection if it was described under such terms. The Messiah, however, is careful to point out that in reality this was to misunderstand altogether the nature of the resurrection and the resurrection body. But He also meets them on their own ground by His appeal to the Law. How far Sadducees were able to use the Pentateuch in the decision of points of doctrinal difference we have little or no means of judging. But our Lord's appeal in this example is entirely Pharisaic in its method. It is, that is to say, not so much a direct quotation of a proof text as a deduction. The resurrection is not stated in the passage quoted;

---

[1] R. Berachya Ha Nakdan (*Masref*, § 13, ed. Gollancz, p. 320).

it is only deduced from the language used. Hence we may presume that the Sadducees were not the merely mechanical expounders of Holy Writ which we often consider them to have been, for otherwise the Messiah would not have answered them by a method of using Scripture which would have no value in their eyes. God, He means to say, cannot have personal relation with a being who lives only for a time and then perishes. The sentence ' I the God of Abraham, &c.,' He implies, by its very juxtaposition of ' I ' and ' Abraham,' with no time-mark of past, present, or future, to intervene, suggests a timeless relation between God and man. Those cannot cease to be who are thus united to God. St. Matthew presents the Messiah as giving a fresh reason for the belief in the Resurrection, by His insight into the Law. The sentence there, He says, was spoken to you,[1] you Sadducees who acknowledge the Law, and you ought to have perceived the force of it.[2]

In the three other passages, as I have already said, the Sadducees are not named alone, but in connexion with the Pharisees.

First, chap. xvi. 1–4. These are Sadducees in Galilee, who either have come down from Jerusalem to interview the new Teacher, or, and more probably, have been living there already. They disregard the ordinary miracles of our Lord, and ask for a sign out of the sky, showing a strange ignorance of what the true signs of the Messiah are. Their worldliness was no safeguard against the demands of superstition.[3]

---

[1] Τὸ ῥηθὲν ὑμῖν; cf. Zahn in loco.

[2] When R. Gamaliel II was asked to prove the Resurrection from the Bible, he referred his inquirers to Deut. xxxi. 16, Isa. xxvi. 19, Cant. vii. 10, and finally convinced them from Deut. xi. 9, or iv. 4 (T.B. Sanh. 90b; see Bacher, Die Agada der Tannaiten, 1903, p. 82).   [3] Vide infra, p. 78.

THE PSALMS OF SOLOMON

Secondly, in xvi. 5-12, our Lord warns His disciples against the leaven of the Pharisees and the Sadducees —that is, not any specific doctrines, but the general tone of their life and religion, which corrupted everything they did, making it unfit to be offered to God.[1]

Thirdly, iii. 7-12, the Baptist's denunciation of the Pharisees and Sadducees. He calls them the offspring of vipers; asks who it was that suggested to them that they should flee from the wrath that was about to come; summons them to show repentance in their lives; bids them not trust to ancestral privileges. With the Pharisees we have nothing to do for the moment, but it is instructive to remember that the authors of the *Assumption of Moses*, as we have already seen, and of the *Psalms of Solomon*, speak of the Sadducees in no less bitter terms. We have heard the former (p. 57); listen now to the latter:[2] ' Let God destroy them that live in hypocrisy in the company of the saints, yea, destroy the life of such an one, in the corruption of his flesh and in poverty. Let God lay bare the deeds of men that are men-pleasers, yea, the deeds of such an one in derision and scorn. . . . Let ravens pick out the eyes of the men that work hypocrisy' (iv. 7, 8, 22). And again: 'They went up to the altar of the LORD when they were full of all uncleanness; yea, even in their separation they polluted the sacrifices, eating them like profane meats' (viii. 13). If the Sadducean priests of our Lord's time were like those of some eighty or ninety years earlier we cannot be surprised at the

---
[1] Lev. ii. 11; *vide infra*, p. 79.
[2] The extreme limits of the date within which these Psalms were written are stated by Ryle and James as 70 B.C. and 40 B.C. (p. xliv).

invective of John the Baptist.[1] The Sadducees held the first position in the nation, and abused it. It is not by accident that, although we find many Pharisees acknowledging Jesus as the Messiah, among them one of surpassing ability and energy, we never read that a single Sadducee was converted. The lack of moral earnestness prevented any attention to the warning of the Baptist or the invitation of the Messiah. The presentation of the Messiah in the Gospel according to St. Matthew shows us His forerunner inveighing against them, and the Messiah Himself refusing their demand for an unnatural and unprofitable miracle, warning His disciples against their teaching, reproving them for their lack of spiritual insight and their ignorance of the very scriptures which they professed to accept.

III. The third of Josephus' three sects of philosophy is that of the Pharisees. But before speaking specifically of these it will conduce to clearness if we consider those with whom they are often closely connected in the gospels, namely the Scribes.

Briefly, the Scribes stood for those learned Jews whose profession was the study of the Law of Moses, especially in its application to the needs of the day. They represented at once, that is to say, the guardianship of the letter (which even as early as our Lord's time appears to have been held in peculiar veneration, or there is little point in His statement that not a

---

[1] Dr. Oesterley and Canon Box indeed are of opinion that ' the words of rebuke addressed to them by the Baptist are not intended for them more than for others,' on the strength of statements in St. Luke's account (*R.W.S.* 1911, pp. 123 *sqq.*). But there is no doubt as to what St. Matthew himself means to say. The invective is the result of the appearance of 'many of the Pharisees and Sadducees,' and it is extremely unnatural to refer the 'them' to anyone else.

ORAL LAW A NECESSITY

jot or a tittle of the Law shall perish), and the working of it out in practice. For this present audience, of all congregations in the world, will understand, that however carefully a written law may be framed it will require explanation, and careful study, if its effect is to be all that its authors intended it to be. It is impossible that a written law can fit all the circumstances, changing as they do from age to age, unless its meaning is interpreted with due regard to the alteration of the times. In laws the letter often killeth, and it is only the spirit that giveth life.[1]

We remember this with regard to law to-day. We are apt to forget that the principle was true of old. Yet the more we study ancient religions, and the system of daily life in ancient times, which, in a large number of cases, was closely bound up with religion, the more we see how impossible it was that written laws could ever have sufficed. We learn that in all religions, and the cruder and more elementary they are the truer is the statement, there were always bodies of persons who were the depositaries of traditional explanations, and the directors of development of practice along the lines sanctified by precedent.

Rabbinic teachers have invariably asserted that this was the case with regard to the Law of Moses, and have been much ridiculed for their assertion. But it is hard to understand why. The more we know of early law, both in its customs and in its ritual, the more we see the necessity that the Bible laws, summary statements of practices often already ancient in the time of Moses, but hallowed then by

[1] *Cf.* Lectures IV, p. 148; V, p. 186.

the express command of God, should be supplemented by the oral explanations of their custodians. We may in fact assume to-day that from the first promulgation of the Law by Moses, its written statutes were only guides to the verbal instruction in ritual and in practice, and even in doctrine, which was presupposed to be available from qualified persons.[1]

The title by which such persons were called in Scripture was that of Scribes, no doubt because primarily their task was to attend to the writing and copying of the Law. For, as is acknowledged now by all scholars, the Israelites were able to write at least as early as the time of their exodus from Egypt. And probably, nay certainly if we are able to believe the Higher Critics, there was never a time when the Scribes were only copying out the Law, and not also recording, in greater or less degree, the development that it was receiving under their guidance. We cannot wonder therefore that Jeremiah complains that some Scribes were introducing into the sacred scriptures their glosses and interpretations in a way of which he did not approve.[2] For there were plainly Scribes and Scribes, and though, if the Higher Critics do not misinform us, some of them were guided to develop the Law aright, yet

---

[1] This is the truth underlying such fanciful representations as *Shmoth R.* § 28, on Exod. xx. 1. '"And God spake all these words, saying"—R. Isaac said: Whatever the prophets were about to prophesy in every single generation, they received from Mt. Sinai. For thus says Moses to Israel (Deut. xxix. 14 (15)): "Neither with you only do I make this covenant and this oath; but with him that standeth here with us this day before the LORD our God, and also with him that is not here with us this day." The last clause does not contain "standeth," because it means the souls that were about to be created, who as yet could not be said to stand.'

[2] Jer. viii. 8. See further the admirable account in Oesterley, *op. cit.* pp. 113-129.

THE SCRIBES

others introduced errors, which we may charitably hope were not permitted to survive.

The great impulse, however, to the growth of professional students and teachers of the Law was given by Ezra, who illustrates in his own person the close connexion that existed between the priests and the Scribes. The coming of ' Ezra the priest, a scribe of the law of the God of heaven,' [1] set in motion a more systematic study of the written word. This combined closer attention to the faithful transmission of it,[2] with the more thorough consideration of the methods of adapting it to the requirements of the post-exilic community, different as these were from those of their forefathers.

It was but natural that the Scribe at first was always a priest. But if we may judge from the language of Jesus the Son of Sirach, the profession of the Scribe was regarded as distinct from any other as early as the third century B.C. After speaking of sickness, the physician and death, he turns to the various occupations of life, contrasting them with the work of the Scribe : ' The wisdom of the scribe cometh by opportunity of leisure ; and he that hath little business shall become wise.' The ploughman, the artisan, the blacksmith, the potter, have no time for study. ' Not so he that hath applied his soul, and meditateth in the law of the Most High ; he will seek out the wisdom of all the ancients, and will be occupied in prophecies. He will keep the discourse of men of renown, and will

---

[1] Ezra vii. 12.

[2] Some centuries had to elapse before such transmission became accurate. The Rabbis accused the Samaritan 'scribes' of falsifying the sacred documents, in the Siphrê, on Deut. xi. 30, ed. Friedmann, p. 87*a*. See Bacher, *Terminologie,* i. pp. 50, 134, note 4.

enter in amidst the subtilties of parables. . . . He shall shew forth the instruction which he hath been taught, and shall glory in the law of the covenant of the Lord. Many shall commend his understanding; and so long as the world endureth, it shall not be blotted out : his memorial shall not depart, and his name shall live from generation to generation.'[1]

In any case, from one cause or another, by New Testament times the Scribes as a body appear to have been laymen, who perhaps, as Schürer suggests, were moved originally by some antipathy to the Hellenistic proclivities of the pre-Maccabæan High Priests.[2] Yet as a whole they were not antagonistic to them, for in the New Testament they are often mentioned together. Some may even have belonged to the party of the Sadducees,[3] but there is no direct evidence for this.[4] They were the professional scholars of the time, having, no doubt, their headquarters in Jerusalem, but not dwelling there only. There were some in Galilee also, perhaps in certain cases acting as schoolmasters, as is expressly stated to have been the case in the next century,[5] but having for their primary occupation the study of the Law, both in itself, and in its application to the immediate

---

[1] Ecclus. xxxviii. 24 ; xxxix. 1, 2, 8, 9.

[2] *G.J.V.* ii. 313.

[3] This is the natural deduction from Mark ii. 16, Luke v. 30, Acts xxiii. 9. See Schürer, *G.J.V.* ii. 320,

[4] Hölscher flatly denies the existence of Sadducean Scribes (*op. cit.*, 1906, p. 18). Chwolson, however, writes: 'Ein grosser Theil des Synhedrions bestand ja auch aus Priestern, die meistens Sadducäer waren, und als Mitglieder dieser hohen Behörde auch schriftgelehrt sein mussten' (*Das letzte Passamahl*, 1908, p. 113, note).

[5] See Bacher, *Terminologie*, i. 135. *Cf.* Büchler, *The Political and Social Leaders of the Jewish Community of Sepphoris in the Second and Third Centuries*, 1909, *passim*, and *Die galiläische 'Am-ha-'Areṣ des zweiten Jahrhunderts*, 1906, pp. 274 *sqq.*

SCRIBE—A NEUTRAL WORD

occasion. It is therefore only natural, as we shall see, that the majority of them were in sympathy with the Pharisees, and that therefore the conjunction of the terms 'scribes and Pharisees' expresses the plain fact, and gives the key to the general relation between them.

For we may assume that the great leaders of the Pharisaic party, such as Hillel and Shammai (about 30 B.C. to 10 A.D.), and Gamaliel I (? 10–40 A.D.), were 'Scribes,' even though perhaps they did not copy out a line of the Scriptures, and although the name 'Scribe' does not appear to have been directly applied to them. But Gamaliel is called a teacher of the Law[1] in Acts v. 34, and certainly all three would be included among the Sopherim (Scribes) to whose authority the Mishna appeals.[2]

We have seen therefore that in itself the word Scribe was neutral, and had no bad connotation. The Scribe as such was not necessarily opposed to Christian truth. He represented, on the contrary, the progressive party, which was prepared to accept fresh developments in the meaning of the Scriptures, if the necessity for them could be shown.

A Scribe who accepted Jesus of Nazareth as the Messiah might still continue the essential part of his work, and bring out the application of the Old Testament to the needs of Christian believers. Thus we find our Lord giving to His preachers the name of 'Scribes' in Matt. xxiii. 34: 'I send unto you prophets and wise men [a semi-technical term for scholars] and scribes.' Also in xiii. 52 our Lord appears to contemplate the conversion of Scribes, saying that every Scribe, if he has become

[1] νομοδιδάσκαλος.   [2] Schürer, *G.J.V.* ii. 314.

an adherent of the Kingdom of Heaven, and has been instructed in its character, is like a householder who produces out of his strong-room treasures which he has recently acquired, and also such as he has long had in store.

We can, however, understand that a Scribe, whose ordinary task lay in study and meditation rather than in active life, should shun the hardships which would be his lot if he followed Christ. Hence when a Scribe came up to our Lord and said: 'Teacher, I will follow thee whithersoever thou goest away,' His reply, free from fanaticism, and scrupulously fair and open, was: 'The foxes have holes, and the birds of the air shelters, but the Son of man hath not where to lay his head' (viii. 19, 20). The result we are not told, but presumably that Scribe withdrew from the physical difficulties in which his enthusiasm had nearly entangled him.

In all the other passages in this Gospel the Scribes are distinctly on the Jewish and anti-Christian side. We can, for example, understand that their professional keenness in religious Law would make them quick in scenting out blasphemy (Matt. ix. 3). For the claim to assert with authority that the sins of the paralytic were forgiven appeared to some of the Scribes who were standing by to mean that the prerogatives of God were being infringed.[1] It should be observed, however, that by his express mention of the fact that only 'some' of the Scribes

---

[1] Blasphemy, 'profanation of the Name' (חִלּוּל הַשֵּׁם), originally meant only the profane use of the actual Name itself (Lev. xxiv. 11), but as early as the days of Amos (ii. 7) it included words or actions which brought that Name into contempt. It would be a very short step to include under it the making of a false claim to be empowered by God with any of His attributes. *Cf.* Lecture IX, p. 315.

INDICTMENT OF THE SCRIBES

said this within themselves, St. Matthew suggests that there were others who were not so mistaken.

Again, in xvii. 10 we find that to the disciples' mind the Scribes are the leaders in sound religious expectation. The Lord has just spoken of His death and resurrection, and the disciples ask : Why, if Messiah must die, do our religious teachers expect the coming of Elijah to put all things right before He comes ? If that be so, there will be no need for Him to die. Christ acknowledges the force of the objection, and says that the aim of the coming of Elijah is indeed to restore all things to their ideal unity, but adds that Elijah had come already, although by the refusal of the learned men of the time to recognise him he was stopped in his work of restoration. In the same way as he suffered, shall the Son of Man suffer at their hands. The Messiah is here portrayed as bringing a heavy indictment against the Scribes, precisely in their position as leaders of religious opinion, because they rejected John, and because they would also take up a wrong attitude towards Himself. The justification for this charge we shall see later.[1]

So far we have considered only those passages where Scribes are mentioned alone. But there are many where other classes are named with them. They themselves evidently stood for the learned part of the Sanhedrin. Hence they are named in conjunction with the High Priests, who represented the Temple officials, and with the Elders (xvi. 21)—

[1] Here perhaps we may notice that the Evangelist remarks in vii. 29 that the various classes of people felt the difference between the teaching of Jesus and that of their Scribes. These taught out of tradition and mere learning, He as One having authority in Himself to deliver His message, and to expound the Scriptures from His own knowledge of their true meaning.

men who, it appears, were respected for their experience and age, or even for their learning. These last no doubt sometimes included persons who were also Scribes. Thus we see that when Herod made inquiry as to the place where the Messiah should be born (ii. 4), he gathered together ' all the high priests and scribes ' of the Holy People. Again, in xxi. 15, when, in the precincts of the Temple, immediately after the Cleansing, ' the high priests and the scribes' saw the miracles that He did, and the children crying out there, and saying Hosanna to the Son of David, they were so annoyed that they asked Him if He heard what these were saying. They received the calm reply : Yea, you study the Scriptures, did you never read these words addressed by the Psalmist to God : ' Out of the mouth of children and babes thou didst lay the foundation of thy defence against thy foes, of thy reputation and praise among men ' ? The Messiah is represented as calling the Scribes back to their own studies, and bidding them see in the Psalmist's words, as they might legitimately be expounded, the truth that the innocence of children guarantees the acceptability to God of the praises that come from their lips.[1] The wise are bid become like the children to whom God had revealed His truth (xi. 25).

In xvii. 12 (*vide supra*, p. 69) the Lord Jesus said that He would suffer at the hands of the Scribes. He says the same in xx. 18, where He associates the High Priests with them, and in xvi. 21, where He mentions the Elders as well. All three classes are to be the means of His suffering and death.[2] Similarly, when the Messiah was hanging on the cross the High

[1] Ps. viii. 2. *Cf.* Lect. VII, p. 269.   [2] *Cf.* Lect. XI, p. 379.

SCRIBES AND PHARISEES

Priests were mocking, together with the Scribes and Elders.[1] The Pharisees, it will be observed, are not named. The Scribes, however, as we have already seen in part, and shall see more clearly, were closely allied to the Pharisees.

For although we have thus far considered those passages of the Gospel which speak of the Scribes either alone or in conjunction only with the High Priests, or with the High Priests and the Elders, there are several which connect them directly with the Pharisees. Thus our Lord in v. 20 tells His followers that their righteousness must exceed that of 'the scribes and Pharisees.' Here they are regarded as one body. And rightly enough, with the subject under consideration. For righteousness was the special study of the Scribes, and the special aim of the Pharisees, who endeavoured to carry out in life the theories set before them by the Scribes. The Messiah, however, demands of His followers a higher grade of righteousness than that attained by the Scribes and Pharisees. The most learned, and the most zealous, members of the nation of Israel were to be surpassed in their own province by the adherents of the Messiah. St. Matthew therefore makes it plain that the demands of the Messiah upon His followers were extraordinarily high, and yet suggests that they were not beyond their powers. We shall have to return to this subject in a later Lecture; here it is enough to say that the righteousness demanded by Christ was greater than that of the Scribes and Pharisees, in as far as the inner character surpasses the totality of separate actions.[2]

[1] xxvii. 41-43.
[2] *Cf.* Lectures IV-VI. Other passages in which Scribes and Pharisees are mentioned together are xii. 38-45, xv. 1-14, and xxiii., *vide infra.*

THE HEBREW-CHRISTIAN MESSIAH [LECT.

We turn now to the Pharisees as such. They appear to be the direct descendants of the Assideans, or Chasidim, who in the first days of the Maccabæan revolt, 167 B.C., gathered to Mattathias and his sons, ' mighty men of Israel, every one that offered himself willingly for the law ' (1 Macc. ii. 42).[1] Thus, as was to be expected, they were, through all their history, zealous adherents of the Law of Moses, and of Jewish traditional customs, in contrast to those Jews who accepted Hellenistic practices and opinions, and acquiesced later in the rule of the Herods or of Rome. The Scribes, generally speaking, were Pharisaic, the distinction between the Pharisaic Scribes and the Pharisees themselves being that the former were leaders, and the latter the ordinary members of the party, who, from lack of opportunity, were not able to make for themselves a close study of the Law and its demands, and could only put the precepts of their leaders into practice.[2]

The name Pharisee is characteristic of their attitude towards religion and daily life. They were the Separatists, answering in their tone of mind to those who as far back as the days of Nehemiah (444 B.C.) ' separated themselves from all strangers ' (Neh. ix. 2), even as God separated light from darkness (Gen. i. 4), Israel from the nations (Lev. xx. 24), and the Levites from the people (Num. xvi. 9).[3]

[1] *Cf.* Charles, *Eschatology : A Critical History of the Doctrine of a Future Life*, 1913, pp. 171 *sqq.*; Montet, *E.R.E.*, vi. 526, *s.v.* Hasidæans.

[2] 'Die nach Tausenden zählenden Pharisäer waren die Partei der nach Hunderten zählenden Schriftgelehrten ' (Zahn, on Matt. v. 20).

[3] In the Targum the Aramaic P-R-SH represents the Hebrew B-D-L in these passages. See Mr. J. H. A. Hart's *Ecclesiasticus*, 1909, p. 275. Dr. Oesterley, following Leszynsky (*op. cit.* pp. 25, 123), derives the name from another root, P-R-SH, with the meaning ' explain,' ' expound,' in reference to the Pharisees expounding Scripture in the interests of the Oral Law (*The*

EARLY HISTORY OF PHARISEES

Perhaps the term was given them first in derision, but at least it accurately expressed their attitude, and was freely accepted by themselves. Apparently also they formed a separate organisation; the members of which were *Chaberim*, Associates, in contradistinction to rich or poor, learned or unlearned, who were not Pharisees.[1]

For our purpose it is unnecessary to say more than a few words about their early history. Josephus implies that they existed by name as early as the time of Jonathan, 153 B.C. (see *Antt.* xiii. 5. 9), but the first incident recorded is the objection raised by a Pharisee to the appointment of John Hyrcanus as High Priest in 135 B.C., and the consequent persecution of them.[2] They were, in fact, generally in opposition to the governing body, because while rulers consider the expedient rather than the good, the latter was the aim of the Pharisees. Hence, with the exception of a few years in the reign of Alexandra Salome, in 78–69 B.C.,[3] they never acquired the leading position

Books of the Apocrypha, pp. 130 *sqq.*). His argument that the Pharisees, so far from being Separatists, were closely allied with the people, does not allow enough for the effect of the principles of the 'unco' guid' upon their own minds. See also Loewe, *E.R.E.* vii. pp. 588 *sq., s.v.* Judaism.

[1] Schürer, *G.J.V.* ii. 399–403. Canon Box writes: 'This association or *ḥabûra*, which probably was already organized in the New Testament period, was a league that pledged its members to the strict observance of Levitical purity, to the scrupulous payment of tithes and other dues to the priest, the Levite, and the poor, and to a conscientious regard for vows and for other people's property' (*The Churchman*, Sept. 1911. 'Who were the Pharisees?' p. 666).

Dr. Mendelsohn, however, insists that only those Pharisees were *Chaberim* who joined a special society (*Jewish Encyclopedia*, vi. 121), perhaps limited to men of learning.

[2] Mr. J. H. A. Hart, in his very stimulating essay on 'The Pharisaic Recension of the Wisdom of Ben-Sira' (*Ecclesiasticus*, 1909, pp. 272–320), appears to argue that Pharisaism existed at an earlier date in its distinctive doctrines.

[3] See in particular L. Ginzberg, *Jewish Encyclopedia*, i. 359.

in the State. This was held by their opponents, the Sadducean party. Yet, omitting for the moment all consideration of Christianity, the Pharisees represented the permanent element in the Jewish nation. For with the fall of Jerusalem in 70 A.D. the Sadducees perished,[1] and the Pharisees came to their own.

It was they who organised Judaism, and drew up the official records of the traditional Law. Judaism, as we know it to-day, is the product of Pharisaic teaching and influence. Putting the case broadly and generally, all Jews from 70 A.D. have been Pharisees.

There are, however, two points of extreme importance for the right understanding of the history of the New Testament, which must now be mentioned.

First, it is necessary to insist on the fact already noticed that in the time of our Lord the Pharisees were inferior in power to the Sadducees. They had no voice in the government, and had no authority in the affairs of the Temple. For until the last decade of the Second Temple, say until 63 A.D., its ritual and its management were in the hands of the Sadducees.[2] It is obvious that this may prove to be of great importance when we come to consider certain events in the life of our Lord.

Secondly, and even of more importance for our purpose, is the fact that the Pharisees themselves were

---

[1] *I.e.* technically and officially. Many of the distinctive tenets of Sadduceeism survived among individual Jews. See Lauterbach, *Jew. Quart. Rev.*, Oct. 1915, pp. 308 *sqq.*, who, however, tries to prove too much.

[2] Büchler, *Die Priester und der Cultus*, 1895, pp. 118, 145, 156; Chwolson, *Das letzte Passamahl Christi*, 1908, pp. 86 *sq.*, 186. Hölscher denies this, but only by straining his authorities (*Der Sadduzäismus*, 1906, *passim, e.g.* pp. 53, 59, 70). See Schürer's note upon him, *G.J.V.* ii. 418. *Vide infra*, p. 378, n. 1.

SHAMMAITES AND HILLELITES

divided. Their great Scribes, Hillel and Shammai (see p. 67), left successors, hardly known to us by name, but referred to under the titles of the House of Hillel and the House of Shammai. While these held the same general principles of opposition to everything that savoured of Gentilism, whether in the persons of the Herods or in the powers of Rome, they were very different in character. It is true that we have only the records drawn up by the winning side, and perhaps if Shammaite writings are ever found they will throw new light on the two parties, but with our present information the difference is clear.

The Shammaites were like their founder, hard and unyielding, bitter and harsh in all their demands and rules. They may not indeed be identified with the party of the Zealots, but they had historical connexion with them (for with Judas of Gamala was joined Zaddok, a Pharisee),[1] and they rejected all kinds of compromise with Rome. They were the extremest of the Separatists properly so called.

It was otherwise with the Hillelites. Hillel himself was typically gentle, and his followers imitated him. The decrees passed by them were, so their writers declare, always on the broader and kinder side. But—and this is the important point for our purpose—the Hillelites became supreme only after all opposition to Rome was found to be useless. Until the fall of Jerusalem the Shammaites were the upper party among the Pharisees. Their power may be estimated from the terrible day soon after 44 A.D. when at a gathering of Pharisaic Scribes in the upper chamber of Hananiah, son of Hezekiah, son of Garon (Mishna, *Sabbath*, i. 4), the Sham-

[1] Josephus, *Antt.* XVIII, i. 1, § 9.

maites not only passed eighteen rules contrary to the wishes of the Hillelites, but even used physical force, and killed many of the latter.[1] Hence in New Testament times the typical Pharisee was more likely to be a follower of Shammai than of Hillel.[2]

Let us now consider the description of the Pharisees given by the Messiah, according to the presentation of Him in this Gospel.

1. First, the Pharisees are ostentatious in their religion. 'They make broad their phylacteries, and enlarge the borders of their garments, and love the chief place at feasts, and the chief seats in the synagogues, and the salutations in the market-places, and to be called of men, Rabbi' (xxiii. 5–7). Similarly, 'the hypocrites' make a display in giving alms, in praying in the sight of men, in fasting (vi. 2–4, 5, 6, 16–18).

2. Secondly, the Pharisees insist unduly upon ceremonial. They are, for example, shocked that the disciples pluck the ears of corn, and, rubbing them in their hands, eat them, upon the sabbath day (xii. 1, 2). They are grieved that people are healed by the Lord Jesus on the sabbath day (xii. 9–14). They are astonished that the disciples eat without first washing their hands, thus transgressing the tradition of the elders (xv. 1, 2). In fact, they put the tradition above the written Law (xv. 3–14). So also they take endless trouble to secure a proselyte, though the result is disastrous (xxiii. 15).

---

[1] It was said that that day was as hard for Israel as the one in which the Golden Calf was made. See Weiss, *Dor dor w'dorshaw*, 1871, i. pp. 186 *sq.*, and especially T. J., *Sabb.* i. 4, p. 3c.

[2] *Vide infra*, pp. 85 *sqq.*

FAULTS OF PHARISEES

3. Thirdly, with all their punctiliousness they neglect those matters that are of greater importance, whether in doing good or in avoiding evil. They 'tithe mint and anise and cummin, and have left undone the weightier matters of the law, judgment and mercy, and faith.' On the other hand, they strain out a gnat, and do not mind swallowing something that seriously pollutes them, presumably some gross sin which they take no trouble to avoid (xxiii. 23, 24). Again, they attend to the outside of things rather than the inside, the appearance more than the reality. In fact, their actions and lives are typified by their treatment of tombs, which they whiten so that men may not be contaminated by touching them by accident, yet all the while the tombs themselves remain full of all corruption (xxiii. 25–27).

4. Fourthly, they make great profession of the knowledge of God, yet in reality their actions and modes of thought are conditioned by ignorance both of Him and His Word. They are, in fact, destitute of spiritual perception. Their decisions about oaths, making, as the Pharisees do, wrong distinctions between swearing by the temple and by its gold, and, again, by the altar and by the gift upon it, proceed on wrong lines, lacking the common sense of the devout believer (xxiii. 16–22). They are indeed blind guides (xv. 14, xxiii. 16, 17, 24; *cf.* 19, 26).

Again, they are surprised that the Lord Jesus eats with publicans and sinners; but this is due to their failure to perceive that it was fully in accordance with the Divine character, as revealed in Scripture, to show mercy, rather than to insist on the minutiæ of ritual (ix. 11). Similarly, as we have already seen, He reproved the High Priests and Scribes for their ignorance of the will of God that the children should acknowledge Him (xxi. 12-16. See p. 70). It is with somewhat of the same kind of reproving tone that He propounds to the Pharisees the question how it is that David gives to the Messiah, his son according to fleshly descent, the title of Lord (xxii. 41-46).[1] So again He convicts them of ignorance of the true meaning of Scripture, when, prompted by a desire to put Him in a dilemma, they ask Him whether divorce is allowable (xix. 3-12), and also of ignorance of the nature of the government of God when they propound to Him the other dilemma, whether it is lawful to give tribute to Cæsar (xxii. 15-22).

5. Fifthly, when they came to Him asking for a sign, no mere miracle performed on earth, but a sign produced out of the sky, to satisfy themselves, as it seems, before they could acknowledge His pretensions, His replies indicate that He thought them worthy representatives of an evil and adulterous generation, who did not deserve that any new sign should be given them. They were more unbelieving than the godless men of Nineveh, less desirous of truth than the heathen Queen of Sheba. It was the will that was deficient in them. Their natural powers which enabled them to understand the signs of the weather were sufficient to interpret the meaning of the moral events that were happening—if only they chose to study them (xii. 38-42, xvi. 1-4).[2]

[1] See Lectures VII, pp. 270-272, and IX, pp. 321 *sq.*

[2] *Cf.* Lecture III, p. 111, *vide supra*, p. 60. Merx on xii. 38 gives an interesting parallel from T.B., *Sanhedrin*, 98a. R. Jose ben Qisma is asked for a sign

IGNORANCE OF PHARISEES

6. Sixthly, the Messiah bade His disciples beware of the doctrine of the Pharisees, which was so far like that of the Sadducees as to resemble leaven in its all-pervading power. It was unfit to be offered to God, corrupt and corrupting (xvi. 5–12).[1] Further, we can hardly be wrong in including the Pharisees among those whom the Messiah calls the wise and understanding, from whom the knowledge of God was hidden (xi. 25).

Again, regarding them as the professed teachers of the truth to Israel, He says that they turn the key of knowledge upon men lest they should enter into the Kingdom, neither entering in themselves nor allowing those that had already begun to enter in to enter (xxiii. 14).

7. Seventhly, what wonder, then, that with this ignorance they show direct opposition to all that is good! When the Messiah performs a miracle in driving out demons, the Pharisees are so indifferent to the sense of spiritual realities that they accuse Him of doing it in the power of Beelzebub, forgetful of the fact that their own followers also exorcised demons. But this, as Jesus shows, is to speak against the very power of the Holy Spirit in the world, and to deny the root-principle of religion. For such persons there can, in the nature of things, be no forgiveness (ix. 34, xii. 22–32).[2]

8. Lastly, they are like the wicked husbandmen in the parable, who do not scruple to remove those

of the coming of Messiah. He at first refuses, but afterwards says that when Messiah comes the waters in the cave at Paneas (the source of the Jordan) will be turned into blood. This took place at his own death.

[1] *Vide supra*, p. 61.   [2] *Cf.* Lecture VIII, p. 295.

who, as they think, stand in the way of their own advancement. Indeed the Pharisees recognise that Jesus spoke this parable against them, and immediately proceed to prove the truth of the application by trying to seize Him (xxi. 33–41, 45, 46; *cf.* xii. 14). Remembering this we cannot be surprised that He should have accused the Scribes and Pharisees of adorning the tombs of the prophets, and yet resembling in character those who murdered them (xxiii. 29–32).

For the closing sentence of the Messiah upon the 'scribes and Pharisees, hypocrites!' is that there is no escape for them: 'Ye serpents, ye offspring of vipers, how shall ye escape the judgment of hell?' (xxiii. 33). Jerusalem must perish, and all the blood of the martyred prophets is to come upon them and that generation (xxiii. 34–36).

To sum up, ostentation in religion, punctiliousness in details, with neglect of that which is of real importance, ignorance of the spirit of Scripture and the character of God, unwillingness to use the means of true knowledge, together with wilful opposition to spiritual work, and with cruelty towards God's messengers—these are the marks of the inbred poisonous viciousness of the Scribes and Pharisees. It is a tremendous indictment.

Such is the verdict of the Messiah upon the Scribes and Pharisees, as presented in the Gospel according to St. Matthew. That of modern Jewish scholars is very different.

The following extracts from Dr. Kohler's article in the *Jewish Encyclopedia* are typical: 'The object of the Pharisees was to render the Sabbath "a delight"

(Isa. lviii. 13), a day of social and spiritual joy and elevation rather than a day of gloom. . . . The Pharisees transformed the Sabbath and festivals into seasons of domestic joy, bringing into increasing recognition the importance and dignity of woman as the builder and guardian of the home. . . . The aim and object of the Law, according to Pharisaic principles, are the training of man to a full realization of his responsibility to God and to the consecration of life by the performance of its manifold duties. . . . The acceptance of God's Kingship . . . means a perfect heart that fears the very thought of sin; the avoidance of sin from the love of God; the fulfilment of His commandments without expectation of reward; the avoidance of any impure thought or any act of sin that may lead to sin. . . . The ethics of the Pharisees is based upon the principle, " Be holy, as the LORD your God is holy." . . . It is a slanderous misrepresentation of the Pharisees to state that they " divorced morality and religion," when everywhere virtue, probity, and benevolence are declared by them to be the essence of the Law. Nothing could have been more loathsome to the genuine Pharisee than Hypocrisy. " Whatever good a man does he should do it for the glory of God." '[1]

Another eminent Jewish scholar, Professor Chwolson, who was a Christian as well as a Jew, writes as follows: ' The kernel and quintessence of the teaching of Christ consists, as is generally recognised, in the spiritualisation of religion, in pointing to the fact that its true nature lies in love to God and men, and not in the punctilious observance of the ceremonial laws. . . . This conception of the true nature of religion

[1] *s.v.* Pharisees, ix. 663–665.

was not at all strange to Judaism in general, and to the nobler and better of the Pharisees. I need only remind theologians, who are acquainted with the Old Testament, of the words of the prophets Samuel, Isaiah, Micah, Jeremiah, and several of the Psalmists, who proclaimed with one voice that love to God, the practice of righteousness, care for the weak and poor, &c., is the essence of religion, and that through such actions one can obtain the favour of God, but not through sacrifices and vows. The Pharisees walked partly in the footsteps of the old prophets, strove for the holiness of the whole people and against the exclusive character of the priesthood, and perceived that love to God and men was the essence of religion, without however desiring to do away with the ceremonial laws.'[1]

No less favourable account is given by Canon Box, one of the few Gentile scholars who can speak from a knowledge of the Talmudic sources of Judaism at firsthand. He writes: ' The Pharisees were for

[1] *Das letzte Passamahl Christi*, 1908, p. 89. ' Der Kern und die Quintessenz der lehre Christi besteht, wie allgemein anerkannt wird, in der Vergeistigung der Religion, in dem Hinweis darauf, dass das Wesen derselben in der Liebe zu Gott und zu Menschen und nicht in der peinlichen Ausübung der Ceremonialgesetze liege. . . . Diese Auffassung vom Wesen der Religion war dem Judenthum überhaupt und den edleren und besseren unter den Pharisäern durchaus nicht fremd. Die Theologen, welche mit dem Alten Testament bekannt sind, brauche ich nur auf die Worte der Propheten Samuel, Jesaia, Micha, Jeremia und mehrerer Psalmisten hinzuweisen, welche einstimmig predigten, dass Liebe zu Gott, Gerechtigkeit üben, sich der Schwachen und Armen annehmen u.s.w. das Wesen der Religion sei, und dass man durch solche Thaten das Wohlwollen Gottes sich erwerben könne, aber nicht durch Opfer und Gelübde. Die Pharisäer gingen theilweise in den Fusstapfen der alten Propheten, kämpften für die Heiligkeit des ganzen Volkes und gegen die Exclusivität der Priesterschaft und sahen es auch wohl ein, dass die Liebe zu Gott und zu den Menschen das Wesen der Religion sei, aber ohne dabei die Ceremonialgesetze abschaffen zu wollen.' See also pp. 187-189, with the touching picture of Chwolson's own home in his childhood.

a long period the party of progress within Judaism ; they fought strenuously and passionately—if not always wisely—for great causes, and won them. They championed the cause of pure monotheism against the Hellenizing movement; they built up religious individualism and a purely spiritual worship; they deepened the belief in a future life; they carried on a powerful mission propaganda; they championed the cause of the laity against an exclusive priesthood ; they made the Scriptures the possession of the people, and in the weekly assemblages of the Synagogue they preached to them the truths and hopes of religion out of the sacred books (not only out of the Pentateuch, but also out of the Prophets and Hagiographa). . . . The Pharisees consistently strove to bring life more and more under the dominion of religious observance. But observance —and ceremonial—was valued mainly because of its educational worth. By carefully formed habits, by the ceremonial of religious observance, religious ideas and sanctions could be impressed upon the people's mind and heart. But the outward was subordinated to the inward.' [1]

We cannot wonder that Josephus should tell us that 'the cities gave great attestation to the Pharisees on account of their entire virtuous conduct, both in the actions of their lives and their discourses also.'[2]

In view of these statements how can we explain the severity of the language employed by the Messiah, according to the presentation of Him in the Gospel according to St. Matthew ? The question is of

[1] *The Churchman*, Sept. 1911, pp. 665, 670. Dr. Oesterley and he use very nearly the same language in *R.W.S.* 1911, pp. 126 *sq*.
[2] *Antt.* xviii. i. 3, § 15.

the greatest importance; perhaps the answer is to be found in more than one direction.¹

First, it has been suggested that the text is corrupt. Dr. Chwolson, for example, is of opinion that in some passages the original reading was only the word 'Scribes,' and that later copyists added, or substituted, 'Pharisees.' If this were so then the Lord Jesus may have intended only to blame those Scribes who were Sadducees, and not those who belonged to the Pharisaic party.² Dr. Büchler again thinks that sometimes 'Priests' was the original word, not 'Pharisees.'³ So also Dr. Kohler writes: 'Owing to the hostile attitude taken towards the Pharisaic schools by Pauline Christianity, especially in the time of the emperor Hadrian, "Pharisees" was inserted in the Gospels wherever the high priests and Sadducees or Herodians were originally mentioned as the persecutors of Jesus.'⁴

Even supposing, however, that it could be proved that in a few passages the word 'Pharisees' had crept in instead of 'priests' or 'scribes,' it is very unlikely that there should have been such wholesale corruption as this theory requires. It alone is quite insufficient.

Secondly, it is thought, especially by Chwolson

---

¹ Mr. Herford in his painstaking work, *Pharisaism*, 1912, writing from a Unitarian standpoint, says: 'I yield to no one in my reverence for Jesus; he is, to me, simply the greatest man who ever lived, in regard to his spiritual nature' (p. 114), but adds: 'If there was on the part of the Pharisees a complete inability to comprehend the religious position of Jesus, there was also on his part an inability to comprehend the religious position of the Pharisees' (p. 170). It is easier to cut the knot than to unravel it.

² *Das letzte Passamahl*, 1908, pp. 113 sq.

³ *Die Priester und der Cultus*, 1895, pp. 81–88. He refers in particular to Matt. xii. 1, 5; xv. 5; xxiii.

⁴ *Jewish Encyclopedia*, s.v. Pharisee, ix. 665.

II] EXPLANATIONS OF CHRIST'S INVECTIVE

and Canon Box, that our Lord's invectives were not aimed against the Pharisees as a class, but only against comparatively few of them, who lived unworthily of their profession. There are black sheep in every flock, and we know from the Jewish writings themselves that it was so with the Pharisees. There is no object in repeating the often quoted list of the seven kinds of Pharisees mentioned in the Talmud, only one of which comes up to the ideal of a true Pharisee, separate in heart and life from sin and the world.[1] Nor is it necessary to do more than allude to another passage, which speaks of 'painted' Pharisees.[2] Here again, while it is quite possible that in one or two verses the Lord Jesus had such Pharisees solely in His mind, the general description of the Pharisees in the Gospel is too far-reaching to be satisfied by this theory. The suggestion of the Gospel that the Pharisees as a whole were wrong, and not only a small fraction of them, cannot be so easily dismissed.

Thirdly, it is pointed out that, quite apart from the question of the existence of hypocritical Pharisees, as we generally use the word hypocrisy, there were two distinct parties among the Pharisees.[3] For it may be that the opponents whom the Lord Jesus had in mind were the followers of Shammai, and not those of Hillel. This, it is said, will account for the fact that some of the relations of the Lord Jesus with Pharisees were quite friendly.[4] Did He not preach in the

---

[1] The list may be found with full references in Chwolson, *op. cit.* pp. 116-118. *Cf.* 98, 120, and more briefly in Oesterley and Box, *op. cit.* p. 127' and in Loewe, *E.R.E.*, vii. p. 588.

[2] See Chwolson, *op. cit.* pp. 114 *sq.*, 189.   [3] See above, p. 75.

[4] *Cf.* Oesterley and Box, *Religion and Worship of the Synagogue*, 1911, pp. 124 *sq.*; Chwolson, *op. cit.* pp. 90, 95. *Vide infra*, pp. 88, note, 151, 209.

synagogues, where, it is asserted (though the assertion may be doubted), the Pharisees were supreme ? And was He not asked to dine with a Pharisee, and warned by Pharisees of danger from Herod ? Besides, did not many Pharisees become believers in Him, as is recorded in the Acts of the Apostles ? These, however, it is suggested, were only followers of Hillel, while it was the followers of Shammai who had the real power in Jerusalem until long after the death of the Lord Jesus. May then it not have been the Shammaite section, and the Shammaite section only, whom He attacked ?

There is, in fact, some corroborative evidence for this. It appears that the regulation about washing the hands before eating was a subject of dispute between the Shammaites and the Hillelites during the greater part of the first century of our era, and was not finally settled until its close. It was the Shammaites who insisted upon it ; and few, if any, of the Hillelites did so. When then in Matt. xv. 1–20 our Lord defends His disciples for eating without having observed this ceremonial washing, and blames the Pharisees for insisting upon it, He must, it is said, have had the Shammaites only, or at least preeminently, in His mind. In view, therefore, both of this and of the comparative powerlessness of the Hillelites in the time of our Lord, it is suggested that His invectives were aimed at the followers of the stern and narrow Shammai, not at those of the peaceful and tolerant Hillel.[1]

[1] Box, *Churchman*, Sept. 1911, pp. 671 *sq.* Oesterley and Box, *op. cit.* pp. 128-130. It is well to note one interesting result if this opinion should be proved correct. It is this, that if a Christian writer thought it was worth while to record the words of Jesus against the Shammaites, this must have been because they were still a power in the land. But they lost their power

WAS HE ATTACKING SHAMMAITES ?

Before, however, we accept this theory, certain considerations must not be overlooked. The differences of the House of Shammai and the House of Hillel consisted only in details, not in principles.[1] We find, for example, that the Shammaites insisted that a maiden who was betrothed in her childhood by her mother or brother should accept their decision, but that the Hillelites permitted her to refuse, if she did not like the man whom they had chosen for her. So, again, the Shammaites allowed divorce only for a serious moral fault; the Hillelites for almost any cause, if the man disliked his wife. Save that the House of Hillel was less dependent on the letter of the Mosaic Law, and tried to discover more means whereby its rigorousness should be softened, we can find no fundamental difference in their tenets. Both were Pharisees of the Pharisees. Speaking generally, what was true of the one party was true of the other.

More evidence for what we may call the Shammaite theory has been thought to lie in their persecuting spirit. It has been suggested, for example, that the opposition in the Gospels to the Pharisees was due to the bitterness that existed between them and the early Christians.[2] The latter had suffered at the hands of the former. It is further supposed that if the Christians were persecuted by Pharisees these must have been the Shammaites, not Hillelites. For

after 63 A.D., as we have already seen. Therefore these portions of the Gospel which attack the Shammaites must spring from a time anterior to that. In other words, the more plainly the Gospel lays stress on feelings and parties that passed away before 70 A.D., the more evident it becomes that the substance of the Gospel is earlier than that date, however much later certain critics may place its composition as a whole.

[1] Weiss, *Dor dor w'dorshaw*, i. 177-187.   [2] *Cf.* p. 84.

THE HEBREW-CHRISTIAN MESSIAH [LECT.

we find Hillelites up to the very end of the second century treating Christians in a kindly fashion.[1]

Yet this is to forget certain plain facts. We do know that not very long after the Lord's crucifixion a persecution arose, organised, it would seem, by the High Priests—that is to say, the Sadducaic party, but supported by one young Pharisee at least, whose zeal as inquisitor took him as far as Damascus. No doubt, it will be said, the man was a Shammaite; a follower of Hillel would not have acted thus. The Hillelites, gentle souls, would never have persecuted Christians. Unfortunately for the theory he was not. His teacher was, in fact, the son, or possibly the grandson of Hillel himself. Saul of Tarsus, the pupil of Gamaliel, cannot have belonged to the party of the Shammaites, but must have been a Hillelite.[2] Yet, as we know from his own statements in the Epistles,[3] as well as from the more detailed account in the Acts of the Apostles,[4] he persecuted the Church to the uttermost. The fact is that when we assume that the greater liberality of the Hillelite school, in regulations affecting the daily life, passed over into the realm of doctrine, and made it less intolerant of divergence from the recognised faith of Pharisaic Judaism, we are going farther than our evidence warrants. In short, the theory that our Lord's invectives against the Pharisees were limited to the Shammaites, is, upon the whole, to be rejected.

[1] That this is true of even R. Jehudah ha-Kadosh himself (at least in one instance) see Chwolson, *op. cit.* pp. 104, 105.

[2] In this connexion it should be remembered that when St. Paul's training by Gamaliel began he was probably old enough to make a deliberate choice of his teacher. See Sir W. M. Ramsay's illuminating article on *The Thought of Paul* in the *Expositor* for Dec. 1911, pp. 481-489.

[3] 1 Cor. xv. 9; Gal. i. 13; Phil. iii. 6; 1 Tim. i. 13.

[4] Acts viii. 3; ix. 1, 13, 21; xxii. 4, 19; xxvi. 10, 11.

THE TRUE EXPLANATION

Even the best and purest part of the Pharisees, and such a position we gladly accede to the Hillelites, justified by its actions the language of the Lord Jesus.

This leads us to what, in all probability, is the true explanation of His indictment. It is that He used the word 'hypocrite' in a somewhat different sense from that which we ordinarily attach to it.[1] Ours is true as far as it goes, but it does not go far enough. We use it in the narrow sense of a person who deliberately and consciously says, or does, a thing with the intention of deceiving others, and perhaps also himself. Now it is quite true that sometimes the Lord employs the word in precisely this way. Take, for example, these verses in the Sermon on the Mount: ' When therefore thou doest alms, sound not a trumpet before thee, as the hypocrites do in the synagogues and in the streets, that they may have glory of men. Verily I say unto you, They have received their reward. . . . And when ye pray, ye shall not be as the hypocrites: for they love to stand and pray in the synagogues and in the corners of the streets, that they may be seen of men. Verily I say unto you, They have received their reward. . . . Moreover when ye fast, be not, as the hypocrites, of a sad countenance: for they disfigure their faces, that they may be seen of men to fast. Verily I say unto you, They have received their reward ' (vi. 2, 5, 16).

[1] ' A painted people,
Who paced around with steps exceeding slow,
Weeping, and in their look tired and overcome.
Cloaks had they on, with hoods, that fell low down
Before their eyes. . . .
Outward all gilded . . . dazzling to view,
Within all lead. . . . O weary mantle for eternity.'
DANTE, *Inferno*, xxiii. 58-67.

Again, when the Pharisees try to place the Messiah in a dilemma with regard to paying tribute to Cæsar, under pretence that it was against the Law of Moses, 'Jesus perceived their wickedness, and said, Why tempt ye me, ye hypocrites?' (xxii. 18).

On the other hand, He sometimes uses the word in a wider sense. In vii. 5, to the man who volunteers to remove the atom of dry twig from his brother's eye, while all the time he himself has a whole plank of wood in his own eye, Jesus says : 'Thou hypocrite, cast out first the beam out of thine own eye ; and then shalt thou see clearly to cast out the mote out of thy brother's eye.' So again in xv. 7-9, after blaming the Pharisees for making the written word of God inoperative because of their system of oral tradition, He adds : 'Ye hypocrites, well did Isaiah prophesy of you, saying, This people honoureth me with their lips ; but their heart is far from me. But in vain do they worship me, teaching as their doctrines the precepts of men.' We may compare our Lord's words in Luke xii. 56 : 'Ye hypocrites, ye know how to interpret the face of the earth and the heaven ; but how is it that ye know not how to interpret this time ?' So also Luke xiii. 15, when the ruler of the synagogue objected to men coming on the sabbath day to be healed: 'The Lord answered him, and said, Ye hypocrites, doth not each one of you on the sabbath loose his ox or his ass from the stall, and lead him away to watering ?' Our Lord seems to use the word 'hypocrite' in these cases when the life is inconsistent with the profession made, but without any connotation of wilful and conscious deceit.

In other words, the Lord Jesus is accusing the Pharisees of what we should call shallowness in religion.

SHALLOWNESS IN RELIGION

They lacked the depth which is the mark of the true believer in God.[1] For the picture of the Pharisee in the parable of the Pharisee and the Publican, recorded by St. Luke, states the case accurately. The Pharisee described there was a good man, if goodness is plumbed by a short line.[2] But the religion of the Publican went fathoms deeper. From this point of view we can understand that the religious pride of the Pharisees was as bad as the religious indifference of the Sadducees, and that therefore John the Baptist was right when he classed them together (Matt. iii. 7), and cried out : ' Ye offspring of vipers, who warned you to flee from the wrath to come ? ' For unless they, even the leaders of the Hellenising and the Judaising parties, came to God in true repentance, there was no hope for them (vv. 9, 10).

In the same way the Messiah, addressing Himself solely to the most religious portion of the community, cries : ' Scribes and Pharisees, hypocrites ! ' Your religion, He means to say, is so shallow, in spite of all your observances and all your conscientiousness, and the effect of it is so unsatisfactory, so actually harmful to the cause of true piety, that you are, in reality, opposed to godliness, and may be compared to poisonous serpents. ' How shall ye,' unless ye repent, ' escape the judgment of hell ? ' (xxiii. 33).

We remember St. Paul's verdict on the Jewish nation, and especially on its leaders, of whom he had had close personal experience : ' I bear them witness,' he writes, ' that they have a zeal for God,

---

[1] It was the lack of moral earnestness in the High Priests and the Elders that made the Lord refuse to answer their question about His authority (xxi. 23-27).

[2] The same may even be said of most of the prayers composed by Pharisees which Mr. Herford has collected, op. cit., pp. 298-309.

but not according to knowledge. For being ignorant of God's righteousness, and seeking to establish their own, they did not subject themselves to the righteousness of God' (Rom. x. 2, 3). They had zeal, but they lacked submission to God and His way of salvation. They lacked, therefore, the one condition by which salvation was obtained. Christ's words are only so far stronger in that they show the logical result, the inevitable outcome, of refusal to yield the heart. 'He that is not with me is against me; and he that gathereth not with me scattereth' (xii. 30).[1]

May I also add that the verdict of St. Paul and of the Messiah holds good to-day? It is not that Jewish scholars and teachers say one thing and mean another, God forbid, for it never was so even in St. Paul's or our Lord's time. It is not that they then preached rightly, and wilfully transgressed; but that although they professed the knowledge and love of God they did not humble themselves before Him, so as to accept the one way of pardon and reconciliation which He offers to sinful men. So also with us. Unless we, whether Jews or Gentiles (it makes no difference), have a deep sense of our own sinfulness (I do not say only of our sins), our religion is but shallow, and we are in the position

---

[1] A lack of humble faith has always tended to produce persecutors, either so-called Christians who persecute Jews, or Jews who persecute Jewish converts. Matthew the publican had probably experienced both social and religious persecution (ix. 9-11). This experience of St. Matthew and his fellow Jewish believers may account in part for the much more severe attitude towards the Jewish leaders exhibited by the writer of the First Gospel than by St. Luke. The Jewish Christian has always had much to bear from non-Christian Jews. The pity is that he has not invariably shown a Christian spirit himself.

II] THE RIGHTEOUSNESS DEMANDED BY MESSIAH

which the Pharisees of old held in the sight of John the Baptist, of St. Paul, and of the Messiah. The presentation of the Messiah in the Gospel according to St. Matthew is that He demands a righteousness higher, a religion deeper, than ever Pharisee or Sadducee, be he Gentile or be he Jew, can grasp, at least until, like the erewhile persecutor, he has a vision of Jesus, and submits himself to Him.[1]

---

[1] One last suggestion may be made. It is that St. Matthew may also have had Pharisaic Christians in his mind when he recorded the Lord's words to Pharisaic Jews. He may have felt that although some Pharisees, when they accepted Christ, left, like St. Paul, Judaism far behind them, there were others of whom this could not be said. Hence he thought it to be his duty to warn his Pharisaic fellow-believers of their danger. In other words, he himself occupied much the same position as St. James, the chief aim of whose Epistle was, as it seems, to caution his readers, Jewish Christians, against shallowness in religion. Both St. James and St. Matthew might, no doubt, personally be in favour of keeping the Jewish Law—that is not the point immediately under consideration—but, in any case, they perceived the danger in which ceremonialists stood, and uttered the most solemn admonitions against it.

Lecture Three

THE MESSIAH—THE HEALER OF DISEASE

'They brought unto him all that were sick, holden with divers diseases and torments, possessed with devils, and epileptic, and palsied; and he healed them.'— MATT. iv. 24.

Lecture Three

THE MESSIAH—THE HEALER OF DISEASE

TWENTY years ago a learned Christian apologist could write: 'Men do not now believe in Christ because of His miracles: they rather believe in the miracles because they have first believed in Christ.'[1] To-day we are reverting to the earlier order of the process of belief—an order which, after all, was that of more than nineteen centuries of faith, and are admitting miracles once more to an important place among the reasons why we believe in Jesus as the Christ. The miracles of Jesus, as we study them to-day, bring us a strong and fresh conviction of the unique character of Jesus the Messiah.

It will be convenient to consider in this Lecture, first, the position of miracles in St. Matthew's presentation of the Messiah to the Jews of his own time; and, secondly, the position of Christ's miracles in the evidences of Christianity for ourselves, whether we be Jews or Gentiles.[2]

---

[1] A. B. Bruce, *Apologetics*, 1892, p. 376. Even Trench goes as far as to say, ' It may be more truly said that we believe the miracles for Christ's sake,' but he recognises the other side also (*Notes on the Miracles of Our Lord*, 8th ed., 1866, end of the preliminary essay, p. 96).

[2] I purposely give no definition of a miracle. The word in itself means only a marvel, and to attempt to make a closer definition at this point would be to prejudge the whole question under discussion. The Lecture will, I trust, clearly show the result to which we are brought.

THE HEBREW-CHRISTIAN MESSIAH [LECT.

I. The position of Miracles in St. Matthew's presentation of the Messiah to the Jews of his own time.

It is probable that those who come to the Gospels with the prepossessions of the modern man are, at first sight, amazed at the prominence given in them to miracles. Neither is this astonishment removed by any further critical study of the documents themselves. Not very long ago, indeed, it was supposed by many scholars that it was possible, by a close examination of the text, to discover a Christ who, no doubt, taught wondrously, and lived a strangely holy life, but performed no mighty acts, or at least no acts, the wonder of which might not easily be explained away. To-day that is changed. The Gospel according to St. Mark is acknowledged to be the earliest of the four, and yet, early though it is, it is full of miracles. Neither can the highest lens of the critical microscope so distinguish the wonderful works from the Personality as to remove those and leave this uninjured. In fact, if we cut the miracles out from the narrative, there remains only a report quite unjointed and unintelligible. 'We cannot contrive any theory by which we may entirely eliminate the miraculous, and yet save the historicity, in any intelligible sense, of those wonderful narratives,' writes the present Archbishop of Dublin.[1] 'If,' says Mr. T. H. Wright, 'excision be made from the Evangelic records (1) of all that directly narrates His unique action as a healer and wonder-worker, (2) of all that presupposes the possibility and actuality of such unique action, (3) of all that testifies to His authority and power due to a unique relation to God—the Gospels are left

---

[1] Dr. J. H. Bernard in Hastings' *D.B.* iii. 389*b*.

MIRACLES INSEPARABLE FROM THE GOSPELS

bald and bare and mutilated beyond description. The very warp and woof of the fabric is destroyed.'[1]

The objection, however, may be raised that the earliest Gospel, the Gospel according to St. Mark, seems to have been written for Christians who were of Gentile origin, whether they had come to the true faith after passing through the stage of proselytism to Judaism or not. As Gentiles by upbringing they may well be thought of as more ignorant and superstitious than Jews, and therefore more ready to accept tales of the miraculous. The Gospel of St. Matthew, however, was certainly written for Jewish Christians, and although we find that a much larger portion of it than of St. Mark is taken up with discourses and parables, yet the miraculous element is no less striking.

In the Gospel for Jewish Christians, as in those for Gentile Christians, the life and work of Jesus the Messiah are so intimately bound up with miracles that it is impossible to obtain a clear picture of Him without them. In fact, all responsible scholars of to-day will accept this statement.

In other words, after doing our best to discover the true historical circumstances of the life of Jesus, discriminating between what He did, and what He did not, we are forced to believe that He did work miracles. The Jews themselves, including those to whom St. Matthew wrote, never denied this.

Now the Jews, be it remembered, were not so ignorant of medicine as not to be able to distinguish

[1] In Hastings' *D.C.G.* ii. 189a. *Cf.* also Heitmüller in *Die Religion in Geschichte und Gegenwart*, 1911, iii. 372. 'Es gehört zur ältesten, uns erreichbaren Ueberlieferung, dass Jesus sich in wunderbare Weise als Arzt betätigt hat. An der Geschichtlichkeit dieser Kunde zu zweifeln, haben wir kein Recht.'

between the ordinary and the extraordinary. It is true that we do not possess Jewish writings of the first half of the first century of our era, from which we can acquire direct information as to the state of medical knowledge among them at that period. But it is not probable that they made much progress in medicine or surgery during the next four or five hundred years, when the Talmud was in process of being compiled. We are, that is to say, justified in arguing back from the Talmud to the time of our Lord, and in believing that we can thus obtain a fairly clear conception of the state of medical knowledge then. As a layman reads the lists showing the anatomical knowledge of the Jews of the Talmud, whether they refer to the bones or the muscles, or the larger organs, he is amazed at their fullness.

Again, he reads that those Jews had learned already what is, after all, only a comparatively modern discovery for Western doctors, that ' the symptoms of all diseases are merely outward manifestations of internal changes in the tissues.' Again, he finds that in major operations the surgeon gave the patient a kind of anæsthetic, and that operations included not only bleeding and cupping, but also amputations, trephining, the extirpation of the spleen, and the insertion of false teeth, made of hard wood, gold, or silver.

Besides these things they distinguished between many forms of diseases of the eye ; they mentioned, or discussed, diseases of the ear, rheumatism, forms of heart-disease, chest complaints, gout, stone, fevers, skin diseases, and many others. Again, their remedies were of the greatest possible variety, by no means

JEWISH KNOWLEDGE OF MEDICINE

confined to the ignorant methods of the superstitious. It is probable that there was no very great difference between the medical knowledge of the physicians and surgeons of our Lord's time and that of four or five hundred years ago.[1]

It is therefore the more noticeable that while they possessed a passable knowledge of medicine and surgery, they recognised the limits of their own science, and yet claimed to perform miracles. In particular they asserted that by the use of magical formulæ they were able to cure diseases.[2] This claim is definitely referred to in Matt. xii. 27, and our Lord is not careful to decide whether the claim was true or false. He found that the learned men of His day made the claim in the persons of their 'sons,' that is, presumably their disciples, and He argued with them *ad hominem*.[3]

[1] See Krauss, *Talmudische Archäologie*, 1910, i. pp. 252 *sqq.*; Spivak in the *Jewish Encyclopedia, s.v.* Medicine. Something also may be learned from W. Ebstein, *Die Medizin im N.T. und im Talmud*, 1903, though, on the whole, this is a very disappointing book. Edersheim, with reference to Matt. viii. 14, writes: 'A sudden access of violent "burning fever," such as is even now common in that district, had laid Peter's mother-in-law prostrate. . . . The Talmud gives this disease precisely the same name (אשתא צמירתא, *Eshatha Tsemirta*), "burning fever," and prescribes for it a magical remedy, of which the principal part is to tie a knife wholly of iron by a braid of hair to a thornbush, and to repeat on successive days Exod. iii. 2, 3, then ver. 4, and finally ver. 5, after which the bush is to be cut down while a certain magical formula is pronounced' (*Jesus the Messiah*, 1887, i. pp. 485 *sq.*, referring to T.B. *Sabb.* 67a). See also Ebstein, *op. cit.* pp. 221 *sq.* For Assyrian-Babylonian medicine, see R. Campbell Thompson in Hastings' *E.R.E.* iv. 744-746. See also Budge, *The Syriac Book of Medicines*, 1913.

[2] For examples see, besides the last note, Edersheim, *Jesus the Messiah*, ii. 774-776. A convenient selection of Jewish miracles is contained in F. Fiebig's *Rabbinische Wundergeschichten des neutestamentlichen Zeitalters* (Lietzmann's Kleine Texte), 1911; but the last three words of the title are to be understood very liberally.

[3] Compare also the statement by our Lord that men would claim to have wrought miracles in His name, although He would deny all 'knowledge' of those who wrought them (vii. 22, 23).

While, however, the Jews were quite able to distinguish between cases of ordinary healing and those of an exceptional kind, effected by means quite insufficient in themselves; and while they asserted that they, or their disciples, brought about cures of the latter kind as well as of the former; and, further, while they did not deny that our Lord wrought extraordinary cures, they attributed these to the wrong cause. They said, as we are told in xii. 24, that it was only in union with Beelzebub, prince of the demons, that He cast out the demons.[1] They refused, as our Lord pointed out to them, to see the viciousness of their logic (as if Satan would ever cast out Satan !), and they attributed a malevolent origin to the work of Jesus (in spite of their claim for their own adherents); and, lastly, they set their face against recognising the good, and professed to believe that health and salvation had their origin in evil.

An echo of the same monstrous statement of the source of our Lord's miracles is found in the Talmud, not, however, as it would appear, in the Mishna or the Tosephta, or in the Palestinian Gemara, but only in the Babylonian. For although we find in the Tosephta, and the two Gemaras, the assertion that by writing letters on his own body a certain Ben Stada brought magic out of Egypt,[2] it is not until the time of the Babylonian Gemara that we find Ben Stada identified with Ben Pantera, the name given to our Lord.[3]

---

[1] So also ix. 34, according to many authorities.

[2] Tosephta, *Sabb.* xi. (xii.) 15 (p. 126); T. J. *Sabb.* xii. 4 (13d); Bab. *Sabb.* 104b. These and the passages in the two following notes may be studied most conveniently in Strack, *Jesus, die Häretiker und die Christen*, 1910. See in particular his notes on § 7.

[3] Bab. *Sabb.* 104b; *Sanh.* 67a. In Bab. *Sanh.* 43a, Jesus of Nazareth is said to have practised magic. See further Strack's notes on § 1. Also on the name Pantera, § 3, note 3, and Box, *Virgin Birth*, p. 201.

III] MIRACLES AMONG THE HEATHEN

We have therefore no direct confirmation from Jewish writings prior to 400 or 500 A.D. of the Gospel statement that the Jews attributed our Lord's miracles to magic.[1]

It is the less strange that the Jews should believe in miracles when we remember that miracles were taking place among the heathen. Even if the tradition of the cures wrought by magical incantations of Ea and Marduk among the Assyrians and Babylonians[2] had died out in Judaism (and in virtue of the remnant that still remained in Babylonia this is hardly probable), there were still in districts nearer Palestine devotees of Esmun,[3] while, if they looked a little further abroad, they would see the temples of Serapis and Isis[4] thronged with suppliants, entreating divine aid for their sickness. In particular they would hear of the many cures effected by the worship of Æsculapius.[5]

---

[1] The earliest evidence outside the New Testament for this appears to be Justin Martyr, *Dial.* § 69. So also Pionius, 250† A.D., and Origen (Strack, *op. cit.* pp. 8* sq.).

[2] R. Campbell Thompson in *E.R.E.* iv. 742. See further Baudissin, *Adonis und Esmun*, 1911, pp. 311–324.

[3] On the probability that Esmun, who was specially worshipped at Sidon, was a god of healing, see Baudissin, *op. cit.* pp. 242–245. One text has been discovered in which the sick man is bid ask Tammuz to drive out from him the demon of sickness (p. 374).

[4] Lucius, *Die Anfänge des Heiligenkults in der christlichen Kirche*, 1904, p. 254.

[5] 'The revival which attended the cult of Æsculapius during the Imperial age. As far back as 290 B.C. Æsculapius of Epidaurus had been summoned to Rome on the advice of the Sibylline books. He kept his sanctuary on the island in the Tiber, and close to it, just as at the numerous shrines of Asclepius in Greece, there stood a sanatorium in which sick persons waited for the injunctions which the god imparted during sleep. . . . From Rome his cult spread over all the West, fusing itself here and there with the cult of Serapis or of some other deity, and accompanied by the inferior cult of Hygeia and Salus, Telesphorus and Somnus. . . . People travelled to the famous sanatoria of the god as they travel to-day to baths. He was appealed to in diseases of the body

It is indeed difficult for us at this distance to discern with accuracy either the nature of the diseases of which cures were effected at the heathen shrines, or indeed to estimate with certainty the truth of the affirmation in any particular case. But when we bear in mind (1) the directness of the statements made at, or near, the time; (2) the evidence that the healing powers exhibited at the temples were in many places continued after the Christian religion had taken these over; (3) the very large amount of apparently immediate and trustworthy evidence that this healing power continued not only in the early centuries, but also throughout the Middle Ages (as, for example, on the death of Becket, or by the means of Catharine of Siena); and (4), lastly, the fact that such miracles occur down to our own day, as, for example, at the exhibition of the Holy Coat at Trèves in 1891, and in churches and shrines in Greece and Eastern Europe every year (to say nothing of Lourdes, or of the work of Faith Healers in our own land)—we can hardly deny that in the beginning of the first century of our era, as in all other times, cures took place of diseases which had been pronounced incurable by the best physicians and surgeons of the day, and were performed only after prayer, or something equivalent to it. To such cures has been given in all ages the generic name of miracles.[1]

and of the soul, the costliest gifts were brought him as the ΘΕΟCCWTHP ("God the Saviour"), and people consecrated their lives to him, as innumerable inscriptions and statues testify. In the case of other gods as well, healing energy was now made a central feature. Zeus himself and Apollo (cp. *e.g.* Tatian, *Orat.* viii.) appeared in a new light. They, too, became "saviours." No one could be a god any longer, unless he was also a saviour' (Harnack, *Expansion of Christianity*, 1904, i. 127–129). See also the Appendix to this Lecture.

[1] For examples see the Appendix to this Lecture.

III] DISEASE TO BE OVERCOME IN MESSIANIC TIMES

Postponing until the second part of this Lecture the question of the differences between our Lord's miracles and those of others, let us now consider how far St. Matthew regarded His miracles as evidence for His Messiahship.

In doing so it is, of course, necessary to be very careful lest we introduce into the Evangelist's mind thoughts that properly belong to our own, whether by way of addition to his mode of regarding facts, or (and perhaps this is the more likely) by omission of what he really did believe.

In the first place, the Jews were accustomed to look up to Jehovah as the Healer of the diseases of His people.[1] It would therefore be but natural that the Jews should expect that when Messiah, His great representative, should appear, men's diseases should be healed.[2]

The people did, in fact, expect to see such a sudden improvement in health, such wonderful victory over infirmity and disease, in Messianic times.[3] For life and human vigour would then be at its highest, and sickness must flee away.[4] If later Jewish thought could tell of the healing of the blind and the lame when the Law was first given at Sinai,[5] how much

[1] For the fullest treatment of this subject see Baudissin, *Adonis und Esmun*, 1911, pp. 385 *sqq*.

[2] The fact that they were accustomed to regard individual angels as the special agents through whom meanwhile He exerted His healing power would not militate against this. On the facts see Bousset, *Die Religion des Judentums im neutestamentlichen Zeitalter*, 1906, p. 378.

[3] Isa. xxxv. 5, 6.

[4] Compare the hyperbolical description of the development of the human frame painted by R. Meir about 150 A.D. See Klausner, *Messianische Vorstellungen*, pp. 108 *sq*., 112 *sqq*. A summary of the hopes expressed in the pseudepigraphic books may be found in Bousset, *loc. cit*.

[5] Quoted from the Siphre by Rashi on T.B. *Sabb*. 146a. So too the Mekilta on Exod. xix. 11 (ed. Friedmann, p. 64; ed. Weiss, p. 72): '"In the

greater would be the expectation of healing power at the coming of the Messiah! It must, however, be remembered that there appears to be no direct evidence that these miracles were to be performed by the immediate agency of the Messiah. It is one thing for healing to be effected, as a result of the blessed change consequent on the coming of Messiah, quite another for cases of cures to be performed by Him Himself.[1] There is, however, some indirect evidence which ought not to be forgotten. Josephus seems to attribute such power of miraculous healing to a king whose coming was promised, and could hardly be anyone but Messiah.[2] Further, it is difficult to understand why the sight of the miracles performed by our Lord should have made the multitude cry out that He was the son of David, unless they expected this promised monarch to perform miracles of healing.[3] In spite, therefore, of the apparent absence of direct evidence, we can hardly be wrong in thinking that, in at least some quarters of Judaism, the Messiah was expected to heal the sick, to restore vigour to the infirm.

Indeed, the assumption of such an expectation underlies the words of our Lord to the messengers of John the Baptist. He bids them report to John the sights that they had seen, and the words which they had heard, while they were actually with Jesus. He tells them this, too, in such a way that their witness

eyes of all the people," teaching us that there was no blind among them,' to which Rashi adds 'for they were all healed.'

[1] 'Der Messias wird im tannaitischen Schriftthum niemals als Wunderthäter *ex professo* betrachtet' (Klausner, *Die Messianische Vorstellung*, u.s.w., p. 108).

[2] *Antt*. xvii. ii. 4 (§ 45). Compare *Encyclopædia Biblica*, c. 4324.

[3] xii. 23; *cf*. ix. 27; xx. 30, 31. *Cf*. also John vii. 31; *cf*. Lect. VII, pp. 266 *sqq*.

SIGNS FOR JOHN THE BAPTIST

was to be linked on to the words inaugurating the kingdom which the prophet had of old put into the mouth of the servant of the LORD: 'Blind men are recovering their sight, and lame men are walking, lepers are being cleansed, and deaf men are hearing, and dead men are being raised up, and (last of all, as most decisive sign of all) poor men are having the good news brought to them.' Our Lord thought the evidence was sufficient to show John that He really was the One who was to come, the One into whose mouth the description of the new kingdom had been placed. John was not to be misled if Jesus did not correspond to the common, but mistaken, expectation of a fighting Messiah who should lead the nation to victory over earthly foes, for He was in fact accomplishing the predictive utterance of one of the greatest of the prophets.[1]

It is worthy of remark that, among the miracles to which our Lord called the attention of the messengers of John, the casting out of demons finds no place. Perhaps there was no instance of it during the time that they were with Him. However that may be, it is certain that in the mind of the Evangelist such cures were of great importance. There is no occasion for us now to consider whether demoniacal possession was and is a reality, or only a false explanation of serious mental disease.[2] It is well established that in the first century A.D. men

---

[1] xi. 5, 6. In *vv.* 20-24 our Lord again insists on the evidential value of His miracles.

[2] For several acute remarks against the presupposition that the existence of hurtful supernatural powers is impossible, see *Christus Futurus*, 1907, pp. 192-195. See also Sir W. M. Ramsay's reference to Nevius' *Demoniac Possession* in the *Expositor*, Feb. 1912, p. 151.

generally, Jews [1] as well as the Gentiles,[2] conceived of the air as peopled with living creatures invisible to man, many of whom were hurtful to him, who by means of their intelligence could not only dispose him to moral evil, but even take up a kind of physical abode within him and injure his body.[3] This dread of the unseen powers, this obsession of their awful presence, under which man was powerless, was, says the Evangelist, overcome by the Messiah, and by those who believed on Him. St. Matthew presents to us One, before Whom the demons tremble, Whom they acknowledge as their judge, Whose word they obey, even though it is to their own destruction. To every reader of St. Matthew's time, whether Jew or Gentile, this good news would bring the greatest possible hope, where before there had been only despair. The believer is no longer at the mercy of the demons! One has come who had proved Himself superior to them! He has, moreover, given to some of His followers power to cast them out![4] We to-day, with our superior knowledge, real or fancied, do not easily grasp the enormous significance of this fact for those early believers.[5]

Here perhaps it is convenient to recall certain other points in St. Matthew's presentation of the Messiah. For example, His healing of disease was

[1] H. Loewe affirms: 'Galilee was the centre of Palestinian Demonology, and it will almost invariably be found that *Galilæan* teachers *accepted*, while *Judæan* teachers *rejected*, the existence of spirits' (*Encyclopædia of Religion and Ethics*, iv. 613). Mesopotamian Rabbis, he adds, agreed with the Galilean.

[2] *Cf.* Harnack, *Expansion of Christianity*, 1904, i. 160 *sqq.*

[3] *Jubilees*, x. 12, 13, and often. See Bousset, *R.J.N.Z.* ch. xvii.

[4] x. 1, 8.

[5] And for the converts from the heathen of our own day. See the memoir of Pastor Hsi; and Warneck, *The Living Forces of the Gospel*, 1909, *passim*.

III]   THE COMPASSION OF MESSIAH

as much a part of His daily work as teaching and preaching. The statement in iv. 23, 24, sets this forth in but longer and more explicit terms than elsewhere : ' And Jesus went about in all Galilee, teaching in their synagogues, and preaching the gospel of the kingdom, and healing all manner of disease and all manner of sickness among the people. And the report of him went forth into all Syria : and they brought unto him all that were sick, holden with divers diseases and torments, possessed with devils, and epileptic and palsied ; and he healed them.'[1]

Again, the motive that moves the Messiah is compassion. His exceeding tender-heartedness, and His accessibility to those who crave from Him relief, form an important part of the Evangelist's delineation : ' He came forth, and saw a great multitude, and he had compassion on them, and healed their sick ' (xiv. 14). ' Jesus called unto him his disciples and said, I have compassion on the multitude, because they continue with me now three days and have nothing to eat : and I would not send them away fasting, lest haply they faint in the way ' (xv. 32).[2] ' And Jesus, being moved with compassion, touched their eyes : and straightway they received their sight, and followed him ' (xx. 34). So also He actually stretched forth his hand and touched a leper, disagreeable though it must have been to do so. He shrank, indeed, from nothing which could enable Him to bring health to sick folk, even though it meant for Him that

---

[1] *Cf.* ix. 35 ; xii. 16 ; xiv. 34-36 ; xv. 29-31 ; xix. 1, 2.
[2] Although the 4000 fed on this occasion were, in all probability, mostly heathen (*v.* 31).

in some sense He bare upon Himself their sicknesses:
'that it might be fulfilled which was spoken by
Isaiah the prophet, saying, Himself took our infirmities, and bare our diseases' (viii. 17).[1]

Again, His miracles were not effective *ex opere
operato*, regardless of any personal relation between
Himself and the sick, or, at the least, between Himself and those who brought them. Where there
was unbelief (speaking of the community in general)
there He could work but few miracles (xiii. 58).
It was when He saw the faith of those that bore
the paralytic that He addressed Himself to him
(ix. 2). It was necessary to draw out the faith of
the Canaanite woman before He healed her daughter
(xv. 21–28). The faith might be mixed with superstition, as with the poor woman who thought that
virtue resided in the holy 'fringe' on His garment,
but the issue of her blood was staunched (ix. 20–22).
The faith too in many of those healed, probably in
most, must have come very far short of spiritual
submission to our Lord, or the multitudes of those
who were healed would have formed a prominent
part of those who actually became His disciples.
But, so far as we can judge, this was the case with
very few of them. Some faith, however feeble
and mixed though it might be, was necessary. The
Messiah, as depicted for us in the First Gospel,
was no mere thaumaturge, performing His wonders
regardless of the moral condition of those upon
whom He worked them.

This leads to another consideration. The Messiah
was absolutely free from any measure of self-seeking.
Mere reputation as such He did not desire (viii. 4,

[1] See below, p. 125.

ix. 31). Neither can we suppose that He who bade His disciples perform their cures without payment could for a moment have thought of receiving any Himself (x. 8).

With this is closely allied His consistent refusal to make an exhibition of His powers. No miracle of His was performed with the single object of impressing those who beheld it. On the contrary, when He was told that a sign from heaven would convince He vehemently blamed the applicants for their worldliness and unbelief. They had turned away from God as a bride from her husband; they were worse than the ungodly men of Nineveh, or the heathen Queen of Sheba. They repented not at the message they heard; they sought not the true wisdom from Him who was greater than Solomon (xii. 38-42, xvi. 1-4). In saying this St. Matthew no doubt intended his readers to learn that, whether they saw strange wonders wrought in Christ's name or not, they themselves had full cause to turn to God in true repentance, and possessed abundance of spiritual wisdom in Christ upon which to draw.

There is, it will be noticed, no trace of an endeavour on St. Matthew's part to argue from the miracles that our Lord was divine, much less to suggest that He worked them by His power as God. The Evangelist does not seem even to regard them as direct evidence of the reality of the new revelation brought to mankind through the Messiah.[1]

[1] Dr. Illingworth writes: the Jews of the first century 'had God's wondrous works of old time recorded in their history; and they expected miracle to be the credential of a divine message' (*The Doctrine of the Trinity*, 1907, p. 226), but this is not quite the same thing. See further below, pp. 128-131.

He only considered that the miracles so far showed that Jesus was the Messiah in that the working of them was consistent with what the Messiah might be expected to do. In fact, miracles appear to St. Matthew to be the logical, and, so to speak, natural outcome of His personality. True that St. Matthew describes Him as unique by birth and therefore by nature, but according to him He consistently refused to exercise this divine nature in working miracles either for Himself, or, as it seems, in a sphere, such as the heavens, outside human influence. Yet, in spite of this refusal to employ His inherent divinity in such mighty works, the force of His personality and character was such that miracles, as it were, flowed forth from Him. Miracles in the case of the Messiah were the product of perfect love unfettered by the frailty, selfishness, and sin with which the ordinary person is hampered. The Messiah, according to St. Matthew's presentation of Him, gladly spent Himself that He might succour suffering humanity to the utmost, and He found no hindrance in doing so save in the failure of the sufferers to accept His services. 'O Jerusalem, Jerusalem, which killeth the prophets, and stoneth them that are sent unto her! how often would I have gathered thy children together, even as a hen gathereth her chickens under her wings, and ye would not!' But to those that will He says: 'Come unto me, all ye that labour and are heavy laden, and I will give you rest'—sending you forth refreshed, and vigorous for new work.[1]

---

[1] It is not impossible that a subordinate reason for the frequent mention of miracles in the First Gospel is that St. Matthew desired to remind his readers of the conditions under which they themselves might expect to be either the recipients, or the agents, of them.

THE VALUE OF MIRACLES TO US

II. To St. Matthew and his earliest readers no question would arise as to the strictly supernatural character of our Lord's miracles. Nature in those days seemed to be so alive with divinity, so responsive to the touch of God, so continually affected by Him, that all extraordinary occurrences represented the work of God.[1] To us, however, who have been taught to regard nature very differently—whether rightly or wrongly I do not now inquire—the question of the character and source of the power by which the miracles were produced is of extreme importance. Were they the immediate result of divine action, or were they the result of human powers, or is there a third way?

Upon our answers to these questions depends the position in which we must place Christ's miracles among the evidences to Him.

It will conduce to clearness in considering the subject if (1) we classify our Lord's miracles; (2) we consider how far they can be explained as regards the recipients of them; (3) we inquire into the relation of our Lord Himself to them; (4) and finally endeavour to state clearly the position which His miracles hold in the evidences to Him.

(1) The classification of our Lord's miracles. The bulk of them, it is plain, were miracles of healing. And, if we take the usual division accepted by medical men, the diseases cured by our Lord were either

---

[1] Compare O. Weinreich, *Antike Heilungswunder*, 1909, p. vii.: 'Uns erscheinen Wunder und ein nach unwandelbaren Gesetzen sich vollziehendes Naturgeschehen als Gegensätze. Die Alten dagegen konnten jedes göttliche Handeln als Wunder bezeichnen, auch wenn es in natürlichen Bahnen verlief. Alles was geschah, konnte als Wunder aufgefasst werden. Die Grenzlinie zwischen Wunder und Nicht-Wunder ist in der Antike keine feste, die Entscheidung darüber liegt im Menschen.'

'functional' or 'organic.' In the first class, the 'functional' diseases may, no doubt, be included some of the cases of lameness, paralysis, and occasionally even blindness and deafness (with its accompanying dumbness). Also under this head many would place possession by unclean spirits.

It is, however, difficult to believe that among multitudes who were healed by Christ functional diseases formed either all, or even the majority of the cases. Blindness and deafness are more commonly organic than functional, so also are even lameness and paralysis. Leprosy, in particular, is not functional, and fever is the result of organic disease.

Lastly, there is the raising of the dead, of which only one specific instance is given by St. Matthew, though he mentions it as (presumably) a frequent occurrence (xi. 5; *cf.* x. 8).

Besides these miracles of healing there are a few which were performed not on persons, but on inanimate nature, such as the feeding of the five thousand, the stilling of the winds and waves, the walking on the water, the withering of the fig-tree. Here also we may place the finding of the stater in the fish's mouth, and the commission about the ass and its foal.[1]

(2) Can any explanation of Christ's miracles be given? The examples of healing functional disorders occasion no great difficulty. Such cures in which, as it appears, the nerves are influenced directly by the

[1] I expressly omit the rising of certain saints at the Crucifixion (xxvii. 51–53), which is depicted as the result of events independent of the volition of the Lord Himself. For the Transfiguration see Lecture XII. It, like the Virgin Birth and the Resurrection, stands in a different category from the miracles proper, and belongs entirely to the personal life of our Lord.

mind, are common in all ages. Dr. R. J. Ryle gives an extreme case : ' A girl had suffered from an injury to the foot causing temporary lameness. She took to a crutch and said she was perfectly unable to use her foot. She persisted in this belief after repeated assurances that the foot ailed nothing. She was advised to see Sir James Paget, and she promised to put implicit confidence in his opinion and to act upon it. She went to his house, explained her case, and was informed by him that there was nothing the matter with the foot. She thereupon threw down her crutch, walked across the room, and left his house without it.'[1] It is quite possible that some of our Lord's cures were of a similar kind. The strength of His personality was sufficient to summon up the latent, and quite ordinary, will power, and lo! the man was healed. But to dismiss all our Lord's cures as due to this cause and this method, is to go far beyond the evidence. For, after all, such cases form a very small part of illnesses either with us or in the East, and we cannot suppose for a moment that it was otherwise in our Lord's time, when sick persons were brought to Him in multitudes and were restored by Him to health.[2]

[1] *The Hibbert Journal*, v. (1906–1907), pp. 583 *sq*.

[2] Dr. R. J. Ryle writes: 'Whether we test the Neurotic Theory by the general references to the exercise of powers of healing, or by the accounts of special cases of the exercise of these powers, the result is the same. We do not find reason to believe that the works of healing were instances of faith-healing. The cases are too numerous, and they are not of the sort among which we look for cures of the faith-healing kind ' (*loc. cit.*). He also says : ' The persons who may be fairly supposed to have constituted the bulk of the " possessed " are not, as a matter of fact, the sort of persons to be straightway healed by a word. . . . They are the subjects who lend themselves least of all to the modern remedial measures of hypnotism and suggestion ' (*op. cit.* p. 579).

I am allowed to make the following extract from an unpublished paper

What, then, are we to say of the miracles in which our Lord healed the second class of diseases, the organic ? This, in the first place ; that although the distinction into the classes of functional and organic is very convenient in actual medical practice, it does not pretend to be more than empiric, and to rest upon observation made with somewhat coarse and unsatisfactory instruments. A division which calls catalepsy functional, and an ordinary boil organic, has not much to recommend it from the point of view either of the man in the street, or of the philosophic thinker. Both one and the other feel convinced that the distinction between functional and organic, convenient though it is at present, is only superficial, and will prove on closer examination to be non-existent.[1]

on the Diseases of Palestine, written by Dr. E. W. G. Masterman, Head of the London Jews' Society's Hospital in Jerusalem : 'The writer has seen, during many years in Palestine, many thousand cases of disease among just the same class of people, chiefly Jews, living under very similar social and geographical conditions, and he has never seen "neurotic" or "hysterical" disease produce morbid symptoms comparable with those described in the Gospels. Indeed most of the cases reported in these narratives are just those which are the despair of the modern medical man. As far as can be judged from the particulars given, the larger proportion of the cases would be considered too hopeless for admission to any of our hospitals, where it is necessary to select from a vast number of the sick those cases only which we have a good hope of curing or of permanently benefiting. Such cases as the imbeciles, the paralysed, epileptics, the deaf and the blind, would have to be passed over. In many villages in Galilee the writer had been compelled to leave on one side dozens of such unfortunates to deal with the more hopeful cases of fevers, dysentery, and surgical affections.'

[1] 'It is more difficult to believe that while many diseases may be cured by the right mental conditions there are others over which such mental conditions have no influence, than to believe that all diseases come under the same natural laws, however powerless we may yet be to apply these laws' (*Christus Futurus*, 1909, p. 222). 'Probably all functional diseases would show some organic defect, were methods of examination adopted sufficiently skilful and sufficiently minute' (Black's *Medical Dictionary*, 1906, *s.v.* Functional Diseases).

INFLUENCE OF MIND ON BODY

Secondly, it appears that evidence is forthcoming in ever-increasing quantity that the mind and the body are so closely connected that it is impossible to separate off any part or organ of the latter, and to say that it cannot be affected by the former. If a chance remark heard by a maiden will cause the capillaries of her cheeks to be suffused with blood; if meditation on the sufferings of our Lord can produce stigmata on the hands; if a drop of cold water on the arm of a clairvoyant subject can by suggestion to her make a blister like that due to a drop of burning sealing-wax; if the edge of a matchcase pressed on the right arm, and suggested as red-hot, can produce a blister and a permanent scar,[1] it is not unreasonable to think that in certain circumstances the mind may send blood with fresh and unaccustomed vigour to any part of the body, or, again, withhold it to some extent from a part that already has too much, and thus vital changes may be effected in the body through the action of the mind.[2] Something of this kind at least must lie at the basis of the fact known by every doctor,

[1] See P. Dearmer, *Body and Soul*, 1909, pp. 27-35; Worcester, *Religion and Medicine*, 1908, p. 95; D. H. Tuke, *Illustrations of the Influence of the Mind on the Body*, 1884, i. 119-126 (stigmata); F. W. H. Myers, *Human Personality*, 1903, i. 495-497; Krafft-Ebing, *Hypnotism* (translated by C. G. Chaddock, 1889), p. 28 *sq*. The case of an unheated pair of scissors producing a burn, with a suppurating wound, described in the last volume (pp. 21, 29), and elsewhere, rests on very indirect and unsatisfactory authority.

[2] 'The brain receives help from every other organ, but it also largely controls the working of each. By its mental action alone it can hurry the heart's beat or slow its pace; it can make the skin shrivel or flush, it can quicken or stop the digestion, it can stop or change the character of all the secretions, it can arrest or improve the general nutrition of the body. Every organ and every vital process is represented in the structure of the brain by special "centres" and groups of cells that have a direct relation with such organs and processes, and through which they are controlled' (T. Clouston, *The Hygiene of Mind*, pp. 7 *sq*., N.D., but 'first published in 1906').

and invariably acted upon by him, that it is all-important that the patient should be of good hope if he is to recover from whatever illness he may have. At present we know nothing of the way in which mind touches matter, and very little of the extent to which it can influence it, but every day adds to the reasonableness of the belief that such action is both continuous and all-pervading. It is true that this influence in all probability is far greater in the case of the unconscious than of the conscious part of our mind, but this is hardly relevant to the present inquiry. It appears that there have been cases of extraordinary cures of confessedly organic diseases, which, after resisting medical skill, and deemed incurable by all known means, were nevertheless cured through the mind.[1] There is then some reason for thinking that even in those cases of organic disease which were healed by our Lord the cure may have been due to the action of the minds of the sufferers upon various parts of their bodies.[2]

[1] See the Appendix to this Lecture. It should be noted that no monstrous cure is attributed to our Lord in the canonical Gospels. He never, for example, restored the missing eyeballs to the sockets (as at Epidaurus, fourth or third century B.C., No. 9; see Fiebig, *Antike Wundergeschichten*, 1911, p. 5; M. Hamilton, *Incubation*, 1906, p. 20; at the church of St. Fides, Conques, in the tenth century A.D.; M. Hamilton, *op. cit.* pp. 169 *sq.*), or restored a cancer-eaten leg of a living man by giving him instead a sound leg from a dead man (a miracle by St. Cosmas and St. Damian. See M. Hamilton, *op. cit.* p. 124).

[2] It is indeed only right that in the present state of comparative ignorance about the nature of cancer the medical profession should strongly resist the raising of any false hope in the patient which is likely to lead him to postpone an operation until it is too late. The knife is still the only known means of extirpating cancer. Yet if cancer (as many think) is a disease of old age, it would seem but reasonable that if through the action of the mind a fresh supply of energy could be directed towards it cures would be effected. Perhaps this is the real explanation of those cures of cancer which admittedly do sometimes take place through causes as yet unknown.

The Emmanuel Movement again, which has done so much in America,

RESTORATION OF THE DEAD

There is indeed one form of our Lord's miracles of healing to which this will not apply, the restoration of the dead to life. The only definite example in the First Gospel is, as has been said, that of Jairus' daughter, but reference is made to other examples of which no details are given. In her case she had not been dead more than an hour, as it would seem. Yet even her restoration is inexplicable at present, on the supposition that she was really dead, which we can hardly doubt. May, however, the explanation be that until dissolution has actually begun restoration is still possible ? [1]

and is attempting something in our own land, is undoubtedly acting wisely in limiting its operations to functional cases, and in undertaking these only after the recorded diagnosis of skilled medical men. 'We believe that the modern refinements of diagnosis should be exhausted in the study of all doubtful cases before the treatment is begun, and thanks to our faculty of consultation we leave no stone unturned in this respect, and we admit no patient to the class until we are assured on good medical authority that he or she is likely to be benefited by the treatment' (E. Worcester and others, *Religion and Medicine*, 1908, pp. 5 *sq.*). See also Worcester and McComb, *The Christian Religion as a Healing Power*, 1910, pp. 17 *sq.*, 51-53. It is in the refusal to act independently of medical men that, on its practical side, the Emmanuel Movement differs from Christian Science.

[1] It is not certain that dissolution had begun in the case of Jairus' daughter, or even in that of the young man at Nain, who doubtless had died the same day in which he was restored (Luke vii. 11-15), or even in the crucial case of Lazarus, if we suppose that the prayer to which our Lord refers as having been uttered by Him had been offered immediately after Lazarus' death. Martha's hasty outcry against opening the tomb proves nothing at all as to what had really happened, in spite of Mr. J. M. Thompson's curious assertion (*Miracles in the New Testament*, 1911, p. 109). Sir W. M. Ramsay writes: 'In the physical sense, how difficult it is to predicate death as final and absolute. . . . I know the circumstances of a case in which a man was pronounced dead by some of the best physicians in Europe after typhoid fever; and yet was brought back to life after many hours of effort by non-medical belief and activity' (*Expositor*, Feb. 1912, viii. 3, p. 149). Science, it must be remembered, distinguishes two stages in death, first, the Systematic or Somatic, in which all the functions of the body have ceased; and, secondly, molecular death of the tissues, in which decomposition of parts begins. See J. Dixon Mann, *Forensic Medicine and Toxicology*, 1908, p. 40.

The other class of miracles, the Nature miracles, is much more extraordinary, and as yet entirely beyond us. We are not aware of any force by which we are, or are ever likely to be, able to bid the winds and waves obey us, or to rise superior to the ordinary power of gravitation and walk upon the water. Hence it is not strange that some scholars have endeavoured to explain all such miracles away by saying that they are either inventions, due to the crystallisation of sayings of our Lord into hard facts, or else allegorical tales, never intended to be taken literally.[1] Yet they are as closely interwoven into the warp and woof[2] of the narrative as those miracles which are easier to understand. There is therefore little doubt but that the Evangelist and his earliest readers regarded them as incidents which actually took place. Probably it is wiser, and more consistent with true criticism, for us to regard them in the same way. The fact that we are beginning to understand something of the method by which the greater number of our Lord's miracles were performed, suggests that the time may yet come when we shall receive fuller light about those which at present are altogether unintelligible to us.[3]

(3) After having endeavoured to classify the

---

[1] G. Traub, *Die Wunder im Neuen Testament*, 1907, pp. 55–65; J. M. Thompson, *Miracles in the New Testament*, 1911, p. 50.

[2] See above, pp. 98 *sq*.

[3] 'The effect, therefore, of scientific progress, as regards the Scriptural miracles, is gradually to eliminate the hypothesis which refers them to unknown natural causes' (Mansel, *Aids to Faith*, p. 14, quoted by J. B. Mozley, *op. cit.* p. 277). Mozley himself, however, can say: 'The greater miracles . . . interpret the lesser ones,' but he seems to be thinking of the Resurrection and Ascension, with regard to which his remark is doubtless true (*op. cit.* p. 168). See also Dr. F. B. Jevons in the *Interpreter*, Oct. 1909, p. 45.

III] HOW WERE NON-BIBLICAL MIRACLES WROUGHT

miracles, and after considering the light thrown upon them by history and science, in particular with regard to the recipients, we turn to inquire into the relation of our Lord Himself to them.

Now, in non-Biblical cures influence of one of two kinds was always apparent. Either there was a remarkable human personality active on behalf of the sufferers, as, for example, Apollonius of Tyana among the heathen, or Catharine of Siena among the Christians, or else, and in the great majority of cases, the cures took place after prayer by the patients. Such prayer, whether formal or informal matters not, was offered either in places consecrated to the service of deity (as in all forms of incubation, ancient and modern), or at a time when there were special reasons for the thoughts of the patients being fixed on divine things, as, for example, immediately after the death of St. Thomas of Canterbury.[1]

By what power, then, was it that these non-Biblical miracles were wrought?

Did God hear the prayers of the Christians, and even of the heathen, ignorant though these were of Him, and, in answer, perform the miracles by His almighty potency? Perhaps so, but if so it is evident that we cannot affirm that the performance of miracles is in itself a witness to the truth of the revelation brought by Christ. If miracles are wrought in the name indeed of heathen deities, but in reality by the power of God, miracles wrought in the name of Christ, or of the true God, are no longer in themselves witnesses to the truth of Christ, or of God, in the unique way often claimed for them.

[1] See the Appendix to this Lecture.

Again, granting that it be true that the heathen and post-Biblical miracles were wrought ultimately by God, yet God's usual method of activity is to employ what we call natural means and methods. Were not some then employed in these cures? If there were, as surely is probable, what were they? We can hardly help acknowledging that the persons through whom the miracles were wrought possessed special powers, and were personalities of striking character, and, on the other hand, that a patient who was of specially receptive mind (not necessarily weak, often indeed the very reverse, but receptive) received the impress of such strong characters. If so, it appears probable that God uses the human means of strong personality on the one hand, and, as we have already seen, humble receptivity on the other, when He allows miracles to be performed among either Christians or heathen.

In this connexion it is important to notice that in almost every case such extraordinary cures, heathen or Christian, are associated with the highest side of life. It is very rare that they are performed by mere quacks. Even Apollonius of Tyana, though his biographers have done their best to prejudice him in the eyes of Christians, appears to have been a moral and kindly personage relative to his spiritual knowledge. It is rarer still that the patients use means that are not closely linked on to religion.

This suggests that it is through the highest spiritual effort of which a person is capable, whether he be the patient or the worker, that the blessing of restoration to physical health is given.

We are now in a position to consider the specific case of our Lord.

III]   HOW DID MESSIAH WORK MIRACLES

In the first place, as has been said already,[1] there is no evidence in this Gospel that He claimed to perform His miracles by His own power as God. Jesus the Son of God, the Second Person in the Blessed Trinity, did not, as such, so far as we can learn, work the miracles. To have done so, we may say further, would have been a repudiation of the circumstances in which it pleased Him to carry out His mission on earth, and of the plan and purpose of the Incarnation as we understand it. This, no doubt, is the popular notion of the rationale of Christ's miracles, but it must be dismissed from our minds. Jesus did not work the miracles because He was God.[2]

Secondly, there is an aspect of the Lord Jesus, which has become strangely unfashionable of recent years, yet ought not to be relegated to the lumber-room of worn-out doctrines; that form which He presents to us as the Ideal Man, or, to use a nearly synonymous term, the Second Adam. If indeed the application of the title of the Second Adam to Christ appears strange to those evolutionists who are accustomed to regard the first man before the 'fall' as little superior to a well-behaved ape,[3] we may remind them that the term implies likeness in two respects

[1] P. 111.

[2] Even though Mr. R. A. Knox can allow himself to write: 'Orthodox theology explains all the miracles recorded of our Saviour under one single hypothesis, that he was omnipotent God' (*Some Loose Stones*, 1913, p. 49). But Mr. Knox expressly disclaims being a theologian (p. vii).

[3] Contrast the description in M. Luzzatto, *Hebrew Glosses and Notes*, edited by Gollancz, 1911, pp. 11, 12: 'In the very name of the first man ADM there is a covert reference to three personages, *A*dam, *D*avid, *M*essiah. This is borne out by the saying of the Sage that "Adam reached from earth to heaven," for he knew all the treasures of the world: he was perfect in knowledge, in stature, and outward beauty, intellectually and morally perfect.'

only, viz. immediate relation to God, and the formation of a new line of descent. It thus leaves room for immeasurable superiority to the first Adam. Not only so, but it submits to us the thought of that archetypal Man into which, and not only from which, men are growing, and into which, from the very first conception of God's plan for them, they were intended to grow. If this be true it is only reasonable that the Second Adam should combine in Himself all those powers which are ultimately to be developed in the human race. Hence the fact that any, or all, of the powers possessed by the Lord Jesus Christ may ultimately be shown to belong to men generally does not detract from the superiority of Him who combined them all in His own person, and this centuries, or, it may be, millennia, before individuals shall have possessed more than fragments.[1]

It is possible also that as it has been with the doctrines of Christianity, so will it be with the miracles. Theologians used to find the evidence for Divine inspiration in the difference of New Testament sayings and doctrines from those existing elsewhere. But in view of the fact that very many, if not all, of these were known before Christ came, and even before the revelation on Mount Sinai—as *disjecta membra*, it is true, but still there—theologians now perceive that the Christian doctrines are divine for the very reason that they were adumbrated beforehand. The doctrines of our Faith do correspond, that is to say, with human yearnings and expressions. Comparative religion, instead of being an enemy to Christianity, is now becoming its firmest ally.

So with miracles. The purely human *provenance*

[1] *Cf.* Moberly, *Atonement and Personality*, 1911, pp. 95–97, 102.

MIRACLES AND SELF-SACRIFICE

of many tends to show that those performed by Jesus were but the more perfect form of powers inherent in humanity.[1]

Thirdly, the explanation suggested by the Evangelist is that our Lord's miracles were the result of His self-sacrifice. 'They brought unto Him many possessed with devils : and he cast out the spirits with a word, and healed all that were sick : that it might be fulfilled which was spoken by Isaiah the prophet, saying, Himself took our infirmities, and bare our diseases.'[2] St. Matthew means, as it would seem, that Christ did not merely perform miracles by His human powers, but that He took them upon His own shoulders, receiving in Himself the sickness and disease that He removed. This suggests something far deeper and more awful than anything experienced by His followers.[3]

---

[1] *Cf.* Mansel, *Aids to Faith*, p. 14, quoted in Mozley, *On Miracles*, Lecture VI, note 3. Take the case of telepathy, the truth of which is vouched for by so many trustworthy witnesses that we cannot but credit its existence. St. Catherine of Siena appears to have possessed in a remarkable degree the power of knowing what her spiritual sons and daughters were doing. See examples in E. G. Gardner, *Saint Catherine of Siena*, 1907, pp. 54 *sq.*, 87 *sqq.*, 93, 114, 183. 'Telepathy is only wireless telegraphy between brain and brain. The ever-vibrating molecules of the living cortex send their undulations through ether like all other oscillating particles, and some brain that synchronises in its period of vibrations receives the "message"' (Joseph McCabe, in *Religion and the Modern World*, 1909, p. 88). Perhaps so ; but what must He have been who at His pleasure was able to cause His brain to receive the 'message' from any particular individual or set of individuals ? Trench, however, is very severe upon this theory of our Lord's miracles in his Preliminary Essay, v. 5 (1866, p. 73).

[2] viii. 16, 17.

[3] See Lecture XI, pp. 390–392. For the thought of diseases as punishments for sins see (besides Biblical passages) many Talmudic references in Mr. H. Loewe's article on Disease and Medicine (Jewish) in Hastings' *E.R.E.* iv. 756 *sq.* See also Büchler, *Die galiläische 'Am-ha-'Areṣ des zweiten Jahrhunderts*, 1906, pp. 27, 30. The realisation of this by the paralytic would make our Lord's words in Matt. ix. 2 the more necessary.

Fourthly, Christ's own explanation, not indeed of the miracles wrought by Himself, but of those wrought by disciples, is that they were dependent upon the worker's faith. ' Then came the disciples to Jesus apart, and said, Why could not we cast it out ? And he saith unto them, Because of your little faith.' [1] For this reason, it is to be presumed, some writers have thought that our Lord worked miracles in precisely the same way as did the Apostles. ' Miracles,' one has said, ' ascribed to the incarnate Christ are to be regarded as wholly upon all fours in respect of their nature with similar miracles ascribed to Apostles and Saints ; they do not diminish from the truth of our Lord's humanity ; they are to be interpreted as Divine answers to His human prayers.' [2]

Excluding, then, the first of these four explanations, viz. that our Lord performed miracles by His own Divine power, He may have wrought them (*a*) by the human powers belonging to His personality ; (*b*) by bearing on Himself the sicknesses and diseases which He cured ; (*c*) by His faith on God, who worked the miracles at His request. It does not, however, appear to be necessary to exclude any of these three methods. All three may well have been combined.

(*a*) For, first, the spiritual gifts bestowed on one or other of Christ's followers, including the healing of disease, are (as is plain from the list of them given in St. Paul's Epistles [3]) not gifts without

---
[1] xvii. 19, 20 ; *v.* 21, with its mention of prayer and fasting, has been added in some authorities, from a corrupt text of Mark ix. 29. In any case fasting is a form of prayer.
[2] A. E. J. Rawlinson, in the *Interpreter*, Oct. 1911, p. 34.
[3] 1 Cor. xii. 4–11, 28–30.

III] THE IDEAL WORKER OF MIRACLES

any relation to powers possessed by other persons. On the contrary, they are only the intensification of 'natural' gifts. The gift of healing among believers is therefore a 'natural' power intensified through the faith of its possessor. (b) Secondly, its action has always depended upon sympathy and self-sacrifice. The ideal worker of miracles, if we may judge from the fragmentary examples of early days down to our own time, must possess boundless love and complete willingness to share the misery of those whom he endeavours to relieve.

(c) Thirdly, he must have faith on God. Now, we have already seen that the performance of miracles is closely allied to spiritual knowledge and personal piety. Hence the greater the miracles the more we should expect to find piety in him who performs them. But the greater the piety the more impossible it is that the person should perform them without reference to God. He cannot, just in proportion to his piety, do the simplest thing without referring it to God, much less do such actions as include utter selfishness towards others, and the consequent release of them from their physical troubles. The perfect, the Archetypal Man, therefore cannot possibly act independently of God, but must, by virtue of His very perfection, bring everything into relation to Him, and live in continual touch with Him. Hence, although we may ask the question whether Christ performed His miracles by His human powers or not, yet practically the question has no force, for He would continually be living by faith on His heavenly Father, and continually be drawing strength from Him. Therefore we must suppose that God was ever working these cures and other marvels in Christ's life, in answer to His prayers and faith, however great His human powers may have been. Yet this is not to accept the theory that God worked through Him as through His disciples. Far from it. For Christ brought all His own human powers, which immeasurably exceeded those possessed by any of His followers, to be used by His Father.[1]

Human potentialities at their height, love for others in the greatest possible intensity, and utter abasement before, and confidence in, His Father in heaven, must all be included in the one and only method by which the Messiah performed His miracles.[2]

(4) Where, then, exactly must we place our Lord's miracles among the evidences to the truth of our religion ? We can no longer say that they are so wonderful, so unique, that they are, for that reason, direct credentials of His divine nature, or even direct proofs that God was giving a new revelation through Him. For, as we have seen, the occurrence of other miracles, not differing essentially in character from

---

[1] 'His greatest works during His earthly life are wrought by the help of the Father through the energy of a humanity enabled to do all things in fellowship with God' (Westcott, *Hebrews*, 1889, p. 66). See also Bishop F. Weston, *The One Christ*, 1914, pp. 270-272.

[2] This suggests that in the last instance human nature, especially sinless human nature such as that which our Lord took, may become not merely not contradictory to God, but rather so permeated by the Divine as to do nothing by its own powers apart from God. All the man does God does, so intimately is God present in his thoughts, words, actions. In him the immanence of God is complete. Observe that this is not Pantheism. For the personality of the man is distinct from God, probably never so distinct, and indeed unique, as when it acts and reacts under the Divine influence. Compare the words of Drs. Worcester and McComb : ' Man does not stand over against God in self-enclosed independence ; rather is he so organically related to Him that his whole being, psychical and physical, is saturated with Divine energy, and apart from it must faint and fail. Prayer is the recognition of this inviolable organic bond' (*The Christian Religion as a Healing Power*, 1910, p. 77).

III] THE EVIDENTIAL VALUE OF THE MIRACLES

His, prevents this, as does also the increasing possibility, not to say probability, that in the future every one of His miracles may be performed by ordinary human means. Besides, evidential value of this kind is never attributed to them in the First Gospel. According to St. Matthew, the miracles were evidence that Jesus was the One to come (xi. 4, 5), and that since Jesus cast out demons the kingdom of God had arrived (xii. 28). Miracles, that is to say, are not adduced by the Evangelist as evidence that God was giving a revelation, but as witnesses to the Messiahship of Jesus of Nazareth, and also, from their peculiar character of opposition to evil spirits, to the fact that the promised change in God's dealings with the world had begun. They suggest that the Lord Jesus was the fulfilment of prophecy, and the Deliverer from the Evil One. They are therefore evidence to our Lord on the predictive side, and on the moral.[1] They do not as such testify to His Divinity or even to the Divine character of His teaching.

This estimate of the evidential value of our Lord's miracles, it will be observed, is quite different from the ' credential ' theory as ordinarily stated,[2] but it is

---

[1] 'The ancient Jew saw in his own dispensation an imperfect structure, the head of which was still wanting—the Messiah : all pointed to Him ; its ceremonial was typical ; and the whole system was an adumbration of a great approaching Divine kingdom, and a great crowning Divine act. The very heart of the nation was thus the seat of a great standing prophecy ; all was anticipation and expectation ; prophets kept alive the sacred longing ; miracles confirmed the prophetical office ; and in prospect was the miraculous outbreak of Divine power in the great closing dispensation itself' (J. B. Mozley, *Miracles*, 1872, pp. 159 *sq.*).

[2] Even Bishop D'Arcy in his very valuable little book, *Christianity and the Supernatural*, 1909, p. 20, writes : ' If, in order to bring the life of Christ into line with what we now know of the working of such forces, we minimise the miraculous element in the Gospel narrative, we are pulling down the mighty

none the less important. Miracles direct attention to Jesus, not as the wonder-worker, but as the promised Messiah and the conqueror of sin. They are not irrefragable proofs of His Messiahship, much less of His Divinity, but they bid us consider the personality of Him who wrought them.

So far, therefore, from our believing in miracles 'because we have first believed in Christ,' we 'believe in Christ because of His miracles.' [1]

For we should expect, on the analogy of history, that He, as a very holy person, would perform miracles, and the performance of miracles by Him strengthens our belief in Him. Had He not wrought them, history would teach us to be doubtful of His claims and His promises. We should have suspected that there was something radically wrong with Him, in spite of the excellence of His words, if He did not release the physically afflicted and drive out the agents of Satan (xii. 28; *cf.* Luke xiii. 16). Proofs, in the strictest and almost mathematical sense, miracles are not, when they are considered in themselves only; but evidences to the character and work, and thus the claims, of Jesus, they are.[2]

They bring before us One, the motive of whose life was to relieve men from their afflictions, bodily, mental, and spiritual; One who was unwearying in

works to the level of everyday experiences and depriving them of all evidential value. What is essential to the function of miracles in the witness to the Divine mission of the Christ is, not that they should be shown to be in every instance an employment of supernatural powers, but that they should have the stamp of superhuman authority.' This seems to make too sharp a distinction between natural and supernatural.

[1] See above, p. 97.

[2] J. B. Mozley is right in pointing out that the doctrine connected with Christ's miracles 'did not leave mankind as it found them, but was a fresh starting-point of moral practice' (*Miracles*, p. 135).

III] APPENDIX—NON-BIBLICAL MIRACLES

His efforts, or rather, though wearied, still continued in them ; One who was able to do such mighty cures because He did not shrink from taking upon Himself the suffering from which He relieved men ; One who was ever in living contact with His Father in heaven. Hence they bid us not only listen to His teaching as to the words of Him who by His power and His life was unique in the history of the world, but also cast ourselves upon Him, for salvation both of soul and body, as on One who can be altogether trusted, whose promises and invitations deserve on our part the fullest acceptance.

APPENDIX

A FEW EXAMPLES OF NON-BIBLICAL MIRACLES OF HEALING [1]

Inscriptions in the Temple of Apollo Maleatos and Asklepios at Epidauros, about the Fourth Century B.C.

No. 3—'A man, whose fingers, with the exception of one, were paralysed, came as a suppliant to the Temple. While examining the temple tablets, he expressed incredulity regarding the cures and scoffed at the inscriptions. In his sleep he saw the following vision. He thought he was playing at dice near the Temple, and as he was going to cast the dice,

---

[1] In all cases, unless otherwise stated, these are taken from apparently contemporary evidence. Full accounts of the majority may be found in Miss M. Hamilton's admirable *Incubation, or the Cure of Disease in Pagan Temples and Christian Churches*, 1906. The original of the older examples is given at length in P. Fiebig, *Antike Wundergeschichten* (Lietzmann's Kleine Texte), 1911, and also in various parts of O. Weinrich's learned but inconveniently arranged *Antike Heilungswunder*, 1909.

Summaries of works of healing in the Christian Church down to the present time may be found in Dr. P. Dearmer's suggestive book, *Body and Soul*, 1909, pp. 231–286, 299–315, 339–395.

the god suddenly appeared, seized his hand and stretched out his fingers. When the god stood aside from him, the patient thought he could bend his hand and stretch out all his fingers one by one. When he had stretched them all out, the god asked him if he would still be incredulous as to the contents of the inscriptions on the tablets. He answered that he would not, and the god said to him : " Since formerly you did not believe in the cures, though they were not incredible, for the future your name will be ' The Unbeliever.' " When day dawned, he left the sacred hall cured ' (Hamilton, *op. cit.* p. 18).

No. 5—' A dumb boy came as a suppliant to the Temple to recover his voice. When he had performed the preliminary sacrifices, and fulfilled the usual rites, the temple priest who bore the sacrificial fire, turned to the boy's father and said : " Do you promise to pay within a year the fees for the cure, if you obtain that for which you have come ? " Suddenly the boy answered, " I do." His father was greatly astonished at this, and told his son to speak again. The boy repeated the words, and so was cured ' (Hamilton, *loc. cit.*).

Among other cases are blindness (Nos. 4, 11), stone (No. 8), a spear-point in the cheek for six years (No. 12), for one year causing blindness (No. 32), an arrow-point in the lung for a year and a half (No. 30), tape-worm (No. 23). (Hamilton, *op. cit.* pp. 18–25.)

Also at Epidauros, in the second half of the second century A.D. A chronic invalid, and suffering from dyspepsia. In this case the god told him to use various means, such as exercise, attention to food, &c. (Hamilton, *op. cit.* pp. 40 *sq.*).

Inscriptions in the Temple of Æsculapius on the Tiber Island

Of about the time of Augustus.

' To Asklepios, the great god, the saviour and benefactor, saved by thy hands from a tumour of the spleen, of which this is the silver model, as a mark of gratitude to the god : Neochares Julianus, a freedman of the imperial household ' (Hamilton, *op. cit.* p. 67 ; Weinreich, *op. cit.* p. 30).

APPENDIX—ANCIENT MIRACLES

Of the second century A.D.

'Lucius suffered from pleurisy, and had been despaired of by all. The god made a revelation to him that he should go and lift ashes from the triangular altar, and mix them with wine, and lay them on his side. He was saved, and he offered thanks publicly to the god, and the people rejoiced with him' (Hamilton, *op. cit.* p. 68; Weinreich, *op. cit.* p. 115).

Other cases are blindness, hæmorrhage (apparently of the lungs).

Aristides' *Sacred Orations*, probably written in 175 A.D. (Hamilton, *op. cit.* pp. 44–62; P. Fiebig, *op. cit.* pp. 21–23).

He had a long illness, with complication of many illnesses, earache, fever, asthma, toothache, rheumatism, lumbago, convulsions. His cure was effected by various intimations of Asklepios at his different shrines—baths in cold water, riding, drugs of all kinds, &c.

Examples of Cures in Christian Churches

In the Church of Cosmas and Damian, at Constantinople (date of writing uncertain, sixth, fifth, or fourth century A.D.). A man with a fistula on his thigh.

'Since miracles of this kind were performed every day, constant crowds of sick people came to the church' (Hamilton, *op. cit.* p. 122). A woman's ulcerated breast was healed through prayers of her husband to St. Cosmas and St. Damian, though she and he were in Phrygia (*ibid.* p. 123). 'A man, suffering from arthritis, promised Cosmas and Damian a waxen offering, and recovered his health' (*ibid.* p. 126).

In the Church of St. Therapon, at Byzantium, in the beginning of the seventh century A.D.

A decarch of military rank, whose body was terribly distorted, remained in the church several days, and then heard an 'unseen voice' telling him to have himself anointed with olive oil 'by an official of my church.' Healed at once. (Hamilton, *op. cit.* p. 132.)

Other cases are cancer, a withered hand.

St. Cyrus and St. John, at Menuthes, near Canopus, in Egypt. Seventy of their miracles are related by Sophronios, patriarch of Jerusalem, who died *c.* 640 A.D. He describes things done in his own time, some of them seen by himself. The cult of these two saints succeeded to the cult of Isis.

The saints say, ' We are not masters of the healing art. . . . Christ is dispenser and guardian . . . we offer intercession for all alike, and Christ decides whom we shall cure ' (Hamilton, *op. cit.* p. 146).

Among their cures are a demoniac, blind men, broken bones, cancer.

In the Church of St. Julian, at Arvernus, in the time of Gregory of Tours, sixth century. (Hamilton, *op. cit.* p. 161.) Woman cured of paralysis after eighteen years.

At the fountain by his tomb at Arvernus: blind men, fever patients, demoniacs restored; Gregory of Tours himself cured of headache, his brother of fever.

In the Church of St. Martin of Tours, about the same period. (Hamilton, *op. cit.* pp. 161 *sqq.*) Gout for a year, blindness, paralysis of fingers.

At the tomb of St. Maximinus, near Trèves, eighth century. Charles Martel cured of fever (Hamilton, *op. cit.* p. 163); erysipelas cured by oil taken from the lamp before the altar; demoniacs.

At the tomb of St. Fides, at Conques, in Rouergue (Hamilton, *op. cit.* pp. 166 *sq.*), told by Bernard of Angers, *c.* 1012 A.D., as cures in his own time: dumbness, blindness, paralysis, arm wounded and power lost but restored, wounds.

Dr. E. A. Abbott has made a long and careful study of the miracles connected with St. Thomas à Becket in his *St. Thomas of Canterbury*, 1898, and comes to the conclusion that it is impossible to resist the evidence that many really did take place. St. Thomas was murdered on December 29, 1170.

William, a monk of Canterbury, who was present at the martyrdom, ' began to compile the Book of Miracles seventeen months (May, 1172) after the martyrdom. . . . Most of the important miracles towards the end of William's book took place in 1174. . . . His book on Miracles must have

III]   APPENDIX—MEDIÆVAL MIRACLES

been published before 1189 (the year of Henry [the Second's] death' (§ 17).

Benedict, another monk of Canterbury, ' probably wrote the present narrative [of the martyrdom] in 1171, but revised it when he prefixed it to his Book of Miracles, which was probably completed, in its first form, before 1175 ' (§ 18). The evidence, therefore, for such miracles as are included in this ' first form ' stands almost, or quite, unequalled for nearness in date to the events described.

In § 453 Dr. Abbott gives two lists of the first thirty cases of miracles recorded severally by Benedict and William.

Among those most worth mentioning are the following :

(a) § 410. On the third day after Becket's death the wife of a knight, who had weakness and blindness connected with it, prayed to Becket ; within half an hour she had her sight restored, and by the sixth day rose from her bed.

(b) § 454. On the fifth day after the martyrdom a woman at Gloucester invoked St. Thomas' aid on behalf of her daughter (aged about sixteen), whose head swelled every month. She was cured, and the narrator, Benedict, saw them both himself.

(c) § 456. A knight in Aeinesburna, in Berkshire, hears of the saint's murder, prays him to deliver him from ' terrible pain in the left arm,' which was badly swollen. He had been in bed for three months. He slept, was refreshed, found his pain gone, and the arm well.

(d) § 457. On January 4, a blind woman in Canterbury had her sight restored by the application of a rag which had been dipped in the martyr's blood.

Catharine of Siena (1347–1380)

(a) The restoration of Father Matthew from plague.

' I asked if medical aid could not save him. " We shall see," replied Dr. Senso, " but I have only a very faint hope ; his blood is too much poisoned." . . . Catharine, however, had heard of the illness of Father Matthew, whom she loved sincerely, and she lost no time in repairing to him. The moment she entered the room, she cried, with a cheerful voice, " Get up, Father Matthew, get up ! This is not a time to be lying idly in bed." Father Matthew roused himself, sat up on his bed, and finally stood on his feet. Catharine retired ; at the moment she was leaving the house, I entered it, and ignorant of what had happened, and believing my friend to be still at the point of death, my grief urged me to say, " Will you allow a person so dear to us, and so useful to others, to die ? " She appeared annoyed at my words, and replied, " In what terms do you address me ? Am I like God, to deliver a man from death ? " But I, beside myself with sorrow, pleaded, " Speak in that way to others if you will, but not to me ; for I know your secrets : and I know that you obtain from God whatsoever you ask in faith." Then Catharine bowed her head, and smiled just a little; after a few moments she lifted up her head and looked full in my face, her countenance radiant with joy, and said : " Well, let us take courage; he will not die this time," and she passed on ' (Josephine Butler, *Catharine of Siena*, 1881, p. 97).

(*b*) ' Gerard Buonconti one day brought to her a young man of twenty years of age, whose system was shattered by the long continuance of a quotidian fever from which he was then suffering. He had consulted many physicians in vain ; he was so weak as scarcely to be able to stand to salute her. Filled with pity for him, and seeking an interview alone with him, she laid her hand on his shoulder, and gently whispered to him concerning the weight which she saw to be pressing on his soul. He was a stranger to prayer, to true faith, and to peace. She charged him at once to pour forth his heart in confession of all his past sins and negligence. He met her advice with truthfulness and simplicity, and conferred for some time after with good Friar Thomas della Fonte, to whom Catharine had commended him. He began at once to feel his soul lightened and his body strengthened. She then said to him, " Go, my son, in the peace of Jesus Christ, who will hear thy prayer. This fever will no more torment thee." Not many days after, he returned in restored health, to render thanks to her and to God ; his countenance was full of happiness and joy, and he walked with a firm, elastic step. Raymond saw him some few years later on a journey through Pisa, and affirmed that he had become so robust that he could not have known him, had he not explained who he was. He continued to be a faithful follower of Christ. Raymond says, moreover, "I was witness of this work of healing, and can say, like St. John, 'He who hath seen beareth witness'"' (Josephine Butler, *op. cit.* pp. 139 *sq.*).

(c) 'One of the women, who was very retiring and careworn in appearance, carried in her arms her sick baby, a pitiful object, but *her* treasure. She besought the friends of Catharine to ask her to take the infant in her arms and cure it; "for," she said, "she has power with God, and can heal diseases: she can restore to me my baby which is dying." The message was taken to Catharine, but she declined to undertake this, or to appear; for she dreaded the publicity of the occasion. But the entreaties and sobs of the poor mother, whose petitions were seconded by the other women, were too much for her compassionate heart: she came out of her chamber, and said, "Where is the little one?" The mother pressed forward, and Catharine, full of pity, took the baby in her arms, and pressing it to her breast, she prayed earnestly and with tears to Him who said, "Suffer the little children to come unto me." From that moment the child revived, and the whole city was witness of its rapid return to health, and the joy of the poor mother' (Josephine Butler, *op. cit.* p. 191).

(d) 'In a few days Neri was quite well. But Stephen, worn out by his fatigues in nursing the patients, and by his anxiety about his beloved friend, was attacked by a violent fever. "As every one loved him," says Raymond, "we resorted to him to try and console him, and all nursed him by turns." Stephen himself gave the following account of it: "Catharine came, with her companions, to pay me a visit, and asked me what I was suffering. I, quite delighted at her sweet presence, answered gaily, 'They *say* I am ill; but I do not know what it is.' She placed her hand on my forehead; and shaking her head and smiling, she said, 'Do you hear how this child answers me?—They *say* that

I am ill, but I do not know of what;—and he is in a violent fever!' then she added, addressing me: 'But, Stephen, I do not allow you to be ill; you must get up and wait upon the others as before.' She then conversed with us about God, as usual, and as she was speaking I began to feel quite well. I interrupted her to tell them so, and they were all in astonishment, and very glad. I arose from my bed the same day, and I have enjoyed perfect health since that time "' (Josephine Butler, *op. cit.* pp. 194 *sq.*).

'When the Holy Coat was displayed at Trèves in the year 1891, the sight of the relic, seen with the eye of faith, did, as an actual fact, according to the perfectly trustworthy evidence of German physicians of unimpeachable reputation, effect in eleven cases cures for which no other medical reasons whatever could be offered, though in twenty-seven other cases another explanation of the cure did not seem to the physicians to be excluded. The eleven cases for which no medical explanation could be offered included atrophy of the optic nerve of many years' standing, lupus, paralysis of the arm as a consequence of dislocation, complete loss of the use of the arms and legs as a consequence of rheumatic gout, St. Vitus' dance, a serious abdominal complaint, blindness of one eye and paralysis of one arm as a consequence of brain fever, chronic intestinal disorder, a cancerous tumour, caries of the spine, and a chronic inflammation of the spinal marrow.'

O. Holtzmann (*The Life of Jesus*, E.T. 1904, pp. 193 *sq.*), referring to Korum, *Wunder und göttliche Gnadenweise bei der Ausstellung des heiligen Rockes im Jahre* 1891, Trier, 1894.

Examples of Cures at the Present Day

At Tenos, on the day of the Annunciation, March 25 (old style) (M. Hamilton, *Incubation*, pp. 191 *sqq.*). Usually eight or nine miracles each year. Church records contain many hundreds of examples: *e.g.* paralysis, especially blindness (one case seen by Miss Hamilton, p. 199), insanity.

In Rhodes, at Kremastos (Hamilton, *op. cit.* pp. 209 *sq.*), *e.g.* deaf and dumb.

APPENDIX—MODERN MIRACLES

At the monastery of St. Luke, in Phocis (Hamilton, *op. cit.* p. 213), lepers, blind.

Miss M. Hamilton, in her *Greek Saints and Their Festivals*, 1910, gives many examples of marvellous cures in Greece in the last few years.

In 1907 a paralytic who was quite unable to move was laid before the ikon. He said that in the night a dark woman (the ikon had a black face) issued from the picture, and told him thrice to move out of the way. At the third time he tried, and found himself cured (p. 47).

In 1909 a girl who had been blind for two months had her vision restored, and a man who was deaf and dumb became able to hear and speak (p. 48).

Another case 'just before our visit' was that of a lame man who was restored to health by means of oil which had been taken from the lamp hanging in front of the ikon (p. 50).

A vivid description of the excitement of the worshippers, and the crowds of sick people, together with the cure of some, at a church near Jahce, on the Vrba, in Bosnia, St. John Baptist's Day, June 24, 1900, is recorded in Ebstein's *Die Medizin im N.T. und im Talmud*, 1903, pp. 61 *sq.*

At the temple of Mar Sergius, near Urmi, in Eastern Kurdistan, incubation is still practised with great success. 'The fact is at all events past question, that a very fair proportion of those who submit to the discipline come out cured.' Sometimes incubation is performed there by proxy. See W. A. Wigram, *The Cradle of Mankind; Life in Eastern Kurdistan*, 1914, p. 206. On Lourdes, see H. Thurston, *E.R.E.*, viii. 148–151.

To note 1, on page 117, may be added: S. Bernardino of Siena (*ob.* 1444) 'notes the powerful action of the mind upon the body, and observes that S. Francis' continual meditation on the Passion would be a predisposing cause of such an effect as the appearance of the Stigmata' (*Life*, by A. G. F. Howell, 1913, p. 271, who also describes the miracles that took place at Bernardino's death, pp. 208 *sqq.*).

Lecture Four

THE MESSIAH AS TEACHER—HIS ORIGINALITY

'He taught them as one having authority, and not as their scribes.'—MATT. vii. 29.

Lecture Four

THE MESSIAH AS TEACHER—HIS ORIGINALITY

WE now turn to the study of the Messiah as the Teacher, remembering, consistently with our subject, that we have to study Him not as the teacher of us Gentiles, but as He is presented to us in relation to the Jews. In other words, the primary question for us is not, What in reality was Jesus Himself as Teacher, but What was He in the eyes of the writer of this first Gospel, whom it is convenient for us to call St. Matthew?

I. What was the preparation received by the Messiah which qualified Him to be a Teacher? Formal and scholastic training He had none. We must therefore put the question into other words, and ask, What were the currents of thought at that time likely to influence Him? We do not ask, What were the sources from which He derived His knowledge, for no one seriously supposes that Jesus was an eclectic, culling, from this side and from that, herbs for His healing draughts, and flowers for the fair garlands of His sweet discourse. With Him it was not a matter of selecting and picking. But, living as He did in an atmosphere of active thought, it was impossible but that He should breathe it, and make it His own. Currents of thought there were from different quarters, mingling and commingling so close that we cannot hope to distinguish them, either in themselves or in their effect. But they were there, and it is useless to expect to understand either the teaching of our

Lord, or His influence upon His people, unless we recognise their presence. 'Even the Prophets and Apostles would have preached to deaf ears if the substance of what they proclaimed had not had links of union with the circle of ideas already present to their audience . . . even they were children of their time, even in them could the new thoughts which they were to announce only be engendered by the support of those which already existed.'[1] This is true universally. Jesus, the perfect Man, the Messiah, was no exception, either for Himself or for those to whom He came.

We cannot, however, be far wrong in eliminating from our inquiry all currents directly emanating from non-Jewish sources. It is true that the advocates of Buddhism have brought forward not a few points in common between the life and teaching of Buddha and those of our Lord, such as the nature of His birth and the events of His childhood, the murder of the Innocents, the early visit of the Boy to the Temple, the Baptism, the Temptation, the Sermon on the Mount, the Miracles, the Transfiguration, the Betrayal, and even the doctrine that evil is inherent in the world.

But against all this must be set the uncertainty of the date of those parts of Buddhist tradition which bear most resemblance to the Gospels, and also the fact that in some of the supposed parallel actions and precepts the coincidence is not so striking as to preclude accident. Lastly, the general tendencies of the two religions, the one introspective and negative, the other positive and energetic, are completely

---

[1] Schürer, *Die Predigt Jesu Christi in ihrem Verhältniss zum alten Testamen und zum Judenthum*, 1882, pp. 3 *sq.*

NON-JEWISH INFLUENCE ON OUR LORD

different. While then it may be granted that Buddhists had visited Alexandria before the time of our Lord, there is no sufficient evidence that their religion was known in Judæa, and no sign that it influenced either the Messiah or those whom He addressed.[1]

The case is otherwise with Parseeism. When we compare the Old Testament, in particular the oldest portions of it, with the New, we cannot but take account of the change in much that refers to the unseen world, and matters of eschatology. The doctrine of angels, for example, especially of evil angels, perhaps even of the devil, marks a whole realm of expansion in belief, and is probably due to contact with Persia. The intercourse, however, did not take place in our Lord's time, but three or four centuries earlier, and to Him and His contemporaries the new doctrines had become a normal part of Jewish theology. The religion of Persia as such had no direct connexion with our Lord.

What then of Greek thought? Perhaps He could speak Greek, but the ordinary people even of Galilee do not appear to have known it well,[2] and in any case it can hardly have been His mother-tongue, or He would not have fallen back on Aramaic

---

[1] The worthless platitudes of *The Unknown Life of Christ*, by Nicolas Notovitch, 1895, may please those for whom they were invented. If Dr. Timothy Richard is right, in his beautiful translation of the Buddhist works, *The Awakening of Faith*, and *The Essence of the Lotus Scripture*, contained in his *The New Testament of Higher Buddhism*, 1910, the most striking coincidences between Buddhism and Christianity are due to Ashvagosha, who lived some fifty years after St. Paul, and incorporated much of his teaching into the Mahayana form of Buddhism. On the subject generally see also Karl von Hase, *Neutestamentliche Parallelen zu buddhistischen Quellen*, 1905.

[2] Schürer, *G.J.V.*, 1907, ii. 63 *sqq*.

in time of stress and profound emotion. Besides, Greek religion, as such, with its love of nature-worship and its disregard of morality, can hardly have presented much attraction to one brought up in the pure and holy precepts of the God of the Old Testament. Greek philosophy, on the other hand, pure and undiluted, has certainly not left much trace on the teaching of our Lord. Non-Jewish thought, then, whether from India, or from Persia, or from Greece, had, so far as we are aware, no direct influence upon Him or on those to whom He ministered.

While, however, Greek thought as such had little or no effect upon our Lord, that form of it called Hellenism had much. Yet here again we must distinguish. There were two kinds of Hellenism—one philosophic, the other practical. The former, though it had made in Alexandria no little progress before the birth of Christ, and was to attain its zenith in the writings of Philo within a few years after His death, demands close attention by the student of the Fourth Gospel, but may almost be ignored by the student of the First. It is otherwise with what we may call practical Hellenism. For this may underlie not a little of the great Apocalyptic writings, the extent of whose influence upon the New Testament is becoming increasingly evident. In any case the reader of St. Matthew must continually bear in mind the possibility that his Gospel may owe much to parts of the Apocrypha and the Pseudepigraphic Writings. So far, indeed, as they are distinctively eschatological, the consideration of them must be reserved for the tenth lecture. Here it is enough to point out that one object of the

iv] INFLUENCE OF THE O.T. UPON HIM

Apocalyptic authors was to produce a freer attitude towards the Law than was presupposed by Pharisaism. Hence they contribute comparatively little information about technical matters of the Law, while saying much on the practical side of religion in their expectation of the swift vindication by God of His people, and, as occasion served, on the manner of life which alone is worthy of His servants.

It is, however, important for our purpose that we should remember that while Apocalyptic books are due both to Alexandrian and to Palestinian thinkers, those of the latter most influenced our Lord, doubtless because they adhered more closely to the teaching of the Old Testament.

For with our Lord, as with every Jew, the Old Testament was the court to which, in the last instance, all appeal was made. It was the head from which flowed the waters of spiritual life in unadulterated purity and strength. With Him again, as with every Jew of Palestine, the limits of the Old Testament did not exceed those of the present Hebrew Canon.[1] He would hear the lesson from the Law, and the lesson from the Prophets, read in the synagogue sabbath by sabbath in Hebrew, together, perhaps, with an explanation of them in the native tongue, the Aramaic of the period.[2]

Further, we may assume that our Lord's home was saturated with religious belief and practice derived directly from the Old Testament. But when we try to be more precise in our knowledge of this,

---

[1] Possibly they were not then quite so large, for there were doubts about Ecclesiastes and the Song of Songs until the Council of Jamnia *c.* 90 A.D.

[2] It would seem, therefore, that He knew at least three languages—Hebrew, Aramaic, and Greek.

and endeavour to state accurately the nature of the influence brought to bear upon Him there, we are, in reality, more at a loss than is generally supposed. Detailed pictures have been drawn of the home-life of Jesus, upon the supposition that it was that of a child trained in such ways as commended themselves to Talmudic scholars. But everything points to the probability that among pious Jews the doctrines of the Apocalyptic literature found ready acceptance, and did much to mould the mind of the rising generation. It is further probable that this was especially the case in Galilee.[1]

Yet, with this reservation, it can hardly be wrong to assume that the Lord Jesus was well acquainted in His home at Nazareth with the teaching of the Pharisees, both in practice and theory, and, in particular, with its insistence on the Traditional Law.

Now we are in no little danger of despising this element of the religious life of that time, and because it had its weak side, and easily lent itself to abuse, are apt to forget its value.

For then, as always, it fulfilled an indispensable function by enabling Judaism, the observance of the Law as a code, to maintain its existence as a living religion. For it was prompted by a sincere desire to determine how the will of God, as revealed in the Pentateuch (to which all other parts of the Bible were but explanatory), could be brought into touch with later life.[2]

We have already seen that with a code some such system of interpretation is necessary, if it is not to become a mere dead weight of unmeaning observance. Once assume that a book, believed to

[1] See Lecture X, p. 351.   [2] See Lectures II, pp. 62-64; V, p. 186.

IV] INFLUENCE OF THE ORAL LAW

be infallible, contains minute and specific directions for daily life, then, as a consequence, there arises the necessity of rules, and of methods of interpreting it, in order to bring it into touch with the practical needs of each day. One must, as the Rabbis say, 'Turn it about, and turn it about, for all is in it' (*Pirqe Aboth*, v. 32). So much painstaking endeavour had been expended on the interpretation of the written Law before our Lord's time, and so great a body of oral explanation had in fact been formed, embracing in its inquiry ritual, social, ethical, theological, and even spiritual matters, that it must have had a considerable share in the preparation of the Lord Jesus for His work as Teacher.

Yet when we endeavour to define more closely the nature of the influence exerted upon Him by the Oral Law we find ourselves in this difficulty, that we are not able to state accurately the contents of that Law at that time.

For indeed at no time have its contents been so rounded off that it has been possible to say: These, and these only, are the precepts of the Oral Law; much less can we affirm what they were at so comparatively early a stage in its history as 25 A.D. when the School of Hillel was still disputing with that of Shammai. Possibly, no doubt, zealous Scribes had already begun to tabulate it,[1] but even this is far from certain, and it is more probable that for the first beginnings of at least the written form of the Oral Law we must wait until the very end of the first, or even the earlier part of the second century.[2] Not until we come to the year 200, or

---
[1] *Jewish Encyclopedia*, viii. 610.
[2] Strack, *Einleitung in den Talmud*, 1908, p. 10, *cf.* p. 20.

thereabouts, are we on sure ground, when R. Jehudah, the Prince of the Jewish community in Babylon, framed the collection of traditional Law known as the Mishna. We grant, however, that this claims to be based on ancient precedent, and gives in many cases the names of those earlier Rabbis who made the decisions which it records, some of whom were living in the first half of the second century, and a few even in the first century itself, approximately, that is to say, in the time of our Lord.

On the other hand, both the Talmuds are later than the Mishna, the earlier, that of Jerusalem or Palestine, dating from about 400 A.D; the later, written in Babylon, from about 500 A.D.[1]

The enumeration of these dates is sufficient to show that when we try to determine the contents of the Oral Law in the time of our Lord, we cannot feel the same certainty about the results at which we arrive as if our material were contemporary with Him. It has ever been a temptation to students, Jewish and Christian alike, to foist in upon us any and every statement of the Mishna and even of the Talmuds, as an illustration of the life and thought of the Jews in the early part of the first century. Nothing can be more absurd. At least some attempt ought to be made first to trace out critically any such tradition to the earliest source attributed to it, namely, the person by whom it was first spoken, and even then the criticism of the trustworthiness of such sources is as yet in far too incipient a form to enable us to place much trust in its conclusions. Still more

---

[1] Strack, *Einleitung in den Talmud*, 1908, pp. 63, 68. On the pre-Talmudic Midrashim, *i.e.* the Mekilta, the Siphra, and the Siphre, see Oesterley and Box, *The Religion and Worship of the Synagogue*, 2nd edition, 1911, pp. 81 *sqq*.

iv] CONCLUSIONS AS TO INFLUENCES UPON HIM

uncritical is it to quote sayings that are found only in yet later Jewish books, as though they were representative of Jewish teaching in the time of Christ. The burden of proof at least lies on those who do quote these passages, not on those who fear to use them.[1]

Lastly, we may not overlook the possibility that certain sayings common both to the New Testament and the Rabbis may have been taken over by the latter from the former, especially if Chwolson is right in affirming the existence of friendly intercourse between Jews and Hebrew-Christians so late as the time of R. Jehudah.[2] It must be confessed, however, that such borrowing of Jews from Christians, on any large scale, is very improbable, in view of the horror which most of the official teachers felt of reading Jewish-Christian books, or of applying to Jewish-Christians for advice.[3]

The conclusions to be drawn from these considerations are, first, that non-Jewish forms of thought had only an indirect effect on Christ, by being already incorporated into the intellectual activity of Palestinian Judaism; secondly, that the influence of the teaching now preserved to us in the Apocryphal and Pseudepigraphic books was, in all probability, in exact ratio to the closeness of its relation to that

---

[1] Dr. Abelson in his illuminating book, *The Immanence of God in Rabbinical Literature*, 1912, may be right in claiming that 'the mediæval Kabbalah is really an integral portion of Talmudism. It is part of its flesh and blood' (p. 2); 'it is really the literature of Jewish mysticism from about the first pre-Christian century until almost recent times' (p. 3); but the critical study of it has made little advance since Zunz affirmed in 1832 that the Zohar was composed about 1300 A.D., and partly compiled out of very late material (*Gottesdienstliche Vorträge*, p. 405). See also H. J. Holtzmann, *N.T. Theologie*, 1911, i. p. 50.

[2] *Das letzte Passamahl Christi*, 1908, pp. 101–107. See Lect. V. p. 209.

[3] *Vide infra*, p. 162.

of the books of the Old Testament, which were certainly to Him the chief source of intellectual and spiritual truth; thirdly, that He came under the Pharisaic treatment of the Law, only so far as this affected the daily life of those many pious Israelites who were not professedly members of the Pharisaic Society; and lastly, that we must, as careful students of evidence, be on our guard against identifying Rabbinic teaching, as we know it, with the instruction given in our Lord's day; unless indeed the existence of some specific portion at that time be shown to be probable by direct statements in Rabbinic literature which are proved to be trustworthy, or by testimony contained in other works of a date not later than the first century of our era.

II. Having considered the currents of thought likely to have influenced our Lord, we turn to consider Him as Teacher. What does St. Matthew tell us of this? For he tells us much, more perhaps than we should have expected. For we have been so accustomed to regard the Lord Jesus as the Deliverer from sin, that it requires on our part some little effort to understand the reason why the Evangelist sets Him before us as the Teacher. Why did St. Matthew say so much of this side of Christ's work? However great may have been his hope that his treatise would be of help to future generations (and what author is there in whose innermost heart such a hope has no place?), yet he must have written primarily for the men of his own time. What, then, moved him to record so much of our Lord's words? This, no doubt, that he desired to draw out the contrast between Him and the other teachers of his nation.

IV] THE SUPERIORITY OF MESSIAH AS A TEACHER

The war was over. The Sadducees had perished. The Essenes had passed into oblivion. The Zealots as such remained discredited for half a century. But the teachers of Israel, the Scribes with their attendant Pharisees, were remoulding religion, and were courageously endeavouring to maintain the faith of Judaism, and rivet the precepts of the Law in the hearts of all Jews who had survived the horrors of the siege and the blandishments of heathen worship. We cannot praise too highly the conscientious attempts of R. Jochanan ben Zakkai and his fellow-leaders to maintain Judaism as they knew it, and to develope the Oral Law in the new circumstances of a State destroyed and a Temple consumed in the flames. They were earnest men, who acquired by their consistency the respect of all, and by their ability ensured to Pharisaic Judaism a long life, down to our own day.

They were great as teachers. But to the Evangelist, living as he was in the same land as they, nay, perhaps in the self-same district, for Jamnia, the new centre of their learning, was nigh unto Lydda and Joppa,[1] they appeared but small in comparison with Jesus. He was a teacher of a standing far higher than theirs. Resembling them in much, He differed from them in more. He was, St. Matthew felt, immeasurably superior to them all.

St. Matthew, that is to say, desired to bring out in his treatise the significance of the Messiah as Teacher, and he did this, whether intentionally or not I cannot say, by showing that both in manner and in matter He was at once dependent and independent, being indeed a great Teacher, original and supreme.

[1] Acts ix. 32–43.

There was much in common between the manner of the teaching of Christ and that of the official leaders of the people. Listen to the following:

'It is like to a king, who invited his servants to a supper, but did not appoint the time. The wise among them adorned themselves, and sat at the door of the king's house. For they said: Can anything be lacking in the house of the king (*i.e.* the supper may be ready at any time)? The foolish among them went to their work. For they said: Can there ever be a supper without preparation? Suddenly the king asked for his servants: the wise among them went in before him, adorned as they were. But the foolish went in, dirty as they were. Then the king rejoiced over the wise, but was wroth with the foolish. He said: These who have adorned themselves for the supper may sit down and eat and drink; these who have not adorned themselves for the supper may remain standing and look on' (T.B., *Sabb.* 153*a*).[1] We might almost be reading a parable in the New Testament, might we not? In reality it is one spoken by R. Jochanan ben Zakkai. Further it is only a specimen (a good one, I grant) out of the many hundreds or even thousands of parables contained in Rabbinic writings. The fact that parables are there so abundant, and are found in connexion with every kind of subject, shows the extreme improbability of the opinion, which some scholars would urge upon us, that the Jewish teachers knew nothing of parables

---

[1] From Fiebig, *Die Gleichnisreden Jesu im Lichte der rabbinischen Gleichnisse*, 1912, p. 18. Perhaps the fullest collection of Rabbinic parables is that of Giuseppe Levi, translated into German by L. Seligmann, *Parabeln, Legenden und Gedanken*, 2nd edition, 1877, but it makes no attempt at chronology or criticism.

IV] THE EXTERNAL FORM OF HIS TEACHING

until the Lord Jesus had opened the way.[1] On the other hand, to see in our Lord's parables only imitations of those already spoken by Jewish doctors [2] and others is to overlook the crucial differences of the one class from the majority of the other. For about our Lord's parables there are a freshness and an obviousness wanting to those of the Rabbis, with the absence of triviality either in subject or in expression, and of the smack of book-learning which too frequently mars their most solemn thoughts.[3]

Passing from our Lord's parables to His teaching generally, we need hardly mention His use of metaphor and hyperbole, so dear to all Jewish and Eastern teachers, for though illustrations such as that of the camel and the needle's eye often appear ridiculous to the crass logic of our Western minds, they are quickly grasped and greatly valued by the more subtle imagination of the oriental.[4]

Whether indeed the prevalence of short pithy sayings in the Gospel gives an accurate impression of the real nature of our Lord's instruction may be doubted, for it may be due to the fact that such remarks were more easily retained in the memory of those that heard them than the argument of which they formed a part.[5]

But at least they have a curious likeness in form to much that we know of the methods of Jewish teachers. Indeed, one treatise of the Mishna, the far-famed *Pirqe Aboth*, ' The Ethics of the Fathers,'

---

[1] Jülicher, *Die Gleichnisreden Jesu*, 1910, i. 168 *sq.*, in Fiebig, *ibid.* pp. 124 *sq.*
[2] Drews, *The Christ Myth*, 1910, p. 253.
[3] *Cf.* Fiebig, *ibid.* pp. 271, 276 *sqq.*
[4] Contrast the crude acceptance of Talmudic Haggadoth by English writers as statements intended to be understood literally.
[5] Compare Heinrici, *Die Bergpredigt*, i. 1900, pp. 16-18, 78.

contains little else. Two quotations will suffice : ' Be not as slaves that minister to the lord with a view to receive recompense ; but be as slaves that minister to the lord without a view to receive recompense ; and let the fear of heaven be upon you ' (Antigonus of Soko, in the first century B.C.). ' The day is short, and the task is great, and the workmen are sluggish, and the reward is much, and the Master of the house is urgent. It is not for thee to finish the work, nor art thou free to desist therefrom ; if thou hast learned much Torah, they give thee much reward ; and faithful is the Master of thy work, who will pay thee the reward of thy work, and know that the recompense of the reward of the righteous is for the time to come ' (R. Tarphon in the end of the first century A.D.). Such utterances are not unworthy to be compared with those of our Lord for their pregnant terseness.

Yet the First Evangelist himself reports discourses. Yes, but even these are hardly elaborate arguments like those recorded in the Fourth Gospel, and are made up of so many short sayings, not a few of which recur in other connexions in the Synoptic Writers, that it is not easy to say whether they were ever spoken at one and the same time, or whether the present arrangement of them is not due to our Lord's followers more than to Him Himself. It is quite intelligible that for easy recollection in daily life, and for the better instruction of others, it was thought well to place great utterances of the Messiah in more or less logical setting, which would demonstrate in unmistakably clear language His teaching on matters of supreme interest to those for whom the Evangelist wrote.

IV]   THE MESSIAH'S USE OF THE O.T.

If this is what took place, then the discourses as they now stand represent summaries of our Lord's teaching, based perhaps upon notes of speeches actually delivered by Him, but enlarged by the inclusion of cognate matter spoken at other times.[1]

If this be so it is evident that although the responsibility for each separate saying rests upon our Lord, the final arrangement and interdependence of the utterances are due to the Evangelist. Occasions may arise, and have been thought to arise, in which this distinction is important. It will, however, be remembered that the discourses as they stand are the deliberate representation by St. Matthew of what he conceived our Lord to mean. They are, that is to say, part of that presentation of the Messiah to the Jews which he desired to draw, and we to-day are endeavouring to trace.

In no particular is that presentation of Him as a Teacher more important than in His relation to Holy Scripture. For a Jewish audience (and this, through his Jewish-Christian readers, St. Matthew ever held in mind) must have expected that the Messiah would refer to Holy Scripture, and expound its attitude to Himself and His work. How stands our Lord's use of Scripture when it is compared with that of the Jewish teachers? Generally speaking, we may say that His methods are theirs. Scholars have not always perceived this. Christian theologians ignorant of Judaism have been content with saying that Christ cared for the spirit of a passage and Jews for the letter, while Jewish controversialists

[1] *Cf.* Heinrici, *op. cit.* pp. 38, 39; B. W. Bacon, *The Sermon on the Mount*, 1902, p. 23.

have been only too glad to seize on apparent differences, and have accused our Lord and His disciples of either wilful, or, more often, unintentional, perversion of the meaning of the original Hebrew. Happily times are changing. Christians are beginning to see that statements in Talmudic writings are not always what they appear to be on the surface, and Jews to appreciate the thoroughly Jewish methods of Christ and the writers of the New Testament. For Scripture is quoted with extraordinary freedom in the religious literature of post-Biblical Judaism, and every method of New Testament quotation may be illustrated from it.[1]

There was, then, much in common between the form and methods of our Lord's manner of teaching and those of the Rabbis. But in one point, and that fundamental, there was a difference. The affirmation of a Jewish teacher had no weight at all in matters of legal rule (Halacha) unless he was either fully accredited, or able to affirm that he had derived his decision from an earlier and recognised authority. Of the two qualifications the latter was the chief. Hillel himself, to take the classic example, in his debate with the Sanhedrin on the question whether a passover lamb ought to be slain on the Sabbath, he himself upholding the affirmative, could not secure acquiescence in his opinion until he was able to show that he had received such a tradition from his predecessors, Shemaiah and Abtalion.[2]

---
[1] *Cf.* Lecture I.
[2] Grätz, *Geschichte der Juden*, 3rd edition, 1877, iii. pp. 227 *sq.*, 673; Weiss, *Dor dor w'dorshaw*, i. 1871, p. 158; Beer, *Der Mischnatraktat Sabbat*, 1908, p. 9: 'Was sich als brauchbares Gesetz für die Gegenwart anbietet, muss sich einer Art Ahnenprobe unterziehen' (quoted in H. J. Holtzmann, *N.T. Theologie*, 1911, i. 41).

IV] HIS INDEPENDENCE AS A TEACHER

Similarly we read in T.B. *Megillah*, 15a : ' He who saith a thing in the name of him who said it earlier brings redemption into the world.' So also in *Aboth*, vi. 6, we find that Torah is acquired by forty-eight things, among them : ' He that considers what he has heard, and tells a thing in the name of him who said it.' [1] These sayings, it is true, doubtless refer primarily to Halacha, and not to Haggada, in which the Jewish teachers were much more free.[2] But they illustrate the tone of mind in which official Judaism regarded the past, the dependence which each felt on those honoured names that had gone before him.

With the Messiah, as St. Matthews suggests (vii. 29), it was quite otherwise. Not His *jurare in verba magistri*. There was something in Him which struck out a line different from that which was characteristic of the Jew, the Semite, the Oriental, even the whole ancient world, and dared to state facts, and pronounce judgements regardless of those which had already been adduced.[3]

Closely connected with this independence in method is our Lord's originality of treatment. There is no sign of eclecticism in Jesus of Nazareth.[4] His knowledge was not bookish ; the lore of the past, recent or long gone by, whether already crystallised into writing or not, did not, as such, appeal to Him.

---

[1] Compare also R. T. Herford, *Pharisaism, its Aim and its Method*, 1912, p. 135.

[2] B. W. Bacon, *The Sermon on the Mount*, p. 30, writes : For Haggadah ' no precedent or authority needed to be cited, no literary expedient of allegory, fiction, or legend was excluded.' But the first clause rather overstates the case if the Haggadah referred to a doctrine of importance.

[3] See H. J. Holtzmann, *N.T. Theologie*, 1911, i. 296.

[4] On the Lord's Prayer, see below, pp. 162 *sqq*.

His learning was acquired from intercourse with men, with Nature, and with God. So, again, there is no sign that He endeavoured to frame any system of truth for Himself, or to set the truth systematically before others. In measure, indeed, this was characteristic of Rabbinic teachers of His time. Great systematisers among the Jews belong to a later date. The Saadiahs,[1] the Maimonides, the Bechais, the Albos, represent a phase of thought completely foreign to the Palestinian Jews of the first century. Had Jesus shown any inclination to formulate religion into plan and order, head under head, and clause by clause, He would have been a monstrosity, so utterly out of touch with His people would He have shown Himself to be. Neither was He a theologian in the ordinary sense of the word. Rabbis around Him disputed over separate points in practice and (to some extent) in theology, but with Him everything like painful endeavour to arrive at truth by comparison and deduction is absent.

In His case it was religious intuition rather than religious learning. Truth for Him was no result of study, conscious and profound. He appears to have assimilated perfectly each new thought which taught Him more of God; to have absorbed, if we may put it so, the atoms of truth floating in the atmosphere round Him, with each breath of His spiritual life. Nay, more than that. As of the nine circles in Dante's Vision, that one had the clearest flame which was least distant from the central point of light: 'Because, I take it,' writes the poet, 'it sinketh deepest into the truth thereof';

---

[1] *Cf.* Abelson, *The Immanence of God in Rabbinic Literature*, 1912, p. 362; Gaster, *E.R.E.* iv. 43b.

and again: 'All have their delight in measure as their sight sinketh more deep into the truth wherein every intellect is stilled';[1] so Messiah kept ever near the great Centre of all truth, receiving from It as He had necessity, thus maintaining within Himself that supreme knowledge, and that perfect sympathy, which enabled Him to respond to every call, to answer every doubt, to meet every question brought before Him, raising all He touched to a higher plane, because He brought it into the eternal light. Hence His authority. The asseveration 'But I say unto you' sprang ultimately, not, as too many have supposed, from His consciousness as God, but from that inner relation which He, the perfect Man, held uninterruptedly with the Divine.

Thus we come near that final secret of His teaching, that entelechy of His doctrine, His character and personality. For, as we are all well aware, the best teacher to-day is not he who hands on to his pupils with greatest accuracy the instruction which was given to him, or even he who selects and imparts to others only the highest portion of what he has received; but he whose personality is so strong to vitalise every word he speaks that his pupils catch his spirit, and one by one move forward to sound education. This is the more true in proportion to the importance of the subject taught, and to the closeness with which it touches the character and the will. To understand Messiah as Teacher is to understand His personality. But who shall grasp the personality of Jesus?[2]

It appears, then, that in our consideration of the presentation to the Jews of Messiah as Teacher we

[1] *Paradiso*, xxviii. 37–39, and 106–108 (Wicksteed's translation).
[2] See Lecture IX.

can trace both the influence of current thought upon Him and His independence towards it, for in spite of all that He owed to others He was supremely original. These two sides of His position may be illustrated from almost every page of the First Gospel. But we must limit ourselves to the Sermon on the Mount, and at first to two short portions of it, the Lord's Prayer, and His great Commandment of Love.

That the Lord's Prayer owes much to current Jewish thought is acknowledged by almost all scholars,[1] whether it is regarded as a whole or in detail.

We may grant at once that the structure of the Prayer, as found in the liturgical services of the Christian Church,[2] is precisely that of the long set of prayers known as the Eighteen Benedictions (*Shemoneh Esreh*).[3] The first three of these refer directly to God and His holiness, the following twelve

---

[1] Dr. E. Bischoff indeed (*Jesus und die Rabbinen*, 1905, pp. 73–82) has attempted to show that our Lord in this as in other parts of the Sermon on the Mount derived nothing from Jewish teachers, but his argument is quite unconvincing. He bases his case entirely on the fact that most of the asserted Jewish parallels are, as they stand, confessedly of later date than our Lord. But he does little to explain the presence of such tones on the lips of Jewish teachers if they were but lingering notes of the Lord's Gloria.

Mr. G. Friedlander, in his learned but somewhat narrow-minded work, *The Jewish Sources of the Sermon on the Mount*, 1911, goes to the opposite extreme, and hears in the Prayer nothing but feeble echoes of the Jewish oratorio.

[2] The addition of the Doxology to the form recorded in Matthew doubtless represents primitive custom. Its omission in the New Testament may be due either to the fact that the wording of it was not fixed when the Gospels were written, or to the presupposition that some such words would be added by the worshipper. Cf. Dr. Thirtle's suggestive *The Lord's Prayer, an Interpretation*, 1915, p. 163.

[3] The Palestinian and the Babylonian forms of the original are to be found conveniently in Dalman's *Die Worte Jesu*, 1898 (German edition only). The current but inaccurate form is given in Singer's *Authorised Daily Prayer Book*, pp. 44–53; see also Mr. Abraham's notes, pp. lv–lxx, and especially Dr. Hirsch in the *Jewish Encyclopedia*, xi. 270–282.

THE LORD'S PRAYER

(now thirteen) are petitions, and the last three are utterances of thanksgiving and praise. It is indeed not proved that the *Shemoneh Esreh* were in existence as early as the first quarter of the first century of our era, but their date cannot be placed much later, and their framework may fairly be taken to illustrate what was in our Lord's time felt to be fitting and usual in prayer to God.

If the structure of the Prayer is Jewish, so also are the individual sentences. For, in the first place, it has been shown [1] that nearly all of these are based upon expressions found in the Old Testament, which have been turned into prayer.[2] In the second, the parallel clauses in prayers scattered through many Jewish books are so numerous that, unless we postulate wholesale borrowing on the part of Jews, we are compelled to come to the conclusion that not a single article of the Prayer is original, in the sense of being previously unknown, though we willingly grant that it is impossible to prove in every case that sentences adduced as parallels are earlier than the time of our Lord.

Was He then only a plagiarist, as certain Jewish writers would have us believe? Have we all been mistaken, these many centuries, in attributing to

---

[1] See in particular Heinrici, *Die Bergpredigt*, ii. 1905, pp. 66 *sq.* Some of his examples, however, are somewhat far fetched. These I have omitted.

[2] Father, Mal. ii. 10; 1 Chron. xxix. 10; the hallowing of His name, 1 Chron. xvii. 24; Isa. xxix. 23; the coming of the kingdom, Obad. 21; Dan. ii. 44; Zech. xiv. 9; the realisation of God's will, Ps. cxxxv. 6; xl. 8; daily bread, Prov. xxx. 8; forgiveness of sins, Isa. xxii. 14, xxxiii. 24, lv. 7; Ps. xxxii. 1; preservation from extreme temptation, and deliverance from the Evil One, Ps. xxxiv. 19 (LXX); Ps. cxxiv. 7; Jer. xx. 13.

Mr. G. Friedlander, *Jewish Sources*, pp. 164 *sq.*, endeavours to show that the Lord's Prayer is 'merely an adaptation' of Ezek. xxxvi. 23–31, but he will find few readers to agree with him. Yet *cf.* Box, *Expositor*, July, 1916, p. 23.

Him not only brilliancy of expression, but also originality of thought ? Originality, to be sure, is a misleading term. In its absolute sense it can be used only of God, and even of Him not later than the first moment of creation, if we may judge from our experience of His actions. For these are ever the result of earlier materials, arranged no doubt in a fresh way, but not new in themselves. When, however, we speak of originality we are not pedantic. We use the word of a combination of materials ordered as never before, to the best of our belief, and we determine the amount of originality by the proportion of newness in the arrangement, and the brilliancy of the consequent effect. We do not deny originality to Bach, Beethoven, Wagner, because they utilise chords and phrases found in other scores ; nor do we hesitate to place Leonardo da Vinci or Michael Angelo on their pedestals of fame because every detail of their work may be matched somewhere among the paintings or the sculptures of their predecessors. Yet these illustrious masters have produced nothing so incomparably superior in their own arts as is the Lord's Prayer in religion. That in Christian forms of worship nothing approaches it every one will allow ; and, if brevity and comprehensiveness be taken into account, the view of even the best of Jewish prayers entering into serious competition with it is a mere dream, scattered by the light of acquaintance with them.

Besides, even the Eighteen Benedictions, for all their length,[1] and for all their beauty, contain no

---

[1] Delitzsch's Hebrew translation of the Lord's Prayer, including the Doxology, contains forty-four words ; the Eighteen Benedictions contain some two hundred and eighty-five in the shortest Palestinian form (see Dalman, *op. cit.* p. 299).

IV] THE EIGHTEEN BENEDICTIONS INADEQUATE

prayer for daily food, expressive though this is of the believer's peaceful trust in the providing care of his heavenly Father.[1] Nor do they connect the forgiveness of our own sins by God with our forgiveness of the sins of others against us. On the other hand, they include a prayer against Christians, originally Hebrew-Christians, no doubt, which, to meet the squeamish good-nature of these degenerate times, is toned down into the formula, ' and as for slanderers let there be no hope, and let all wickedness perish as in a moment.' The original Palestinian and the early Babylonian forms were very different : ' As for apostates, let there be no hope for them ; and the religion of pride do Thou quickly root out ' ; to which an addition was made at least as early as the second century : ' And let the Christians and the heretics perish as in a moment, let them be blotted out of the Book of Life, and let them not be written among the righteous.' The early and late forms of the petition close alike with a note of triumph : ' Blessed art Thou Who humblest the proud.'[2] The Christian, when he recites ' Our Father,' breathes a very different spirit.

It matters little, however, what we call the faculty which produced the Lord's Prayer, whether ability to use existing material, or independence of thought, or originality, or transcendent insight into the things of God and the needs of man ; the fact remains that in it, as in no other prayer, short enough for a child to remember and so simple that a fool can grasp the

[1] The ninth, indeed, is a prayer that God may bless the year and make it fruitful, but this is far less direct and personal than ' Give us this day our daily bread.'
[2] No. 12. See Dalman, *op. cit.* p. 300. Compare also Heinrici, *op. cit.* ii. p. 67.

central thought of every clause, there are embodied the great principles of all religion, social and individual.

But there is more to be said than this.

There is no part of the whole Gospel which reveals more plainly the aim of the Evangelist. The Lord's Prayer portrays the attitude which, in St. Matthew's opinion, the Christ desired His followers to hold towards God and man. They were to show unwavering trust in their Father in heaven; to have complete consecration to Him, with a longing for His glory, for the fulfilment of His purposes, for the manifestation of His rule; to maintain a conscious, but restful, dependence on Him for the needs of each day; to possess a poignant sorrow for sin, and expectation of pardon, conditioned by their own return for wrong-doing received; to feel a heart-felt conviction of weakness in view of moral evil and the tempter, with the confidence that God would deliver them from him. All this, and much more, is contained in the compass of the few sentences which we call the Lord's Prayer. And as they stand, in word and plan and spirit, they form the very antithesis to Pharisaism, the official Judaism of St. Matthew's time and our own, with its dependence on human power, its congratulation of personal success, its assurance of self-righteousness. For the sense of sin, and the consciousness of personal weakness against temptation, never take root in human hearts until men find them met and satisfied in the Saviour and Deliverer, Jesus the Christ.[1]

[1] It may be questioned whether they who reject doctrinal Christianity, and yet glibly assert that they accept the Sermon on the Mount, always remember that this includes the Lord's Prayer. For Christ would teach us that the attitude of the soul in prayer is the test of true religion.

In the Lord's Prayer, then, we see both the indebtedness of the Messiah to current thought and the independence of His attitude towards it. So also is it with the second portion that we have chosen out of the Sermon on the Mount, the famous precept: 'Ye have heard that it was said, Thou shalt love thy neighbour, and hate thine enemy: but I say unto you, Love your enemies' (Matt. v. 43, 44).

A fierce battle has been waged round these words; on the part of Christians to prove that the Jews knew nothing of the precept, 'Love your enemies'; on the part of Jews to show that it contains nothing new, for Jews have always taught it, and practised it much better than Christians.

It may, however, be questioned whether either party in the strife has taken the trouble to recognise certain facts, and it may, therefore, be worth while to attempt to state the more important of these.[1]

The first is that at the time when Christ quoted the precept: 'Thou shalt love thy neighbour, and hate thine enemy,' it did truly represent the common teaching and practice of men in general. No one will deny this in the case of the non-Jewish nations;[2] and, unless their statements about the Jews are wholly

[1] Observe that when our Lord quotes the words, 'Thou shalt love thy neighbour, and hate thine enemy,' He does not say by whom this saying was uttered. He does not even add, as He does in vv. 21 and 33, that it was said 'to them of old time.' This is important, for, if we assume with many Jewish writers, that He was speaking directly of the contents of the Law of Moses, we are going further than the language warrants. It is more probable that He had in His mind the popular teaching of His time, which, however, as we fully grant, made the claim to have been handed down from of old.

[2] Among them 'preparing for enemies things of enmity' (ἐχθροῖς ἐχθρὰ πορσύνων, Æsch. Agam. 1374) was both the normal state of a man and also his duty; as Euripides says: πρὸς σοῦ μὲν, ὦ παῖ, τοῖς φίλοις εἶναι φίλον, τά τ' ἐχθρὰ μισεῖν, 'Be it thine, my son, to be friendly to thy friends, and to hate thine enemies' (Herc. Fur. 585, quoted by Wetstein).

untrustworthy, the impression produced by Jews upon non-Jews was in accordance with it. Jews did appear to Gentiles to be kind to members of their own race, but to them only.[1] Further, we all know that in the early days of the Hebrew nation, when public justice was weak, much was left to the action of the individual, and he who was wronged satisfied justice by personal retaliation on his enemy, his private enemy, though not one of the enemies of his nation, nor necessarily an enemy of his God.[2] It is true that in the time of Christ public justice was better administered than of old, but it was very far from perfect, and there is no reason to think that the common doctrine and practice of Jews towards other Jews was greatly altered. 'Thou shalt love thy neighbour, and hate thine enemy' did represent the popular teaching and practice of the day.

The second fact is that in the atmosphere in which the Lord Jesus was brought up there were currents breathing the warm air of love towards all men. It cannot be denied by fair-minded scholars that this precept of 'Love your enemies' is found essentially, both as theory and as practice, in the Old Testament,

[1] As Tacitus says: 'With each other resolute trust, ever-ready pity: but towards all others enmity and hatred' ('apud ipsos fides obstinata, misericordia in promptu, sed adversus omnes alios hostile odium,' *Hist.* v. 5). Consider also Ecclus. xii. 4.

[2] Something has already been said about the feeling on the part of Jews that it is legitimate to hate others if they differ in religion, and thus show themselves, in Jewish eyes, as opponents of God (see p. 165). This is also borne out by T.B. *Taanith*, 7b. 'Rabba bar Huna said: "In the case of any man who is arrogant, it is permissible to call him 'wicked,' for it is said, 'The wicked man hath hardened his face'"' (Prov. xxi. 29). R. Nachman bar Isaac said: "It is permissible to hate him, for it is said 'The hardness of his face is changed'"' (Eccles. viii. 1); read not, 'is changed' (יְשֻׁנֶּא), but 'one shall hate' (יִשְׂנָא); *i.e.* one shall hate the hardness of his face.

THE LORD TEACHES SUCH LOVE

as well as in other Jewish teaching earlier than the time of Christ. Read Exod. xxiii. 4, 5: 'If thou meet thine enemy's ox, or his ass going astray, thou shalt surely bring it back to him again. If thou see the ass of him that hateth thee lying under his burden, and wouldest forbear to help him, thou shalt help with him.' Read Lev. xix. 17, 18: 'Thou shalt not hate thy brother in thine heart: thou shalt surely rebuke thy neighbour, and not bear sin because of him. Thou shalt not take vengeance, nor bear any grudge against the children of thy people, but thou shalt love thy neighbour as thyself: I am the LORD.' True, that in this last passage the reference is exclusively to fellow-Hebrews, 'the children of thy people,' and therefore we may *not* find in it a direction to treat all men kindly, in spite of their enmity, and regardless of whatsoever nationality they may possess, but for the moment we are not considering this. The point is that the Jew is directed by the Law to show love towards his personal enemy. So again the words of Job tell us that anything like joy at disaster to such an enemy is contrary to the mind of God, for we find Him saying: 'If I rejoiced at the destruction of him that hated me, or lifted up myself when evil found him' (Job xxxi. 29). That this kind of instruction did not remain only a matter of theory, but was carried out into practice by the best men, is seen by the behaviour of David to Saul twice over (1 Sam. xxiv. and xxvi.). A later passage of Scripture teaches us the same duty, though it appends two reasons which hardly belong to the highest strata of ideal ethics: 'If thine enemy be hungry, give him bread to eat; and if he be thirsty, give him water to drink: for thou shalt heap coals of fire upon his head, and the LORD shall reward thee' (Prov. xxv. 21, 22). Yet at any rate this is better than the very worldly-wise advice of Prov. xxiv. 17: 'Rejoice not when thine enemy falleth, and let not thine heart be glad when he is overthrown: lest the LORD see it, and it displease him, and he turn away his wrath from him.'[1]

Similar teaching may be found in post-Biblical Jewish books which were written either before the time of Christ, or approximately at the same time. In Ecclus. xxviii. 2 we read: 'Forgive thy neighbour the hurt that he hath done thee; and then thy sins shall be pardoned when thou prayest.' Still plainer examples are to be seen in the Testaments of the Twelve Patriarchs. Issachar vii. 6: 'I loved the Lord; likewise also every man with all my heart.' Zebulun viii.: 'Have, therefore, yourselves also, my children, compassion towards every man with mercy, that the Lord also may have mercy upon you. . . . For in the degree in which a man hath compassion upon his neighbours, in the same degree hath the Lord also upon him. . . . Do not set down in account (*i.e.* as a ledger account), each one of you, evil against his brother.' Dan v. 3: 'Love the Lord through all your life, and one another with a true heart.' Gad vi. 1, 3: 'And now, my children, I exhort you, love ye each one his brother, and put away hatred from your hearts, and love one another in deed, and in word, and in the inclination of the soul. . . Love ye one another, therefore, from the

---

[1] It is, by the by, worthy of notice that in the best texts of Aboth iv. 19 (26), R. Samuel the Little, or the Younger, makes this passage his own, without the addition of the last two clauses. It may be that by this time (about 125 A.D.) higher motives were generally accepted. But this did not prevent him from composing the curse on the heretics in the Eighteen Benedictions (see p. 165).

heart; and if a man speak against thee, cast forth the poison of hate and speak peaceably to him, and in thy soul hold not guile; and if he confess and repent, forgive him'; vii. 7: 'Put away, therefore, jealousy from your souls, and love one another with uprightness of heart.' Joseph xvii. 2: 'Do ye also love one another, and with long-suffering hide ye one another's faults'; xviii. 2: ' And if any one seeketh to do evil unto you, do well unto him, and pray for him, and ye shall be redeemed of the Lord from all evil.'

Still more striking is the saying in the *Book of the Secrets of Enoch*, l. 3. 4, which is thought to be not later than 50 A.D.: ' Every wound, and every affliction, and every evil word and attack, endure for the sake of the Lord. And when you might have vengeance do not repay, either your neighbour or your enemy. For God will repay as your avenger in the day of the great judgement. Let it not be for you to take vengeance.' So again Philo writes (on Exod. xxiii. 4; *de Humanitate*, § 15, Young's translation iii. 439): ' If you see the beast of one who is thy enemy wandering about, leave the excitements to quarrelling to more perverse dispositions, and lead the animal back and restore him to his owner; for so you will not be benefiting him more than yourself: since he will by this means save only an irrational beast which is perhaps of no value, but you will get the greatest and most valuable of all things in nature, namely, excellence. And there will follow of necessity, as sure as shadow follows a body, the dissolution of your enmity.' We know very little of Hillel, but the following sentence may, no doubt, rightly be attributed to him : ' Be of the disciples of Aaron; loving peace, and pursuing peace; loving mankind, and bringing them nigh to the Torah' (Aboth i. 12 (13). So also his charge, good enough as far as it goes, 'What is hateful to thyself do not to thy fellow: this is the whole Torah, and the rest is commentary' (T.B. *Sabb.* 31a), following in the wake of Tobit iv. 15, 'What thou thyself hatest, do to no man.'

Can, however, this be said of the Talmud and later Jewish writings, which claim to have absorbed the essence of pre-Christian Judaism? Can such a spirit of love be attributed to them? On the whole, yes. I am indeed well aware that passages are often quoted from the Talmud, as well as from Maimonides and other writers, to the effect that Gentiles are to be treated unscrupulously, and the commonest actions of ordinary humanity are not to be shown them. But in some of the cases cited the rules were due to fear of complicating matters with the Gentile authorities, who were ever on the look-out for opportunities of accusing the Jews of proselytising, and in others they represented only the opinions of individual teachers.[1]

Something, no doubt, must also be attributed to the arrogance of certain Rabbis, especially in their relation to those co-religionists who expressed opinions contrary to their own. No sensible man to-day, it is true, whether Jew or Christian, will claim that the Talmud is a miracle of kindliness, but much less will he affirm that it is the concentration of brutality and ignorance. The prayer at the Daily Morning Service has not been in vain: 'Oh my God! guard my tongue from evil and my lips

---

[1] See also the catena on the subject in the *Jewish Encyclopedia, s.v.* Gentile, v. pp. 617 *sqq.* On the Golden Rule see C. Taylor, *Pirqe Aboth*, 1897, p. 142.

BUT IT IS NOT POPULAR

from speaking guile; and to such as curse me let my soul be dumb, yea, let my soul be unto all as the dust' (Singer, p. 54).

It may then be fully granted that the saying, 'Love your enemies,' or its equivalent, was both known to Jews and practised by them before it was spoken by the Lord Jesus, and that, in some degree, it has always been a part of Jewish ethics from the very first.

If so, how is it that our Lord can say in so many words: 'Ye have heard that it was said, Thou shalt love thy neighbour, and hate thine enemy: but I say unto you, Love your enemies'? Yet why should He not? For though love to enemies was taught in the Law (and He does not say the contrary), and though it was taught by individual Jewish leaders before our Lord's time, or independently of Him about the same time, there is no reason to think that it was ever the popular theory or practice. So far from this, it may be pointed out that the precept 'Love your enemies' is not the popular theory or practice even now, either among Jews or Christians. The religion of an ordinary man down to this twentieth century has always permitted hatred of a private enemy.

Popular religion has ever said, 'Love thy friend and hate thine enemy.' There is still need for Christ to add: 'But I say unto you, Love your enemies.'[1] If, however, Christ were to come to us

[1] 'Der berühmte christliche Maler Anselm Feuerbach mahnt, nach folgendem Grundsatz zu handeln: "Wenn dich einer auf die rechte Backe schlägt, so gibihm dafür zwei auf die linke"' (*Ein Vermächtnis*, 11-14 Auflage, Berlin, 1911, p. 258, quoted by J. Scheftelowitz in the *Monatschrift für Geschichte und Wissenschaft des Judentums*, 1912, p. 369). 'He is a fool,' said Frederick the Great, 'and that nation is a fool, who, having the power

Christians and utter these words now there would be this difference from His language to the Jews of old. He would add : Remember what you have heard from your earliest youth ; you have been brought up as Christians, and the essence of Christianity is the news of God's love to men, the very worst of men. You as Christians, and because you are Christians, must endeavour to imitate God. More than this. You as Christians profess to have accepted as your own the wonderful love which God has shown you ; surely then you feel your own hearts moved with love to others ? Afterwards perhaps He would quote statements of the New Testament to the effect that love is in reality the greatest of all principles (1 Cor. xiii.) ; that it sums up the whole Law (Gal. v. 14) ; and that every one that loveth is begotten of God, and knoweth God, while he that loveth not, knoweth not God, for God is love (1 John iv. 7, 8).

We grant, of course, that in Judaism, past and present, love to others is a duty ; but in Christianity it is the very central duty of all. We affirm that while the golden thread of love as a moral obligation is visible here and there in the Old Testament and in Jewish books, it enters into the very web and woof of Christ's teaching and of Christianity. The prayer : ' Father, forgive them, for they know not what they do,'[1] may not be part of the original form of the Third Gospel, but at least it represents

to strike his enemy unawares, does not strike and strike his deadliest ' (J. A. Cramb, *Germany and England*, 1914, pp. 42 *sq*.). Mr. G. Friedlander, by the by, rightly calls attention to the fact that the phrase, ' But I say unto you,' is found at least once in Philo, *Quod det. pot.* § 43, Cohn's edition, § 158 (*Hellenism and Christianity*, 1912, p. 122).

[1] Luke xxiii. 34.

IV] LOVE IS THE CENTRE OF CHRISTIANITY

the feeling of the early Christian Church, a feeling due to Christ's teaching. His whole existence here on earth, and His endurance of the Cross, were, according to the New Testament (and it is the Jesus of the New Testament whom alone we know), the outcome of love for us sinful men, Jews and Gentiles alike. There is no such transcendent emphasis on love in any other religion. Christianity alone is the religion of love, based on love and carried out by love. But it is not a religion which can be learned by rote; it is not a religion simply of the head. Only so far as it becomes part and parcel of our very life does it become real. Hence, unless an individual Christian appropriates to himself the love of God in Christ, he has not learned in truth what Christianity means, and he may very easily come terribly short in love to others, and treat them with shocking cruelty. Still, in spite of all the failings of its followers, Christianity has been, and still is, the one active religion of love in the world, the one religion that urges its professors to do all, and suffer all, from love to God and man. Jews have never shown a tithe of the activity of love to men which Christians have shown. What is the cause? Love is not the centre of Judaism; it is the centre of Christianity. To quote a well-known commentary on the Epistle to the Romans: ' In Christianity this principle, which had been only partially understood and imperfectly taught, which was known only in isolated examples, yet testified to a universal instinct, was finally put forth as the paramount principle of moral conduct, uniting our moral instincts with our highest religious principles. A new virtue, or rather one hitherto imperfectly understood, had become recognised as the root of all virtues, and a new name was demanded for what was practically a new idea.'[1] Christ desired to enforce the law of love towards all, whatever might be the relation in which any of His followers stood to others, and whatever the treatment they received. The popular religion was: ' Thou shalt love thy neighbour and hate thine enemy.' The Messiah added : ' But I say unto you, Love your enemies.'[2]

Was He not then a great Teacher ? Was He not superior by far to those many doctors who were disputing and quibbling, straining out gnats and swallowing camels—conscientious, if you like, but ignorant of great principles, bound by the steel bands of human traditions, stretch them as they would ? They were preserving the accumulated wisdom of generations of thinkers like themselves, and endeavouring so to attract their contemporaries as to unite them by rule and ritual to the religion

[1] Sanday-Headlam, *Romans*, 1896, p. 376.

[2] It will be apparent that our Lord's words are interpreted above as referring primarily to the current and popular conception that hatred of an enemy is allowable, or even praiseworthy, whether he be national or personal. But two other explanations may be mentioned. One, earnestly advocated by the present learned Dean of Lichfield, Dr. Savage, is that our Lord was defending the best Jewish teaching and practice of the time, as regards duty to a foreign nation, and was opposing all hatred of Gentiles, especially of the Roman conquerors (*The Gospel of the Kingdom*, 1910, pp. 126-134. *Cf.* also Malwyn Hughes, *The Ethics of Jewish Apocryphal Literature*, 1909, p. 121). But there is nothing to limit the reference of the words to this. The second explanation is that our Lord was speaking against the bitterness of one Jewish sect towards another, as, for example, of the Pharisees towards the Sadducees ; or of factions among the Pharisees themselves, as, for example, of the followers of Hillel towards those of Shammai, or again of both Pharisees and Sadducees towards less orthodox sects, as for instance, the Essenes. But again this interpretation limits the meaning of Christ's words. In reality, He desired to enforce the law of love towards all, whatever might be the relation in which any of His followers stood to others, and whatever the treatment they received.

of their fathers, that thus they might keep the nation whole, and at last throw off the yoke of the heathen. He was concerned rather with eternal verities and fundamental facts, the love of God to the sinner and the sinner's awful need, sure that if the relation of individuals to their Father in heaven were but put right all else would follow as noonday the dawn, every social need being satisfied, every national aspiration being more than met—for God would care for His children. Parable and paradox, hyperbole and gnome, quotations and adaptations of Law and Prophets, prayers of Liturgy and visions of Apocalypse, jewels from Palestine and treasures from Egypt, alike served Him, and fulfilled His purpose.

He taught, not as the Scribes, but with authority, for they were in touch with dead men, He with the living God.

Lecture Five

THE MESSIAH AS TEACHER—THE PERMANENCE OF THE JEWISH LAW

'*Think not that I came to destroy the law or the prophets: I came not to destroy, but to fulfil. For verily I say unto you, Till heaven and earth pass away, one jot or one tittle shall in no wise pass away from the law, till all things be accomplished. Whosoever therefore shall break one of these least commandments, and shall teach men so, shall be called least in the kingdom of heaven: but whosoever shall do and teach them, he shall be called great in the kingdom of heaven.*'—MATT. v. 17–19.

Lecture Five

THE MESSIAH AS TEACHER—THE PERMANENCE OF THE JEWISH LAW

'THINK not that I came to destroy the law or the prophets : I came not to destroy, but to fulfil. For verily I say unto you, Till heaven and earth pass away, one jot or one tittle shall in no wise pass away from the law, till all things be accomplished. Whosoever therefore shall break one of these least commandments, and shall teach men so, shall be called least in the kingdom of heaven : but whosoever shall do and teach them, he shall be called great in the kingdom of heaven ' (v. 17-19).

Then the Messiah is no iconoclast ! This is evident. St. Matthew tells us that to Jesus the Messiah the Law was a precious possession which was to endure ' until all things be accomplished,' in other words, until the end of the world.[1]

This is a statement which raises several questions, of varying degrees of importance, but all worthy of some consideration, such as : What is the Law of which the Messiah here speaks ? What is the kind

---

[1] 'The phrase "till heaven and earth pass away" does not define a *terminus ad quem*, but means "for ever," in the sense that He has no pronouncement to make as to a time when the Law shall be no longer valid. . . . The second phrase "till all things be accomplished" is parallel to "till heaven and earth pass away," and in meaning can only be synonymous with it ' (Votaw in Hastings, *D.B.* v. 24). The best text of the Talmud, the Munich MS., quotes *v.* 17 in the form, ' Not to take from the Law of Moses am I come, but to add to the Law of Moses am I come,' where for the word ' but ' the common texts have ' nor ' (*Sabbath*, 116*b*). Our Lord took the opposite side to those who were denying the Divine origin and the binding character of the Law. *Cf.* Bergmann, *Jüdische Apologetik im neutestamentlichen Zeitalter*, 1908, pp. 97 *sq.*, 108 *sq.*

of permanence which He attributes to it ? Did He intend to suggest any necessary distinction between His Jewish and His Gentile followers in their observance of it ? Are, on the other hand, Jewish believers at liberty, if they like, to observe it more literally than others ? What is the relation in which the statement of the Messiah stands to certain famous utterances by St. Paul ? What, lastly, is the relation in which the teaching and message of Messiah as a whole, the Christian ' Gospel,' stands to the Law ? In other words, is it, or is it not, a Second *Law* ?

It is to these questions that we must now direct our attention.

I. The first question, *What does the Messiah here understand by the Law?* admits of an easy answer. The contrast implied in the phrase ' the Law or the Prophets ' makes it clear. The Prophets can only mean the collection of Former and Latter, containing the canonical books from Joshua to Kings, and Isaiah to Ezekiel, with the Book of the Twelve, or the Minor Prophets ; and the Law can therefore be only the Five Books of Moses, the Pentateuch. When therefore the Messiah is represented as saying that ' one jot or one tittle shall in no wise pass away from the Law,' He plainly means that every part of the Pentateuch, however small, and however apparently unimportant, is to remain in perpetuity ; that none of its commandments is to be broken.[1]

[1] Chrysostom strangely supposes that the Law whose permanence is here stated is not the Law of Moses, but the New Law of Christ. Ὅτι γὰρ οὐχ ὑπὲρ τῶν παλαιῶν νόμων τοῦτο εἴρηκεν, ἀλλ' ὑπὲρ ὧν αὐτὸς ἔμελλε νομοθετεῖν, ἄκουσον τῶν ἑξῆς (*Matt. Hom.* xvi. 4, p. 207D ; Gaume, vii. 237). *Vide infra*, p. 201 *sq.*

II. When we come to the second question, *What is the kind of permanence which the Messiah attributes to the Law, i.e. to the Five Books of Moses?* we find ourselves in some little difficulty. More than one answer has been given, and at the best we can but weigh probabilities in the balance, and humbly endeavour to come to a right conclusion. What is the permanence which the Messiah ascribed to the Law?

Did He desire to maintain it in its literal force, filling it up as an empty vessel [1] by observing every detail of its commands, literally understood? 'Certainly,' affirm the Orthodox Jews, 'that, and that alone, can have been His intention, if He was really a Jew. It is unthinkable that any real Jew would deny the perpetuity of the Law of Moses in the literal meaning of its ordinances.' [2]

Yet it seems incredible that Christendom, from almost the very first, can have erred so utterly about the subject-matter of our Lord's message as this opinion implies. Can it be possible, in spite of the

---

[1] There is no suggestion of *enlarging* it.

[2] The real expectation of Orthodox Jews is seen in such statements as *Wisd.* xviii. 4, 'the incorruptible light of the law'; *Baruch.* iv. 1, 'the law that endureth for ever'; Talm. Jer., *Megillah*, i. 5 (7), 70d, 'the Prophets and the Holy Writings will cease, but the five books of the Law will not cease.' Yet certain sporadic utterances appear to assert that the Law will be forgotten (perhaps during the pains of the pre-Messianic times). So *Mekilta*, on Ex. xii. 26, ed. Friedmann, 13a top; ed. Weiss, p. 16a. 'Finally the Law will be forgotten' (שסוף התורה עתידה להשתכח). But there appears to be no evidence of such sayings before the latter part of the second century, after the depression caused by the Hadrianic war: see Klausner, *Die messianischen Vorstellungen des jüdischen Volkes im Zeitalter der Tannaim*, 1904, pp. 53–56. On the other hand, the saying in *Pesikta Rabbathi*, c. 15 (ed. Friedmann, 75a), that 'the Law will again become new,' התורה חוזרת לחידושה (quoted by Klausner, p. 53), certainly means that it will return to its pristine vigour and force after being forgotten. A fourth-century teacher says in T.B. *Niddah*, 61b, 'In the future the commandments will cease.' Compare also the late Midrash Tehillim on Ps. cxlvi. 7.

general tenor of the narratives of our Lord's sayings to the contrary, that He really ordered the literal observance of the Law of Moses ? If He did, one can never trust again the records of the teaching of any person, sacred or profane.

The reply, no doubt, may be urged—it has often been urged—that this did truly represent the intention of Jesus at the beginning, and that He altered His teaching afterwards. At first He desired His followers to observe the Law literally, and only the failure of his early enthusiastic plans led Him to permit, or even command, its non-observance.[1] But if this be the case how came it about that the Evangelist recorded these earlier statements of Christ at all ? He wrote long after Christ had changed His plan; why did he mention the earlier, and discarded, sayings ? Surely he could not fail to perceive that they did not fit in with the many sentences he relates, which, as we shall see, are against such literal obedience as this explanation demands. It is then quite improbable that when our Lord taught the permanence of the Law He meant to enforce its literal observance.

Did He then desire to reform the Law, caring only for the greater and more important parts of it, and content to let the rest fall into oblivion ? In spite of the obvious contradiction of such an interpretation to the words themselves, which plainly insist upon the

---

[1] So Mr. Gerald Friedlander, *The Jewish Sources of the Sermon on the Mount*, 1911, p. 32. H. J. Holtzmann (*N.T. Theologie*, 1911, i. pp. 204 *sqq.*, *cf.* 505 *sqq.*) thinks Jesus had two contradictory modes of teaching, one enforcing literal, the other more spiritual, observance to the Law. *Vide infra*, p. 200. Even Votaw thinks *vv.* 18, 19 could not have been spoken by Jesus, and are at best the result of an Apostolic misinterpretation of an original nucleus, which taught the duty of preserving truths already received (Hastings' *D.B.* v. 24 *sq.*).

observance of minute details, this answer has been acceptable to not a few Jewish writers, who would gladly see their own opinions of the value, and the worthlessness, of different parts of the Jewish Law confirmed by the greatest of the sons of Israel. The Reform party in modern Judaism cares little for the observance of the details, nor indeed, if the truth must be told, even for the supremacy of the books of Moses over the other parts of the Bible. Its interest lies in what are deemed the greater principles, and doctrines, and observances, though even in these it is very far from holding any rigid or orthodox opinion. Circumcision, for example, is valuable, but a Jew is born a Jew, not made such by circumcision, which is therefore not indispensable.[1] The Sabbath ought certainly to be kept, but modern conditions of commercial life (so it is asserted) preclude its observance with any very great strictness.[2] The Feasts may be treated in the same way. Monotheism no doubt is all-important, naturally a kind of monotheism framed with the express object of excluding Christian doctrine.[3] If we add the doctrine of the election of Israel to be a pattern to the nations of all that is good and holy (for stress is rightly laid on the fact that all privileges imply duties),[4] and that of the potential resemblance of all men to God, with never a trace of original sin,[5] we have stated the principal tenets of reformed Jews, and we may well ask if it is possible that there

[1] Dr. E. G. Hirsch, *Jewish Encyclopedia*, x. 351.
[2] *Principles of Liberal Judaism* adopted by sixty-seven Rabbis at Frankfort-on-Maine in September 1912 (see the *Jewish World*, Oct. 11, 1912).
[3] Morris Joseph, *Judaism as Creed and Life*, 1903, pp. 72, 78; *Principles, ibid. Cf.* Dr. E. G. Hirsch, *op. cit.* p. 350.
[4] Kohler, *Grundriss*, p. 20; Morris Joseph, *op. cit.* pp. 153 *sqq.*, 166, 513.
[5] Kohler, *Grundriss*, p. 21; *Principles* (as above).

can be anything in common between the aspirations of such teachers and the emphatic statements of Christ. The representation of Jesus as a pious young Jew who desired to reform the Judaism of His time, and unfortunately perished in the attempt, is singularly inadequate, when it is confronted with His actual words, and the tenor of His whole life.

It has, however, been supposed that when our Lord inveighed against the observance of details in literal form (xii. 1–8, and elsewhere) He had in mind only the rules manufactured by the Scribes, the Oral Law in fact, and that He was quite prepared to accept the literal observance of the Written Law as such. But this is an impossible position to defend. Given a code, there must be explanations of it, as has already been shown,[1] and the nature and extent of its observance in literal fashion must be determined by qualified lawyers trained for the purpose. The minutiæ of the Oral Law are for the most part only logical deductions from the crude ordinances of the written code. If Christ taught the literal observance of the latter, He must in consequence have taught also the literal observance of those innumerable details which make up the daily life of even a strictly pious Jew, to-day. You cannot make a distinction, in practice, between the written Law and the oral.

But the perpetuity the Messiah inculcated was different. To Him as a Jew the Pentateuch was the revelation of God, standing higher in His eyes than the messages of the Prophets, if we may judge from the attention He paid to it, and as the revelation of God it was to be obeyed. How it was made known

---

[1] Lectures II, pp. 63 *sq*., and IV, pp. 148 *sq*.

THE PERMANENCE OF TRUTHS

to men was of little importance, and He does not touch on the subject.

Whether it was all given in one piece, as it were, at Mount Sinai; or revealed to Moses portion by portion as occasion served; or framed out of primitive customs selected and sanctioned by the Spirit of God, and woven into legislation; whencesoever the details were derived, howsoever they were incorporated, they became the living expression of the Divine will. Yes, certainly, it may be replied, the expression of the Divine will for those days, but not for later ages. But I ask whether it may not be that to the Messiah, the Anointed of God, the incarnate Wisdom, and the living Word, whatever once bore the stamp of the Divine will ever retains something of its origin, never loses altogether its permanent value? Must it not always enjoy something corresponding to ultimate truth? If this be so, we can understand that Christ's eye, piercing below the surface, saw in the tiniest atoms of the Mosaic legislation fragments of the feast prepared by God for the lasting refreshment of His people, and, forbidding the well-meant efforts of those who would cast them away, enjoined respect and preservation of them for ever.

Such perpetuity, then, of the Law of Moses which the Messiah had in view was not, as it seems, that of the punctilious observance of ritual and ceremonial regulations, much less that of the retention of the more important, and the surrender of the less important, portions of them, but the maintenance of all alike in their fundamental truths. Jesus did not encourage, it will be noticed, merely spiritualisation of the Law—that was not at all His intention—but the practice of it in its real, as contrasted with its temporary, or even its apparent, meaning. He desired that His followers should go back to the principles that underlay each article of the code of Moses, that thus it might be carried out in reality, and not so as to satisfy its outer form alone.[1]

Some examples of such treatment by our Lord in the Sermon on the Mount will come before us in the next Lecture. Here let me remind you of five passages from the Pentateuch that are quoted elsewhere in this Gospel. The Lord applies the phrase 'at the mouth of two witnesses, or at the mouth of three witnesses, shall a matter be established' (Deut. xix. 16), not to the usage of the law-courts, but to the prudent and kindly action of a believer in his dealing with an offended brother (xviii. 16). Again, He recognises the command in Deut. xxiv. 1–3 to give a bill of divorce when necessary, but at the same time points out that the permission must be considered in connexion with another phrase, also in the Pentateuch, which is of very much wider significance, and implies the permanent union of man and wife. For whereas the former was only a concession to human selfishness, which refused to yield to the claims of God, the latter states once for all what was God's ideal of marriage, what the reason for its institution. To keep the former without reference to the latter was in reality to destroy its meaning.

Again, in xix. 18, 19, He enforces the sixth,

---

[1] '"Fulfilment" is the completion of what was before imperfect; it is the realisation of what was shadowy; it is the development of what was rudimentary; it is the union of what was isolated and disconnected; it is the perfect growth from the antecedent germ' (Kirkpatrick, *The Divine Library of the O.T.*, 1891, p. 134).

v] PERMANENCE OF THE INNER MEANING

seventh, eighth, ninth, and also the fifth commandments, adding the comprehensive charge, from the Pentateuch again (Lev. xix. 18), 'Thou shalt love thy neighbour as thyself,' and in *v.* 21 assuredly does not abolish them, but puts them on a firmer basis than ever, when he bids the poor selfish young man, who was so rich in this world's goods, part with all he had, and give the proceeds in charity. For whatever might be the case with others, that young man could observe the Law only by giving up all that belonged to him for the service of the poor. The principle is much the same in xxii. 32, where Jesus reminds the Sadducees of what looks at first sight like a bald historical statement, and then unfolds to them its inner meaning: if God can speak of Himself as the God of Abraham, Isaac, and Jacob, this implies that the relation in which He stood to them holds good still, He to them and they to Him. Death cannot part God and His people; they live with Him eternally.

These are a few passages outside the Sermon on the Mount, and from other parts of the Gospel in which the truth of the perpetual validity of every word of the Law is taught by Christ, whether it refer to things moral, or, as we say, only to ceremonial.

That the moral, the ethical, part of the Law is of permanent validity needs no demonstration, and required no enforcement by Christ. The permanence of the ceremonial Law, and of the narrative of the historical facts enshrined in the Pentateuch (for we cannot omit this from our survey) emphatically did. But now (after Christ's words) to the Christian as much as to a Talmudic Jew, every paragraph and phrase of the Law was to bear the imprint of the heavenly; and to him was to belong the privilege of learning its true intent, and of fulfilling it in his life. Thus, and thus only, as the Master says in the immediately succeeding verse, shall his righteousness exceed that of the Scribes and Pharisees. For these, standing on a lower plane of Divine knowledge than the Christian, are not able to learn the will of God, or do it, as perfectly as he.[1]

It must not be supposed that perpetuity of this kind has been unknown to the Rabbis. The frequent assertion by them that fasting takes the place of sacrifices is an example.[2] They have also maintained, with perfect truth, that there is much more in the Law than its *prima facie* meaning, and they have, consistently with this supposition, endeavoured to bring out the principles upon which many of the precepts are based, doing so, sometimes, no doubt, in order that, by determining these principles, they may be able to apply them to cases of casuistry not directly mentioned in the Law itself. This, however, was not the case with Philo, who made a sincere endeavour to understand the deeper intention of the Divine Lawgiver, although he was hampered by his devotion to Greek forms of thought. 'Like rain and light,' Dr. Schechter tells us, ' the Torah was a gift from heaven of which the world is hardly worthy, but which is indispensable to its maintenance. The gift was a complete one, without any reserve whatever. Nothing of the Torah, God assures Israel, was kept back in heaven. All that

---

[1] *Cf.* Martensen, *Christian Ethics: General*, § 125; also the quotations from B. Weiss and Tholuck given by Votaw in Hastings' *D.B.* v. 24*b*.

[2] So primarily orthodox Jews, but in spirit it is even more true of reformed, who do not expect the restoration of sacrifice.

follows is only a matter of interpretation. The principle held by the Rabbis was that the words of the Torah " are fruitful and multiply." Thus the conviction could ripen that everything wise and good, be it ethical or ceremonial in its character, the effect of which would be to strengthen the cause of religion, was at least potentially contained in the Torah. Hence the famous adage, that everything which the student will teach at any future time was already communicated to Moses at Mount Sinai, as also the injunction that any acceptable truth, though discovered by an insignificant man in Israel, should be considered of as high authority as if it had emanated from a great sage or prophet, or even from Moses himself. It requires but an earnest religious mind to discover all truth there. For the Torah came down from heaven with all the necessary instruments : humility, righteousness, and uprightness—and even her reward was in her. And man has only to apply these tools to find in the Torah peace, strength, life, light, bliss, happiness, joy, and freedom.' [1] Of course the Rabbis, so far as they have been Orthodox, have always insisted on the literal observance of the ceremonial laws where it has been possible to keep them, but they often allowed themselves strange liberties with the literal meaning of a text, in order to bring it under their rules.

III. Directly we begin to discuss the question of the perpetuity of the Law a cognate inquiry suggests itself to us, Whether such a perpetuity, in whatever sense that perpetuity holds good, is of

[1] *Some Aspects of Rabbinic Theology*, 1909, pp. 134 *sq.*

force for Gentile Christians as well as for Jewish. To us who are members of the later, but incomparably larger, division of the Church, it matters not so much how believers from the stock of Israel are to regard the Law, as how we Gentiles ought to regard it. Is there, then, anything in our Lord's words which can be of guidance to us ? Did He, for example, make a distinction between Jewish and Gentile believers ? Did He wish the inference to be drawn that whereas the former were bound to observe the Law, the latter were at liberty to reject it ? The truth is that He was not likely to make any distinction between the two classes of His followers because He was not directly concerned with Gentile believers at all. He virtually had none in His lifetime. Nor, it must be added, was the Evangelist. St. Matthew indeed knew of their existence (see especially xii. 18, 21), but he took little interest in their special conditions, or the problems of their Christian life. We may therefore conclude without any doubt that neither our Lord nor His biographer referred to their relation to the Pentateuch. If they kept the Law it was not because Christ or St. Matthew definitely included them in the command to do so. St. Matthew was not writing for them.[1]

Our Lord, then, is depicted here as thinking only of Jewish believers, and St. Matthew therefore must have desired to impress on these the fact that the Law was to be a perpetual possession, in its true and fundamental meaning.

[1] It is therefore doubly absurd for Jewish controversialists to use these verses as proof-texts in their argument that Gentile followers of Christ ought to observe the Law literally.

IV. This raises a rather curious point. If our Lord, as portrayed by St. Matthew, did not insist upon the literal observance of the Law of Moses by any of His followers, is it, on the other hand, permissible for Jewish-Christians to observe it thus if they like? Are they at liberty, if they so desire, to carry out the ritual and ceremonial ordinances of the Pentateuch, preserving of course their faith in the Creeds of orthodox Christianity? It is evident that this is a question which is of interest to very few people to-day, and will therefore appear to many readers to be only academic. In fact, however, there are certain persons among both Jews and Gentiles who take sides rather hotly in the discussion of it. For some Jewish Christians of our time, who, in their earlier years, were consistent members of the ordinary Jewish community, believe the question to be almost vital, and think that if they may but observe the ritual of the Law, while enjoying the spiritual treasures of the Gospel, they are far more likely to win over their other brethren of the house of Israel to the true faith, than if, like most Jewish converts, they entirely neglect it.

A brief discussion of this question will be found in the Appendix. Here it must suffice to say, in the first place, that literal observance of the Law, as has been shown above, is not in accordance with the meaning intended by our Lord; and, in the second place, that, notwithstanding the hopes of those who favour it, it is an impossibility in the present condition of things. If the Jews once more possess a country of their own, with a temple for ritual worship, and lands wherein legal enactments may be carried out, the case may be different.

V. Christ then says that the Law is to endure for ever. But if so how does His language tally with that of St. Paul, who describes it as temporary, and the strength of sin ? Although, strictly speaking, it is no part of our present duty to discuss the teaching of St. Paul, yet it would appear as though the subject were being shirked if it were not mentioned, and perhaps a brief statement of how the case stands may contribute to a clearer comprehension of our Lord's meaning.

Briefly, we may say that there is no real opposition between the two sets of utterances. St. Paul had in mind the immediate effect of the Divine regulations upon men ; Christ the contents of the Law as Divine. St. Paul regarded the Law as law in the strict sense of the word ; Christ had in view the whole manifestation of Divine truth which it contained.

The argument has been raised that St. Paul quite misunderstood the meaning of the Hebrew word *Torah* when he translated it as *Law*, and also misrepresented the way in which it was regarded in his time. Now *Torah*, like every word that has a long history, lies under the disadvantage of having many meanings. The question is whether St. Paul was right or wrong in attributing to it a legal, not to say a codic, force, at the time when he lived, and for the people to whom he wrote.

Dr. Schechter, no doubt, tells us : ' The term *Law* or *Nomos* is not a correct rendering of the Hebrew word *Torah*. The legalistic element, which might rightly be called the Law, represents only one side of the Torah. To the Jew the word *Torah* means a teaching or an instruction of any kind.' Again : ' It is the Torah as the sum total of the contents of

THE MEANING OF TORAH

revelation, without special regard to any particular element in it, the Torah as a faith, that is so dear to the Rabbi.'[1] Dr. Bacher too says : ' *Torah* denotes in its widest meaning the totality of Jewish teaching, whether as the basis of religious perception and practice, or as the object of study.'[2]

So again Dr. Kohler: *Torah* ' signifies spiritual and moral instruction or teaching quite as well and often as Law ; religious tuition and enlightenment quite as much as legal standard; and, especially in post-biblical times, comprised the whole of the subject-matter of Judaism as the object of education and scientific study.'[3]

Far be it from us to criticise the dicta of such specialists in Rabbinic literature. For saturated as these scholars are with the deepest and most religious thought to be found in Jewish learning, their statements that this wide and comprehensive meaning of the word *Torah* does in truth represent the best Rabbinic usage, must be accepted once for all. Yet not all Rabbinic teachers, much less all the ordinary

---

[1] *Some Aspects of Rabbinic Theology*, 1909, pp. 117, 127.

[2] 'תוֹרָה bezeichnet in seinem weitesten Sinne die Gesamtheit der jüdischen Lehre, sei es als Grundlage des religiösen Erkennens und Handelns, sei es als Gegenstand des Studiums ' (*Die exegetische Terminologie der jüdischen Traditionsliteratur,* 1905, i. 197).

[3] ' Tora, das ebenso wohl und ebenso häufig geistigsittliche Unterweisung oder Lehre als Gesetz, ebenso sehr religiöse Belehrung und Aufklärung als Gesetzesnorm bedeutet und besonders in der nachbiblischen Zeit den gesamten jüdischen Lehrstoff als Gegenstand des Unterrichts und wissenschaftlicher Forschung umfasste ' (*Grundriss einer systematischen Theologie des Judentums auf geschichtlicher Grundlage*, 1910, p. 267). See also Herford, *Pharisaism*, pp. 58, 71, 74; C. G. Montefiore, *Rabbinic Judaism and the Epistles of St. Paul* in the *J.Q.R.*, 1901, pp. 161 *sqq.*; *Judaism and St. Paul*, 1914; *The Synoptic Gospels*, 1909, p. 499 : ' The Pauline theory of the bondage of the Law is unhistorical. Certain enactments may have pressed heavily upon certain people, but the Pauline bogey of "THE *Law*" did not press heavily, for it is a bogey, and bogeys are light and unreal.' See also his *Religious Teaching of Jesus*, 1910, pp. 23-58.

members of the nation, breathe that high spiritual atmosphere which such an interpretation implies. ' The feature of Judaism which first attracts an outsider's attention,' confesses Dr. Israel Abrahams (and his personal knowledge of the subject is hardly surpassed by that of Dr. Schechter), ' is its " Nomism " or "Legalism." Life was placed under the control of Law. Not only morality, but religion also, was codified. "Nomism," it has been truly said, "has always formed a fundamental trait of Judaism, one of whose aims has ever been to mould life in all its varying relations according to the Law, and to make obedience to the Commandments a necessity and a custom " (Lauterbach, *Jewish Encyclopedia*, ix. 326). . . . For many centuries, certainly up to the French Revolution, Religion as Law was the dominant conception in Judaism. . . . Conduct, social and individual, moral and ritual, was regulated in the minutest details. . . . Law seized upon the whole life, both in its inward experiences and outward manifestations. . . . The Word of God was to occupy the Jew's thoughts constantly ; at his daily employment and during his manifold activities ; when at home and when at rest. And, as a correlative, the Law must direct this complex life, the Code must authorise action or forbid it, must turn the thoughts and emotions in one direction, and divert them from another. . . . This was realised in a Code. Or rather in a series of Codes.' After enumerating some, Dr. Abrahams adds : ' Finally, in the sixteenth century, Joseph Caro (mystic and legalist) compiled the *Table Prepared (Shulchan Aruch)*, which, with masterly skill, collected the whole of the traditional law, arranged it under convenient heads in chapters and paragraphs, and

TORAH AND NOMOS

carried down to our own day the Rabbinic conception of life. Under this Code, with more or less relaxation, the great bulk of Jews still live.'[1]

It is true that Dr. Abrahams himself proceeds to qualify his language by showing that beneath this legality there lay a deeper principle, lacking which the term Torah would fail to be fully understood. He is perfectly right. But his eloquent pages are quite enough to show that those great scholars quoted above pass over too lightly an aliquot part of the contents of Torah when they minimise its legal character, and in effect draw attention to its highest and best connotation only, disregarding the lower.

If then 'Nomism,' as Dr. Abrahams terms it, was always so important, and, we may say, so predominating, a part of the Torah, surely the translators of the Septuagint can hardly be blamed (as they are blamed by Dr. Schechter when he blames St. Paul[2]) for rendering *Torah* almost invariably by *Nomos*.[3] The latter word, indeed, does not appear to have precisely the full legal force of the Latin *Lex*, but it at least means direction and decision, which, it would seem, is also the basic meaning of Torah.[4] For if scholars are right [5] in their conjecture that the root

---

[1] *Judaism*, 1907, pp. 13–18.

[2] And by Dr. Perles in *E.R.E.* vii. p. 856.

[3] The word *Torah* seems to occur about 212 times in the Hebrew Bible, in 194 of which it is represented by *nomos* in the Septuagint. Even in Isa. xlii. 4, quoted in Matt. xii. 21, it is probable that the original translation was νόμος, which has been corrupted into ὄνομα.

[4] The root-meaning of *lex* may be 'bind,' 'oblige'; that of νόμος 'assign' or 'apportion.' It is, by the by, not unimportant to remember that *Torah* never stands for the principle of law in the abstract. From failure to bear this in mind many an interpreter of the Jewish writers of the New Testament has gone astray. *Cf.* Lukyn Williams on *Galatians*, ii. 16.

[5] See in particular Robertson Smith, *O.T.J.C.*², pp. 299 *sqq.*; Driver in Hastings' *D.B.* iii. 64 *sqq.*

from which *Torah* is derived means 'cast' or 'shoot,' and the word itself primarily described the casting of lots, or the shooting of arrows, whereby to determine the Will of God, the analogy of such rites in primitive religion suggests that the performance of that Will, when ascertained, became the immediate and imperative duty of the consultant. In those early days, which struck the key-note of the word for ever, *Torah* was the direction of God to do this or that action, or to do it not.

Nor can we have much hesitation in defining the subject-matter of such a *Torah* at that time if the study of Comparative Religion is to be our guide. Not instruction in ethical truth, not direction in moral practice, much less enlightenment in theological or spiritual verities, but discharge of ritual, exactness in ceremonial, now avoidance of tabu, and now consecration to a holy war—these, and such as they, will have been the *toroth* imparted to those early worshippers. A change would come, did come, as both Bible and Science tell us, when both priest and people thought on guidance in higher matters, when, to the pious inquirer, or the worshipping multitudes, the minister of the Divine Oracle proclaimed nobler truths, announcing these in their turn as the direction of the Almighty, the *Torah* of the living God. With this the word lost none of its binding force; it only enlarged the circle of its contents. When, finally, both kinds of *toroth* were united, ritual and ethical, either in the memory or in the written word, the collection retained the momentum of its origin, the innate energy of its early existence, and men still recognised in the Law of Moses the stringency of legal obligation. The Torah, in its essence, its reality, is religion conceived as duty, towards man and God.

Was not St. Paul right, then, when he regarded the Torah as a Law, a Nomos, and the more right in that he was not composing in any of his letters, no, not even in the Epistle to the Romans, the most elaborate of them all, a treatise for divines, men highly trained in theological inquiry ? If those whom he addressed had been the Dr. Schechters or Dr. Bachers of his day he might well have taken other lines of argument, and, leaving all thought of the legal side of Old Testament truth, have compared, for instance, the revelation given in a book with the fuller revelation manifested in a Life. But he was writing to simple people, many of them slaves, most of them poor, a few belonging, as we should say, to the middle classes, and only here or there one rich or noble. Great was St. Paul as a scholar, no one denies it, but greater still was he as a man of affairs, a level-headed man of business, whose one aim and vocation were to spread the knowledge of God in the Lord Jesus Christ, and make the Gospel understood by Christians. It was to the populace, to the man in the street—the Christian man in the street, the Christian populace, *bien entendu*—that St. Paul wrote. His phraseology and mode of thought were theirs. To them, whatever Rabbinic theologians might say, the Torah in practice was strictly a Law, and he made no mistake when he treated it as such.

St. Paul then, if we may judge from the typical phrases of his Epistles, regarded the Torah as *Lex*, in the proper meaning of the word, a Law to be obeyed, sanctioned by punishment if it were broken. Of the Messiah this cannot be proved. For Jesus, in the presentation of Him recorded in this Gospel, nowhere defines the Torah, and, in fact, is not concerned with its nature. In so far as it was a manifestation of the Will of God it was permanent, in His eyes, with the kind of permanence portrayed above, but more cannot be said.

While St. Paul took what may be called a low, because a practical, view of the Torah (for he found persons teaching his converts that it was binding in the literal observance of all its details, and he laboured therefore to show that even the sense of duty which it called forth only led men to see their sinfulness more clearly in proportion as their consciences understood its claims [1]), Jesus, the true theologian, not of system or logic, but of heart-union with God, hinted at the existence in it of profounder depths and loftier peaks, which, when lit up by the fresh rays of the new light, were to be recognised, and to be attained, by His faithful followers. These were to despise no part of the Law of Moses, but were to observe in each its final and intrinsic character.

The Law, generally and in particular, in its substance and its details, was to stand for ever. The followers of the Messiah were to make it their own, and thus, both in perception and in accomplishment, were to surpass the highest measure ever attained by the religious among the community, the learned Scribes, and the earnest Pharisees.[2]

---

[1] Yet St. Paul sometimes indicates the permanence of the principles taught in the Pentateuch, *e.g.* that circumcision was a seal and witness of faith (Rom. iv. 11, 12), and a parable of the death to sin which every believer must undergo (Col. ii. 11, 12).

[2] *Vide supra*, p. 190. *v.* 20 is omitted in Codex Bezæ, but, as it seems, in no other authority. Perhaps the omission was due to *homoioteleuton* with *v.* 19. It can hardly be an interpolation, as Mr. Gerald Friedlander bluntly

THE GOSPEL NOT A NEW LAW

VI. This brings us to the consideration of the fundamental difference that there is between the Torah of Moses and the Evangel of the Apostles. Men write, and speak, and think of the Gospel of Jesus Christ as though it were a new Law, claiming comparison with the old, and ousting this from its position. Nothing can be more untrue, nothing more subversive of the principles of Christianity.

No doubt if the word 'law' be employed inaccurately, with that wide and lax usage which denotes either mere sequence of events, or a principle of action, or a standard of conduct in a particular case, or even the revelation of the Divine character and will in general terms, we can speak of the Law of Christ. So indeed wrote St. Paul himself in Gal. vi. 2 : 'Bear ye one another's burdens, and so fulfil the law of Christ'; and in somewhat similar language in Rom. iii. 27 : 'Where then is the glorying? It is excluded. By what manner of law? Of works? Nay, but by a law of faith' (R.V.). And so also St. James commends to us 'the perfect law, the law of liberty' (i. 25, compare ii. 12). In the same way we find the author of that early document, the Epistle of Barnabas, saying : 'The new law of our Lord Jesus Christ, which lays on us no yoke of compulsion' (ii. 6),[1] where the second clause, by the very fact of its addition, demonstrates the inadequacy of the term 'law' in the first to express the writer's meaning properly. Many an instance

calls it (*Sources*, p. 35). But to see in it a cheap sneer at hypocrisy is due to misunderstanding. H. J. Holtzmann, on the other hand, considers it 'eine vollkommen zutreffende Ueberschrift' to *vv*. 21–48 (*N.T. Theologie*, 1911, i. 204), but he thinks it contradicts *vv*. 18, 19. *Vide supra*, p. 184, note.

[1] This appears to be the meaning of the curious phrase: ἄνευ ζυγοῦ ἀνάγκης ὤν. See further Harnack *in loco*.

might also be quoted from the Greek Fathers to the same effect, notably from Chrysostom, who, in one brilliantly oratorical passage, does not hesitate to insist that Christ came to give us new laws,[1] extending to our very thoughts.

To speak of the Gospel as a Law rhetorically and inexactly was in itself harmless. But when once Christian people became accustomed to use the phrase 'the Law of Christ,' there was a danger of attributing to the Gospel the very qualities which belonged to the Law actually in force around them, the law of Rome, with its system of rules and ordinances, sanctioned by punishment upon their violation.

In the Greek-speaking world, to be sure, some centuries elapsed before this danger took effect. The Law of Christ was regarded by Eastern Christians less as a system to be obeyed than as a revelation to be learned. Christ was more of the Teacher than the Lawgiver. But in the West it was otherwise.

The early training of a certain lawyer in North Africa had far-reaching issues. For the brilliancy of Tertullian's epigrams, the originality of his definitions, centred round Law as he knew it, the greatest of all powers in the Roman world, nay, the ruling force in earth and heaven. To Irenæus, his earlier contemporary, who wrote and thought in Greek, the conception of the Gospel as redemption was of supreme importance; to Tertullian as Divine Law.[2] All religion, he felt, must have the character of a fixed law, and presupposed definite regulations.[3]

---

[1] ξένους νόμους. *Act. Hom.* v. 4 (Gaume, ix. 54 *sq.*). Cf. *supra*, p. 182.
[2] Harnack, *History of Dogma*, ii. 16.
[3] *Ibid.* ii. 103, note 1.

v]   BUT WAS TREATED AS SUCH

'Through the agency of Tertullian,' Harnack writes,[1] 'by his earlier profession as a lawyer, all Christian forms received a legal impress. He not only transferred the technical terms of the jurist into the ecclesiastical language of the West, but he also contemplated, from a legal standpoint, all relations of the individual and the Church to the Deity.'

The seed thus sown by Tertullian fell on fruitful soil, and the legal character of the Gospel of Christ was more and more elaborated in the West. Even Augustine's doctrine of Grace itself took a legal tone,[2] and finally Gregory the Great stamped all Roman Christianity with the form of Law.[3] In this way the doctrine of human merit, obtained by the performance of good actions (however closely in the minds of the theologians this was connected with grace bestowed through Sacraments), dominated the Christian religion, as it was now understood, and, save for the change of name, and of the subject-matter of the regulations, the new Gospel became the old Law writ large.

After all, this was but natural. For Law comes more easily to the human mind than Gospel. Until a man knows his sinfulness, and the impossibility of making atonement for himself or for others, he catches at the vain hope of compounding for evil by good, and of acquiring such righteousness as shall balance, yes, more than balance, his sin. No doubt the Church, like the Synagogue, bade the sinner repent, and obtain from God the strength for such a meritorious life, but in neither case was the

[1] Harnack, *History of Dogma*, v. 16; cf. 52.
[2] *Ibid.* v. 52.
[3] *Ibid.* v. 263; cf. also pp. 265 note, 267, 271.

principle affected. If Judaism on such conditions was a Law, so was Christianity. The pardon offered freely in Christ was set aside; the power to be found only in Christ was forgotten. Christianity became a system of duties, a counterpart and a rival to the Law of Moses.

That, let it be stated once more, is a parody, nay, a contradiction, of its true character. For Christianity is the Good News of the coming of Him who was called Jesus, because He should save His people from their sins (i. 21); who bade believers know that their iniquities were pardoned, although they had not acquired merit (ix. 2); whose attitude to sinners was such that they could always be sure of a welcome from Him; whose miracles not only brought health to the body, but also portrayed in living action the way in which He freely healed the soul.

This Gospel of St. Matthew describes Jesus, not as the Lawgiver, no, not even in this Sermon on the Mount, but as the One to Whom men came with their difficulties and their trials, with their desires and their longings, their humble inquiries and their timid expectations, to find their hunger satisfied, and the energy they lacked, fully supplied in Him.

Not a system, but a Person, is the subject of the New Testament; and therefore not directions, but principles; not a Law, but a Gospel. The Law stands unrivalled as a direct statement of the will of God, binding, and therefore condemning. Christ came not to destroy it, or to place another Law in its stead, but to bring about its accomplishment, by revealing the character of God more completely, announcing the Good News of His love in receiving sinful men, and of the ensuing power for a holy life.

The Gospel is no new Law, in the strictest sense of the words Lex, Nomos, or Torah. They, properly speaking, represent religion as duty to be performed. But so far as the Law contains the revelation of God, so far is it permanent, and its permanence is but increased and confirmed by the fuller revelation of God's mind and will, and of the grace given to us by Him, in His Son Jesus the Messiah, who is 'the effulgence of his glory, and the expression of his being' (Heb. i. 3).

'Do we then make the Law of none effect through faith? God forbid: nay, we establish the Law' (Rom. iii. 31).

'Think not that I came to destroy the Law or the Prophets: I came not to destroy, but to fulfil.'

APPENDIX

A HEBREW-CHRISTIAN CHURCH

By 'a Church' I understand a branch of the Catholic Church, in which the pure word of God is preached, and the Sacraments are duly ministered. By 'Hebrew-Christian' I understand that the members of this Church are believers from among the Jews, the term 'Hebrew' being employed in preference to 'Jewish,' as savouring more of nationality than religion. The whole phrase, 'A Hebrew-Christian Church,' denotes an organisation more or less distinct from any other, the members of which are recognised as Christians by all persons, whether Jews or Gentiles, and yet are also recognised on all sides as Hebrews, *i.e.* of Hebrew race, or, as we might say, as Jews except in religion, this twofold recognition being continued to the children and descendants of the actual converts.

To put the case slightly otherwise; what is desired by many is something more than the popular acceptance of the fact that certain Jews who retain Jewish customs are also Christians, for this is so already. What is desired, if I understand the matter aright, is, first, an official pronouncement by the officers of the Church, in particular the officers of the Church of England, that such persons are recognised as Christians; and secondly, the appointment of a Christian officer, preferably a bishop, and of course of Jewish birth, who shall himself practise such Jewish customs, and shall act as shepherd and guide to such Hebrew-Christians.

Two things indeed must be sorrowfully confessed. First, at present there is very little demand by Hebrew-Christians for such an officer; and secondly, Hebrew-Christians belonging to the Episcopal Church are far outnumbered by others; in fact, Episcopalian Hebrew-Christians form but a small minority of the whole of those Jews who have been brought to acknowledge the Saviour.

Let me at once say that all of us must feel sympathy with this proposal, for there can hardly be a person interested in Missions to the Jews who has not felt strongly drawn towards it. If, after thinking it over, we find ourselves compelled to believe that any attempt to bring about a Hebrew-Christian Church now is likely to end in failure and do more harm than good, it is with sincere sorrow that we are compelled to say so.

I. Let us recall, so far as we can, the arguments adduced in support of such a Church, together with statements of what it implies.[1] Afterwards we will consider the objections to it.

1. The proposition offers, in particular, two advantages. In the first place it hopes to remove one of the greatest hindrances to the acceptance of the Gospel by the Jews. For to Jews Christianity is worse than only a change of religion.

[1] *Cf.* The Declaration by two Hebrew-Christians presented to the International Jewish Missionary Conference at Stockholm in 1911. See the *Year-Book of the Evangelical Missions among the Jews*, edited by Professor Strack, 1913, pp. 15 *sqq.*

v] APPENDIX—A HEBREW-CHRISTIAN CHURCH

To them it is treachery to the nation. Many a Jew would be ready to change his religion (I speak in popular language) if there were not added to it the forsaking of his nation. Christians do not sufficiently recognise the strength of the national feeling that exists among the Jews. The more that Jews are persecuted, the more they are knit together by the strongest bands of national feeling, and the more despicable they find it in any one to forsake them in their need.

The hope, therefore, is that if a Hebrew-Christian Church were formed there would be something to which we Christians could point and say: You see it is not necessary to give up your Jewish (or rather, according to the nomenclature preferred, your Hebrew) customs. We, at any rate, whatever the non-Christian Jews may say, have no desire that you should break away from your nation.

There is also another advantage. Not only would the non-Christian Jews find it easier to become Christians, but also those who have already acknowledged the Lord Jesus would be more likely to remain faithful to Him. For, disguise the fact as we may, the proportion of those who fall away is much too high. The strain on Hebrew-Christians, it is asserted, would be minimised if a Hebrew-Christian Church could be established. As things are now, they feel the strain of separation from their own people. The *Heimweh* for their nation is strong within them, and sometimes, alas, is overpoweringly strong.

2. Let us, however, be quite clear as to what membership of a Hebrew-Christian Church implies.

It means, first, the observance of Hebrew ceremonies and customs. Such, for example, are Circumcision and the Sabbath, both of which, it is urged, are very much older than the time of giving the Law to Moses. Then there is the keeping of the Dietary Laws, which may be defended partly on the ground of health. Then the Jewish Festivals, and perhaps some of the Fasts, will not be neglected. Passover will be observed, as in remembrance of the deliverance of the nation from Egypt; Shebuoth, or the Feast of Weeks, will be kept, in sign of the early part of the harvest, and the giving of the Law; Tabernacles, in remembrance of the booths on the way out from Egypt, and the full ingathering of fruit; Chanuka, in joyful memory of the Feast of the Dedication in the time of the Maccabees; Purim, for the escape through Esther. All these, and perhaps one or two of the Fasts connected with the destruction of Jerusalem, will be retained because of their historical interest, and their importance to the nation as a whole. Further, with some of them at least, Christian thoughts will be interwoven. For example, Passover will remind the believer of the death of the true Passover Lamb, and also of the Lord's Supper; Shebuoth, or Pentecost, of the outpouring of the Holy Spirit; even Chanuka of Christmas or perhaps Epiphany. It is however presupposed, unless I am mistaken, that the observance of all these ceremonies and customs is to be on purely Biblical lines, and not in the form and degree sanctified by traditional teaching. To this I will return presently.

Secondly, prayers will be available in Hebrew, and this not as a direct translation from the English Prayer Book, such as is common now, but in a form adapted from the specifically Jewish prayer-books. Our own Book of Common Prayer is a compilation from so many sources that we can make no objection to this in principle.

Thirdly, Hebrew-Christians will be encouraged to use the Hebrew language as much as possible. To this also no objection can be raised.

Fourthly, Zionism, on lines independent (if necessary) of the form accepted by those who are non-Christian Jews, will be given an important place in the affections and interests of Hebrew-Christians.

3. While it is proposed that Hebrew-Christians observe these things, it is further claimed that such a body of Hebrew-Christians will not be an entirely new experiment. For, it is said, many believers in the first two centuries of our era practised these customs. Did not the ideal Hebrew-Christian, the Lord Jesus Himself, keep them? Undoubtedly He did; nothing else was possible for Him. But did He not teach His followers, in particular His followers from among the Jews, to observe them also? I own that this is a difficult question, and confess that so learned and orthodox a scholar as Zahn

v] APPENDIX—A HEBREW-CHRISTIAN CHURCH

argues that He did. See Zahn's comments on Matt. v. 17–20, in particular pp. 221 *sq.* of the third edition of his commentary.

Yet Homer sometimes nods, and I cannot think that we ought to follow even a Zahn in his exposition here. The true meaning of our Lord's words in Matt. v. 17–20 appears to be that He is coming forward as a Teacher showing the inner meaning of the Law, which is not necessarily at all the same as its outward observance. Not a jot or a tittle of the Law was to pass away, but, on the contrary, to receive a meaning, and accomplish a purpose, far beyond anything achieved by the minute righteousness of the Scribes and Pharisees. No doubt our Lord would not have opposed, and did not oppose, the external observance of the Law by Jewish-Christians, but that He bade them so observe it, and made arrangements for their doing so, seems to be quite contrary to the spirit of His acts and words.

It may be granted also, indeed it cannot but be granted, that nearly thirty years after the Crucifixion, the Christian Jews of Palestine observed the Jewish customs (see Acts xxi. 20), and also that on occasion St. Paul did likewise; witness his circumcision of Timothy, and his sacrifices in Jerusalem (Acts xxi. 21–26).[1]

Further, it cannot be denied that during the second, and even the third centuries there were certain Christians of Jewish race, of different degrees of Christian orthodoxy, who maintained Jewish customs. In particular it may be noticed that if, as is possible in some cases, these were identical with the Minim of the Talmud, they were, notwithstanding, recognised by Jewish teachers as Jews in nationality, though not in religion. Most striking of all the examples which Chwolson, for instance, mentions, is the case of the Min whom R. Jehudah himself, the editor of the Mishna, the patriarch, the spiritual and political head of the Jewish nation in the end of the second century, welcomed to his table, permitting him to say the blessing after the meal.

---

[1] Only 'on occasion.' Normally he appears to have lived like a Gentile. For example, he did not keep the dietary laws, see Gal. ii. 11-14.

This blessing is in four parts, of which the second contains thanks for the deliverance from Egypt, for the sign of the covenant (circumcision), for the Law, and the ordinances. The third contains a prayer for God's mercy on Jerusalem, and for the rebuilding of the temple.[1]

4. Lastly, upholders of the proposition to establish a Hebrew-Christian Church point to the fact that a certain number of Hebrew-Christians in the nineteenth and twentieth centuries have observed Jewish ceremonies and customs, and have remained faithful and devoted Christians. They also tell us with no little gratification that the American Episcopal Church has formally accepted the principle.

This last argument would carry more weight if it could be shown that the American Episcopal Church made the very slightest effort to rise to the immense possibilities of evangelistic work that lie immediately before it in the crowded Jewry of New York. The neglect of the Jews by American Christians is extraordinary, and suggests serious reflections as to whether they have thought deeply over the question whether it is the duty of the Church to endeavour to win the Jews to the Master whom they themselves adore and love.

II. Let us now consider the objections to the proposition.

One very common objection, however, is due to a misunderstanding. Many suppose that St. Paul's language in his Epistle to the Galatians is contrary to the idea of a Hebrew-Christian Church as now proposed. He refused to circumcise Titus, and he strongly attacked those who advocated circumcision. But it is forgotten that he was not considering the case of Hebrew-Christians at all. Far from it. He was attacking those who urged that Gentile Christians should be circumcised, a wholly different thing. It seems to be quite indefensible to adduce St. Paul as an opponent of a Hebrew-Christian Church, at any rate in his Epistle to the Galatians.

---

[1] See Lect. IV, p. 151; see also Strack, *Jesus, die Häretiker und die Christen*, u.s.w., 1910, § 22 c. T.B. *Chullin*, 87a.

v] APPENDIX—A HEBREW-CHRISTIAN CHURCH

The real objections to the proposal are of a different kind.

1. First, the Jewish ceremonies and customs which it is proposed that Hebrew-Christians should observe have always been regarded by Jews as religious as well as national. Mr. Philip Cohen indeed writes:[1] 'Circumcision can only be regarded as an oath of allegiance or as a kind of registration in the Hebrew state similar to what all nations impose on the birth of a child, or to the oaths imposed on those admitted into special office.' His second alternative seems, by-the-by, not to march strictly with his first. But he produces no sufficient evidence for his statement. No doubt a Jewish child would not be reckoned, in either ancient or modern times, a member of the Jewish nation if he were not circumcised, but there seems to be no evidence at all that the rite was regarded as only secular. This would, in fact, be contrary to all that we know of the nations of antiquity, and the Semitic nations in particular, who did nothing apart from religion. Circumcision seems always to have been regarded as inauguration into the religious system of the Jewish nation, as well as the record of nationality. So also with the other customs, such as the Feasts and Fasts, that have been mentioned; there never was a time in which they were only secular and national, and not religious.

2. Secondly, it is proposed to separate the Biblical from the Rabbinic methods of observing these customs, and to keep to the former while rejecting the latter. 'It is not proposed to continue Rabbinical Judaism,' writes Miss Dampier in *Church and Synagogue*, 1911, p. 37. I venture to think that this is an impossible position, and for this reason. We know next to nothing about the way in which these ceremonies and customs were observed in strictly Biblical times, and, in fact, almost nothing about the daily, practical life of Judaism apart from Rabbinical Judaism. Is it not probable that from the very beginnings of Israel's history there was some definition of the Sabbath, when (exactly) it began and ended, what (exactly) might be done,

[1] *The Hebrew Christian and His National Continuity*, 1910, p. 119.

and what might not be done, upon it ? How is it proposed now to draw the line ? Again, take the Passover. Is the leaven to be hunted out or not ? If it is, how will you determine which Rabbinical rules you will accept, and which reject ? So also with the Dietary Laws. We are told that these will not be so minute. Why not ? On what principle will you go ? Is it not, in fact, probable that the laws and rules given in the Bible are in most cases merely summaries of practices which had a long history behind them, and therefore were determined by oral rules existing already when the summaries were incorporated in the Law of Moses ? It is very easy to say : We will keep the written Law, but will reject the oral. But let us not deceive ourselves, we are attempting an impossibility.[1]

3. Again, it is to be feared that such an observance of Jewish customs will put too heavy a burden upon Hebrew-Christians. One of two things will happen. If the Hebrew-Christian does his best to observe the customs with due care and consideration, there is a grave danger that he will, little by little, be led back into Judaism. It hardly seems right indeed to speak, as some of our friends do, especially in Germany, of ' Ebionitism ' in Missions to the Jews, but the term does put in a nutshell the danger that is to be feared. On the other hand, if the man is careless about the customs, the tendency will be for him gradually to give them up. In this case we arrive at the present condition of things. As has already been implied, these dangers are not imaginary. They represent what actually took place among the Jewish Christians of the first three centuries. Many fell back into Judaism. Others became, gradually but eventually, indistinguishable from Gentile Christians. The history of the obscure and useless sects of Hebrew-Christians in the first three centuries, so far as we know it, is not pleasant reading.

---

[1] The history of the Karaites confirms rather than contradicts this. Their customs and ceremonies are governed as much by an oral Law as those of the Rabbanite Jews, and are often harsher and more difficult to keep. So also with the Samaritans, and even the Sadducees.

v] APPENDIX—A HEBREW-CHRISTIAN CHURCH

It may be replied that the same results are not likely to be found under present conditions. This remains to be seen. It is asserted, I know not with how much truth, that the majority of those Hebrew-Christians who have attempted to retain their Jewish customs in the nineteenth and twentieth centuries have found it impossible to remain faithful to both sides, and at last have either become Jews, or become merged among the Gentiles. The path between the two precipices has been too narrow.

III. Yet, say our friends, there are Chinese Christians and Japanese Christians, why not Jewish, or Hebrew, Christians, recognised as such by all? True; and when there is a Judæa, or a Hebrew State, as there is now a China and a Japan, then there will be readily enough Jewish or Hebrew Christians. When, that is to say, the Jews are once more settled in Palestine as a race, when they have what Mr. Philip Cohen calls 'a true centre of their own,'[1] then the name will be so distinctly racial and national that it will be attached to Jews who even become Christians. Then a Hebrew-Christian's child, though baptized, will still be reckoned as a Jew.[2] But until the race and nation inhabit a home of their own the scheme is, I fear, Utopian, and even harmful. Neither does it seem that anything can now be done to prepare the way for it, save to encourage the restoration of the People to the Land.

[1] *The Hebrew Christian and His National Continuity*, 1910, p. 37.

[2] Unless Dr. Gaster's narrow *dicta* are accepted: 'A Jew who changes his faith is torn up by the roots. There is no longer any connection between him and other Jews. He has practically died.' 'There cannot be Christian and Jewish Jews' (*Zionism and the Jewish Future*, edited by H. Sacher, 1916, pp. 91, 94).

Lecture Six

THE MESSIAH AS TEACHER—THE ETHICAL
DEMANDS IN THE SERMON ON THE
MOUNT

'Blessed are the poor in spirit: for theirs is the kingdom of heaven.'—MATT. v. 3.

Lecture Six

THE MESSIAH AS TEACHER—THE ETHICAL DEMANDS IN THE SERMON ON THE MOUNT

WE now come to the very heart of the Sermon, the Ethical Demands made by the Messiah upon His followers, and we must endeavour to think of these demands, not as they seem to us, but as they appeared to Jewish-Christians, and other Jews, who lived in the last quarter of the first century.

The method to be pursued is this. After briefly recalling the fact that much was already accepted by Jews, whether Christian or non-Christian; and then mentioning a few of the requirements which (as is asserted) seemed to them strange and even impracticable, we shall consider at greater length whether there is not some misapprehension both of the nature of the demands themselves and of the persons to whom they were addressed. In this way we shall arrive at a better understanding of the true character and aim of the Sermon on the Mount, and the requirements of the Great Teacher.

I. First, then, much of these demands was already well known to Jewish-Christians before they believed in the Lord Jesus. They had been taught it, either orally or in books.[1]

---

[1] It is not easy to determine the trustworthiness of the different witnesses to the ethical knowledge of Jews in the first century. On the one hand, we are apt to forget that the Old Testament did not necessarily mean the same to them as to us, and on the other the claims of modern Jewish writers to represent an unchanging tradition is hardly consonant with facts. Their

Take, for example, our Lord's words about purity in v. 27–30. The son of Sirach had said already: 'Turn away thine eye from a comely woman, and gaze not on another's beauty' (Ecclus. ix. 8). And the sayings now found in the *Testaments of the Twelve Patriarchs* can hardly have been unknown to the Jewish reader: 'Pay no heed to the face of a woman.... Pay no heed to the beauty of women, nor set your mind upon their affairs' (Test. Reuben iii. 10; iv. 1); 'I command you, my children, not ... to gaze upon the beauty of women' (Judah xvii. 1); 'The single-minded man ... looketh not on the beauty of women, lest he pollute his mind with corruption' (Iss. iv. 4); 'I never committed fornication by the uplifting of my eyes' (Iss. vii. 2); 'Flee evil-doing and cleave to goodness. For he that hath it looketh not on a woman with a view to fornication; and he beholdeth no defilement; for there resteth upon him a holy spirit' (Benj. viii. 1, 2, in A.). We may compare the later words of the Talmud: 'A man must not look on a beautiful woman, even if she be single' (*Abodah Zarah*, 20a).[1]

Again, it is a serious matter for an Oriental to be expected to keep his mouth clean from oaths. For they form part of his ordinary conversation. It is therefore no wonder if St. Matthew is careful to record the fact that in this respect the Messiah

glasses are at least as tinted as ours, though with a different shade. Neither can the statements of the Talmudim and the Midrashim be trusted for a period so much earlier than their own. Even the Mishna, and the Tosephta, ascribed to the end of the second century, must be used with caution. Probably after the New Testament itself (which by the nature of the case is hardly available for our present purpose) the most satisfactory material is that of the Apocryphal and Pseudepigraphic books, which range from the second century before, to the first century after, the beginning of our era.

[1] In *Jub.* xx. 4 the reference is to flagrant sin.

made great claims upon His followers (v. 33–37; xxiii. 16–22). Yet it must not be supposed that teaching upon this subject was new to Jewish-Christians. 'Accustom not thy mouth to an oath,' writes the author of *Ecclesiasticus* (xxiii. 9–11), 'and be not accustomed to the naming of the Holy One. For as a servant that is continually scourged shall not lack a bruise, so he also that sweareth and nameth God continually shall not be cleansed from sin. A man of many oaths shall be filled with iniquity, and the scourge shall not depart from his house.' Indeed, it was a Jewish commonplace to warn the pious against so evil a practice. Philo treats of it at some length. In his essay *On the Ten Commandments*, § 17, he says: 'That being which is the most beautiful, and the most beneficial to human life, and suitable to rational nature, swears not itself, because truth on every point is so innate within him that his bare word is accounted an oath.'[1] The godly man, that is to say, will not swear at all. Let him avoid oaths altogether, if possible. But in his treatise *On the Special Laws*, § 2, he is not so strict: 'However, if a man must swear and is so inclined, let him add, if he pleases, not indeed the highest name of all, and the most important cause of all things, but the earth, the sun, the stars, the heaven, the universal world; for these things are all most worthy of being named, and are more ancient than our own birth, and, moreover, they never grow old, lasting for ever and ever, in accordance with the will of their Creator.'[2] The quasi-

---

[1] Yonge's translation, iii. 155.
[2] Yonge, iii. 256. In *Shebuoth* iv. 13 (Talmud, 35a) there is a discussion whether certain appellations (such as heaven, earth, &c.) contain a reference

permission to ordinary folk to live on a comparatively low level is very characteristic of Jewish teachers, and the concessions made by Philo approach very closely to those pilloried by our Lord.

In the *Secrets of Enoch* (xlix. 1), on the contrary, a higher standard is raised : ' For I swear to you, my children, but I will not swear by a single oath, neither by heaven, nor by earth, nor by any other creature which God made. God said : There is no swearing in me, nor injustice, but truth. If there is no truth in men, let them swear by a word, yea, yea, or nay, nay. But I swear to you, yea, yea.'

We may also compare the later phrases of the Talmud : ' Let thy yes be true, and thy nay be true.' [1] But this perhaps only inculcates truthfulness, and has no immediate reference to swearing. In *Shebuoth*, 36a, even the repetition of the affirmative or the negative is said to be an oath.[2]

So with charity to the poor : ' Give to him that asketh thee, and from him that would borrow of thee turn not thou away ' (Matt. v. 42). The charge is thoroughly Jewish, and would present little difficulty to Jewish-Christians of St. Matthew's time. Recall Deut. xv. 7, 8 : ' If there be with thee a poor man, one of thy brethren, within any of thy gates in thy land which the LORD thy God giveth thee, thou shalt not harden thine heart, nor shut thine hand from thy poor brother : but thou shalt surely

to God or not. In the Shulchan Arukh, *Yore Deah*, § 237. 6, the negative is affirmed. Hamburger, *Real-Encyclopädie*, 1870, s.v. *Eidesformel*, has many references to Jewish standard works bearing on the subject. See also J. Lightfoot on Matt. v. 33–37.

[1] *Baba Mezia*, 49a. The passage is a play on the words in Lev. xix. 36.

[2] This is derived from the twofold ' not ' in Gen. ix. 11. Chwolson, *Das letzte Passamahl*, p. 94, has an interesting note showing the abhorrence with which pious Jews still regard oaths, even true ones.

VI]   AND INCULCATED

open thine hand unto him, and shalt surely lend him sufficient for his need in that which he wanteth.' The whole passage to the end of the eleventh verse breathes the same spirit of free-hearted charity. Lev. xxv. 35, 36, is very similar : ' And if thy brother be waxen poor, and his hand fail with thee ; then thou shalt uphold him : as a stranger and a sojourner shall he live with thee. Take thou no usury of him or increase; but fear thy God : that thy brother may live with thee.' Ecclesiasticus iv. 4, 5, is even more to the point : ' Reject not a suppliant in his affliction ; and turn not away thy face from a poor man. Turn not away thine eye from one that asketh of thee.'

Closer still is the command of Tobit to his son (Tobit iv. 7) : ' Give alms of thy substance ; and when thou givest alms, let not thine eye be envious : turn not away thy face from any poor man, and the face of God shall not be turned away from thee.' The spirit, however, of true charity is that which is put into the mouth of Zebulun in the *Testaments* (Zeb. vii. 2–4) : ' Do you, my children, from that which God bestoweth upon you, show compassion and mercy without hesitation to all men, and give to every man with a good heart. And if ye have not the wherewithal to give to him that needeth, have compassion for him in bowels of mercy. I know that my hand found not the wherewithal to give to him that needed, and I walked with him weeping for seven furlongs, and my bowels yearned towards him in compassion.' [1]

So with Christ's demands about riches, in vi. 19–34, where He bids His followers to lay up treasures,

[1] On the need of personal kindness in bestowing alms see the quotations in the *Jewish Encyclopedia*, iii. 669.

not upon earth but in heaven; for no man can serve two masters; and not to take anxious thought for the morrow, but to remember the birds and the flowers, whose simplicity of life receives the perfection of God's care.

'I command you, my children, not to love money. . . . Beware, my children, of the love of money. . . . For he is a slave to two contrary passions, and cannot obey God, because they have blinded his soul, and he walketh in the day as in the night. My children, the love of money leadeth to idolatry' (Test. Judah xvii. 1; xviii. 2, 6; xix. 1). 'Work righteousness, my children, upon the earth, that ye may have it as a treasure in heaven' (Test. Levi xiii. 5).

Lastly, it may be noticed that although it was permissible to pray in the street (vi. 5), and a man who so prayed ought not to interrupt his prayer for 'ass or driver or seller of pots,'[1] yet Hillel himself, at about the time of our Lord's birth, forbade anything like ostentation in all that one does.[2]

It will be evident from these few examples of the way in which much of our Lord's demands was already known to Jewish disciples, that He did not come to give entirely new orders, but rather desired to impress more firmly upon the minds of His hearers all that was best in what they had already learned. And this was a necessary part of St. Matthew's presentation of the Messiah. For, in fact: 'It was of the utmost importance for them . . . that they should realise that the fundamental convictions of the religion whence they had emerged were not shaken. The new teaching of Jesus was really

---

[1] Tosephta, *Berakoth*, iii. 20.   [2] *Ibid.* ii. 21.

vi] ARE PARTS OF THE SERMON IMPRACTICABLE ?

continuous with the truths by which their forefathers had lived, yet it so widened and deepened them that the religion of a nation was not only capable of becoming the faith of the world, but must inevitably become such, as was happening before the eyes of the readers of this Gospel. They would see that the contemporary Jewish slander, which accused Jesus of Nazareth and His followers of disloyalty to the Old Testament revelation, was false, and that in Him was its only true fulfilment.' [1]

II. Much, then, of the Sermon on the Mount must have been well known to pious Jews before ever our Lord delivered it, and to Jewish-Christians after the Fall of Jerusalem before they were brought into the Christian fold. But not a little must have been new to them, and part must have been so strange and contrary to their habits of thought and life as to seem impracticable, and perhaps not desirable even if it were carried out. So at least portions of it strike some of our Jewish contemporaries who have considered the Sermon, with a sincere desire to understand it.

Against our Lord's demands in respect of purity of thought (v. 27–32) modern Jewish critics appear to have nothing to say. But they strongly object to His supposed commendation of celibacy, especially in xix. 10–12, a passage which is closely connected with words on the holiness of marriage, when He is speaking against divorce.

It is not necessary, for the purpose of these Lectures, to enter upon the thorny question of whether our Lord did, or did not, forbid divorce

[1] Dr. H. U. Weitbrecht, *St. Matthew*, pp. 132 *sq.* (Madras, 1912).

entirely.¹ His standard was considerably higher than that of His contemporaries. Let that suffice. But the outcome of His words was that His disciples said unto Him : ' If the case of the man is so with his wife, it is not good to marry,' to which He replied that His saying was intended only for certain persons, and that there were some who did not marry for the kingdom of heaven's sake.²

We are, however, told by our critics that ' the Church had to deal all along with ordinary human beings, and found it quite impossible to follow the lines laid down by Jesus.' ³ ' He tried to abolish divorce, but he failed. Human nature, being what it is, requires divorce as a necessary and expedient consequence of the sin of adultery.' ⁴

So, again, Mr. Montefiore writes : ' It cannot be alleged that the ascetic element is wholly wanting in the teaching of Jesus. There is a tendency to regard abstention as higher than temperate enjoyment, just as it is considered higher to have no money than to use money well. There is a tendency to put celibacy above marriage ; there is a tendency to suggest that the highest religious life necessitates the abandonment of ordinary family ties. The result of this tendency has been seen, in its full fruitage, in the monastic institutions and life of the Roman

---

¹ If πορνεία (v. 32, xix. 9) is taken in its strict meaning of antenuptial sin, as is not improbable, the clause refers to Deut. xxiv. 1 with xxii. 14-21, and, whether actually spoken by our Lord or not, forms no exception to his prohibition of divorce as usually understood.

² Jews surely would be the last to find fault with this saying if they remembered that Jeremiah was expressly forbidden to take a wife (Jer. xvi. 1, 2). He is precisely one of those cases to which our Lord refers.

³ G. Friedlander, *Sources*, p. 55.

⁴ *Ibid.* p. 58.

Catholic Church. No student of history, no observer of facts, can deny the noble characters which this tendency has produced. But, at the same time, none can deny its dangers and its evils. Judaism has, on the whole, been opposed to it. The phrase " to live in religion," meaning to live outside the family, is the antithesis to Jewish conceptions of religion and morality. Thus this tendency of the teaching of Jesus is off the Jewish line. . . . Married life is, according to the main stream of Jewish teaching, a higher thing than celibacy or self-mutilation.'[1]

With regard to oaths, two difficulties are felt by Jewish students of our Lord's words. First, Christian scholars have often supposed that Jewish teachers permitted men to use different kinds of oaths, with the express intention of feeling themselves bound to speak the truth only if they mentioned the name of God. Now this is plainly a very serious accusation against the truthfulness of the Jewish nation in the time of Christ, and we cannot be surprised that it is resented.[2] That indeed there were at that date casuistical distinctions to be seen in forms of oaths can hardly be disputed, in view of the examples adduced above, but the reason for them appears to be, not that the use of lesser oaths might be the means of deception of men, but that they might not be the profanation of God. Reverence for Him, not trickery of fellow-creatures, appears to have been the motive for swearing by heaven instead of by God.[3] Our Lord, however, sweeps

---

[1] C. G. Montefiore, *The Synoptic Gospels*, p. 507. .

[2] G. Friedlander, *Sources*, pp. 60–65.

[3] That this might lead to wilful deception in cases is evident, but there is no evidence that our Lord attacked it on this ground.

away all such sophistry, reminding His hearers that heaven is God's throne and the earth His footstool, and that to invoke either the one or the other, or, in fact, to employ any of the lesser terms of adjuration, is the same thing as invoking Him who is very King and Lord of all. He shows that Jewish casuistry fails in its own purpose, besides being, at the best, unworthy of true believers.

The second objection is that, in spite of the prohibition by Christ of all oaths, He Himself did not refrain from them, and allowed their force. For He was accustomed to strengthen His own utterances by the use of the solemn asseveration 'Amen,'[1] and also submitted to being put upon His oath at His trial (xxvi. 63, 64).

But surely an interpretation which thus makes our Lord flagrantly contradict His own teaching is itself faulty somewhere. It rests on the presupposition that when our Lord forbade swearing He was giving an absolute and legal command on the subject. If this was not the case, as will be seen later, much of the difficulty comes to an end.[2]

To turn to the question of charity to the poor. ' Give to him that asketh thee, and from him that would borrow of thee turn thou not away!' (v. 42).

---

[1] R. Jose, in the name of R. Chanina, argues in *Shebuoth*, 36a, that it contains an oath.

[2] Mr. Friedlander proposes to lay the burden of the inconsistency on the Evangelist, who, as he supposes, was influenced by the Essene objection to oaths (pp. 62 *sq.*). But he forgets that the Essenes themselves did not hesitate to take an oath when occasion demanded it (Josephus, *War*, II, viii. 6, 7, §§ 135, 139-142). For their entrance into the order was only by taking a very solemn oath indeed. Neither they, nor, therefore, according to his theory, St. Matthew, objected to swearing *per se*, but only to its use unnecessarily. That their prohibition extended, as it seems, to courts of law, is not in reality a matter of principle, but of detail.

vi]   ALMSGIVING

What ! Are we to imitate the practice of the Russian nobility in the earlier half of last century, who, as Tolstoy tells us in the reminiscences of his boyhood, were accustomed to set a servant on the front of the carriage in which they drove, whose duty it was to scatter coins to poor persons whom they passed ?[1] Is that to obey Christ's demands ? No doubt to do so is better than miserliness, and may lead in time to higher conceptions of what true almsgiving is, but it is so strangely primitive a form of charity that for Christ to have taught it would have shown that He Himself had attained to a very low level of ethical experience. Yet His words, taken by themselves, have been understood to mean this !

So with the demands He made upon His followers with regard to wealth. 'If thou wouldest be perfect,' says Jesus, 'go, sell that thou hast' (xix. 21). 'This is impossible in everyday life,' we are told, and 'it has led to belief that wealth is accursed, whilst poverty ensures blessedness.'[2] ' In the Gospel money is considered to be tainted. This is the reason why it is called "the mammon of unrighteousness"' (Luke xvi. 9).[3] 'Ye cannot serve God and mammon' (Matt. vi. 24). 'Jesus denies the right to possess wealth. His command is "Lay not up treasure"' (Matt. vi. 19).[4] 'Shall we be wrong,' our critic asks, 'in attributing the antipathy of Jesus to wealth to the fact that he and his followers were in abject poverty ? '[5]

[1] *Adolescence*, chap. ii. ; English translation, 1894, pp. 159 *sq.*
[2] G. Friedlander, *Sources*, p. 89.
[3] *Ibid.* p. 170.   [4] *Ibid.* p. 173.
[5] *Ibid.* p. 174. Observe that this is a wholly gratuitous assumption They may have thought it right to become poor, but they were not so at first *Vide infra*, p. 236 note.

Similarly, it is said : ' Not only must the disciple of Jesus avoid wealth, but he must not even have a care for the material needs of ordinary daily life. Not only should he be heedless as to what he will eat, or wear, but he is not to attempt to obtain these bare necessities of life. Jesus had only one concern —the coming kingdom—"Seek ye first his kingdom and his righteousness, and all these things shall be added unto you " (Matt. vi. 33). This absolute faith in Providence, unaccompanied by *any* effort on man's part, is not Jewish doctrine.' [1]

Even Mr. Montefiore writes in much the same strain : ' Jesus had a bias against the rich.' [2] ' It is considered higher to have no money than to use money well.' [3] ' That Jesus had a real antagonism to wealth and earthly goods is pretty certain. He regarded money as an evil in itself, a spiritual and moral danger for him who owned it.' ' As Pfleiderer points out,' Mr. Montefiore continues, ' he agreed with most ancient thinkers in supposing riches to be not a means for productive moral action, but a mere source of pleasure and enjoyment. With many other pious Jews of his age, he saw in the rich, as a social class, the oppressors of the poor, the children of " this world," the enemies of the divine Kingdom (*Urchristentum*, i. p. 650). What M. Loisy says seems entirely accurate : "The incompatibility between the service of God and the pursuit of riches is absolute. It would be arbitrary to understand the text in the sense that a man ought not to serve God and Mammon at the same time, or that it is permissible to seek or keep riches, on condition of not

---

[1] G. Friedlander, *Sources*, pp. 187 *sq*.
[2] *The Synoptic Gospels*, p. 477.   [3] *Ibid.* p. 507.

being a slave to them. The possibility of such a condition is just what it is desired to exclude. In this sentence, as everywhere else, and especially in the discourse which follows, Jesus puts himself at the ideal point of view of evangelical perfection, as it ought to be found in those who are waiting for the coming of the Kingdom of Heaven and preparing themselves for it. Such persons are not only spiritually separated from riches, they ought also to be actually separated from them. It is impossible for him whose thoughts are occupied with earthly wealth to belong entirely to God " (*E.S.* i. p. 614).

'J. Weiss rightly says,' adds Mr. Montefiore, 'that Jesus must have thought that he saw in riches a sort of demonic power, hostile to God, and the concentrated essence of the "world" as opposed to the Kingdom. "No reformer of the moral life of the world speaks here, but a prophet, who has finished with this world to prepare the way for a higher and different order."'[1]

So also another writer, who represents the opinions of many orthodox Jews, tells us that 'Jesus made poverty a distinctly pronounced, if not decisive, test of discipleship.'[2]

Was then the Messiah, according to the presentation of Him in this Gospel, only an enthusiastic visionary, whose schemes for the reformation of manners took no account of human nature, so unfitted for human life, so grossly unpractical, have they proved in effect to be? Must we dismiss the higher and more stringent portions of the Sermon on the Mount, and other sayings in the Gospel that

---
[1] *The Synoptic Gospels*, p. 541.
[2] P. Goodman, *The Synagogue and the Church*, 1908, p. 274.

resemble it in tone and tension, to the limbo of the vagaries of an eccentric, and the ravings of a madman?[1] Or are they, at best, fitted for a small, very small, community, living an other-worldly life in very primitive surroundings? If we are shut up to either of these alternatives it is evident that the Christian world has been grievously mistaken from the very first, and the sooner it shakes itself free from the incubus of so dead a weight upon its ethical progress, the better for both it and mankind in general.

III. There are, however, certain considerations to be borne in mind which may well modify such impressions of the 'unpractical' nature of Christ's demands.

In the first place, it is not unreasonable to think that the Jewish-Christians of those early days were in a better position to understand them than we are. They were Orientals, to whom figures of speech and hyperbole of statement were matters of course. It would never have occurred to them to suppose that if their right eye, or their right hand, was a cause of sin they were intended to pluck it out, or cut it off, literally (v. 29, 30).[2] Even our grosser Western minds do not imagine that our Lord's charge not to let our left hand know what our right hand doeth when we give an alms can be carried

---

[1] A. Schweitzer reviews modern arguments adduced to show that Jesus was the subject of mental delusions, and decides against them on purely medical and psychical grounds (*Expositor*, Oct., Nov., Dec., 1913).

[2] No Jew would have followed Origen in mutilating himself (xix. 12). But Origen knew no Hebrew till some forty years later. It is strange that they who insist on the necessity of poverty for believers do not also insist on their being blind (John ix. 41).

out verbally (vi. 3). Neither is it likely that those early believers would have dreamed that the Master meant them to give to every one who asked them, regardless of their knowledge of the person in question.

Besides this primary advantage of the early Jewish believers, which they share with Orientals in general, they also had personal experience of the pressure of the Law, certainly of the Mosaic and Oral, possibly even of the moral, in a stronger degree than most of us to-day. The burden, for that in a real sense it was a burden has been shown in the preceding Lecture, had rested so heavily upon them that they were more prepared than we are to grasp the truth of the liberty of the Gospel, and therefore less likely to misunderstand the demands of the Messiah, and to see in them so many fresh clauses of a new and stricter code. Law, alas, came into the Church, and largely spoiled the Gospel, as we have seen, but it is probable that the Jewish-Christians for whom St. Matthew wrote were better able than we to disentangle the two, even although some of them thought that it was desirable to observe certain precepts and ceremonies to which they had been accustomed from their youth up. This, however, was something very different from imagining that the demands in the Sermon on the Mount formed paragraphs and sections of a new code.

Secondly, it is of supreme importance for the right understanding of the Sermon that we should not detach single demands from their context, or fail to consider them in relation to the Sermon as a whole.

No doubt it is especially to the Sermon as a whole that objections have been made. It omits so much, we are told. There is, it is said, in all the New Testament, 'no adequate place for the knightly virtue of actively redressing wrong'[1]—a strange taunt, surely, when the chivalry of mediæval Christianity claimed to be prompted by Christ's teaching, and, as far as it actually was free from self-seeking, did undoubtedly draw its inspiration from it. The demand: 'All things therefore whatsoever ye would that men should do unto you, even so do ye also unto them' (vii. 12), is, after all, not a bad substitute for details of rules of redressing wrong, even if it does not, as probably it does, lie at the very foundation of all the improvement effected in social life since it was first uttered.[2]

But, it is urged, 'the nineteenth chapter of Leviticus is a far more complete moral code than the Sermon on the Mount, in spite of the important Jewish teaching that makes up the greater part of the contents of the Sermon.'[3] There is no accounting for taste, and every one must be allowed to have his own opinion of the comparative moral worth of a chapter which seems to place the rounding of the corners of the head, and the marring of the corners of the beard, on as high a pedestal as fearing one's mother and father (the order is that of Lev. xix. 3). But even if the case were made out that Leviticus contained a 'more complete moral code,' what of it?

---

[1] Paulsen, in Montefiore, *The Synoptic Gospels*, p. 518.

[2] Would the objectors have been satisfied if Christ had taught the principles of Bushido, 'the Way of Fighting Knights,' viz. loyalty, politeness, bravery, faithfulness, and simplicity, together with a sincere spirit? Are not these all contained in that one demand? See the article on Ethics and Morality (Japanese) in the *Encyclopædia of Religion and Ethics*, v. 499 *sq.*

[3] G. Friedlander, *Sources*, p. 85. See also Montefiore, *The Synoptic Gospels*, p. 522.

JEWS INDICT THE SERMON

Is there any sign in the Sermon on the Mount that it claimed to present a complete code, or even a code at all? We cannot but think that objections brought against it on the score of omissions are due to a complete misunderstanding of its nature.

A much more serious indictment is that the demands of the Sermon are too high for the average man. 'It is,' says a modern Jewish writer, 'the distinction of the Mosaic rule of life that it requires no impossible, superhuman effort, no seclusion or morbid saintliness, to carry out our duty to God and man, while it leaves at the same time a wide field for our spiritual development, so that, like the Jewish prophets, we may rise to the noblest conceptions of our purpose in life.'[1] Or again: 'The vision of Jesus was that of an apocalyptic dreamer, his message was eschatological, and therefore of little practical value for everyday life.'[2] And once more: 'It is contended by Jewish critics that the defect in the ethical teaching of Jesus is that it is strung so high that it has failed to produce solid and practical results just where its admirers vaunt that it differs from, and is superior to, the ethical codes of the Pentateuch, the Prophets and the Rabbis. . . . The bow is so bent that it snaps altogether. . . . The injunction, "Love your enemies," is an injunction which has failed to produce a result. It was conspicuously violated by Jesus himself, who, if he had loved his enemies, would not have called them vipers, or enthusiastically predicted their arrival in hell;[3] it has always been conspicuously

---

[1] P. Goodman, *The Synagogue and the Church*, p. 277.

[2] G. Friedlander, *Sources*, pp. 262 *sq*.

[3] I keep the phrase, shocking parody though it is of our Lord's solemn utterances.

violated by his disciples. . . . What, then, are we to say of a teaching which has so conspicuously failed in practical result ? " By your fruits shall ye be judged, " said Jesus, and by its fruits his new and superfine teaching stands condemned.'[1] ' It is contrary,' writes another Jewish scholar, ' to sound human nature to love a man who has made himself hated by his infamous behaviour. Even Jesus and his disciples who taught " Love your enemies " did not act in agreement with their saying.'[2] The Sermon is unpractical for the average man. Now we may freely grant the truth of this indictment. For the average man—the man, in fact, in whom the love of the world predominates—will always find the demands set forth by Christ too exacting for him. He is certain either to pass them by, regardless of them altogether, or vainly to endeavour to tone them down to his own capabilities and desires.

But—and this merits particular attention—were these demands ever intended for the average man ? Are they not rather addressed to those who are desirous of doing the will of God from the heart, and meant for them as long as life shall last, and up to, and including, every stage of progress that they shall make ? Are they not intended for the most advanced, the most spiritually perfect, of Christ's followers, to the end of all time ?

---

[1] Montefiore, *The Synoptic Gospels*, pp. 523 *sq.* See also his *Outlines of Liberal Judaism*, 1912, pp. 341–343. It should be observed that Mr. Montefiore, speaking in his own person, says : ' How far is all this criticism just and fair ? Some of it seems beside the mark.' See below, p. 243.

[2] Scheftelowitz, in Brann's *Monatschrift*, 1912, p. 367. For the last sentence see also Montefiore, *The Synoptic Gospels*, p. 525. ' He rather reviled the Scribes than prayed for them ; he returned their antagonism with antagonism, and his denunciations show anything rather than love.'

vi] **THE SERMON ADDRESSED TO BELIEVERS ONLY**

We are told, forsooth, that the Sermon 'sets forth the indispensable characteristics of all who would enter the Messianic kingdom.'[1] 'Indispensable!' Where is this in the Sermon? And in what meaning is it true? If it be meant that no one can become a member of the kingdom unless he fulfils all the demands made upon him in the Sermon, then indeed the so-called Gospel of Jesus of Nazareth was no good news at all, but the harshest of harsh laws and conditions. Then, indeed, the Church has made a fatal error in her whole conception of the life and work of Him whom she worships as her Saviour from sin and Deliverer from the bondage of the Law.

But if it be meant that the characteristics enjoined in the Sermon will be found eventually to mark every one of the perfected saints, whether he be in heaven or on earth, we cannot quarrel with the term 'indispensable.' For in this sense it is true, true gloriously and eternally, and to the praise of God.[2]

For when we consider the Sermon as a whole, we see that it is addressed to true believers in God, men who venture themselves wholly upon Him, and *to them alone*.

Mindful of the Baptist's cry, 'Repent ye; for the kingdom of heaven is at hand,' and of his warning

[1] G. Friedlander, *Sources*, p. 91.

[2] The Law of Moses is said to be practical, and easy to be kept by ordinary people. Certainly, if it be taken at its surface value only; but certainly not, if its meaning be examined conscientiously, and its principles be understood aright, with a true perception of the far-reaching nature of its claims. It is one of the vital differences between popular Judaism and true Christianity that the former fails to appreciate the Law of Moses at its true worth, and the latter magnifies it and makes it honourable. See further the writer's *Manual of Christian Evidences*, §§ 173–179.

of the approach of One who would cleanse His threshing-floor, gathering the wheat and burning the chaff (iii. 2, 11, 12); mindful also of the proclamation by the new Teacher Himself: 'Repent ye; for the kingdom of heaven is at hand' (iv. 17); the multitudes gathered round Him on the mountainside to hear the demands He made upon His followers. What did they expect to hear? What did they desire? Do this? Do that? Observe these ceremonies? Keep those rules? Avoid this and that sin? Practise certain good actions? They did hear nothing of the kind, but ' Blessed are the poor in spirit: for theirs is the kingdom of heaven.'[1] What a contrast! What glorious good news! The Gospel in its freedom, passing the understanding of the clever and the learned, but welcomed by every man, scholar or untrained, dull or brilliant, rich or poor, Gentile or Jew, who was conscious of his need and knew his poverty. Laden with the burden of endless duties, an eloquent writer has said, the multitude stood before Jesus, ready to take on them His uttermost command, and they heard, instead of ' Thou shalt,' a benediction, enfeoffing them with the highest thing there is—on the one condition that they knew their dependence upon God, and hungered and thirsted after Him.[2]

---

[1] Probably *vv.* 4-9 are only an explanation and expansion of this fundamental thought. The necessity of becoming as little children (xviii. 3) is the same truth expressed in other words.

[2] See the very remarkable work by Dr. Johannes Müller, *Die Bergpredigt, verdeutscht und vergegenwärtigt*, 3rd edition, 1911, p. 39. It is true that in St. Luke's account of the Sermon the phrase 'in spirit' is absent, but we are considering St. Matthew's presentation of the Messiah, and, in any case, whatever the original form may have been it is probable that St. Matthew gives the original sense. If so, the gibe that ' as the Sermon was delivered

HUMILITY

Now, it is quite true that Jews felt of old the necessity of humility before God, and were well aware of the grave danger of spiritual pride. In Ecclus. iii. 17, we read: 'My son, go on with thy business in meekness; so shalt thou be beloved of an acceptable man. The greater thou art, humble thyself the more, and thou shalt find favour before the Lord. For great is the potency of the Lord, and he is glorified of them that are lowly.' It was no new thing, therefore, for Christ to insist upon this. Nay, did not Jewish teachers of the next century (and they may well have been repeating the words of His contemporaries) forbid Jews to stand on anything raised, even a footstool, when they prayed to God, that thus their thoughts might be kept humble? [1] The same fear of anything that might induce pride directed the pious man not to take hasty steps or walk upright: For 'Mar said, he who walks upright even four cubits is as though he pressed down the feet of the Shekinah, for it is written: all the

---

only to the narrow circle of disciples, who were very poor people, the first message is to encourage them' (G. Friedlander, *Sources*, p. 18), loses its force. Besides, it may be doubted whether the first disciples were such 'very poor people' (*vide supra*, p. 227, n. 5).

It should be noticed that if the first Benediction gives, as is probable, the key-note of the Sermon, then to speak of the Sermon as standing in the same relation to the New Testament that the Ten Commandments hold to the Old Testament (Gore, *The Sermon on the Mount*, opening words) is misleading. For our Lord's object in it is to bring men to a sense of their own weakness and dependence upon God, and, while maintaining that attitude, to aim at nothing less than likeness to Him.

On the other hand, Jews strangely pervert Christian teaching, when they can write: 'The Church has placed salvation, not on what men do, but on what they believe to have once happened' (P. Goodman, *The Synagogue and the Church*, p. 275). The Epistle of St. James ought to have saved even the most cursory reader from so grave an error.

[1] Tosephta, *Berakoth*, iii. 17.

earth is full of His glory.'[1] Similarly, one should always have a covering on one's head at prayer,[2] and indeed at other times.[3]

The same motive has suggested, in all probability, the habit of bowing at certain of the Jewish forms of Benediction, because to do so tends to increase the sense of unworthiness in the presence of God.[4] For humility was the chief of all graces. 'R. Joshua son of Levi said: Humility is greater than them all, for it is said: The spirit of the Lord GOD is upon me, because He hath anointed me to preach good tidings to the humble. He does not say: To the pious, but to the humble. You see that humility is greater than them all.'[5]

If, then, the importance of humility before God was so frankly recognised by Jewish theologians, why did Christ insist so much on it? For a reason that underlay much of His teaching. It was necessary for Him sometimes to place accepted truths in a different position and setting from that which they already possessed, and sometimes to recall to the religious sense of the bulk of the people what they were in danger of forgetting. It is quite true that there is much in the Old Testament about humility of soul being the only right attitude for a sinful man, and also that there is not a little in the teaching of the Rabbis to the same effect. But he who knows his own heart will be the first to admit that there is no truth, which, in practice, is so easily overlooked or shunned. It is probable that our Lord saw that the teaching of the Old Testament with respect to

---

[1] T.B. *Berakoth*, 43b.   [2] Mishna, *Berakoth*, v. 1; *cf.* ix. 5.
[3] See *Jewish Encyclopedia, s.v.* Bareheadedness, ii. 532.
[4] See Jastrow, *Dictionary, s.v.* שחה, p. 1546b; Tosephta, *Berakoth,* i. 5. The frequent bowings of Aqiba are mentioned in Tosephta, *Berakoth*, iii. 5.
[5] *Abodah Zarah*, 20b.

'POVERTY OF SPIRIT' ESSENTIAL

humility of soul was not being carried out, and therefore He insisted upon it, teaching that poverty of spirit (another phrase for humility in its best and strongest form) was the most necessary of all things for His own followers.

In other words, He acted like many a Mission-preacher in our Churches to-day, who brings no new truths, and says nothing that has not been known, or ought to have been known, long before. Yet often the result of his coming is that the lives of many are changed, and religion becomes quite a new thing to them. So, as regards humility before God, Christ taught nothing that had not been already laid down by Lawgiver, Prophet, and Psalmist, and was to be taught sometimes by Scribe and Rabbi, but He so expounded it that the truth went home to many who had not grasped its significance before, and it was to them the very essence of the Good News which He came on earth to bring.

Hence if passages are adduced from either the Old Testament or later Jewish authorities to show that such humility of spirit was already taught, namely, that true religion consisted not in the doing of good actions as such, but in self-abasement before God, we do not deny it. What we do say is that at the time when the Lord Jesus came, and indeed ever since, the Jewish nation as a whole (we do not speak of individuals) has not accepted this truth, but has proceeded on quite other lines as means of salvation. We Christians cannot boast; we have fallen into the same error ourselves. For centuries and centuries the Church, like the Jewish nation, refused to humble itself before God, and, consciously or unconsciously, looked for salvation as the effect of its own good deeds.

When therefore Mr. Montefiore allows that the Sermon on the Mount 'contains nothing that is essentially antagonistic to Judaism,'[1] we cordially agree, if only we are permitted to interpret the word 'Judaism' in its highest meaning. But not otherwise. For, by the necessity of the case, the Sermon is 'essentially antagonistic' to a great deal that passes for Judaism, as it is to much that is called Christianity. In fact, the whole of it, when rightly understood, is specifically contrary to that conventional notion of religion held by the 'average man,' whether he be a baptized Christian or a circumcised Jew.[2]

If this interpretation of the Sermon be right, that it is addressed not to the average man, but to him who is 'poor in spirit,' it is evident that the punctilious performance of its detailed demands is but unintelligent, and even hypocritical, when the presupposed condition of humble dependence on God is lacking. But if it be present, then the observance of these demands is but the natural result of such a spiritual state.

For, after all, they are the proper outgrowth of love to God, which fulfils itself in many ways, and knows no limit to its activity and expansion. Opponents, as we have seen, say that it is impossible for us to love our enemies. It may rather be doubted whether it is possible for a person who possesses any true love to help loving them. If God loves His foes,

---

[1] *The Synoptic Gospels*, p. 555. On the next page he modifies this remark by enumerating passages which he thinks objectionable, but he evidently regards them as minor blemishes in 'a religious document of the highest nobility, significance, and power.' Mr. G. Friedlander is very vexed with him (*Sources*, pp. 262-266).

[2] It need hardly be mentioned that such a sense of one's own dependence on God stands in no kind of contradiction to true self-respect.

THE IDEAL LIFE

the Christian as such can do no less. If he fails to love them, so far he is not moved by Divine love at all.[1]

It is, however, surely needless to say that Christ contemplates no blind performance of His demands—demands in such a case made by an authority external, and solely external, to him who would do them. Don Quixote is not the ideal of humanity. Love must take into full account the effect of its every action, and if, in any given circumstances, an act of love is likely to prove to be an act of ill, the would-be doer of it cannot but pretermit its doing.

'There is a real danger,' writes the Bampton Lecturer of a few years ago, 'in all hasty and ill-considered attempts to relieve distress; the danger that while we feed the hungry and clothe the naked we may rob them of honesty and self-respect. But that does not mean that we are to make no effort; it means more effort—the very hard and distasteful effort to understand the evils on which our comfort and prosperity are based.'[2] The fact is that Christ's demands, whether they refer to almsgiving, or riches, or marriage, or avoidance of oaths, all contemplate our thoughts and actions under what has been called

[1] *Cf.* Dr. Johannes Müller, *Die Bergpredigt*, p. 171. 'Man kann in Wahrheit nur lieben, wenn man lieben muss. Darum muss auch die Liebe zu den Feinden eine impulsive Äusserung ursprünglichen Empfindens sein, wenn sie echt sein soll.' The whole passage deserves study. Mr. Montefiore appears to be feeling after this philosophical, and therefore Christian, truth in his sympathetic remarks on pp. 343 *sq.* of his *Outlines of Liberal Judaism.* Prof. James Denney writes: 'He is to find in love alone his impulse and his guide, and he is to go all lengths with love' (*The Literal Interpretation of the Sermon on the Mount*, p. 40).

'Dole not thy duties out to God,
But let thy hand be free.'—FABER, *Hymns.*

[2] Peile, *The Reproach of the Gospel*, 1907, p. 110. It may be noted that the bathos of the last clause is not apparent in its original context.

the 'subjugation to a unifying principle which controls the life.'[1] When we are ruled by that, the supreme principle of dependence on God and fellowship with Him, all else in us falls into its proper place. So far, and only so far, as we are receptive of Him, remaining in His love and under His influence, are we able to carry out the ideal life described in the Sermon.[2]

It is then probable that our Lord had no intention of bidding His followers observe the demands contained in these three chapters of the Gospel according to St. Matthew unless they complied with the first and greatest of all—conscious self-abasement before God, and dependence upon Him. For this raises a man's whole tone, and, as a consequence, his one desire is to do the complete will of God. Henceforth he is not satisfied with the performance of duties, even though they were ordered by Christ Himself. He wants to carry out the whole will of God, so far as he can understand it, and he expects to understand it better the more he carries it out. To him directions as such are comparatively unimportant. Words, he knows well, are not commensurate with Divine demands, and cannot adequately express them. The circumstances of life are too many for verbal orders to cover, even if they could be given time after time. He is glad, no doubt, to have such verbal orders, so far as they go, but he knows that to obey them always and *au pied de la lettre* would sometimes be to disobey their import. He is compelled, therefore, to interpret

---

[1] A. E. F. Macgregor in Hastings, *E.R.E.* v. 408, *s.v.* Ethical Discipline.

[2] In contrast to the principle of the world that might is right, the foundation of the social ethics of the kingdom of God is that greatness is commensurate with service to others (Matt. xx. 26). Compare H. J. Holtzmann, *N.T. Theologie*, i. 232. After all, this is but another side of the Prayer Book saying: *Cui servire regnare est.*

them in accordance with the surroundings of his life, and the character of the persons with whom he is brought into contact.[1] No doubt this is much harder than to obey commands literally, however difficult, for he has continually to keep in touch with the Divine Source of life and wisdom, in order to perceive the ' nexte thynge ' that he must do. But this is inseparable from his new position. He has entered on fellowship with God, and he has to apply to the details of his life the superhuman knowledge day by day imparted to him.[2]

That the commands we find in the Sermon on the Mount express the highest form of Divine and therefore Christian morality we do not doubt, but we perceive also with increasing clearness that for us to attempt to keep them literally, regardless of the effect of doing so, would in many cases stultify our lives. The Christian man will prepare for them ; he will hold them ever before him as the ideal of what a Christian life should be, but he will put them into practice in their literal meaning only so far as complete, not partial, opportunities are given to him.[3]

But if the Sermon on the Mount is held as a whole

---

[1] Compare Martensen, *Ethics, Individual*, § 100.

[2] In measure he has the experience of the Son, who 'can do nothing of himself, but what he seeth the Father doing ; for what things soever he doeth, these the Son also doeth in like manner' (John v. 19). Prof. James Denney writes : ' The mind of Jesus will be reached, not when we keep His words as we observe the terms of an Act of Parliament, but when the consciousness of God in our hearts is like what it was in His ' (*The Literal Interpretation of the Sermon on the Mount*, p. 50).

[3] Mr. Montefiore says that the method of the bishop in *Les Misérables*, who by his extraordinary kindness won the heart of the convict, would not always succeed. ' One needs to *be that bishop* to try it with likelihood of good results ' (*The Synoptic Gospels*, p. 517). Quite so ; not a single demand in the Sermon, or several of its demands, but the whole of it, including the first verse, is the condition of influence.

to be unpractical for the individual, it is accused of being utterly subversive of society and the nation. 'Tolstoi says that the doctrine of the Gospel would do away with States and tribunals, property and individual rights. The fact is that Jesus here, as elsewhere, enunciates a principle that would destroy the structure of society.'[1] 'This advice not to show resistance,' writes M. Loisy, 'may suit a small select band in a world which is about to come to an end, or men devoted to an extraordinary mission which requires from them a renunciation of self as extraordinary as their destiny, but not a society which has to live and perpetuate its existence in order.'[2] So again M. Loisy says: 'A country in which all honest folk were to comply with these maxims, instead of being like the kingdom of heaven, would be the paradise of robbers and villains.'[3] Even Dr. Sanday writes: 'The ethical ideal of Christianity is the ideal of a Church. It does not follow that it is also the ideal of the State. If we are to say the truth, we must admit that parts of it would become impracticable if they were transferred from the individual standing alone to governments or individuals representing society.'[4]

Yet the same principle applies to this objection as to the former: and this is what we should expect. For it is a desperate expedient to assert that the ethics of a community or nation are different in kind from those of individuals, and therefore that what Christ demands from the latter He does not contemplate being done by the former.

[1] G. Friedlander, *Sources*, p. 66.
[2] Montefiore, *The Synoptic Gospels*, p. 517.
[3] H. J. Holtzmann, *N.T. Theologie*, i. 230. [4] Hastings' *D.B.* ii. 621b.

NO CHRISTIAN NATION KNOWN

No, it is not possible to find any trace of distinction on Christ's part between individual and social ethics in their character, however wide the variation may be in the scope and theatre of their activity. Indeed for there to be any difference in the ethical laws that finally determine the management of a nation from those that govern an individual would imply the ruin of the latter. The commonwealth being but the aggregation of individuals, the ethics of the constituent parts must surely determine those of the whole. 'The essential unity of individual and social mind'[1] would appear to be an axiom, not requiring proof, but itself the test of every proposition on the subject, theoretical or practical.

The ethics, then, as such are the same. The only question is whether the community or nation is far enough advanced in spiritual life to have made the opening Benediction of the Sermon a reality for itself. If not, it cannot be expected to answer to the further demands of Christ.

It has failed to rise to the opportunity presented to it. For though we have all known Christian men, or men whom, by some stretch of the exact use of terms, it is convenient to call so, we have never seen a Christian nation, much less a Christian world. And, once more, just as it is only in proportion as a

[1] Prof. J. B. Baillie in *E.R.E.* v. 411 on *Ethical Idealism*. He goes on to say that 'Institutions are embodiments of the social spirit, from which individuals themselves derive their moral sustenance and support. . . . Institutions are a more objective and permanent embodiment of the supreme principle in man's life than the actions or the life of a given individual; and conversely we see more fully in institutions what the final end of man is. . . . The operations of the individual mind in realizing its own end, and the operations of the social mind in realizing a common end, proceed on the same plan.' See also Votaw in Hastings' *D.B.* v. 29*b sq.*

nation is Christian that an individual believer can fully carry out the demands of the Sermon, so only in proportion as all the nations are Christian can any one Christian nation do so.

The blame for the present state of things must then not be laid on the Sermon, but on the reception given to the fundamental basis on which its demands rest, to the presupposition underlying them all. Once let an individual be 'poor in spirit,' and maintain as his constant attitude the dependence on God, which that phrase implies, so will he be drawn on to observe the demands with increasing completeness. And thus also will it be with the community, or nation, of such blessed individuals. Let it, in its turn, be truly dependent on God, and it will endeavour to carry out the demands of Christ as far as the condition of the other nations in the world permits.[1]

But when each of these nations, one by one, becomes consciously dependent upon God, and 'the kingdom of the world is become the kingdom of our Lord and of his Christ,' then will the ideal of the Sermon be accomplished, and all alike, whether individuals, or communities, or nations, or the world, will vie in fulfilling the ethical demands made upon His followers by the Great Teacher, Jesus the Messiah.[2]

---

[1] 'Ours till lately was a government of maxims, and perhaps is so in a great measure still. The economists want to substitute a despotism of systems. But who, until the coming of Christ's Kingdom, can hope to see a government of principles?'—A. W. and J. C. Hare, *Guesses at Truth*, 1827 (edition of 1874, p. 236).

[2] It is hardly necessary to point out that as the Sermon is Pauline in its insistence on the sense of dependence on God and His grace, so also is it in making works the final test of character (v. 13-16; vii. 16-27). We may compare the Jewish sayings: 'By their works those who have wrought them are known' (*Secrets of Enoch*, xlii. 14); and 'Whosoever teaches noble things and does them, shall be enthroned with kings' (*Test.* Levi, xiii. 9).

Lecture Seven

THE MESSIAH—THE SON OF DAVID

'Hosanna to the son of David.'—MATT. xxi. 9.

Lecture Seven

THE MESSIAH—THE SON OF DAVID

DURING our study of the presentation of the Messiah to the Jews in the Gospel according to St. Matthew, we have considered Him in relation to the Sadducees and Pharisees, and as the Healer of Disease, and lastly as the Teacher, particularly as He is made known to us in that summary of His doctrine known to us as the Sermon on the Mount. We turn now to three phrases, each of far-extending significance, and each an important part of that picture which the writer of this Gospel desires to portray. These are 'the Son of David,' 'the Son of Man,' and 'the Son of God'; describing Messiah as the ideal Ruler of the Jewish people, the ideal Man in service and in power, and the ideal representative of God Himself.[1]

They are well-known terms, so well known that it is difficult for us to study them dispassionately, without reading into them the connotations given by nearly nineteen centuries of Christian thought, which cannot have been present in full to the mind of the Evangelist. Yet each had a history when St. Matthew selected it for his description of the Christ, and our task now is to try to understand that history, and endeavour to give to each term its rightful meaning, the sense intended by the writer. Each sums up hopes long apparent to the Jewish mind, though

---

[1] The three thoughts are found closely together in xii. 18, 23, 32, and with the substitution of 'the Christ' for 'the Son of David' in xvi. 13, 16; xxvi. 63, 64.

indefinite and vague, but now laid open in the First Gospel in their true significance.

We must consider the phrases separately, doing our best to keep the content of each as distinct as possible from that of the other two. Not indeed that this is easy. For the hopes contained in one tend to run over into those of the others, and when, as here, all three streams plainly and definitely converge on one and the same Person, it is difficult to view them apart, necessary though this is if we would understand their combined strength. For, to change the figure, as it is not possible to appreciate all the teaching of a composite photograph unless we also hold before us the original pictures of which it is made up, so if we are to estimate at its right value the portrait of the Messiah in this Gospel, we must pay the closest attention to each separate delineation of Him, as the nation's King, the perfect Man, the revelation of God.

Thus the subject of this seventh lecture is Messiah the Son of David; that of the eighth will be, Messiah the Son of Man, that of the ninth, Messiah the Son of God. Following these, and closely connected with them, will come one on the Apocalyptists, in which we shall consider the whole question of the relation of the Messiah to the current eschatology of His time.

I. Our theme, then, is: Jesus the Son of David; the King, not of the world (or, if of the world, only so indirectly), but of the nation of the Jews. For a national king was expected, and on the phrase, the Son of David, have been inscribed, as on a register, many and many an expression of the nation's hope, before it was incorporated into St. Matthew's narrative.

VII]   'THE SON OF DAVID'—IN THE O.T.

It is based upon the Old Testament, as, I should suppose, are all other Jewish beliefs and hopes that are of any importance. 'Thus shalt thou say unto my servant David. . . . When thy days be fulfilled, and thou shalt sleep with thy fathers, I will set up thy seed after thee, which shall proceed out of thy bowels, and I will establish his kingdom. He shall build an house for my name, and I will establish the throne of his kingdom for ever. . . . And thine house and thy kingdom shall be made sure for ever before thee: thy throne shall be established for ever.'[1] Starting from this foundation-text the Jews appear to have built up their expectation, that, come what might to the nation, to its city and its polity, there would always be a king, ready to appear in God's good time, a king who should belong to the stock and lineage of David.

So Jeremiah writes: 'They shall serve the LORD their God, and David their king, whom I will raise up unto them.'[2] So also Ezekiel: 'And I will set up one shepherd over them, and he shall feed them, even my servant David; he shall feed them, and he shall be their shepherd. And I the LORD will be their God, and my servant David prince among them; I the LORD have spoken it.'[3] Similarly, he adds later: 'And my servant David shall be king over them; . . . and David my servant shall be their prince for ever.'[4]

Listen again to Isa. lv. 3, 4: 'I will make an everlasting covenant with you, even the sure mercies

---

[1] 2 Sam. vii. 8, 12, 13, 16. The Messianic reference of this passage is assumed by Trypho, and used by him in argument against Justin (*Dialogue with Trypho*, § 68). On v. 14 cf. Lecture IX, p. 313.
[2] Jer. xxx. 9. [3] Ezek. xxxiv. 23 *sq.* [4] *Ibid.* xxxvii. 24 *sq.*

of David. Behold, I have given him for a witness to the peoples, a leader and commander to the peoples.'[1] And we find in Ps. lxxxix. 34–37: 'My covenant will I not break, nor alter the thing that is gone out of my lips. Once have I sworn by my holiness; I will not lie unto David; his seed shall endure for ever, and his throne as the sun before me. It shall be established for ever as the moon, and as the faithful witness in the sky.'[2] The same thought of the certainty of the permanence of the Davidic kingdom underlies passages in Ecclesiasticus and 1 Maccabees: 'The sovereignty was divided, and out of Ephraim ruled a disobedient kingdom. But the Lord will never forsake his mercy; and he will not destroy any of his works, nor blot out the prosperity of his elect; but the seed of him that loved him he will not take away; and he gave a remnant unto Jacob, and unto David a root out of him.'[3] 'David for being merciful inherited the throne of a kingdom for ever and ever.'[4]

The tone of the Pseudepigraphic Writings generally, which (as we shall see in the next Lecture) deal with wider issues than the nation,[5] is not favourable to the mention of the national king.

Yet the seventeenth and eighteenth of the Psalms of Solomon describe Him: 'Behold, O Lord, and

---

[1] Apparently 'the peoples' are non-Jewish.

[2] The signal by which the sight of the new moon was sometimes forwarded to Jerusalem was based on the language of this verse: 'David, the King of Israel, lives and abides for ever' (*Rosh haShanah*, 25a). It may have been, at the same time, a confession of faith in the coming of the Messiah.

[3] Ecclus. xlvii. 21 *sq.* The immediate reference of the passage is, of course, to the permanence of David's line through Rehoboam. *Cf.* the eighth verse of the Hebrew Hymn of Praise inserted after li. 12. See further Oesterley, *The Books of the Apocrypha*, 1914, pp. 281 *sqq.*

[4] 1 Macc. ii. 57.

[5] In this doubtless lies the secret of their preservation by non-Jewish hands.

IN THE PSALMS OF SOLOMON

raise up unto them their king, the son of David,[1] at the time in which thou seest, O God, that he may reign over Israel thy servant. And gird him with strength that he may shatter unrighteous rulers, and that he may purge Jerusalem from nations that trample her down to destruction. . . . With a rod of iron he shall break in pieces all their substance, he shall destroy the godless nations with the word of his mouth; at his rebuke nations shall flee before him, and he shall reprove sinners for the thoughts of their heart. . . . And he shall have the heathen nations to serve under his yoke; and he shall glorify the Lord in a place to be seen of (?) all the earth; and he shall purge Jerusalem, making it holy as of old: so that nations shall come from the ends of the earth to see his glory. . . . And he shall be a righteous king, taught of God, over them, and there shall be no unrighteousness in his days in their midst, for all shall be holy and their king the anointed of the Lord. . . . Blessed shall be they that shall be in those days, in that they shall see the goodness of the Lord which he shall perform for the generation that is to come.'[2]

We may add the following from the Sibylline Books: 'But when Rome shall rule over Egypt as well, as she still hesitates to do, then the mightiest kingdom of the immortal king over men shall appear. And a holy prince shall come to wield the sceptre over all the world unto all ages of hurrying time.'[3]

---

[1] The earliest example of this title of the Messiah (Dalman, *Words*, p. 317).

[2] The translation is from Charles' *Apocrypha and Pseudepigrapha of the Old Testament*, 1913.

[3] iii. 46-50. These verses may belong to the beginning of the first century B.C.

'And then from the sunrise God shall send a king who shall give every land relief from the bane of war: some he shall slay and to others he shall consecrate faithful vows. Nor shall he do all these things by his own will, but in obedience to the good ordinances of the mighty God. And again the people of the mighty God shall be laden with excellent wealth, with gold and silver and purple adornment.'[1] 'But when he (Nero) reaches the zenith of power, and his boldness knows no shame, he shall come fain even to sack the city of the blessed. And then a king sent from God against him shall destroy all the mighty kings and the best of the men.'[2]

In the Syriac Apocalypse of Baruch, written in the end of the first century of our era, we find the following: 'The last leader of that time will be left alive, when the multitude of his hosts will be put to the sword, and he will be bound, and they will take him up to Mount Zion, and My Messiah will convict him of all his impieties, and will gather and set before him all the works of his hosts. And afterwards he will put him to death, and protect the rest of My people which shall be found in the place which I have chosen. And his principate will stand for ever, until the world of corruption is at an end, and until the times aforesaid are fulfilled.'[3]

The Ezra-Apocalypse of about 100 A.D. has a very vivid account of the Messiah, from which the following may be quoted: 'And as for the lion whom thou

---

[1] iii. 652-657. This passage may have been written in the second century B.C.

[2] v. 106-110. This book may have been written in the beginning of the second century A.D. See another quotation in Lecture X, p. 356.

[3] xl. 1-3. See also Lecture X, p. 357.

didst see roused from the wood and roaring, and speaking to the eagle and reproving him for his unrighteousness and all his deeds, as thou hast heard: This is the Messiah whom the most High hath kept unto the end of the days, who shall spring from the seed of David, and shall come and speak unto them; he shall reprove them for their ungodliness, rebuke them for their unrighteousness, reproach them to their faces with their treacheries. For at the first he shall set them alive for judgment; and when he hath rebuked them he shall destroy them.'[1]

The Messiah, however, is for this writer to be a mere man, who shall pass away like other mortals: ' For behold the days come, and it shall be when the signs which I have foretold unto thee shall come to pass, then shall the city that now is invisible appear, and the land which is now concealed be seen; and whosoever is delivered from the predicted evils, the same shall see my wonders. For my Son the Messiah shall be revealed, together with those who are with him, and shall rejoice the survivors four hundred years. And it shall be, after these years, that my Son the Messiah shall die, and all in whom there is human breath. Then shall the world be turned into the primæval silence seven days, like as at the first beginnings; so that no man is left.'[2]

When we turn to the Talmudic and Rabbinic writings, in our endeavour to ascertain what light they throw on the pre-Christian history of the term, we meet the same difficulty as before, that, strictly speaking, they contribute no directly pre-Christian evidence at all. For, as we are well aware, no Jewish

[1] xii. 31-33. Cf. Lecture X, pp. 356 *sq.*
[2] vii. 26-30. On the appellation 'my Son,' see Lecture IX.

uncanonical writing in Hebrew or Aramaic has survived from a date earlier than the first century of our era, save indeed Ecclesiasticus, from which we have already quoted, the lately discovered 'History of Ahikar,' which is of little or no interest in this connexion, and possibly the Fragments of a Zadoqite Work, both the date and the interpretation of which are quite uncertain.

Yet it is evident that if so well known a designation as 'the Son of David' be found not only in Christian books but also on the lips of teachers honoured in the Talmud, it must have been accepted by these earlier than the rise of Christianity. We are justified, therefore, in employing this somewhat late evidence to throw light upon the history of the phrase before the time of St. Matthew.

The important fact is that 'the Son of David' is the one established, as well as the commonest, name for the Messiah in Jewish literature,[1] and although it becomes more frequent in sayings by teachers later than the time of Hadrian than by those who lived earlier, it is sometimes employed by these from Jochanan ben Zakkai (c. 100 A.D.) onwards. He said, 'The Son of David comes not, save in a generation which is all righteous, or all guilty.'[2] So again, Gamaliel II (c. 110 A.D.) teaches, 'As for the generation in which the Son of David cometh the lecture-room will be given up to immorality, Galilee will be laid

---

[1] See Klausner, *Die messianischen Vorstellungen* u.s.w., p. 67. The one exception is the strange idea that He should be of the stock of Levi, to which the fautors of the Hasmonæan dynasty gave expression (*Test.* Reuben, § 6; Levi, § 8; Dan, § 5). See also the *Zadokite Fragments*, ix. 10 (B), 29; xv. 4, and Ecclus. xlv. 23-25 (Hebr.). *Cf.* Oesterley, *The Books of the Apocrypha*, 1914, p. 149, who thinks this was the doctrine of the Sadducees.

[2] T.B. *Sanhedrin*, 98a.

VII] IN THE EIGHTEEN BENEDICTIONS

waste,' and so on.[1] Similarly, in Hosea iii. 5, where the Hebrew reads: 'Afterward shall the children of Israel return, and seek the LORD their God, and David their king,' the Targum has: 'And they will obey Messiah son of David their king.'

Sometimes the connexion with David is expressed slightly differently, or even more directly, though the thought is the same. Thus in the fifteenth prayer of the Babylonian recension of the Eighteen Benedictions we find: 'The Branch of David wilt thou cause to branch forth soon, and his horn shall be exalted in thy salvation.' The Jerusalem Talmud, however, saying 'We pray for David' (*Ber.* ii. 4. p. 5*a*), combines this Benediction with the passage from Hosea. It then continues: 'Our teachers say with reference to this: If king Messiah is among the living, his name is David, if he is among the dead, his name is David.'[2]

But, in fact, the phrase 'the Son of David' was in the Jewish mind so synonymous with 'Messiah' that it is needless to attempt to quote passages from Talmudic and Rabbinic writings descriptive of His work under the former title. It is the more unnecessary as the Talmudic view is the same as that which has been already given. To use the words of a learned Jew: 'In the rabbinical apocalyptic literature the conception of an earthly Messiah is the prevailing

---

[1] *Derek Erets Zuta,* c. 10. In T.B. *Sanhedrin,* 97*a*, the saying is attributed to R. Jehuda; see Bacher, *Die Agada der Tannaiten,* i. 97.

[2] The same remark is found in T.B. *Sanhedrin,* 98*b*, where the clause 'among the living' is illustrated by the case of R. Jehudah the Saint, the compiler of the Mishna, and 'among the dead' by that of Daniel. There is also the addition: 'R. Jehudah reports that Rab said, the Holy One will raise up for them another David, as is said in Jer. xxx. 9.'

one, and from the end of the first century of the common era it is also the one officially accepted by Judaism. . . . His mission is, in all essential respects, the same as in the apocalypses of the older period: he is to free Israel from the power of the heathen world, kill its ruler and destroy its hosts, and set up his own kingdom of peace.'[1]

'The Son of David,' then, sums up an important side of the character and work of Messiah, as He was depicted in Jewish thought of immediately pre-Christian times; namely, that He was to be of the stock of David, and a conqueror like David, leading His nation to victory, giving to the Gentiles peace if they accepted His rule, restoring to Israel itself the blessings of a just government, and material prosperity.[2]

That this was indeed the hope of Israel may be seen further by the character of those who claimed to be Messiahs. For declaring themselves agents of the LORD, they led the people to war against their earthly oppressors. The only two who are little more than names to us are Judas of Galilee and Barcochba, separated indeed by about 120 years, but identical in spirit. Both were zealous for Israel, and for the deliverance of God's people from their enemies. Each secured, either at once or ultimately, a large number of adherents, the former among the untutored inhabitants of Galilee, the latter among all classes,

---

[1] Buttenwieser in the *Jewish Encyclopedia*, viii. 510 *sq*. The general truth of this statement is unaffected by the later figment of a Messiah ben Joseph, who was to be killed by the Gentile hosts, while Messiah ben David (after suffering, but not dying) was in turn to conquer these. The earliest evidence for this legend is R. Dosa (c. 250 A.D.) in T.B. *Sukkah*, 52 *a, b*.

[2] It is not necessary to show that the books of the New Testament outside the First Gospel fully confirm the prevalence of a hope of this kind.

JESUS THE KING

including even Aqiba, the typical Pharisee, the light and joy of every pious Jew from that day to this.[1] An earthly king, using worldly means, successful in war, restoring political independence and material prosperity, and bringing about everything ideal in government—this was what the Jews meant by their title 'the Son of David,' and such a Messiah they expected. Yet St. Matthew dares to claim that the meek and gentle Jesus of Nazareth was the rightful heir to this title, was in very truth the Son of David, the hope of his people. A bold claim indeed!

The obvious objection of the literalist is that Jesus was never crowned with a golden crown, nor formally installed with human pomp and ceremony; and never reigned in any tangible sense over country or any city.[2] Yet it is undeniable that if a king is one whom persons obey, and is the more fully king in proportion as they who obey him are greater in number and yield completer service, then of men born of women there never has been one to whom the title ought more ungrudgingly to be given than to Jesus of Nazareth. Besides, the orthodox Christian contention, and also, as will appear, the view put forth by the Evangelist, is that Jesus, the Son of David, has not even yet entered into full enjoyment of His title, but is now like an earthly king between the moment of his accession and the day on which he is crowned amid the shouts and applause of his people. The coronation day of the Messiah is still to come.

[1] There is no reason to think that Judas of Galilee was connected with the family of David, and Barcochba certainly was not. But both are examples of the kind of Messiah that was typified to the popular mind by the term 'the Son of David.'

[2] See, for example, R. Isaac of Troki (1533–1594 A.D.) in his *Chizzuk Emunah*, i. §3.

THE HEBREW-CHRISTIAN MESSIAH [LECT.

For this Gospel represents itself as history, and professes to give us facts upon which we can rest our theories. We all know, indeed, that there is in our own day a temporary aberration of philosophical thought, which would attempt to ignore facts, and to insist on spiritual sensations alone, as being the sole evidence of spiritual truths. Spiritual sensations are themselves facts which may not be relegated to the realm of fancy as though they were non-existent. And we dare not, God forbid, underrate the importance of spiritual experience, or forget its supreme importance in the religious life. But it is not scientific to separate such a fact of the spirit from other departments of human life, and say that it is so distinct that it can receive nothing from them, when perhaps it is dependent on them for its very existence. For indeed we may gravely doubt whether ultimately the human mind, as it is, can receive mental and spiritual impressions, save from things altogether external to it. That it must have affinity with them, affinity of some kind, goes without saying. But facts, external and hard facts, are, it may be, the stuff out of which, in the last instance, all spiritual sensations grow. God, the Father of Spirits, uses them, it may be said, as the means whereby He will teach His people of Himself, and give them insight into His nature and character, His methods and His work. If so, we cannot blame the Evangelist for setting forth facts as the foundation of that belief in the Messiah which he desires to build up.

II. 'The book of the generation of Jesus Christ, the son of David.'[1] Although reference was made to

[1] Matt. i. 1.

VII] THE DAVIDIC ORIGIN OF JESUS

these words in the first Lecture, it is necessary to repeat here that in the very opening sentence of the Gospel the writer desires to affirm the claim he is making for Jesus. And he gives, as we have already seen, a whole genealogy to prove his point, arranging it too in such a way as to bring before the minds of the more thoughtful of his earliest readers, Jewish by birth though Christian in creed, the strange vicissitudes of their nation. Generations had come and gone, the visible glory of the Hebrew monarchy had departed, but the line of David had not failed, and the hoped-for scion of the Davidic stock had at last appeared.

Purveyors of paradoxes, no doubt, would fain persuade us that the Davidic origin of Jesus is not a fact at all, nay, that far from being a descendant of David, He had not a drop of Jewish blood in His veins; for, coming as He did from Galilee, He was, without any question, of purely Gentile origin, an Aryan, not a Semite. What are the reasons which have suggested this extraordinary statement, confessedly opposed to the opinion of our Lord's contemporaries, and to that of the whole of history, Jewish and Gentile, until a few years since ? [1]

They appear to be these. Even in the times of the Old Testament Galilee was but sparsely occupied by members of the Hebrew race. Part of it at least was 'Galilee of the Gentiles.' [2] Not only so, but when the Assyrian monarchs had carried off the inhabitants, [3] it was not repeopled by Hebrew blood for several centuries. Even in the time of

---

[1] See the arguments of Professor Paul Haupt of Baltimore quoted in the *Expository Times*, Sept. 1909, pp. 530 *sq*.
[2] Isa. ix. 1.   [3] 2 Kings xv. 29.

Simon the Maccabee (who died in 135 B.C.) the Jews in Galilee must have been but few in number, for they sent to him saying that they were in danger of destruction by their neighbours, and though he went and fought many battles with the Gentiles, and the Gentiles were discomfited before him, he did not dare to leave the Jewish inhabitants there, ' but brought them into Judæa with great gladness.' [1] Nor was it before the reign of Aristobulus I (105–104 B.C.) that Jewish rule was finally established, when many of the Gentile inhabitants were compelled to accept Judaism.[2] From that time, however, the Galileans were considered Jewish. But, as will be observed, the very lateness of the date at which it was possible for many Jewish families to settle there makes it easier to credit the statement of the Evangelist that Joseph was in all strictness a Jew, and of the stock and lineage of David. No long time had elapsed since his family could have lived permanently in Galilee; therefore the ancestral home at Bethlehem was not forgotten.[3] If we have any regard at all for the truthfulness of the statements in the Gospel, it would appear to be impossible that so deeply important a fact as the Jewish origin of Jesus should be a delusion, dependent on a manufactured genealogy, and a more or less conscious exploitation of popular ignorance. The strictly Jewish origin of Jesus of Nazareth appears to be beyond all reasonable question.

It may then be taken for granted that Joseph,

[1] 1 Macc. v. 14–23.
[2] Galilee was at that time part of Ituræa. Josephus, *Antt.* XIII, xi. 3 (§ 319). See Schürer, *G.J.V.* ii. 7.
[3] There are even reasons for supposing that Bethlehem was Joseph's own home. See Canon Box, *The Virgin Birth*, pp. 56–60.

VII] JESUS—JOSEPH'S LEGAL HEIR

the reputed father of Jesus of Nazareth, was in deed and in truth a member of the Jewish race, and also a lineal heir of the founder of the one dynasty which ever reigned over the Jews, David the son of Jesse.

But Joseph was only the reputed father of Jesus, according to the express testimony of our Evangelist. Was then Jesus Himself strictly of David's line? The question of the Virgin birth of our Lord has been already discussed in the first Lecture. Here we must consider it only in so far as it affects the relationship of Jesus to David. Joseph, it may be affirmed, was undoubtedly the descendant of David, but if Jesus was not Joseph's son how is that fact of any interest to us?

Now, it is plain that the right to inheritance in the dynasty was possessed by Joseph, and it would appear from the genealogy that this was complete. If so, the heirship of Jesus was also complete; the unusual character of His birth not affecting it at all. For according to all law, Jewish and Gentile, Jesus being born after, and probably many months after, the marriage, was fully heir to Joseph. No Jew in those days, or, I think, in ours, would seriously deny it. Jesus, then, was in the direct line of inheritance to the throne of David. Whether He was actually the eldest son of Joseph, by the by, matters not. Primogeniture has not that position in the East that it has in England. Bible history may teach us that. Jesus then, born after the marriage of Joseph and Mary, was heir to Joseph.[1]

Yet, if that were all, we in this country, and in

---

[1] Although in Luke ii. 5 Mary is said to be 'betrothed,' this must not be understood in the weak modern sense, for if they had not been married Joseph and she could not have travelled together. See Lecture I, p. 20.

THE HEBREW-CHRISTIAN MESSIAH [LECT.

these days, might still find lurking in our minds an uneasy suspicion that the right of Jesus to be called the Son of David was not justified morally, however much it might be legally. Ideal law is, no doubt, ideal truth. But the English mind is often uneasy about the practical effects of law, and rightly so. St. Matthew was satisfied, as it appears, with having shown the legal relation of Jesus to Joseph. We are not. Is there anything more to be said?

In other words, can it be shown that Mary, the Mother of Jesus, was herself of the Davidic line? I do not ask: Was she in the direct line of legal succession? For that, it may be presumed, she was not. But was she, as well as Joseph, a lineal descendant of David? According to some there was direct evidence in the New Testament, for although the genealogy in the First Gospel was that of Joseph, the one in the Third was Mary's.[1] We can only regret that so easy a method of proving Mary's relationship to David cannot be maintained to-day, and that we are compelled to hold, unless of course fresh evidence should be discovered, that both the genealogies are those of Joseph, St. Luke's giving his natural descent, St. Matthew's his line of inheritance. Direct evidence, then, of the Davidic origin of Mary there is none; the matter was not deemed important by the Evangelists. Yet the balance of probability is that it is true.

For, in the first place, several passages in the New Testament point to this belief. In Luke i. 32 the angel who addresses Mary at the Annunciation tells her that God shall give unto her Son ' the throne

[1] Formally proposed first in 1490 A.D.; but see Irenaeus III. xxi. 9 and xxii. 3.

VII] MARY DESCENDED FROM DAVID

of his father David,' and in verse 69 Zacharias says that God 'hath raised up a horn of salvation for us in the house of his servant David.' So too in Acts ii. 30 St. Peter speaks of God swearing to David that 'of the fruit of his loins he would set one upon his throne,' and applies this promise to Jesus. St. Paul's evidence is especially clear. He, as a learned Jew, knew perfectly well that the Messiah was to be of David's line, yet, though after his conversion he mingled much with Christians who had known the Lord Jesus in the flesh, he never shows the least hesitation in attributing to Him Davidic descent. He writes, for example, in Rom. i. 3 of Jesus: 'who was born of the seed of David according to the flesh.' The New Testament implies, though it does not actually state, the Davidic origin of Mary as well as of Joseph.

Secondly, while it is true that the New Testament may admit of doubt as to the family of Mary, the Christians of the next generation had no doubt at all. They who had seen Apostles and other contemporaries and personal friends of the Lord accepted the Davidic birth of Mary as a fact. See in particular Ignatius (A.D. 110), who says (*To the Ephesians*, xviii. 2), 'For our God Jesus the Christ was conceived of Mary according to the appointment of God, of the seed of David and of the Holy Ghost.'[1]

We may conclude, therefore, that it is probable that, according to the evidence at our disposal, Mary was descended from David, as well as Joseph.

Of the stress laid by the Evangelist on the fact that Jesus was born in Bethlehem, mention has

[1] See the writer's *Manual of Christian Evidences*, §§ 8–13, and the references there.

already been made in the first Lecture. His birth there, though St. Matthew does not say how Joseph and Mary came to be in Bethlehem, was an important part of the argument that Jesus was the Son of David. For this Hope of the nation must fulfil the ancient prophecy connecting the Messiah with Bethlehem, the fount and source of the family of David.

The Evangelist, however, does not only state his own conviction that Jesus was the promised Son of David; he also reports to us occasions when the title was given Him by others. And as we read the examples that he adduces, we can see that the title was known widely among the populace of different parts of Palestine, in Galilee and in Jericho, in the neighbourhood of Tyre and Sidon, and in Jerusalem. We notice also this fact about it, that sometimes the appellation was called forth by the display of miraculous powers.[1]

In particular we notice that in two out of the three cases in which our Lord is addressed by the title 'Son of David' in appeal for restoration to health, the words are uttered by blind men.[2] This suggests that the promises of the prophet in connexion with the Messianic time[3] were interpreted very literally, and that it was expected that when Messiah came He would restore the blind to sight. If so, it was not unnatural that when these poor blind folk were convinced on other grounds that Jesus was that Son of David for whom they were looking, they should appeal to Him for His aid, and ask for restoration

[1] On the question whether Messiah was expected to perform miracles, see Lecture III, p. 105.
[2] ix. 27; xx. 30, 31. The possibility that these two examples are 'doublets' must not be overlooked.
[3] Isa. xxix. 18; xxxv. 5; cf. lxi. 1, R.V. marg.

VII]   THE SON OF DAVID AND MIRACLES

at His hands—and they did not ask in vain.[1] St. Matthew wishes us to understand not only that people addressed Jesus by the title of Son of David, when they were expressing their faith that He could, if He would, perform miracles on them, but that His effective assent showed that He accepted the title and proved it to be true.

The case of the poor Canaanite is not so plain. She had, at least, no verbal assurance in the Old Testament that in the times of Messiah demons were to be cast out. Yet she pleaded with a faith triumphant over apparent rebuff that He, the Son of David, should have pity upon her, for her daughter was 'grievously vexed with a devil.'[2]

Akin to this is the question of all the multitudes who saw Jesus heal one possessed, blind and dumb, 'insomuch that the blind man spake and saw.' In their amazement they said : ' Can this be the Son of David ? '[3] The fact is that whatever may be the reality of possession by evil spirits, and it may be questioned whether science is in a position to affirm or deny this, the belief in them at that time was so closely bound up with the experience of physical disease, that every one felt sure that when Messiah came He would cast out both the one and the other of these tyrants of humanity. If His coming delivered men from illness, and left them still at the mercy of the evil angels, the Messianic age, it was felt, would be little more than a mockery, and the Messiah a delusion. The Son of David, as the Messiah, would certainly set men free from ills of every kind. It was not unnatural, therefore, that the half-heathen woman should appeal to the Son of David in her anxiety

---
[1] See further Lecture III, pp. 106 *sq*.   [2] xv. 22.   [3] xii. 22, 23.

about her daughter, or that the crowds who saw an extraordinary miracle of deliverance performed before their eyes should ask whether indeed this was not perhaps the Messiah for whom they were longing, the Son of David Himself.

At the triumphal entry the case is different. The shout of the multitudes, in front of the Lord and behind Him, is due not to some one display of mercy and health-giving vitality, but to the cumulative effect of all His work, teaching, and life for the past three years amid the Galilean hills. The Prophet Jesus, of Nazareth of Galilee, is now publicly acclaimed as the Son of David : ' Salvation to the Son of David ! Blessed is He that cometh in the name of Jehovah ! Salvation in the highest ! '[1] It would be difficult to determine how far that enthusiastic crowd understood either the life, or the teaching, or the work of Him whom they thus welcomed. We may even express the fear that they had not gone far beyond the aims and intentions of those other Galileans at an earlier stage in His ministry, who (as we are told in the Fourth Gospel) were about to carry Him off by force to make Him king ;[2] but, in any case, our Evangelist's purpose was fulfilled, as he showed that there was something about Jesus of Nazareth which so attracted those who had seen most of Him that they recognised in Him the Messiah, the promised Son of David.

---

[1] xxi. 1-11. 'Hosanna,' meaningless to us, can hardly have lost its force to those whose native tongue was Hebrew or Aramaic. It is another form of the word translated 'having salvation' in Zech. ix. 9, the very prophecy which our Lord was then strangely fulfilling. Whether or not the Galileans perceived this when they cried 'Hosanna' is uncertain. But we may well credit the Evangelist with doing so.

[2] John vi. 15.

vii] THE SON OF DAVID AT JERUSALEM

Nor did the acclamation of the King cease with the entry into the Holy City. Jesus went into the Temple and drove out from God's house of prayer those traders, with their money-bags and their birds, who had presumed to think that the Temple was so safe from all injury that they could treat it as they liked, and then, once more, in that very Temple, but a moment ago the scene of so much worldliness, He healed the blind and the lame, who came up to Him!

Can we wonder that again the cry arises, not this time from rough Galileans, but from the simple-hearted children standing by, 'Salvation to the Son of David'; and that Jesus accepts the title, asking the cavillers if they had never read the eighth Psalm: 'Out of the mouth of babes and sucklings thou didst stablish praise?'[1] As once before our Lord exulted in the revelation of the truth to babes, though it was hidden from the wise and understanding,[2] so now He acknowledges the justice of the application of this title, 'the Son of David,' to Himself, and declares that on the praises of the little ones lies the foundation of witness to His work and character. Jesus, the Evangelist would tell us, Himself accepted the title of the Son of David, and recognised it in the Temple as the salutation not of mere childish minds, but of child-like hearts.

The fact that Jesus accepted the title both earlier in His ministry, as we have seen, and also more particularly in the Temple, is of some guidance to us in our consideration of the next and final occasion on

---

[1] xxi. 12-16. The Hebrew of Ps. viii. 2 is 'strength,' not 'praise,' but the thought seems to be that the strength and majesty of God are made known among men through the utterances of children. *Cf.* Lecture II, p. 70.
[2] xi. 25.

which the words are used in this Gospel. For it has been supposed that when our Lord asked the Pharisees: 'What think ye of the Messiah? Whose son is he?' He did so with the object of showing them their error in answering that He was the Son of David.[1] Jesus, it is said, desired to teach the Jews that the title of the Son of David, which they gave to the Messiah, was mistaken; that it was too closely identified with political and worldly success; that, in fact, the Jewish nation ought to be looking for a Messiah of a very different type, consonant with higher notions of Divine governance; a Messiah who ought *not* to be called by the title ' the Son of David.'[2]

But, frankly, if this supposition is true, why did our Evangelist stultify himself by contradicting what he had already said? He himself shows in the very opening words of his Gospel that he believed that Jesus the Messiah was, in very truth, a descendant of David. Was he in the least likely to say now that Jesus Himself denied it?

Yes, it is replied, that argument is sound. There is no doubt that St. Matthew himself fully believed in the Davidic origin of Jesus, and adduced this discussion with the Pharisees to strengthen his case.[3] But he was wrong; he misunderstood the object with

[1] Matt. xxii. 41-45. So H. J. Holtzmann, *N.T. Theologie*, i. 310-313; *cf.* Wellhausen, *Einleitung in die drei ersten Evangelien*, p. 97; Dalman, *Words of Jesus*, pp. 286, 319.

[2] Those writers, it may be added, who do not believe that Jesus was descended from David, or that He was even of Jewish stock, presumably accept this theory the more gladly, as they are able to see in our Lord's words the implication that it was not necessary for the Messiah to be of David's family at all. Jesus, they say, conscious as He was of His inability to satisfy the popular requirement that the Messiah should be a descendant of David, declared it to be wrong.

[3] See H. J. Holtzmann, *N.T. Theologie*, i. 311, 500.

which the argument was introduced. There indeed I might leave it. For if we grant that the meaning of the Evangelist is plain, that is all that is required for the purpose of these lectures, which endeavour to show St. Matthew's presentation of the Christ. But surely we may in this case go further, and say that it is extremely unlikely that the Evangelist's opinion is mistaken. For unless we repudiate the whole texture of his Gospel, we must allow that the claim to be the Son of David was accepted by Jesus Himself, four or five times over, and willingly and gladly. There is no hint that He blamed those who addressed Him by this title. But He did rebuke the authorities of the Temple for professing indignation with the children for using it of Him, and then He directly commended the children for their utterance. He knew that He was the Son of David, and accepted the term from old and young.

Yet it may be granted that there is this much truth in the new explanation: that Jesus desired to draw the mind of the people away from a merely worldly view of the nature and work of the Son of David. If so, the object of our Lord's questions was not indeed, as used to be thought, to teach directly the fact of His Divine Sonship, but to correct a false impression of the *meaning* of the title. The Messiah, He says, must hold a different relationship to David from that low and carnal imitation which you Pharisees attribute to Him, for He is to be seated at the right hand of God, and David calls Him Lord. ' If David then calleth Him Lord, *how* is He his son ? ' Must there not then be something in Him which is greater than the standard of David's reign, higher than David's character, and perhaps even his nature ? ' The Son of David ' was the most universal, and the favourite, appellation of the longed-for Messiah, but, hints Jesus, the Old Testament, nay, one of the very Psalms attributed to David himself, suggests that He is more. The title of the Son of David, however true it is in itself, does not satisfy the Divine description of the hoped-for Deliverer. That David called Him Lord shows that the title ' the Son of David,' though right and true, is not commensurate with the reality.

This appears to have been the Lord's reason for His questions, and certainly St. Matthew's for recording them. For it is evident that to the Evangelist the phrase ' the Son of David ' seemed applicable indeed to Jesus, but partial and inadequate. He was, no doubt, the King, the National King, but of a kind far above the popular notion of the Son of David. He was no mere politician, no mere conqueror, and no mere lawgiver, who, by force or fascination, was able to secure obedience to His commands. While the connotation of the phrase was wrong, in so far as it credited the coming King with worldly aims and methods, the Evangelist showed that in reality He moved on a higher level, and worked with better-tempered tools.

For the Christ of St. Matthew is different from the Christ of Judaism in this respect ; that whereas the latter appears suddenly, sent by God to accomplish the salvation of Israel, without any regard paid to His previous life and character, these are so interwoven in the First Gospel that the deliverance wrought is the outcome of the previous preparation. In Judaism the work of Messiah is an abrupt display of the power of God, acting through one, who, worthy of all honour, no doubt, for what he does, is only an instrument, showing in his life, apart

VII] AN INCOMPLETE DESCRIPTION OF MESSIAH

from his success, no such attractiveness, or extraordinary personality, as would lead men to risk danger and death for his dear sake. There is nothing lovable about the Jewish Messiah. He is the Son of David, but, if free from David's faults, as confessedly he is, he also lacks his winsomeness; not one mighty man, much less three, would venture a life to draw him water from the well, if he were to thirst for it ![1]

'The Son of David' was in fact an incomplete description of the Messiah. That it was His popular title in Judaism at the time, and has been ever since, does but show an ineffective grasp of the truth foretold about Him, and an unworthy appreciation of His work. It was the aim of St. Matthew to prove that although Jesus was in very truth the expected Son of David, He far exceeded the contents of the title perceived by contemporary thought, in His words and His deeds, His character and even His nature; that He satisfied not political and social hopes alone, but also the fullest claims of ethics and of religion; that He held the highest place as regards both Jews and Gentiles; that, lastly, He was not only the instrument, but also the messenger, of God, to Whom He stood in a relation quite unique; in fact, that if we are to have a true and full conception of the Messiah we must acclaim Him with the titles of not the Son of David only, but the Son of man also, and even the Son of God.

[1] 2 Sam. xxiii. 15, 16. The lack of attractiveness in the Jewish Messiah does not seem so grave a fault to Jews as it does to us. For with them the person of the Messiah does not hold the same commanding position. They think chiefly of the Messianic age, we more of Him who has loved us and given Himself for us, that He may at last bring that Messianic age to pass; Compare Dalman, *Words of Jesus*, p. 316.

Lecture Eight

THE MESSIAH—THE SON OF MAN

'*The Son of man hath not where to lay his head.*'— MATT. viii. 20.

'*The Son of man is lord of the sabbath.*'—MATT. xii. 8.

'*Henceforth shall ye see the Son of man sitting at the right hand of power.*'— MATT. xxvi. 64.

Lecture Eight

THE MESSIAH—THE SON OF MAN

I. IN the rich plain of Shinar, watered then, as in our own near future, by streams drawn from Tigris and Euphrates, the Prophet walked in prayer by Chebar. And as he gazed on the sunset, ever the glory of lea and marsh, the feathering clouds, half-hiding, half-enhancing, the rays, framed themselves before him into a holy vision of things beyond the sky.[1] From a dazzling centre came the likeness of four living creatures, and this was their appearance; they had the likeness of a man. And every one had four faces, and every one had four wings. And they had the hands of a man. And as for the likeness of their faces, they had the face of a man, and of a lion, and of an ox, and of an eagle. They were like burning coals of fire; they ran and returned as the appearance of a flash of lightning. Beside them and beneath them, and in union with them, were four wheels, a wheel within a wheel, perfect in motion they turned not when they went. Above was the likeness of a firmament, like the colour of the crystal, and above the firmament the likeness of a throne, as the appearance of a sapphire: and upon the likeness of the throne was a likeness

---

[1] *The Illustrated London News* of Feb. 8, 1908, contains a picture of a sunset seen not long before by the river Chebar. During the afterglow, Dr. A. Hume Griffith, a medical missionary in Mesopotamia, 'saw the sky lit up with rays of various hues, projecting like the spokes of a wheel from the setting sun. From either side of the sun wings seemed to issue. The period of the year was the same as that referred to in Ezekiel.'

as the appearance of a man upon it above, as of fire, with brightness round about Him like as of the rainbow.[1] 'This was the appearance of the likeness of the glory of the LORD.... And he said unto me, Son of man.'[2]

'Son of man!' Was Ezekiel thus addressed only to make him feel the more intensely his difference from that glorious vision, him, frail man compared with the inhabitants of heaven, and the majesty of God? Or was there not this intention also, to remind him that though he was an exile in a foreign land, far from Zion's temple, and amidst idolatrous heathen, he, as man, not as Israelite or Jew but man, had something in common, not with the highest beings of creation only, but even with Him who sat on the throne, above the living creatures and the living wheels, Him who had the appearance of a man, the Charioteer of all? Son of man! For man the Prophet was, and should have his share of suffering and pain. Son of man! For manhood is in the seraphs and in God Himself! The Prophet should share their glory![3]

---

[1] Called specifically 'the God of Israel' in x. 20; *cf.* xi. 22.

[2] Ezek. i. and ii. 1. '*Adam*, the more generic term for man, is used in every case, not '*ish*, the more specific.

[3] Kimchi is on the right track when he says on Ezek. ii. 1: 'The interpreters have explained the passage to mean that God called Ezekiel Son of man to prevent him being lifted up with pride, and reckoning himself as one of the angels because he had seen this great vision. But the right explanation to my mind is: Because he saw the face of a man (or possibly "of Adam") in the Chariot He told him that he was upright and good in His eyes, and he was the son of a man (or "of Adam"), and not the son of a lion, or the son of an ox, or the son of an eagle.' It should be noted, however, that it is extremely improbable that *ben'adam* in Ezek. ii. is to be translated 'Son of Adam,' for it is impossible that '*adam* can mean Adam in i. 26, and ii. 1 follows too closely to permit a change of meaning. It must be 'Son of man.' Dr. E. A. Abbott (*The Son of Man*, 1910) brings out more plainly

'SON OF MAN' IN DANIEL VII

The Vision of Daniel (Dan. vii.) was different. He saw four great beasts come up from the sea, diverse one from the other. The first was like a lion, and had eagle's wings; the second like a bear; the third like a leopard, having four heads; the fourth beast terrible and powerful, strong exceedingly, and it had ten horns. Then, after these awful forms of brute creation, he beheld thrones placed, and one that was ancient of days did sit: his raiment was white as snow, and the hair of his head like pure wool; his throne was fiery flames, and the wheels thereof burning fire. The judgment was set; the books were opened; the beasts were judged. Then the writer adds: 'I saw in the night visions, and, behold, there came with the clouds of heaven one like unto a son of man, and he came even unto the ancient of days, and they brought him near before him. And there was given him dominion, and glory, and a kingdom, that all the peoples, nations, and languages should serve him: his dominion is an everlasting dominion, which shall not pass away, and his kingdom that which shall not be destroyed.'

The interpretation given to the seer is that the four beasts are four kings, or dynasties, and that, after they are judged, ' the kingdom and the dominion, and the greatness of the kingdoms under the whole heaven, shall be given to the people of the saints of the Most High: his kingdom is an everlasting kingdom, and all dominions shall serve and obey him.'

From this we see that though the heathen

than anyone else the importance of this passage in Ezekiel for the interpretation of our Lord's use of the term. For earlier examples of this interpretation see H. J. Holtzmann, *N.T. Theologie*, 1911, i. 324. D. Völter finds also in Exekiel the basis of many of his sayings (*Die Menschensohn-Frage neu untersucht*, 1916).

kingdoms of this world are as brute beasts, and monstrous ones at that, the people of Israel, the saints of the Most High, are like a son of man, a human being, resembling in form, and therefore presumably in character, Him that sat on the throne of fiery flames with its wheels of burning fire, the ancient of days Himself. Never was made higher claim for the superiority of Israel over the heathen than this; and never was claim more justified. Wild beasts may stand for the heathen; Israel alone can be depicted as a man.

Thus while in Ezekiel the words 'Son of man' hint at both sides of human nature, its weakness and also its association with the highest of created beings, and with God Himself; in Daniel the phrase in the first place is restricted to Israel, and in the second suggests moral eminence and likeness to the Divine. Common to both is the intrinsic greatness of human nature because God shares it, but in Ezekiel the thought of its weakness is also present, and in Daniel its ethical outlook, with the limitation of this to Israel.[1]

There is another change in the Parables, or Similitudes, of the Book of Enoch. All suggestion of weakness is gone; gone also is all restriction of the term to Israel. 'And there I saw One who had a head of days, and His head was white like wool, and with

[1] Gressmann attempts to show that the idea of a Man pre-existing in heaven was known earlier than Daniel, and was adapted by him (*Der Ursprung der Israelitisch-jüdischen Eschatologie*, 1905, pp. 336–349). See also Box, *J.T.S.*, April 1912, pp. 326 *sq.*; *Ezra-Apocalypse*, 1912, pp. 282 *sq.* Similarly Volz, who still maintains that in Daniel the 'Son of man' does not represent Israel but Messiah (*Jüdische Eschatologie*, 1903, § 2, 2*b*; § 35, 1*b*). H. J. Holtzmann gives a good conspectus of the various interpretations of the 'Son of man' in Daniel in his *N.T. Theologie*, 1911, i. pp 88 *sq*. *Vide infra*, p. 304 n.

Him was another being whose countenance had the appearance of a man, and his face was full of graciousness, like one of the holy angels. And I asked the angel who went with me and showed me all the hidden things, concerning the Son of Man, who he was, and whence he was, (and) why he went with the Head of Days ? And he answered and said unto me : This is the Son of Man who hath righteousness, with whom dwelleth righteousness, and who revealeth all the treasures of that which is hidden, because the Lord of Spirits hath chosen him, and whose lot hath the pre-eminence before the Lord of Spirits in uprightness for ever. And this Son of Man whom thou hast seen shall . . . put down the kings from their thrones and kingdoms because they do not extol and praise Him, nor humbly acknowledge whence the kingdom was bestowed upon them.'[1] Again, ' I saw the fountain of righteousness . . . and all the thirsty drank . . . and at that hour that Son of Man was named in the presence of the Lord of Spirits, and his name before the Head of Days. Yea, before the sun and the signs were created, before the stars of heaven were made, His name was named before the Lord of Spirits. He shall be a staff to the righteous whereon to stay themselves and not fall, and He shall be the light of the Gentiles, and the hope of those who are troubled of heart.'[2]

Once more : ' And thus the Lord commanded the kings and the mighty and the exalted, and those who dwell on the earth, and said : " Open your eyes and lift up your horns if ye are able to recognise the Elect One." And the Lord of Spirits seated him on the throne of His glory, and the spirit of righteousness

[1] § 46.   [2] § 48.

was poured out upon him, and the word of his mouth slays all the sinners, and all the unrighteous are destroyed from before his face. And there shall stand up in that day all the kings and the mighty, and the exalted and those who hold the earth, and they shall see and recognize how he sits on the throne of his glory, and righteousness is judged before him, and no lying word is spoken before him. . . . And they shall be downcast of countenance, and pain shall seize them, when they see that Son of Man sitting on the throne of his glory. And the kings and the mighty and all who possess the earth shall bless and glorify and extol him who rules over all, who was hidden. For from the beginning the Son of Man was hidden, and the Most High preserved him in the presence of His might, and revealed him to the elect. . . . And all the kings and the mighty and the exalted and those who rule the earth shall fall down before him on their faces, and worship and set their hope upon that Son of Man, and petition him and supplicate for mercy at his hands. Nevertheless that Lord of Spirits will so press them that they shall hastily go forth from His presence, and their faces shall be filled with shame, and the darkness grow deeper on their faces. . . . And the righteous and elect shall be saved on that day, and they shall never thenceforward see the face of the sinners and unrighteous. And the Lord of Spirits will abide over them, and with that Son of Man shall they eat and lie down and rise up for ever and ever.' [1]

The Son of man, therefore, in the Book of Enoch is no longer the Prophet, as in Ezekiel, nor the ideal nation of the saints of God, as in Daniel, but a

[1] § 62.

IN THE EZRA-APOCALYPSE

Person, eternal, supreme, sitting on God's throne the source of righteousness, and the Judge of all. The description of him is no doubt closely connected with that employed in Daniel, but he is called the Elect One, and even the Anointed or the Messiah [1] He is plainly a Person, who judges the ungodly, and with him the righteous live in blessed fellowship for ever and ever.

Here perhaps we might stop in our endeavour to trace the use of the term before the days of Christ. For indeed I do not know that there is any other instance of it besides those already quoted, apart from isolated expressions in Scripture. But although the phrase, 'the Son of man,' is not used by the author of the Fourth (Second) Book of Ezra, yet the thought is there. 'I dreamed a dream by night: and I beheld, and lo! there arose a violent wind from the sea, and stirred all its waves. And I beheld, and lo! the wind caused to come up out of the heart of the seas as it were the form of a man. And I beheld, and lo! this Man flew with the clouds of heaven. And wherever he turned his countenance to look everything seen by him trembled; and whithersoever the voice went out of his mouth, all that heard his voice melted away, as the wax melts when it feels the fire. And after this I beheld, and lo! there was gathered together from the four winds of heaven an innumerable multitude of men to make war against the Man that came up out of the sea.... And lo! when he saw the assault of the multitude as they came he neither lifted his hand, nor held spear nor any warlike

---

[1] § 48, 10.

weapon; but I saw only how he sent out of his mouth as it were a fiery stream, and out of his lips a flaming breath, and out of his tongue he shot forth a storm of sparks. And these were all mingled together—the fiery stream, the flaming breath, and the . . . storm, and fell upon the assault of the multitude which was prepared to fight, and burned them all up, so that suddenly nothing more was to be seen of the innumerable multitude save only dust of ashes and smell of smoke. When I saw this I was amazed. Afterwards I beheld the same Man come down from the mountain, and call unto him another multitude which was peaceable.'[1] The interpretation given to the seer is: 'Whereas thou didst see a Man coming up from the heart of the sea; this is he whom the Most High is keeping many ages.'[2]

Although this Apocalypse was not written before the very end of the first century of our era, yet the description of the Man has so much in common with that of the Son of man in Enoch that we cannot help identifying the two, and at the same time perceiving that, distinctly Jewish as the Fourth Book of Ezra is, it is describing a Figure which owes nothing to Christian doctrine,[3] and thus deepens in our minds the conviction previously acquired that in the Jewish teaching of the time of our Lord there was the expectation, at least in some circles, of a Person who should come in the clouds of heaven, to vindicate the ways of God, destroying the sinner

---

[1] xiii. 1–13.   [2] xiii. 25.
[3] Except perhaps negatively in the writer's avoidance of the term '*Son of man.*' There are also some Christian interpolations in the form of the book as it has come down to us, but these are generally to be distinguished without much doubt.

vIII]   THE PROBLEM IN THE NEW TESTAMEN

and drawing the godly to Himself. He had no connexion with earth, save to descend and to act as Judge. He was called occasionally the 'Anointed' or Messiah, or the 'Elect One,' but pre-eminently the 'Son of man,' or only 'man.'

II. Now when we turn to the New Testament we are face to face with a strange fact. Our Lord in the earlier part of His public ministry did not proclaim Himself to be the Messiah, and, even after the confession by St. Peter, prevented His followers from using that title of Him. And yet He used the term 'the Son of man' freely of Himself in all stages of His work.[1] How is this? Did He not stultify His endeavour to keep His Messianic character secret if He referred to Himself as 'the Son of man'?

One answer is that the books in which this title was freely employed to designate the expected Judge were the peculiar property of comparatively few people, and were not known to the nation at large. Certainly we may grant that they were not beloved of the leaders of Judaism, who so disliked them that they did their best to destroy them.[2]

But, on the other side, we must remember that an appeal was made to the Book of Enoch by a member of our Lord's family, in a passage intended for ordinary Jewish Christians,[3] and that the presence of certain other phrases in the New Testament, peculiar to them and Enoch, suggests that this book at least was known to a fairly wide circle.[4]

[1] See below, pp. 290 *sqq.*
[2] See Lecture X for both the preceding and the following paragraphs.
[3] Jude 14, 15.
[4] Dr. Charles gives a full list of such phrases, more or less certain, in his *Enoch,* 1912, pp. xcv-ciii.

Besides, when our Lord throws off all hesitation, for the time for concealment had gone, and tells the High Priest openly of the future, the words indeed which He uses may be taken from Daniel, but their application is surely that of Enoch. 'Henceforth ye shall see the Son of man sitting at the right hand of power, and coming on the clouds of heaven.'[1] On the whole it is probable that the Book of Enoch was known to far too many people, and appreciated by them too much, for our Lord to have used the appellation 'the Son of man' on the ground that no one would know that it signified the Messiah, the One to come.

There is another, and a more satisfactory explanation. More than one conception of the nature and work of the Messiah prevailed among our Lord's contemporaries, and although the term Anointed or Messiah is used of the Son of man in the Book of Enoch, and also, as it appears, of the Man in the Fourth Book of Ezra,[2] yet, for the most part, among by far the great majority of the Jewish nation, the Messiah was no being who was to come in the clouds of heaven, belonging entirely to the sphere of the heavenly and the divine, but, as we have already seen in our consideration of the title 'the Son of David,' a man, little, if anything, more than a mere man, who, by his victorious leadership of his warlike people, should secure for them deliverance from their oppressors, and rule so justly as to attract all the nations of the earth to the true worship of the One God. Had Jesus proclaimed Himself the Messiah thousands and thousands of enthusiastic Jews would have flocked round His banner, to be led by Him

---

[1] Matt. xxvi. 64.   [2] vii. 29.

to victory. But when He called Himself only the Son of man, they could see no connexion between Him, the meek and lowly Jesus, hungry at times, and weary, and at times scorned and threatened, with the Son of man who was to come in the clouds of heaven. The title by its very glory was perfectly safe for our Lord to use. No one could possibly suppose, until He Himself made it clear, that He was that Son of man of whom the seers spake.

It is, however, alleged that we must not lay upon our Lord the responsibility of using the term, for not He but the Evangelists employed it.[1] If so, what an extraordinary thing it is that they have been so very careful to restrict the use of it to words said to be uttered by Him, without ever placing it in the mouth of those who addressed Him, or of the narrators of His history. Only in the Acts do we find St. Stephen employing it once, and in the Revelation of St. John we have no title, but only the description 'one like unto a son of man' twice used of the Lord in glory.[2] Yet in each of the Evangelists it is found on the lips of the Lord Jesus again and again. If the early Christian Fathers used it freely, the case would be different. But they do not. They seem to have felt a delicacy in employing it of Jesus, for they loved to think of Him not as the Son of man, but as the Son of God. Yet though there is no evidence for the free use of the term by the early Church, we are told that the four Evangelists, for some inscrutable reason, palmed it off upon us as customary upon our Lord's lips.

[1] Wellhausen, *Einleitung in die drei ersten Evangelien*, 1911, p. 128.
[2] Acts vii. 56; Rev. i. 13; xiv. 14. In Acts the phraseology suggests primarily the Book of Enoch (see below, pp. 300 *sq*., on Matt. xxvi. 64); in the Revelation that of Daniel.

They had, so far as we can see, no temptation to do so. It is easier to suppose that they attributed the use of it to Him because He really did employ it.[1]

But at this point we come to the most difficult and crucial question of all, What did the Lord Jesus mean by this phrase?[2] We should know better if we were sure of the actual words He used. The form in which the term has come down to us is Greek, and it is possible that our Lord, as an inhabitant of Galilee, which was overrun with Greek-speaking people, spoke Greek and Aramaic with equal fluency, and that thus the Greek expression found in the Gospel, ὁ υἱὸς τοῦ ἀνθρώπου, is what He said, syllable for syllable. But in view of the fact that when He was more than ordinarily moved He spoke in Aramaic, it is likely that this latter was, as we say, His native language, and that He thought more commonly in it, even if He sometimes spoke in Greek. Nor can we entirely neglect the bare possibility that He used a Hebrew phrase, especially in the case of a technical term such as ' the Son of man ' may be.

Now there is no reason to doubt that both in

[1] It is quite another question whether there are not a few places in the Gospels where the phrase has been put into our Lord's lips, although in fact He did not actually use it on those specific occasions, but only some other phrase with which it was, as we say, synonymous. The Evangelists added it to make His real meaning plain. The possibility of this must not be excluded, and must be considered later. It is sufficient to say now that even if this hypothesis holds good in one or two places, it does not affect the general result of a more careful enquiry, which is that our Lord did use the term ' the Son of man ' with reference to Himself from an early stage in His ministry, and to the very end, and not only after St. Peter's confession of Him.

[2] The materials for a decision are very numerous, and may be found, in particular, in Dalman, *The Words of Jesus*, 1902, pp. 234–267; Driver, Hastings' *D.B.* iv. 579–589; N. Schmidt, *Encycl. Bib.* coll. 4705–4740.

THE MEANING IN ARAMAIC

Greek and in Hebrew the phrase means what we usually attribute to it in English, the special individual who stands out as the representative of mankind.[1]

But when we turn to the Aramaic, the language which in all probability our Lord employed, we find ambiguity. For we have, in fact, no Aramaic of the precise time, and of the approximate place, in which our Lord conversed. Palestinian Aramaic of the first century of our era does not exist, and we can but guess at the precise expression spoken by our Lord in Aramaic from such forms of the language as were in use elsewhere, or at a later period. This hampers us greatly, for when the most learned perhaps of Christian Talmudists now alive, and perhaps the most deeply read of all living students of Aramaic, Dr. Dalman, tells us that in his opinion the phrase on our Lord's lips must have definitely meant 'the Son of man,' in the usual specific sense, we cannot but regret that he is obliged to resort to analogy and deduction, for lack of direct evidence.

For unquestionably, in such Aramaic as has come down to us, and there is a good deal, but of other locality or of other time, the phrase[2] means, not 'the Son of man,' but 'the Man,' or possibly, but improbably, only 'a man.'[3]

It must, however, be confessed that the last interpretation, 'a man,' is hardly possible in our Gospel, from the simple fact that in some of the places

---

[1] For it is hardly possible that the article can mean 'the man in question,' following a well-known Hebrew idiom, in which case the idiomatic English rendering would be 'a son of man,' *i.e.* 'a man.'

[2] בר אנשא.

[3] 'Der Mensch,' Wellhausen, *Israelitische und Jüdische Geschichte*, 1894, p. 312; *Einleitung in die drei ersten Evangelien*, 1911, pp. 123 *sqq.*; Gressmann, *Der Ursprung der Israelitisch-jüdischen Eschatologie*, 1905, p. 334.

where the phrase is attributed to our Lord, to explain it of a man, a human being generally, would appear to deprive it of any point at all.[1] The Greek plainly distinguishes between ' A son of man,' in this sense, and ' the Son of man,' and often the context also is free from all ambiguity.

In such passages, therefore, it is clear that even though the ordinary Aramaic phrase in itself might be translated ' a man,' our Lord must have excluded this meaning, either by some additional word, or by some difference of intonation. On the other hand, it would seem reasonable that when the context in itself is ambiguous the Greek phrase, all that we actually possess, should be interpreted by the meaning it must have in passages which admit of no doubt.

If our Lord, then, did not mean ' a man,' did He mean ' the Son of man ' or ' the Man ' ? It is not easy to say. But if we judge by the direct evidence, such as it is, and exclude deductions of more or less doubtful validity, we are led to the conclusion that the stress of our Lord's thought was not on the word ' Son ' but on the word ' man.' Perhaps the translation ' the Man ' does not give in English all the connotation of the Aramaic, but it is nearer the truth than that of ' the Son of man,' which with us lays too much weight on sonship and derivation. While therefore it is convenient in this course of lectures still to use the term ' the Son of man,' we must not forget that the emphasis of it is to be found, not in our Lord's relationship to humanity ('the *Son* of man '), but in the actual manhood itself. It is ' the *Man*,' ' the Man ' *par excellence* which the phrase connotes.

---

[1] *E.g.* viii. 20. *Vide supra*, p. 291.

VIII] THE THREEFOLD USE BY OUR LORD

III. Now when we turn to the Gospel we find that the passages in which the phrase occurs are of three kinds.[1] There is the Son of man suffering and dying, the Son of man in His active relation to men and human institutions, and lastly the Son of man coming to judge. Let us take these groups in order.

The first time that the phrase is used is in viii. 20, where the Lord tells the enthusiastic Scribe, who had said that he would follow Him whithersoever He went : 'The foxes have holes, and the birds of the heaven have nests ; but the Son of man hath not where to lay his head.' There is no question about its meaning here. To say that an ordinary man hath not where to lay his head would be folly. It refers to the Speaker, and to Him alone. And He, though 'the Man,' yet, because of His work as man, is worse off for a home than the very beasts and birds ! He shares the weakness and the suffering incidental to human life. So in xi. 19 the same lower side of manhood is expressed, when the Lord says, again indubitably of Himself, 'The Son of man came eating and drinking, and they say, Behold, a gluttonous man, and a winebibber, a friend of publicans and sinners.' He is, in other words, no ascetic, but mixes with men, and behaves at table as do they ; and His reward is that He is accused of self-indulgence in food and drink.[2]

Other passages, however, describe His humiliation more strongly.

The earliest indeed, xii. 40, has its own difficulties, into which we need not here enter, but, as it stands,

---

[1] The usual division into 'two great groups' (Driver in Hastings' *D.B.* iv. 580), *i.e.* my first and third groups, disguises the very important small class which comes between.

[2] On xxiv. 36 see Lecture IX, p. 322.

it speaks of the Son of man being three days and three nights in the heart of the earth. This presupposes His death; which is frankly foretold in the next passage, xvii. 9: 'As they were coming down from the mountain, Jesus commanded them, saying, Tell the vision to no man, until the Son of man be risen from the dead.' The same thought is expressed in *v.* 12: 'Elijah is come already, and they knew him not, but did unto him whatsoever they listed. Even so shall the Son of man also suffer of them.' Verse 22 is fuller, and the result of His death is added: 'The Son of man shall be delivered up into the hands of men; and they shall kill him, and the third day he shall be raised up.' xx. 18, 19, are fuller still: 'Behold, we go up to Jerusalem; and the Son of man shall be delivered unto the chief priests and scribes; and they shall condemn him to death, and shall deliver him unto the Gentiles to mock, and to scourge, and to crucify: and the third day he shall be raised up.' Verse 28 of the same chapter gives the reason for all this suffering: 'Even as the Son of man came not to be ministered unto, but to minister, and to give his life a ransom for many.'

Lastly, there are the repeated predictions in chap. xxvi., in one of which the sufferings of the Son of man are expressly connected with the statements contained in the Old Testament Scriptures, implying that the disciples, and all other Jewish devout students of the Word of God, ought not to be surprised at the suffering and death of Him who was typically the Man, the Son of man. Verse 2: 'After two days the passover cometh, and the Son of man is delivered up to be crucified'; *v.* 24: 'The Son of man goeth, even as it is written of him: but woe unto that man

VIII]   THE SMALL SECOND GROUP

through whom the Son of man is betrayed'; v. 45: 'Sleep on now, and take your rest: behold, the hour is at hand, and the Son of man is betrayed into the hands of sinners.'

Not one of all these passages, we may say, admits of any doubt in the interpretation of its general sense. Each must refer to the Speaker, and to Him alone, and each depicts Him as undergoing suffering, or shame, or death, even though in some places this is represented as but the prelude to triumph, and in one as the means of ministry to others, and of ransoming them from some awful loss not further defined. The weakness and the suffering, and even the death, incidental to manhood, were, the Lord Jesus declared, to be His own lot, as the Scriptures had said. And He freely accepted all, that He might ransom men.[1]

The second class of passages is small in number, but very important. In them He is not the weak and suffering man, but active, strangely powerful in the spiritual sphere, and superior to legislation which seemed able to trace its history to the very beginning of time.

xiii. 37 : 'He that soweth the good seed is the Son of man.' He spreads abroad the knowledge and the source of life. The verse requires no comment.

ix. 6 is harder: 'But that ye may know that the Son of man hath power on earth to forgive sins.' Some have thought that our Lord's intention was to inform the bystanders that even a man could forgive sins, and have supposed therefore that the term here, in the form in which our Lord spoke it, did not contain any reference to Himself as the typical Man. He bade them, it is said, think of

[1] *Cf.* Lecture XI.

the powers that can be entrusted to any man, not of their special gift in Himself.¹ This is possible, and we dare not exclude the thought that what our Lord does may be done by any other man who is in perfect sympathy with the mind and will of God.

But, in view of our Lord's usage of the phrase elsewhere to designate Himself, it is probable that He refers to Himself here as the Man who, in spite of being on earth (in contrast to God in heaven), yet receives power to forgive others. If Jesus wished to say in one phrase that this power was given to man as such, and yet in fact not to any man but only to Himself, it is difficult to see how He could otherwise express His meaning than by using the term the Son of man.

xii. 8 : ' For the Son of man is lord of the sabbath.' The disciples had been accused of profaning the sabbath by plucking ears of corn, and eating them, thus breaking one or more rules made by the Oral Law to prevent the more vital ordinances of the Pentateuch itself being carelessly infringed. The Lord Jesus had defended His followers, first, by an appeal to the case of David and his men, who had not scrupled, in an extremity, to partake of food which had been consecrated to the priests, for human need comes before religious enactments; secondly, by invoking the regulations of the sabbath as given by Moses, which prescribed certain work to be done on it by the priests, when the welfare of the Temple services demanded it; thirdly, by an appeal to the fact that there was then present something greater and more important than the

¹ So, apparently, Wellhausen *in loco*, and in his *Einleitung in die drei ersten Evangelien*, 1911, p. 129, on the parallel passage, Mark ii. 10.

Temple itself, namely, the personal relation of the disciples to their Master, and the necessity of full vigour of mind and body in the service of God. If His opponents, He adds, had only understood the meaning of God's statement contained in the Prophets, that, not external regulations, but heartfelt practice of tender love, was the all-important requisite, they would not have condemned His guiltless followers. 'For the Son of man is lord of the sabbath.' Christ, in fact, was trying to teach the Pharisees two lessons: first, that man as such was above merely external rules; and, secondly, that He, the Man *par excellence*, was therefore all the more above them, and indeed in a position to declare the way in which the Sabbath should be observed.

xii. 32 is another difficult passage, where the Lord Jesus is contrasting words spoken against the Son of man with those against the Holy Spirit. 'Whosoever shall speak a word against the Son of man, it shall be forgiven him; but whosoever shall speak against the Holy Spirit, it shall not be forgiven him, neither in this world, nor in that which is to come.' One thing at least is plain here; the phrase can hardly refer to an ordinary man.[1] What, then, does it mean? It has been explained as saying: Whosoever does not believe in Messiah, the glorious Being of the Book of Enoch, or even of the Book

---

[1] In the parallel passage in Mark iii. 28, which omits the title, 'the contrast is quite obvious, between the offences (slanderous though they may be) of men against their fellows—which can and ought to be forgiven—and deliberate refusal to appreciate the beneficent effects of the operation of the divine Spirit upon their afflicted brethren through human instrumentality—an attitude wholly to be condemned' (Winstanley, *Jesus and the Future*, 1913, p. 189). But Dr. Winstanley allows that in our passage itself 'the Son of man' was intended to refer to Jesus (p. 190).

of Daniel, will be forgiven. But it is hard to see why this belief, or rather unbelief, should suddenly be mentioned, when there is no trace of a reference to it in the immediate context. Or perhaps Jesus intended to say : Whosoever does not believe in Me as the Messiah will be forgiven—a very improbable solution in view of the fact that there is no sufficient reason to think that He ever intended the Pharisees to understand the term 'the Son of man' to refer to Himself as the Messiah. What, then, did He intend by this sentence ? The words 'the Son of man' must refer to Himself, and He means this : Personal abuse of Me, even though I am Man in a sense higher than others can claim, will yet be forgiven, but rejection of the life-giving influence of the Holy Spirit does not permit of forgiveness, for necessarily, and in itself, it excludes that tone and temper of the soul which is the essential preliminary to such an exhibition of God's love.[1]

The last passage of the second group is the question which leads to the confession by St. Peter in xvi. 13 : ' Who do men say that the Son of man is ? ' Here too the reference is undeniably to the Lord Himself, for when the reply has been given : ' Some say John the Baptist; some Elijah; and others Jeremiah, or one of the prophets '; He asks again : ' But as for you, whom say ye that I am ? ' And Peter answered : ' Thou art the Christ, the Son of the living God.' This is even clearer in the form, perhaps the original form, of the question as it is recorded in Mark viii. 27 : ' Who do men say that I am ? ' In either case the

---

[1] The Apostles were very conscious of the work of the Holy Spirit in preaching the Gospel. See 1 Pet. i. 12. He is sent from heaven, and speaks within the heart and conscience. *Cf.* also Heb. xii. 25.

ST. PETER'S CONFESSION

answer is: Not the Messiah, but only one of His forerunners restored to life. The phrase 'the Son of man,' if it was actually spoken by the Lord, did not suggest to the populace the Messiah at all, or even the Figure contained in the Books of Enoch or of Daniel. Jesus, as they knew, called Himself 'the Son of man,' or, if you will, 'the Man,' but the term suggested to the people at most a forerunner of Messiah, not Messiah Himself. St. Peter, however, speaking for all the Twelve, breaks through this lower conception of the work and office of Jesus, and acknowledges Him as the Messiah.[1]

In this second division, then, we have seen that the Son of man spreads the word, has power to forgive sins, is above the sabbath, and that although dishonour to Him is far less serious than the temper which speaks evil of the work of the Holy Spirit, He is, notwithstanding, the very Christ whom the nation was expecting. Others saw in Him, and, alas, still see in Him, a mere forerunner; but they that were taught of God acknowledged Him to be the Christ.

We turn now to the third group of passages. As with the predictions of His death, so with those of His future glory; both one and the other were addressed to the Lord's disciples only. In whatever other way Jesus might hint at the failure of His earthly hopes in the final catastrophe of His rejection by the nation, He reserved, according to St. Matthew's presentation of His teaching, direct statements of it for the ears of His disciples. So was it with His expectation of more than ultimate success. He who

---

[1] See further Lecture IX, pp. 317 *sq.*

was to die was also to rise again. And further, He who died and rose was at last to return in the clouds of heaven with His angels, to execute judgment on all the nations of the earth.

The individual passages which describe His future glory need not detain us long. In x. 23, when sending forth the Twelve to preach, He tells them: 'Ye shall not have gone through the cities of Israel, till the Son of man be come.' The immediate application is obscure, and the discussion of this belongs to the tenth rather than to the present Lecture, but two things are clear.

First, for all that the words say, Jesus and the Son of man might be different persons. Secondly, He assumes a knowledge on the part of His disciples that a Being is to appear suddenly, the purpose of whose coming is suggested. For the object of the saying is plainly to give them an additional incitement to zeal and earnestness in preaching the kingdom of heaven—soon the Judge will come to test them and those to whom they preach.

The next passage is more precise, xiii. 41: 'The Son of man' (who in *v.* 37 had been described as the Sower) 'shall send forth his angels, and they shall gather out of his kingdom all things that cause stumbling, and them that do iniquity. . . . Then shall the righteous shine forth as the sun in the kingdom of their Father.'

So in xvi. 27, the context of which plainly shows that He is referring to Himself, Jesus says that 'the Son of man shall come in the glory of his Father with his angels; and then shall he render unto every man according to his deeds.' He further adds that some of them standing there should not taste of death, 'till they see the Son of man coming in his kingdom.' But the full discussion of this prediction too belongs to the tenth Lecture.

In xix. 28 Jesus promises the Twelve that 'in the regeneration when the Son of man shall sit on the throne of his glory, ye also shall sit upon twelve thrones, judging the twelve tribes of Israel.' Here He is to judge Israel, with the Twelve as assessors.

In xxiv. 27 His coming is to be visible from all parts of the earth, and His angels will come with Him for vengeance on a spiritually dead world, as vultures to devour the carcase.

In *vv.* 30, 31, the sign of Him predicted in Daniel will appear, and the tribes, not merely of the Jews, as Zechariah said (xii. 12), but of the whole earth, shall mourn, 'and they shall see the Son of man coming on the clouds of heaven with power and great glory. And he shall send forth his angels with a great sound of a trumpet, and they shall gather together his elect from the four winds, from one end of heaven to the other.' The coming of the Son of man shall be not only for the judgment of the ungodly, but also for the restoration of His own.

In *vv.* 37 and 44, on the contrary, only the suddenness of His coming is mentioned.

The last occasion on which the Lord uses the term in His speeches to His disciples is xxv. 31, where He begins the parable of the Sheep and the Goats by saying: 'But when the Son of man shall come in his glory, and all the angels with him, then shall he sit on the throne of his glory: and before him shall be gathered all the nations.' He sits there as Judge, and the final state of each man in the world is, as it seems, determined by his attitude towards the servants of the Lord. Higher claim for the position of the Son of man, and for His identification with Himself, the Lord Jesus could hardly have made.

Yet for solemnity, and decisive importance, it is outweighed by the final example of its use in this Gospel (xxvi. 64). The Lord Jesus was surrounded by His enemies, on His trial before the Sanhedrin, and to inquiries put to Him He had answered nothing. Then the High Priest said to Him : ' I adjure thee by the living God, that thou tell us whether thou be the Christ, the Son of God. Jesus saith unto him, Thou (not I) hast said : nevertheless (thou art right, and) I say unto you, Henceforth ye shall see the Son of man sitting at the right hand of power, and coming on the clouds of heaven.' The time is gone by for concealment of His true position ; there is no danger now that the populace will rise and hail Him as Messiah ; He acknowledges, therefore, the truth of the question that He is the Christ ; and adds the warning that judgment will come at last, implying, that though He now stands to be judged by the Sanhedrin, He will one day return in power on the clouds of heaven to execute justice for this His condemnation. You say I am the Messiah, I accept the statement ; I am also the Judge who will come from heaven. But this final revelation of His office and work to the representatives of the Jewish people was treated as blasphemy, and the verdict went forth : He is guilty of death. It seems as though, however unwilling the people were to recognise any connexion between the claim of Jesus to be the Son of man, and their expectation of the Messiah, the High Priest combined the two expressions at once, and saw in the threat of judgment by the Son of man, the endorsement and enhancement of His stupendous assertion that He was Messiah.

Here, as it seems, for the first and last time in our Lord's life on earth, the combination of the two expressions was understood to be claimed by Jesus; He was, then, according to His own account, both the Messiah, whom the Jews expected, and that mysterious Son of man of whom they had heard in teaching which pretended to be derived from the Book of Daniel. If His claim to be the Messiah was rejected, how much more that of being the Son of man!

IV. What are the impressions produced by this short survey of all the passages in the First Gospel where the phrase 'the Son of man' occurs? There are two; of which the first relates to the source from which the Lord derived the words, the second to the value He set upon them.

First, what is the source from which the phrase is drawn? The answer must satisfy all the three ways in which, as we have seen, it is used; namely, the Son of man suffering and dying, the Son of man in His active relation to men and human institutions, and the Son of man coming in glory to judge.

It is too often assumed that the last is decisive, and shows that our Lord borrowed the phrase, if not from Daniel, at least from the current Apocalyptic thought represented to us in the Similitudes of Enoch and the Apocalypse of Ezra. Yet the description of the Son of man in these writings contains but a very little of the life-picture suggested by our Lord's words. Or, perhaps more truly, it gives us the end, but not the earlier portion of that life. It tells us of the Son of man in glory, but never mentions Him as sufferer.

Whence then did this come? No doubt, so scholars would persuade us, the Lord Jesus added it from the Isaianic presentation of the Servant of the LORD, who suffered for man even to the death.[1] But although the Servant is depicted in Isaiah as human, no stress is there laid upon his humanity as such, and we may also well hesitate before attributing to our Lord so solely mechanical a combination of the servant with the Son of man in glory as this theory requires. Besides, it entirely fails to account for the second group of passages in the Gospel.

On the other hand, the beginning of the Book of Ezekiel, the salient parts of which have been already quoted, provides material for a nearly satisfactory answer. For in Ezekiel stress is plainly laid on the weakness of man, involving, as is seen in later parts of the book, much personal suffering, both of body and mind. But certainly also one great purpose of Ezekiel's vision was that he should be upheld in his weakness by the remembrance of the fact that the very nature of man was to be found in angelic beings, and even in God Himself. Man belonged not to earth alone, but to heaven also; glory was his prerogative as well as weakness and suffering. And on this it follows that a man, though weak and liable to suffering, may yet be so much in touch with Divine

[1] Dr. Charles, *Enoch*, 1912, pp. 306-309. The verbal evidence of 'rejected,' 'set at nought,' in Mark viii. 31, ix. 12, compared with Isa. liii. 3, which Bishop Gore adduces (*The Title 'The Son of Man,'* 1913, pp. 13 *sq.*), is quite insufficient, and in any case did not appeal to St. Matthew, who omits it. The use of 'many' in Mark x. 45, Matt. xx. 28, and Mark xiv. 24, Matt. xxvi. 28, is more suggestive, and may point, in truth, to Isa. liii. 12. For certainly the Servant is the most extreme example of human suffering in the Old Testament, and it would be strange if our Lord never referred to its prophecy as completed in Himself. But not with the bare mechanical conjunction implied in Dr. Charles' theory.

power, even while he is on earth, as to be able to be a medium of communication between the higher and lower forms of human existence, and convey to other persons on earth spiritual privileges and experiences, which they, from some lack in their religious life, are not able to obtain themselves. Deeply taught, as certainly the Lord Jesus was, in the experimental contents of Holy Scripture, we cannot suppose that this very elementary lesson of the Book of Ezekiel can have escaped His notice. Ezekiel tells us of the union of weakness with potentiality of strength commensurate with the nature of God, and this provides exactly that combination of qualities and experience suggested in the Gospel. In spite of much weakness, and suffering, and at last death itself, nay, if the truth be told, not in spite of, but by means of these, the Son of man rises above the ordinary limitations of sinful men while here, and will, in the future, enjoy authority unfettered, executing judgment on opponent and on friend. He is the Son of man, nay, Man—nay, Man *par excellence*—ever in close relation to the heavenly beings and the eternal Ruler of all; Man, therefore one with men, sharing their weakness and their sorrows, and able by suffering, and indeed only by suffering, to deliver them from death; but Man for whom glory is assured at last, when He shall appear in judgment.

But here, I confess, the language of Ezekiel is insufficient. While the life of the Son of man on earth is drawn from Ezekiel, and its ultimate postulates are also derived thence, the actual words in which His future work is portrayed are due to those forecasts of the future which had already been painted by seers, who understood that if the Judge of all the earth were to do right, He must be in complete sympathy with men, and in judging exercise that part of His being in which they shared. For 'the Son of man' is the Apocalyptic expression of the fact, that the Charioteer of all has human qualities, and will judge mankind by virtue of these.[1] The source, then, from which our Lord derived the phrase 'the Son of man' was not the Book of Enoch supplemented by that of Isaiah, but the Book of Ezekiel supplemented in little more than phraseology by the Book of Enoch and even by that of Daniel.

The second impression is that for some reason or other 'the Son of man' was our Lord's favourite title for Himself. But why did He like it, and what truth or truths did He desire to convey by His use of it?[2]

What did He Himself mean by the phrase, 'the Son of man'? One answer may be at once dismissed, that He regarded it as summing up all humanity, desiring to convey the notion that in Himself were united all the aspirations, powers, affections, and even spiritual experiences, that mankind can possess.[3]

---

[1] This seems to be the real basis for the conception of the 'Ur-mensch'; see p. 280, note. Compare also John v. 27.

[2] It does not follow, we may remark, that these truths were necessarily perceived by the immediate followers of Christ, for, with so high a superiority as His over the minds and spiritual attainments of others, He might well perceive truths in a phrase, which none else could see at the time, but which He could teach those who after many years of development in Christian thought should attain more nearly to His supreme knowledge.

[3] So, it would seem, Bishop Westcott (*St. John*, c. i., Add. Note on The Son of Man, §§ 10–13), and Wellhausen earlier, but now given up by him. See his *Einleitung*, p. 126. At first sight Dr. Sanday's phrase, 'I believe that He meant Humanity as gathered up in Himself' (*Christologies Ancient and Modern*, 1910, p. 124), implies this, but he is referring only to Mark ii. 28 (Matt. xii. 8), and perhaps means no more than what has been said above on p. 295. *Cf.* the reference to Irenæus in Moberly, *Atonement and Personality*, 1911, p. 344.

vIII]   THE TRUE MEANING OF THE TITLE

For this savours altogether too much of philosophical *finesse* to be consistent with the thoughts of our Lord, as He is depicted for us in this Gospel. Or, put it another way, and the result is the same, without, I think, any unworthy treatment of the Master, such a conception of the Son of man is altogether unlike the character of St. Matthew.[1] The Evangelist would be quite unlikely to perceive a philosophical content in the phrase ' the Son of man.' And therefore he also cannot have intended that his description of the Lord Jesus should convey the impression that Jesus saw, or desired others to see, such a content Himself. The phrase no doubt, to the Evangelist, and so to our Lord, meant something much more simple.

It is this. I, the Lord Jesus would say, am Man, in weakness, in suffering, even unto death. Yet all the time I am in touch with that supreme nature of Man which belongs to a sphere higher than earth. I hold, in a way which sin has not injured, such relationship to the Divine that here on earth I can forgive, and am superior to religious regulations which have in fact but a local or temporary significance. This Manhood, too, is one that will not cease when I have passed through those last stages of suffering and death, which I must endure if I am to accomplish My work. For I shall arise, and I shall take it with Me to the clouds of heaven. On these I shall one day come to restore to earth the equity now hidden under

---

[1] Whoever the writer of the First Gospel was (and, when all is said, there is no absolutely decisive reason why he should not have been St. Matthew) he was a plain painstaking man, showing no special grasp of dialectics or philosophy, and original only in the choice and arrangement of his materials. If we compare him with St. Paul, for example, the contrast is evident at once.

the selfishness and sins of men. I, Jesus of Nazareth, as man, nay, as the Man, will accomplish this.[1]

We are now in a position to understand why the Lord Jesus used the third person instead of the first.[2] To have said 'I,' as He often could have done, when, in fact, He did say 'the Son of man,' would have excluded all presentation of the thought implied in the latter. He wished to lay stress on His Manhood, and this He could not have done if He had not mentioned it. And we can hardly doubt that in doing this He did not wish only to say as much as 'I am Man,' and therefore I have a right to say so, but I am man, and in calling your attention to this I desire you to notice also what a man can be and can do. Man is weak, it is true, and comes to suffering and death; yes, it may be that these are necessary steps in the fulfilment of his task of aiding others; but man also has affinity with the heavenly and even with the Divine. Let him keep in touch with this higher nature, and he shall be crowned with glory and honour.

In modern language, then, one of the reasons why our Lord used the phrase 'the Son of man' was that He desired to teach a deeper anthropology than He found at that time, or even than He finds to-day. Sometimes the glory of man has been

---

[1] *Cf.* Driver, Hastings' *D.B.* iv. 587, § 21, end. St. Paul's term, 'the Second Adam,' may perhaps go back to this teaching by our Lord. *Cf.* Lecture III, pp. 123 *sq.*

[2] It is hard to believe that Gressmann is right when he says of this: 'Auffällig und bis jetzt unerklärt ist allerdings das Problem auf das WREDE (*Z.N.T.W.*, Jahrgang V. 1904, s. 359) aufmerksam macht, dass Jesus von sich statt des Ich die dritte Person mit dem Titel gebraucht. Dieser aussergewöhnliche Sprachgebrauch muss auf irgend welche uns unbekannt (religionsgeschichtliche) Vorbilder zurückgehen' (*Ursprung*, pp. 334 *sq.*).

viii] ITS SIGNIFICANCE FOR OURSELVES

forgotten, sometimes the privilege of suffering. He desired to make us think of the possibilities of human nature in self-sacrifice, and in its reward.

And therefore He teaches the wider and truer meaning of the Messianic hope.

Until He came, most Jews thought that the Messiah was to be of the stock of David, and to resemble David, only with greater power than his, with holier piety, and wider rule over the nations round. But in 'the Son of man' our Lord hints that there is something higher than a merely national leader, however great and good. Manhood is not limited to the Jews; the Son of man will judge all nations. 'The Son of David' is the Jewish Messiah; 'the Son of man' belongs to the whole world—'to the Jew first, but also to the Greek.' A merely national Messiah, then, is inadequate. Jesus the true Messiah is Man and for man. And therefore will He suffer, and therefore will He triumph, and therefore will He judge.

Lastly, may we not venture to see a permanent significance in the phrase 'the Son of man' for our own day and for ourselves?

First, Christ would tell us that suffering due to self-denial is the one means by which we can be of benefit to others; that men are crying out in pain, and we can deliver them, if only we will imitate Christ the Man—'Who came . . . to minister, and to give His life a ransom for many.'

Secondly, that pessimism can find no place in the heart of anyone who remembers that human nature is no separate entity, cut off from all association with higher forms of life, but is represented in heaven and has kinship with God. Our good desires, then, our high aims, our sublime ideals, spring from that identity of nature, of thought, and of will, which we share with the Creator.

Lastly, that our knowledge of life, our insight into human passions and human frailties, our blood-bought experience of the manifold forms of men's actions and motives—and who know these so well as members of this Honourable Society?—shall have so abiding an influence upon us as to equip us for the last great exercise of discernment on the stage of human history, when the Son of man shall come to judge, and all His Saints with Him, and as He says, ' Ye also shall sit upon twelve thrones, judging the twelve tribes of Israel ' (xix. 28), or even, as St. Paul says, judging angels : ' What mean these strange figures, this speech in parable ? ' What else but that in proportion as we resemble Him, who as Man learned sympathy with human life, its sins, temptations, victories, thus fitting Himself to judge actions and weigh motives, and give praise and blame aright, so we—followers of the Man, and ourselves becoming men as in measure we resemble Him—shall take our share in the judgment of the world, assessors in that Supremest Court of all, understanding and approving the judgments pronounced by the Son of man ?

To suffer for men—and save them ; to appropriate the power of God—and live by Him ; to know both God and man—and so judge Jews and Gentiles justly—these are the abiding truths that Jesus the Christ would teach us, both of Himself and of His followers, by His claim to be the Son of man, the Man.

Lecture Nine

THE MESSIAH—THE SON OF GOD

'No one knoweth the Son, save the Father; neither doth any know the Father, save the Son, and he to whomsoever the Son willeth to reveal him.' — MATT. xi. 27.

Lecture Nine

THE MESSIAH—THE SON OF GOD

I. IN the last two Lectures we have seen St. Matthew's portrayal of our Lord as the Son of David, fulfilling the national hopes and aspirations, but raising them to a higher plane; and as the Son of man, the Man, suffering, yet akin to God, and the Judge to come.

We turn now to that supreme title, which suggests to us Christians the deepest truths of our faith, the interpenetration of human and Divine, nay, the Blessed Trinity itself, economic and essential. It is but fitting that we should pause at the threshold of so great a mystery, removing, so far as we may, the defilement of earth, for we stand on holy ground.

I indeed, an orthodox Christian, speaking to orthodox Christians, can say and feel this; but our duty to-day is to investigate the statements of the Evangelist with as little prejudgment as possible, endeavouring to understand his language, and to weigh the meaning that he gives to the phrase ' the Son of God,' as part of his presentation of the Messiah to the Jews.

St. Matthew the monotheist, for monotheist he surely was, tells us that the term ' the Son of God ' was used of Jesus of Nazareth; relates facts about Him which emphasise and expand the expression; and reports sayings by Jesus Himself which illustrate it, and were, perhaps, intended to illustrate it, from the very first. What significance does the Evangelist desire his readers to see in it? What part does the title of 'the Son of God' hold in his presentation of the Christ?

It is all-important for us to remember that it, like the two other terms, had a long history behind it, and this among Jewish people, who were not likely to be, and, so far as we know, had not been, influenced by the hero-worship of the Greeks, or the emperor-worship of the Latins. St. Matthew the Jew, writing to Jews, though they were Jews who had found the Messiah, had abundance of material in Jewish sources from which he could derive the title of ' the Son of God.'

It is true that, strictly speaking, the phrase is not to be found in the Old Testament.[1] The plural occurs fairly often; sometimes in the sense of supernatural beings generally,[2] or, in almost identical phraseology, of judges as endowed with certain functions and powers of divinity.[3] Further, Israel is called by Jehovah ' my son ' in Ex. iv. 22 (J), to which both Hosea alludes in xi. 1, and also the author of the Book of Wisdom, when he writes ' upon the destruction of the first-born they confessed the people to be God's son ' (xviii. 13). In the plural, too, the phrase, ' the sons ' or ' the children ' of God, is used of Israelites generally (Isa. i. 2; Deut. xxxii. 19), and more particularly of the more godly among them (Deut. xiv. 1; Hosea i. 10; *cf.* Jub. i. 24; Psalms of Solomon xvii. 30).[4]

---

[1] In Dan. iii. 25, ' a son of (the) gods' is defined in *v.* 28 as God's angel.
[2] Gen. vi. 2; Job i. 6, ii. 1, xxxviii. 7; Ps. xxix. 1, lxxxix. 6, R.V. marg.
[3] Ps. lxxxii. 6.
[4] Compare the remarkable passages: Ecclus. xxiii. 4: ' O Lord, Father and God of my life '; Wisd. ii. 16, 18: ' He vaunteth that God is his father. . . . If the righteous man is God's son, he will uphold him.'

THE SON OF GOD

For our purpose, however, it is of extreme interest to see that the thought of the sonship of the nation passes over into that of the sonship of the king, and so of the ideal King, the Messiah. Reference was made in Lecture VII to the fundamental passage, 2 Sam. vii. 8–16, but no express mention was made of v. 14: 'I will be his father, and he shall be my son,' where the sonship of David's descendant is half moral and half official. The thought is taken up in Ps. lxxxix., as, for example, in vv. 27, 28: 'I also will make him my firstborn, the highest of the kings of the earth. My mercy will I keep for him for evermore, and my covenant shall stand fast with him.' The reference to this ideal King is even plainer in Ps. ii., to which, however, it will be convenient to refer rather later.

In the Apocryphal and Pseudepigraphic Writings there is but little reference to Messiah as the Son of God. His mission is ordered and directed by God; His work is for the glory of God; and He is the representative of God;[1] but in only two books is He called God's Son. In Enoch cv. 2 we read that the Lord says: 'I and My Son will be united with them (the children of earth) for ever in the paths of uprightness in their lives; and ye shall have peace.' So also in 2 (4) Esdras xiii. 32: 'It shall be when these things shall come to pass, and the signs shall happen which I showed thee before, then shall my Son be revealed whom thou didst see as a Man ascending.' And in v. 52: 'Just as one can neither seek out nor know what is in the deep of the sea, even so can no one upon earth see my Son [or those that are with Him], but in the time of his day.' And lastly, xiv. 9:

---

[1] See full references in Volz, *Jüdische Eschatologie*, 1903, § 35. 9. pp. 233 *sq.*

THE HEBREW-CHRISTIAN MESSIAH [LECT.

'Thou shalt be taken up from among men, and henceforth thou shalt remain with my Son, and with such as are like thee, until the times be ended.'

The thoroughly Jewish character of the title 'the Son of God' in its application to the Messiah may be seen more clearly in the usage of Talmudic and Rabbinic writings, which do not hesitate to refer the second psalm to Him. 'Our Rabbis have taught us in a Mishna,' says the Talmud in T.B. *Sukkah,* 52a, 'with reference to Messiah who is about to be revealed quickly, that the Holy One, blessed be He, saith to him, Ask thee, for it is said, I will declare the decree. Ask of Me and I will give thee nations for thine inheritance.'[1] So also Maimonides, in his introduction to *Sanhedrin*, chap. x.: 'The prophets and saints have longed for the days of the Messiah, and great has been their desire towards him, for there will be with him the gathering together of the righteous and the administration of goodness, and wisdom, and royal righteousness, with the abundance of his uprightness and the spread of his wisdom, and his approach to God, as it is said: The Lord said unto me, Thou art My son, to-day have I begotten thee.'[2] So the *Yalqut* on Ps. ii. 7 (§ 621): 'R. Huna said in the name of R. Idi, In three parts were the punishments divided: one for King Messiah, and when his hour cometh, the Holy One, blessed be He, saith: I must make a new covenant with him, and so He saith: To-day have I begotten thee.' Similarly, with reference to Ps. lxxxix. 27, we find in the *Shmoth Rabba*, § 19 (near the end), on Exod. xiii. 2: 'R. Nathan says, The Holy One, blessed be He, saith

[1] The text is that of the Munich MS.
[2] Both Rashi and Kimchi report the Messianic interpretation of the Psalm, though they do not accept it themselves.

IX]   APPLIED BY JEWS TO MESSIAH

to Moses, As I made Jacob firstborn, for it is said (Exod. iv. 22) "Israel is my son, my firstborn," so do I make King Messiah firstborn, for it is said (Ps. lxxxix. 27) " I also will make him (my) firstborn."'

We can therefore easily believe that the sentence attributed to the High Priest in Matt. xxvi. 63 : ' I adjure thee by the living God, that thou tell us whether thou be the Christ, the Son of God,' was fully in accordance with what we know of Jewish belief about the Messiah at that time. As Mr. Montefiore writes on the parallel passage in St. Mark : ' It is assumed by the high priest that the true Messiah *would* be "the Son of God." Nor was Mark inaccurate in making the high priest use such words. The later metaphysical and more developed conception of " the Son of God " had not yet arisen. The Messiah *was* the Son of God; in the Messianically interpreted second and eighty-ninth Psalms he is actually so called. In the age of Jesus the purely human character of the Messiah was not insisted on by Jewish teachers as it became insisted on after the development of Christianity. Room was given for wide speculations and fancies as to his nature and pre-existence ; he stood in a special relation to God, and was in a pre-eminent sense his Son.' [1] In a word, the Messiah could be called, and was called, the Son of God, whatever the sense was in which the term was used.

It was said above that St. Matthew tells us that the phrase was used of Jesus, relates facts which emphasise and expand it, and reports sayings by our Lord Himself which further illustrate it. To these three groups of passages we must now address ourselves.

---

[1] *The Synoptic Gospels*, p. 351.

The High Priest was not the only person who used the term 'the Son of God' in connexion with Jesus. The two possessed with devils in the country of the Gadarenes 'cried out, saying, What have we to do with thee, thou Son of God?' for they dreaded Him as the judge come to torment them before the time (viii. 29). They that were in the boat—whether disciples or not does not appear—on seeing that the wind sank when He and St. Peter came on board, prostrated themselves before Him, saying: 'Truly thou art God's son' (xiv. 33). The miracle suggested to them not divinity in His nature, but likeness to God at least in power, and perhaps also in character as means to that power, and therefore they bowed down before Him in acknowledgment or even fear.

The same thought of power, and, more evidently in this case, of character also, being inherent in the term, appears to have been the motive that prompted the threefold use of it as He hung upon the cross. In the first two examples there is the further suggestion that Jesus had employed it with reference to Himself. 'Thou that destroyest the temple,' jeer the passers-by, 'and buildest it in three days, save thyself' (that is, put forth the power thou hast claimed), 'if thou art the Son of God' (as thou hast asserted) 'come down from the cross.' The fellowship with God which thou pretendest to possess ought surely to yield thee as much power as this! The priests, with the scribes and elders, saw deeper into what the claim involved, namely, not only fellowship with God for power, but also assurance of the Divine favour and assistance. 'He trusteth on God; let him deliver him now if he desireth him: for he

ST. PETER'S CONFESSION

said, I am the Son of God' (xxvii. 39, 40, 43). But the centurion and his fellows seem to have grasped still more firmly the connexion of portent with holiness, when, on seeing the signs at Jesus' death, they feared exceedingly, saying, 'Truly this was God's son' (v. 54). They would have heard the term applied to Him; they would, probably, have been aware that He had claimed it for Himself; and their consciences affirmed that the claim was justified, for only because of One who was in touch with God would these awful events have happened.

What, then, of St. Peter's confession in xvi. 16, the terms of which so moved the Lord that, according to St. Matthew's record, He answered him: 'Blessed art thou, Simon Bar-Jonah: for flesh and blood hath not revealed it unto thee, but my Father which is in heaven'? When Jesus asked: 'But who say ye that I am?' wherein lay the excellence of the reply: 'Thou art the Christ, the Son of the living God'? First, that, unlike the populace, St. Peter acknowledged Him to be the looked-for Messiah.[1] But secondly, that he said: 'The Son of the living God.' For this can hardly be only epexegetic of 'the Christ.' It is surely no mere synonym containing nothing fresh. Rather is it probable that in St. Peter's untutored mind there was some such thought as this, that Jesus the Messiah stood in quite unique relation to God, I do not say physical, or, if you will, metaphysical, but at least as revealing Him. And the word 'living,' related by St. Matthew, and placed in this position and not only in a formula of adjuration as by the High Priest (*vide supra*), suggests a present interrelation between Jesus and

[1] See Lecture VIII, pp. 296 *sq.*

His heavenly Father, who is the source of all activity and life. Dr. Sanday, then, may well be right when he says of this passage: ' "The Son" is emphatically taken out of the common category of all others who may be described as " sons." And, " the Son of the living God " is as much as to say " the Son of Jehovah Himself," the God of Revelation and Redemption, and the expression of His Personal Being.' [1]

We are on surer ground when we come to statements by the Evangelist. In the first place, he tells us that notwithstanding the human ancestry of the Messiah (of the stock of Abraham and David), He was of unique origin. We have indeed already considered the Birth of our Lord in the first Lecture of this series, as an answer to Jewish calumnies, and as illustrated by Jewish prophecy. Here it is enough to call attention to the greatness of the origin claimed for Him by the Evangelist. He was born of a pure Virgin, of the Holy Ghost.[2]

Again, He received a unique summons to His life-work, and a unique assurance of its value and import. At the Baptism, ' Lo, the heavens were opened unto him, and he saw the Spirit of God descending as a dove, and coming upon him; and lo, a voice out of the heavens, saying, This is my Son, the Beloved, in whom I am well pleased.' [3] The words were repeated at the Transfiguration,[4]

---

[1] Hastings' *D.B.* iv. 574. Dalman's verdict, 'It appears that Jesus was not called "the Son of God" by any contemporary' (*Words*, p. 275), seems to be based on purely subjective grounds, and not on his great Aramaic and Rabbinic learning.

[2] i. 18-25. See Dorner, *System of Christian Doctrine*, § 105, E.T. 1882, iii. 344-349.

[3] iii. 16, 17. *Cf.* Lecture XI, pp. 381 *sq.*

[4] xvii. 5.

IX] THE PREMISS OF MESSIAHSHIP

at the time, that is to say, when it began to be plain that the life-work of the Messiah promised to Him death. Thus, when His public work began, and again when it was entering upon its final stage, came the assurance : 'This is my Son, the Beloved, in whom I am well pleased.' Community of nature with God forms, as it seems, the premiss of His Messiahship, and this in turn, or rather both together, form the reason for the assurance of God's delight in Him. 'The words [the Son of God],' writes a living English theologian, ' come too often, and the stress laid upon them is too great, for a critical reader to be content with the equation which makes " the Son of God " a simple synonym for " the Messiah." '[1] 'The phrase signifies,' writes one of the most careful of German theologians, ' not an official, but a personal relation ; it is not identical with his position as Messiah, but forms the premiss of it. Because Jesus is the only, or the only begotten, Son of God, therefore God has selected him for this, that he should establish the kingdom of God upon earth by spirit and by judgment. Only the Son of God without a peer is fitted for this superhuman task.'[2] There, in this unique relationship to God, a relationship of nature as well as of character, does the Evangelist see the power that enabled Him to carry out the functions of His Messiahship. Whatever men may think of Jesus of Nazareth to-day, this was the explanation of His life accepted and proclaimed by St. Matthew. He preaches no merely human Jesus, but the Son of God, who came into this world without the medium of a human father,

---

[1] Dr. A. J. Mason, in the *Cambridge Theological Essays*, 1905, p. 453.
[2] Zahn, *Das Evangelium des Matthäus*, 1910, p. 150.

and was acknowledged by God both at the Baptism and at the Transfiguration as holding so unique a relation to Him, that therefore He was fitted for His Messianic office.[1]

That St. Matthew meant his readers thus to understand his own belief in the Divine nature of our Lord will appear still more plainly when we consider the language imputed to Him. It is indeed true that Jesus never, so far as we can learn, applied the phrase ' the Son of God ' directly to Himself, yet He made it clear that He did not regard Himself merely as a Son of God, but as the Son of God.[2] He attributes to Himself, that is to say, an entirely unique relation to His Father, a relationship in which the degree (shall we say ?) of sonship stands on so far higher a plane than that of those who are elsewhere called sons of God that no comparison is possible. Men may or may not be sons of God; He is Son of God as none else is, ' the Son of God.' Certainly in one incident, that of the half-shekel for the Temple tax, He places Himself on St. Peter's level, when He says that the sons of kings are free from taxation to their royal parents, and bids the Apostle take the shekel that is to be found and give it to the collectors ' for me and thee.'[3] But this semi-proverbial saying can hardly be misunderstood. His language is very different in two of the parables, the Wicked Husbandmen, and the marriage of the King's Son.[4] In them He claims to be above all the servants and messengers,

---

[1] In ii. 15 also the Evangelist appears to use the phrase in the same high meaning. See further Lecture I, p. 30. In chap. iv. 3, 6, the meaning is more doubtful, for perhaps the Evangelist intended the phrase used by the devil to have solely an official sense.

[2] *Cf.* Dalman, *Words*, p. 280.

[3] xvii. 24-27.   [4] xxi. 37, 38 ; xxii. 1-14.

OUR LORD'S CLAIM

prophets and teachers of every sort, and to be the very Son of the Owner of the Vineyard, who for that reason is the last person sent; and, again, to be the very heir to the throne of the Almighty King, the Son for whom servants are bid summon, once, yea twice, and even constrain, men of every condition, place, and class to attend His wedding. The point of either parable is lost if Jesus did not by 'the Son' intend in each case Himself.

We have already examined our Lord's reference to Psalm cx.,[1] so far as it bore upon the question of His Davidic origin, and we saw that, notwithstanding certain misinterpretations current to-day, there is no reason to hesitate in finding in His words a claim to be descended from David; but we did not finish our discussion so far as it affected His claim to be Divine. 'If David, then, calleth him Lord, how is he his son?' Must there not, I said, be something in Him which is greater than the standard of David's reign, higher than David's character, perhaps even his nature? In fact, if our Lord's answer to the Pharisees was intended to make them think, rather than to solve for them the problem of His origin, He could hardly have proposed a better method than to set their thoughts on lines which should lead eventually to the result at which St. Matthew arrived, that there was in Jesus the Messiah a something which could only be explained in terms of God, not in those of man. 'We see once again,' writes Zahn, 'that Jesus, like His Evangelist, uses the name "the Son of God," not as a synonym with "Christ," but as a designation of a relationship with God, inherent in Him, and belonging to Him alone among all the sons of David

---

[1] xxii. 41–45. See Lecture VII, pp. 270–272.

and the children of men; a personal quality without which He would have been as little fitted for the office of Messiah as Solomon or Hezekiah.'[1]

The peculiar difficulties of the next passage hardly affect our present inquiry. Matt. xxiv. 36 : 'Of that day and hour knoweth no one, not even the angels of heaven, neither the Son, but the Father only.' For the question so often discussed by the orthodox, whether the Lord is speaking of Himself in His human or in His divine aspect, is of no present moment to us. Upon the face of it He knows Himself to be so high above men and the very angels of heaven, that He places Himself almost, I grant not quite, on an equality with the Father. This passage, notwithstanding those difficulties at which I have hinted, is one of the most remarkable assertions of His supremacy in nature over all things created which are to be found in this Gospel.[2]

The baptismal formula, ' baptizing them into the name of the Father and of the Son and of the Holy Ghost ' (xxviii. 19), is so near the high-water mark of the ecclesiastical definition of the relation of the Son to the Father (implying, as it appears to do, the equality of One with the Other, and each with the Holy Ghost), that we can hardly be surprised that attempts have been made to excise it from the text. Yet, in spite of the omission of the full phrase in some passages of Eusebius, there is no reason to doubt that

---

[1] *Matthäus*, p. 647. Dalman writes: 'An unbiased reading of the statement of Jesus cannot avoid the conclusion that the Messiah is in reality the Son of One more exalted than David, that is, the Son of God' (*Words*, p. 286).

[2] Dalman's opinion (*Words*, p. 194), that ' the original was "not even the angels know it," and that the ending "nor the Son, but the Father only" should be regarded as an accretion,' does not appear to be due to his Aramaic learning.

it was always part of our present Gospel. To put it otherwise, the verse expressed the belief of the Evangelist in the complete Divinity of Jesus, and was therefore included in his presentation of Him as the true Messiah.[1]

But one passage [2] has been omitted from our survey which confessedly belongs to that primitive source known as ' Q,' and therefore, on the most approved critical principles, to the utterances of Him whom some are pleased to call ' the Historical Jesus.'

' I thank thee, O Father, Lord of heaven and earth, that thou didst hide these things from the wise and understanding, and didst reveal them unto babes : yea, Father, for so it was well-pleasing in thy sight. All things have been delivered unto me of my Father : and no one knoweth the Son, save the Father; neither doth any know the Father, save the Son, and he to whomsoever the Son willeth to reveal him.'

Observe the intimate standing which the Speaker holds with God ! He addresses Him twice as Father, with thankful acknowledgment confessing the justice and the wisdom of His dealings with men. Then, in

---

[1] For a full discussion of the passage see Bp. Chase, *Journal of Theological Studies*, vi. July, 1905, pp. 481–521 ; viii. Jan. 1907, pp. 161–184 ; Knowling, *Messianic Interpretation*, 1910, pp. 64–73, and especially pp. 81–84 for a discussion of Harnack's unsatisfactory verdict ; Sparrow Simpson, *The Resurrection and Modern Thought*, 1911, pp. 268–284. It is indeed possible that our Lord did not Himself deliver the charge word for word as recorded, and that the formula in its present language may be the result of thought and condensation. But if, as is almost certain, it belongs to the original Gospel and is not an interpolation, it must be so early that those critics who deny its genuineness do not get much support for their theory that the doctrine of the Holy Trinity was unknown to the Apostolic Church. Our Lord might, or might not, have cared to formulate His teaching on the Godhead in the language of this verse, and yet it may legitimately represent the substance of His teaching.

[2] xi. 25–27 ; Luke x. 21, 22.

contrast to the method of Jewish reception of doctrines from human teachers, He solemnly affirms that to Him had been entrusted all things necessary for His work by His Father, whereon follows the amazing passage that no one has thorough knowledge of Himself, the Son, save the Father, and no one has such knowledge of the Father save the Son, and he to whom the Son deems it well to reveal Him. The knowledge of Son and Father by each other is expressed in identical terms, implying equality of position, and, as it seems, of nature.[1]

Here, too, we cannot be surprised that the statement has proved a stumbling-block to many of those critics who are so firmly convinced that Jesus was a mere man and nothing more, as to be able to persuade themselves that Jesus Himself never uttered the words.[2]

One thing seems to be clear, that it was not the Evangelist alone who understood Him to have said this, but also the writer of the earlier source from which, according to modern criticism, the passage was incorporated in our present Gospel. Further, if, as some believe, the author of that source was the Apostle Matthew himself, we could hardly have better witness to the actual sayings of Jesus. For

[1] *Cf.* Dalman, *Words*, p. 283.
[2] See Montefiore, *Some Elements of the Religious Teaching of Jesus*, 1910, pp. 162-164 : ' That mournful Christian particularism which would deny any true knowledge of God the Father except to those who also believe in the Son.' Sanday (Hastings' *D.B.* iv. 573) points out the difficulty of accounting for the rapid growth of theological terms within some twenty-three to twenty-six years from our Lord's death, if it was not the natural continuation of His own teaching. *Cf.* J. Weiss, *Urchristentum*, 1914, p. 28. See also A. J. Mason in the *Cambridge Theological Essays*, 1905, pp. 455 *sq.* ; F. Tillmann, *Das Selbstbewusstsein des Gottessohnes*, 1911, pp. 77-81 ; Knowling, *Messianic Interpretation*, 1910, pp. 62-64. Harnack's study of the passage in *The Sayings of Jesus*, E.T. 1908, pp. 272-310, is important. McNeile (*in loco*) has a valuable summary of the various interpretations.

ST. MATTHEW THE MONOTHEIST

the Apostle had lived continually with the Master for three years.

This passage, then, appears to be the highest of all those that contribute to the presentation of the Divine nature of Jesus, the Messiah, in this Gospel. He claims here that all things necessary for His Messianic work have been given Him, because He stands in the relation, the full and complete relation, of Son to Father, the Sonship and the Fathership being so perfect that each Person is able to know the other in the same degree that He is known. We are brought, as it would seem, to the inner shrine of Christian doctrine, the very Being of the One Eternal God, the essential Trinity.

To sum up what we have learnt of the teaching of the Evangelist. To him the term 'the Son of God' meant unique earthly origin, *i.e.* birth from a woman, without the agency of a human father; also a unique summons to His life-work, and a unique assurance of its acceptance and its value; lastly, full equality with the Father, whether this be expressed in an ecclesiastical formula or in an utterance of filial love. Jesus the Son of God brings the fullest revelation of God, and holds the closest fellowship with Him. There is interrelation of knowledge between them different from that of men. These might know the Father, but only through the medium of the Son.

In other words, the monotheism of St. Matthew proved to be consistent with a belief in the equality of Jesus of Nazareth with the Father. The question for us is: Was this, when all is said, only monstrous idolatry, or was it indeed the very truth of truths? There is no third possibility.

II. How could St. Matthew come to the conviction that Jesus of Nazareth was equal to the living God, Jehovah, and in some degree identical with Him? The belief is amazing, in whatever way we regard it. St. Matthew, a strictly monotheistic Jew, to believe that Jesus of Nazareth was divine, and yet to show no sign of any consciousness that he was committing blasphemy in this belief, or idolatry in worshipping Him!

Now to answer the question by saying that similar beliefs were current among the heathen of that time (for persons like Alexander of Macedon and Augustus of Rome had been admitted by Greeks and Romans into their pantheon), and that St. Matthew and those he represented were influenced by these superstitions, is extremely unsatisfactory from a purely historical point of view. St. Matthew and his friends were not heathen. They were Jews, and not even Hellenistic Jews, though there is no evidence, so far as I am aware, that even these ever thought of deifying men. But he and the first Christians were Jews of Palestine, monotheistic to the backbone, not in the least likely to be affected by heathenism.

Yet they said Jesus was divine, and divine in such a way that not only was He above angels, but also was upon an equality with the Father. How then came St. Matthew to this creed, and when? Of course we can but draw inferences; there is no clear statement in the form of a direct answer to either question. And, further, in the First Gospel, unlike the Fourth, no attempt is made to unfold the history of the progress of belief in the mind of the disciples as they beheld more and more of the glory of Jesus. But this much seems fairly clear;

IX] JESUS' DIVINITY PERCEIVED GRADUALLY

that the Apostle did not arrive at his belief in our Lord's divinity during the earthly life of our Lord. He, with other disciples, wondered at Him, and that increasingly, accepting *ex animo* (it would seem) even St. Peter's acknowledgment of Jesus as the Messiah, the Son of the living God. But St. Matthew could not have meant more by this than St. Peter, and the meaning of the latter seems to have come far short of belief in the full Godhead of Jesus. During the earthly life of Jesus of Nazareth, St. Matthew received the impression of Him as a unique personality, quite above and beyond any other he had seen, but he never regarded Him as God.

The Resurrection must have made a difference, partly by the fact itself, partly by the words of the risen Master. For now the Twelve, with the other believers, knew that Jesus was on so high a pedestal that all authority in heaven and earth was given to Him, and that His presence with His people was assured to them all the days until the completion of this current age. The Resurrection must have enormously increased the belief of the disciples in the supernatural origin of Jesus.

Yet it is probable that the full meaning of the words of the risen Lord, and of that earlier saying in which He expressed in identical terms the mutual knowledge of the Father and the Son, was not perceived until after Pentecost, the promised baptism in the Holy Ghost and fire (iii. 11). Or putting it otherwise, with, as I trust, no suspicion of irreverence, the doctrine of the full divinity of Jesus was the result of holy thought and meditation guided by the Spirit. Then, and only then, after, it may be, weeks or months, or possibly a few years (though we have no hint that the time was so long), the value and the purpose of Jesus' life, words, death, and resurrection were at last understood. To the believers of that day Jesus became known as divine in the fullest sense. In spite of St. Matthew's strict monotheism, which brooked no tampering with the deification of men, the pressure of the events of our Lord's life, together with His teaching, compelled him to come to the amazing conclusion that Jesus was not only the Son of David, and the Son of man, but even the Son of God, in the highest meaning of that supreme title; and one of the reasons that led him to write his Gospel was to strengthen the faith of his readers in this truth.

Yet for us there is a more important question than: Why did St. Matthew believe in our Lord's divinity? namely: *Why do we ourselves believe in it?* It is commonly asserted that it was easier for him to believe it in those days of ignorant superstition than for us. I am not so sure. What little we know of the psychology of the Jewish mind of that date does not suggest that belief in the divinity of Jesus was easy at all, and there are some considerations which tend to make it easier for us to believe it than for St. Matthew.

Why, then, do we believe that Jesus of Nazareth was divine? Not because St. Matthew said He was. Nor because the other Apostles said so. Nor because all the writers of the New Testament said the same thing. Nor, again, because the Church tells us so. We each started with this reason, no doubt. When we were children we were bound

WHY WE ACCEPT HIS DIVINITY

to believe what we were told, if we were to arrive at any creed or knowledge worth holding or knowing. But for grown and intelligent men to believe so stupendous an assertion as the divinity of Jesus solely on the strength of another man's belief, or on the belief of others, countless though these be as the grains of sand along the shore, and united though they are by a spiritual tie so close and living that it is compared in Scripture to that of the various members of a human being—number and size do not count against one immortal mind—is to abdicate the functions of discernment and decision implanted in us by God. By all means let us give weight, due and proper, to the authority of numbers and of moral superiority; but to accept a truth solely because of what others say, without making any effort to understand the principles that have guided them to accept what they now offer us—this is to despise the inheritance of sanity, the awful gifts of will and choice. To accept blindly a *quantum* of dogma at the bidding even of Holy Church is what no man, above all, no Christian man, is called upon to do. That is but a false humility which urges us towards it.[1]

Yet to credit facts related by others, not because they are persons in authority, but because they are historians—facts judged by such canons of history as are applicable to their special subject, and to reason therefrom—is a very different thing. This we may and we must do. We find certain facts related in the Gospels, and we not only are permitted, but are

---

[1] This is the weakness running through Mr. Knox's witty *Some Loose Stones*, 1913, *e.g.* pp. x, 33, 36, 191, 215 *sq.*

actually compelled, to reason out their meaning, and to interpret them as best we can.

It is replied, however, that the facts recorded by the New Testament writers are coloured. But I suppose the question is, not whether they are coloured, but whether they are coloured wrongly. For will you ever find a narrative in which facts are not coloured? The members of this learned body know much more about such matters than I do, but I have always understood that facts are never stated in absolute and naked truth, and that, at any rate, you never find even two witnesses to an occurrence agreeing in every detail of the facts they narrate. Indeed, if there were such minute concord, there might be a grave suspicion that their testimony was concocted.

So far, however, as we can test St. Matthew, we find, at the very lowest estimate of him, that his statements of facts are truthful, and that his records of words are sufficiently accurate to justify us in basing a general argument upon them.

Yet it may be said that as St. Matthew believed in the divinity of Jesus before he wrote his Gospel, and indeed wrote it with that presupposition, his statements are prejudiced and unworthy of credence. His narrative confessedly represents Jesus, not as He appeared to His companions during those three years of visible intercourse, but as He seemed to them to have been some thirty or forty years after His death. But do thought and consideration necessarily vitiate the presentment of history? Lord Haldane has taught us once again that the true historian is no mere photographer, snapshotting event after event, but an artist, catching the essential

THE IRREDUCIBLE MINIMUM

features of his subject and presenting it in a light all the truer because it gathers into one picture not one moment but many.[1] The fact that the First Gospel not only states the mystery of the life of Jesus but also gives the key to its solution, a key wrought out by much thought and toil, does not necessarily lead to the conclusion that the mystery and its facts are wrongly set forth. It may, and personally I believe it does, only assist us in interpreting those facts in the right way.

Can we then, as thinking men, believe in the divinity of Jesus ? I answer that the question is rather : Can we help believing in it, if we accept the Gospel narrative as substantially correct ? And, further, I will say, treat the narrative as critically as you may ; remove, if canons of historical criticism demand it, saying after saying, and explain away miracle after miracle, strictly in accordance with scientific knowledge ; cast everything into the crucible of the severest tests possible, without bias either for or against the miraculous, or for or against Christian dogma, if such freedom from bias can be found, and the residuum is that One still stands out before us unique in history for the powers He displayed over disease and nature ; for the holiness He exhibited in every place and in all circumstances ; for the continuous communion He enjoyed with His Father in heaven ; for the love which prompted Him to give at last His very life for others ; for the triumph He gained after death—One who claimed to be above angels, and even to be on an equality with God ; One upon whom the earliest Christian Church, the society of the first believing Jews,

[1] The Creighton Lecture, *The Meaning of Truth in History*, 1914, pp. 7 *sqq.*

was built, and in Whom, as they affirmed, they obtained pardon and peace and power, in a word, eternal life. Who and what is He, this irreducible minimum of the Gospel story ?

For observe, you explain nothing of all this, no, neither the figure of Christ, nor the genesis of the Christian Church, if you assert that Jesus was only a good Jew, put to death either for His reforming tendencies, or for the odium that He incurred with the Roman authorities. This theory can be held only after the Gospels have been stripped of all that made them Gospels in the eyes of those who wrote them, and of their first readers.

You also explain nothing when you say that Jesus was a man of superior type to us others ; a man in advance of His age, so far in advance, perhaps, that millennia may pass away before other men are like Him ; or even if you suggest that the difference between Him and us was due to the fact that He enjoyed more of the presence of God than we do. For, say what we will, the difference between His experience and ours, *i.e.* between Him and ourselves, is so immense that no comparison is possible.

While, on the other hand, if you grant that the man Jesus of Nazareth received the Divine Spirit so fully that there was in Him no part or corner, as it were, unfilled with the Godhead, then you are drawing so near to the orthodox Christian position that you may well question whether, after all, this does not better represent the truth.

For this at least is clear, that we cannot hold any opinion about Jesus which treats Him as a man raised to a kind of honorary Godhead, without impeaching the Christian Church of idolatry, of

SPIRIT AND MATTER

worshipping a deified man. Whatever opponents may say, nothing can be more abhorrent than this to us Gentile Christians of to-day, or could have been to such Jewish Christians as the author of the First Gospel.

It is not so. The Christian Church feels, and has ever felt, that all the words and actions of Jesus are indeed consistent with the nature of man in the abstract, yet transcend the experience of all other men.[1]

They suggest to us, therefore, the possibility that they are connected with His own claim to equality with God, and make us seriously consider whether this be not the true explanation of the problem of His life—that in very truth He was divine. As with St. Matthew so also with us; the pressure of the life, words, death, and resurrection of Jesus bears upon us so heavily that we cannot but believe Him to be more than man, even the living God.[2]

Yet when we speak of the living God taking human flesh, the reply is made at once: *Can Spirit clothe itself with matter?* But surely this objection, in at least this bald form, is now antiquated. Such

---

[1] Perhaps Dorner brings this out best in his *System of Christian Doctrine*, E.T. 1881, ii. 284–290.

[2] Some recent scholars have even thought that Jesus actually acquired Godhead. But 'faith views Jesus not merely as One who through grace rose to a union with the Highest comparable to that achieved by saints, though far more intimate, but as One whose development in Divine-human personality took place *within* His own native sphere of transcendence. . . . It was because deity was His from before all time that He possessed the unspeakable gift to lay on love's altar. On the other hand, the conception of an acquired divinity stands on a lower ethical plane; it has parted with the aspect of sublimity' (H. R. Mackintosh, *The Doctrine of the Person of Jesus Christ*, pp. 423 *sq.*, *cf.* p. 245). Joh. Weiss, *Das Urchristentum*, 1914, p. 85, writes: 'Adoption ist hier gebraucht im Gegensatz zu der natürlichen Sohnschaft, die von Geburt an vorhanden ist. Es liegt also hier der Gedanke vor, dass Jesus nicht von Anfang an Messias oder, wie dafür auch gesagt werden kann, *Sohn Gottes* war, sondern dass er erst *geworden* ist in einem bestimmten, scharf abgegrenzten Willensakt Gottes.'

force as it once had, even so lately as thirty, or even twenty, years ago, is passed away to-day. For our whole conception of the nature of matter has been revolutionised. We now know that matter, as we see and feel and perceive it, is no dead thing, but instinct with energy, and motion, and a kind of life. The potencies at work within one grain of sand, the primitive elements which constitute it, are, I suppose, beyond the calculation of even mathematical formulæ (save such as are devised to cover our ignorance), for its powers are so stupendous, that it is a very microcosm of the omnipotence of God.

But besides this comparatively simple way of regarding matter, philosophers remind us that we have no knowledge at all of matter existing apart from Spirit; that it is, so far as reason tells us, the form, and perhaps only the form, in which Spirit makes itself known. 'Matter is the name for what moves in space. It is at present believed to consist of atoms which have different chemical characteristics, that may possibly be due to different mechanical arrangements; but here we pass into the region of hypothesis, and beyond all this is hypothetical as to what atoms ultimately are. At any rate, their ultimate constitution is out of reach of our senses; and it remains that matter as we know it is an effect, a phenomenon or appearance, a manifestation of something other than meets either hand or eye.'[1] 'Matter, as being the language of Spirit, is also the medium of its realisation.'[2]

In short, reason tells us to-day that all matter is informed by Spirit, which Spirit must in the last

---

[1] Illingworth, *Divine Immanence*, 1898, p. 8.
[2] *Ibid., op. cit.* p. 11.

IX] INCARNATION—IMPERFECT AND PERFECT

instance not only be personal (or else you and I, as being persons, are higher than It), but, by Its complete freedom from all external force, also be more truly personal than ourselves.[1] Matter, then, what we call Creation, is, according to pure reason, without any reference to revelation, continually the scene and the instrument of Spirit, the sphere of the immanence of that great Personal Spirit, to whom, in religious language, we give the name of God.

If so, is it mere juggling with words, or is it rather the expression in human language of a truth for which other phrases fail, to speak of the immanence and revelation of God in Creation as a kind of incarnation? Such an 'incarnation' is no doubt imperfect, but it is a hint, if you will, and a promise, of what God may do, if He chooses, in making Himself known, not merely within what we term matter, but in a Person, who shall, without any hindrance due to error and failure, theologically called sin, make the true character of God known to the world. Spirit does continually clothe itself with matter. Is it so very surprising that, if occasion arose, it should reveal itself completely, in a Person living on earth, and exhibiting the true nature and character of the Divine Spirit, without let or hindrance—God manifest in the world in the Person of Jesus Christ?[2]

We then regard Jesus of Nazareth as Very and Eternal God. But can it be that the Creator of millions of worlds, each perhaps far exceeding in size this puny earth of ours, selects it out of all for

---

[1] See p. 338, n. 3. *Cf.* W. Temple, *Foundations*, 1913, pp. 258 *sq.*

[2] *Cf.* W. Temple, *ibid.* pp. 245-248. Bishop Weston, *The One Christ*, 1914, pp. 227-232; and Fairbairn, *Philosophy of the Christian Religion*, p. 479, quoted in H. R. Mackintosh, *The Doctrine of the Person of Jesus Christ*, pp. 433 *sq.*

the manifestation of Himself? No doubt, when we put the question so, it does seem improbable. But if we leave terms of space, and consider it in those of ethics, the case alters. As a man is greater than all the stones of earth, than all the myriad insects, fishes, birds, and beasts, taken singly or together, not so much for his body or his brains, as for his power of discerning between good and evil, and the possibility of his moral growth; so is he certainly greater than all the blazing suns in the universe, all the worlds in boundless space, and, so far as we know, may be greater than all the inhabitants of these, if they are inhabited at all.[1]

And there is another, and still more vital consideration. We are each so bowed down with sin and guilt as to be unable to look up with unshamed countenance into the face of God. And it is this side of the Incarnation upon which the New Testament insists. For when we study the Gospel of St. Matthew, it is evident that the Son of God is come not only to exhibit God's holiness and love, but to do

[1] 'When we are complacently told in certain quarters that the Copernican astronomy revolutionized man's view of his relation to the universe, we should remember that to say the least, this is a considerable over-statement of the case. In minds of a materialistic bias, it would have undoubtedly have this effect; but not in those who estimated man by the claims of his spiritual nature, which is as unaffected by the size of his dwelling-place as by the cubits of his stature' (Illingworth, *Divine Immanence*, p. 21).

'Can we believe that a tiny planet known to be but a speck in the stellar immensities was chosen as the scene of the astounding miracle of incarnation? Why this special favour to one world out of myriads? Does not our cosmical insignificance veto the notion as a preposterous incredibility? But this, as has been said, "is simply an attempt to terrorise the imagination" (P. C. Simpson, *Fact of Christ*, p. 116). Its plausibility vanishes when we recall the love of God and the greatness of the soul' (Mackintosh, *op. cit.* p. 443). 'We see the magnitude of matter, but cannot see the magnitude of mind' (Illingworth, *op. cit.* p. 18). *Cf.* also Dorner, *A System of Christian Doctrine*, iii. p. 325.

TO SAVE SINNERS

so with the express object of freeing us men from sin. Whatever may be said for the belief that the Incarnation would have taken place even if sin had had no power over us—and there is much to be said for it—the Gospel of St. Matthew knows nothing of this. We read instead, in the first chapter, that the Son of the Blessed Virgin shall be called ' Jesus, for it is he that shall save his people from their sins '; and in the twentieth, that Jesus Himself says, He came ' to give his life a ransom for many.' To us, sinful people, saved by the Incarnation of the Son of God, and by that alone, His coming is the everlasting subject of our gratitude and praise.

> ' Alas ! shall I present
>   My sinfulness
> To Thee ? Thou wilt resent
>   The loathsomeness.
> "Be not afraid, I'll take
>   Thy sins on Me,
> And all My favour make
>   To shine on thee."
> LORD, what Thou'lt have me, Thou must make me.
> "As I have made thee now, I take thee." '
>   CHRISTOPHER HARVEY, *Synagogue*, 1640, in
>   the *Treasury of Sacred Song*, lxxi.

When therefore we see in Jesus the highest example ever known of holiness and love, and, far more than this, the highest conception we have ever framed of them, or apparently ever can frame, it does not seem unworthy of God to show Himself, not only as Omnipotence in making and preserving creation, but also as holiness and love, living a human life, that by His life lived, His life given, and His life triumphant over death, men might be delivered from sin in its consequences, its powers, and at last its presence.

For we must not forget that if there were a perfect Incarnation of the living God we could not expect to see more in His human life than holiness and love. Omnipotence in action would surely be impossible for One who was to live as man; Omniscience exercised would frustrate any full development save that of the body; Omnipresence enjoyed would be contrary to His very existence amid earthly conditions. But love, with its accompanying holiness—for love without holiness ceases to be love—is the greatest of all forces, and therefore perhaps *is* Omnipotence; the most penetrating of all forms of knowledge, and so perhaps the basis of Omniscience; and overleaps all boundaries in time or space, suggesting Omnipresence.[1]

There does not appear, then, to be anything shocking to our moral sense, or our intelligence, in the thought of incarnate holiness and love, with their exhibition of utter self-sacrifice for men's salvation.[2]

At this point the question may be asked: Wherein lies the personality of Jesus? Was it, is it, human or divine? But, alas, the question, simple though it looks, is itself obscure, because no satisfactory definition of personality has ever yet been given,[3]

---

[1] On our Lord's omnipotence, omniscience, and omnipresence see H. R. Mackintosh, *op. cit.* pp. 477 *sqq.*, 486.

[2] 'Love in essence is desire and will to suffer for the sake of the beloved: to enter his condition, to take his load, to renounce every privilege. Not to send a sympathetic message simply, or appear by deputy, but to come in person, obstacles and counter-reasons notwithstanding. Otherwise love is not known as love. Even of God it is true that he who would save his life must lose it' (*ibid.* p. 425).

[3] 'The conception of the Ego is very perplexing. It is difficult to describe its content, and to discover a fundamental principle which will serve to

IMPERSONAL HUMANITY NON-EXISTENT

and, presumably in consequence of this, the full answer to the question is so delicately poised that it is apt to incline to error or even heresy. If we affirm that our Lord's personality is human we say something very like Nestorianism or Adoptionism, and are near to the denial of His true divinity; if Divine, we must beware lest unconsciously we fall into Eutychianism and into a denial of His manhood. The old formula indeed of one Divine person in two natures, the Divine and the human, may still be the best within our reach,[1] but verbally it assumes the existence of human nature as an entity apart from personality, a thing of which we have no experience whatever, and to which perhaps we can attach no real meaning. As Dr. Moberly writes: 'There is, and there can be, no such thing as impersonal humanity. The phrase involves a contradiction in terms. Human nature which is not personal is not human nature. . . . In so far as He is a Person now humanly incarnate, the word human has become a true attribute, truly predicable of His Personality.'[2] Similarly, Professor Mackintosh says: 'It has no reality our minds can apprehend to say that Jesus matured in mind, in character, in self-consciousness, but that His personality or Ego remained throughout immutably

distinguish it satisfactorily from the non-Ego' (Professor D. Phillips, in *Encyclopædia of Religion and Ethics*, s.v. Ego, v. 227). Some see gradations of personality in brutes, men, and God, depending on the extent to which each is superior to external circumstances, self-determinate and self-bestowing. In this way, while it is still convenient to speak of human personality, in strictness the term belongs to Him alone who is supreme and absolutely free, God Himself. *Cf.* W. Temple, *The Nature of Personality*, 1911, especially pp. 5, 17, 79-81. See also especially Sanday, *Personality in Christ and in Ourselves*, 1911, pp. 8, 13-15, 20.

[1] 'The Son of God did not assume a man's person unto His own, but a man's nature to His own person' (Hooker, *Ecclesiastical Polity*, V, lii. 3).

[2] *Atonement and Personality*, 1911, pp. 93, sq.

behind a veil, as a substratum unaffected by the phenomena of change. The word "person" has no content when we remove moral character, religious consciousness, and the mediatorial function which both subserve.'[1]

We tread in fear and trembling, like travellers on a narrow pass with an awful precipice on either hand. Yet the solid rock beneath us is this, that none less than God became man. Primarily, therefore, Jesus is Divine. But in saying this we must acknowledge that if God is everywhere, as He must be, then in becoming man He submits Himself by self-limitation to human conditions, and takes real, not imaginary manhood, with human growth in complexity of character, in devotion of will, in enlargement of understanding, in even the perception of His own unique nature and His relation to the Father, and of His work of redemption and what it costs, thus possessing (in this self-limitation of the Godhead) only one consciousness, truly human, and (as a conscious Person) even only one will. We cannot, that is to say, postulate in Jesus two Personalities, two Egos, but one, and that Divine, but so self-restrained as to form a man. As Bishop Weston says: 'He did not take a manhood, in the sense that He associated with Himself one human person; for that would have been to redeem one at the cost of the race. But in Mary's womb He took human flesh which, with its own proper and complete soul, He constituted in Himself so that He became truly man, living as the subject or ego of real manhood. Thus His human nature He united to Himself personally. It is manhood assumed by God the Son; and may not be thought of as if it were joined to His divine nature,

[1] *Op. cit.* pp. 495 *sq.*

He Himself being as it were apart from both. It is His own proper nature, constituted in His own divine person as self-limited.'[1]

'Looked at from above, as from the standpoint of the Logos Himself, His consciousness as man must surely bear the marks of self-sacrificing love, of powerful self-restraint. It is the result of the self-emptying of the Son; of His determination to accept, within certain relationships, the fashion of a man and the form of a slave. He willed so to relate Himself to the Father and to men that within these relationships He could not know Himself as unlimited Son of God.'[2] 'The popular teaching that assumes in the Incarnate a full consciousness of divine glory side by side with a consciousness of certain occasional human limitations cannot be too strongly deprecated. It requires three states of the Logos: the first in which He is unlimited and unincarnate; the second in which He is incarnate, and unlimited except when He wills to allow some merely human condition to prevail over Him; and the third in which He is self-limited in that human condition. And the result of such a conception of the Incarnate is to make His manhood unique not only in the degree of its perfection, but also in kind. It makes it utterly unlike ours, and also removes it from all part in the mediation of His self-consciousness.'[3] 'As Eternal Logos He made an Act of Will in virtue of which He entered upon and now lives in manhood; and as Incarnate, He accepts at every moment, personally, through His divine will, all the foreseen, inevitable consequences of His act.'[4]

---

[1] *The One Christ*, 1914, pp. 150 *sq.*
[2] *Op. cit.* p. 173.
[3] *Op. cit.* pp. 174 *sq.*
[4] *Op. cit.* p. 176.

For it was the Son, the Logos, who became man; this is self-evident, and the teaching of Scripture. 'In the beginning,' writes St. John, 'was the Word, and the Word was with God, and the Word was God. . . . And the Word became flesh.' Jesus of Nazareth, that is to say, represents not God *per se*, transcendent above matter, but God as He comes forth in self-impartation in space and time, but still God.[1] It was He, none less than He, who became incarnate, lived once on earth, and lives now in heaven, as Jesus of Nazareth, our ascended Lord. We shall therefore not shrink from adopting the language of our Creed, for, after all, it is the truest exponent of the facts, in language suited to human understanding, and we shall speak of Jesus as the Son of the Father, with filiation more complete, because complete, than any other sonship that ever has been. He is therefore both the Son of God and God the Son,[2] the object of our praise and worship, very and eternal God.

Bearing in mind, then, the daily manifestation of Spirit through matter; the incalculable value of human souls, and the woefulness of their state through sin; and also the power of holy love in its self-sacrifice, hindered, not helped, by other attributes of God; we begin to see a reason and a cause for the unique character of Jesus of Nazareth, and dare to accept His own verdict on Himself, and that of His friends, that He was the Son of God; and, further, in the light of thought and contemplation,

---

[1] Compare Mackintosh, *op. cit.* p. 492. Further, may we not even say God in His human side, with His human attributes, as in the vision vouchsafed to Ezekiel (see Lecture VIII)?

[2] Against Dr. Latimer Jackson, *The Eschatology of Jesus*, 1913, p. 329.

wrought in us, as we humbly trust, by the Holy Ghost, we learn to give to that title the fullest meaning it can embrace, perfect Son of perfect Father, very God of very God; and, rising in our meditation from the economic to the essential Trinity, we confess with our great western Hymn of Praise: 'Patris et Filii et Spiritus Sancti una est divinitas, æqualis gloria, coæterna majestas.'

Lecture Ten

THE MESSIAH AND THE APOCALYPTISTS

'*Therefore be ye also ready :
for in an hour that ye think
not the Son of man cometh.*'
—MATT. xxiv. 44.

Lecture Ten

THE MESSIAH AND THE APOCALYPTISTS

CATASTROPHE, development, catastrophe, appear to be the normal order of our earth. First, as physicists tell us, was the disruption of that molten mass now represented by the moon; then, down to our own time, have been long, slow, sure change, development, and evolution, punctuated with crises, convulsions, and upheavals of a minor kind; to be followed, as it seems, by one all-embracing cataclysm, when, either by its own internal heat, or by the impact of an external body, our earth will experience a sudden conflagration, with, we may presume, a complete reconstruction of its existing material.

But the law of life is one. As with the planet, so with us who live upon it. At our birth, catastrophe; in our life, uniformity; at death, catastrophe again.

And with the spiritual life it is not otherwise. There is conversion, when all things become new; then growth, mostly so slow and gradual that its progress is hardly noted, yet marked at times by sudden bounds and swift, unlooked-for expansion; lastly, that great catastrophic change when the body is sloughed away, and the personality is face to face with the Source of all light and life, receiving the celestial outcome of its terrestrial form, and the final result of its moral probation.

And so, we may presume, is it with the Church. Catastrophe at its origin, slow development with minor crises, and at last the catastrophic end, glorious beyond words.

I. It was on this consummation that the thought of the Apocalyptists fastened. This was the central conception embodied in their terms and illustrations, which to us are quaint, and sometimes barely edifying, and in both substance and form were distasteful to the recognised leaders of their race. For among the many difficult questions affecting the relationship of the Apocalyptists to other Jewish teachers, two facts emerge—first, that their instruction was not esoteric, but popular, and secondly, that it was rejected by that Pharisaic section of Judaism which alone survived the Fall of Jerusalem.

First, their teaching was not esoteric, but popular. A reaction against the growing scholasticism of the interpretation of the Law was bound to make its appearance. Though, as we have already seen in previous Lectures, the insistence on the minutiæ of the code of Moses, and the necessary oral tradition which accompanied it from the very first, did not reach its height until taught by those great men who were in part the survivors, in part the successors, of the Rabbinic doctors of New Testament times, yet Shammai and Hillel, just before our Lord's birth, were themselves the inheritors of some centuries of casuistic teaching, which tended to mark off its devotees more and more strictly from the common and unlearned people.

Yet some thinkers perceived that the strength of true religion lay in the fact that it was intended for the many rather than for the few, and that they who had little time for study and debate, or even

THE APOCALYPTIC WRITERS

for the punctilious observance of innumerable rules of deportment, ceremony, and religious ritual, could and would appreciate the encouragement to be found in fundamental truths, amid the increasing burdens, political and social, now threatening their daily life. And more than this. These Apocalyptists taught that the spiritual world was very near, not only future but present, though hidden from earthly sight. Others might be taken up with political expectations, and the hope of a Messiah belonging to this world only, but for them the supernatural was all-important, and the Messiah was from above, and would come on the clouds of heaven.[1]

Therefore they taught and wrote. They appealed to the feelings rather than to the intellect; they bade their disciples (though of disciples in the narrower and more technical sense they probably had but few) lay stress on the glorious changes possible in the near future for those who served their God, rather than on any such slow improvement as might appear desirable to more worldly men; and, above all, they bore in mind, nay, perhaps they themselves shared, the impatience which is natural to the uneducated, rather than the disciplined hope of the more thoughtful. For, whatever the reason may be, the fact can hardly be denied that belief in the near approach of the end has seldom been a mark of the more philosophic thinkers of any creed.

Not that the Pharisees were philosophers. It is

---

[1] The Apocalyptic literature is a 'Loslösung der messianischen Erwartungen von dem irdisch politischen Ideale und Steigerung desselben in's Uebernatürliche' (Baldensperger, *Das spätere Judenthum als Vorstufe des Christenthums*, 1900, p. 15). M. Friedländer thinks that early Apocalyptic thought owed much to Hellenism, an opinion which is well stated by Oesterley, *The Books of the Apocrypha*, 1914, pp. 90-112. *Cf. supra*, p. 7.

the last title that we can give them, and perhaps the last which they would have cared to receive. They rejected the Apocalyptic books for quite other reasons. One book no doubt they accepted, because both in use and in present form, perhaps even in origin, it belonged to the heroic period of the nation's deliverance from Syro-Greek heathenism, and to the beginnings of Pharisaism. But with this notable exception of the Book of Daniel, almost all the writings of the Apocalyptists, such as the Book of Enoch, the Testaments of the Twelve Patriarchs, the Sibylline Oracles, the Assumption of Moses, the Second or Fourth Book of Ezra, the Apocalypse of Baruch, and others, owe their preservation entirely to Christian, and not to Jewish, copyists. The reason is not far to seek. As Professor Burkitt shows, from a saying attributed to R. Jochanan ben Zakkai, ' It was this world that God revealed to Abraham ; but the world to come he revealed not to him,'[1] the Rabbinic leaders were more occupied in insisting on the duties involved in serving God in this life than in occupying themselves with the mysteries of the world to come. Rightly or wrongly, they tried to leave the future to God, and devoted their attention to His claim upon them here, while the Apocalyptists on the contrary turned away the eyes of their followers from the details of the religious

[1] *Jewish and Christian Apocalypses*, 1914, p. 12, quoting from Bereshith Rabba, § 44 (on Gen. xv. 18). Contrast ' The Most High hath not made one world, but two,' 2 (4) Esdras vii. 50, quoted by Professor Burkitt, *op. cit.* p. 32. I leave this as written, but it is questionable whether we are justified in laying so much stress on R. Jochanan ben Zakkai's haggadic explanation of one verse. R. Aqiba, it may be noticed, takes the opposite view. He came much nearer to the Apocalyptists, in that he was looking for the Messianic age, to which indeed the commentators on the Bereshith Rabba understand ' the world to come ' to refer.

THE ATTITUDE OF THE RABBIS

life on earth in order that they might entrance them with the glories and blessedness of the hereafter. In neither case was the complementary truth forgotten, but the centre of gravity differed. In these circumstances we cannot be surprised that the Rabbis thought the Apocalyptic books were dangerous to that system of painful ceremonial life which they were endeavouring to impress upon the nation.[1]

A more potent reason still lay in the attitude of Christianity towards the Apocalyptic teaching. For the events of the first century showed that the two forms of belief had a great deal in common, or rather, as perhaps we ought to put it, that Christians incorporated a large part of the distinctive doctrines of the Apocalyptists. And, without forestalling what will appear more evident in the course of this Lecture, we may say at once that it is impossible to understand, humanly speaking, how Christianity could have arisen, if it had not built upon the foundations laid by the Apocalyptists. Not only had their hopes and expectations, and even their ethical outlook, already spread among the common people, of whom we are told that they heard the Master gladly, but there is even reason to suppose that the greatest of their books, that of Enoch, had its origin in Upper Galilee. But if Christianity had so close a connexion with Apocalyptics it is readily explicable that the Rabbinic teachers did their utmost to discourage the study of the latter among their followers, and we can hardly doubt that the Pseudepigraphic Books were at least included among those against which the Rabbis from time to time issued special warnings.

Passing over the less important topics of the

[1] See further Box, *The Ezra-Apocalypse*, 1912, pp. lviii *sqq*.

Apocalyptic teaching, as, for example, that of the angels, good and bad, with the parts they played, are playing, and will play, in the history of the world, or, again, that of the nature of the other world, whether it be for the blessed or the damned, it is sufficient to call attention to its main subject, the approaching catastrophic change, and the connexion of this with the Messiah, by whatever name He was called.

Let me quote a few passages. Here is one from the Book of Enoch :

The Holy Great One will come forth from his dwelling,
And the eternal God will tread upon the earth, (even) on Mount Sinai,
[And appear from his camp]
And appear in the strength of his might from the heaven of heavens.
And all shall be smitten with fear,
And the watchers shall quake,
And great fear and trembling shall seize them unto the ends of the earth.
And the high mountains shall be shaken,
And the high hills shall be made low,
And shall melt like wax before the flame.
And the earth shall be wholly rent in sunder,
And all that is upon the earth shall perish,
And there shall be a judgment upon all (men). . . .
And behold ! He cometh with ten thousands of his holy ones
To execute judgment upon all.
And to destroy all the ungodly :
And to convict all flesh
Of all the works of their ungodliness which they have ungodly committed,
And of all the hard things which ungodly sinners have spoken against him.[1]

[1] Eth. Enoch i. 3-7, 9.

x] ENOCH'S PROPHECY OF THE WEEKS

Or turn to Enoch's prophecy of the weeks. He himself, he says, was born in the first week. In the second is the Flood. In the third comes Abraham. In the fourth the Law is made. In the fifth the Temple is built. In the sixth is the Captivity. In the seventh an apostate generation arises, but at its close the actual writer of the book receives instruction from God. In the eighth week sinners shall be delivered into the hands of the righteous, and these at its close shall acquire houses through their righteousness, and a house shall be built for the Great King in glory for evermore, and all mankind shall look to the path of righteousness.

And after that, in the ninth week, the righteous judgement shall be revealed to the whole world,
And all the works of the godless shall vanish from the earth,
And the world shall be written down for destruction.

And after this, in the tenth week in the seventh part,
There shall be the eternal judgement,
In which he will execute vengeance amongst the angels.

And the first heaven shall depart and pass away,
And a new heaven shall appear,
And all the powers of the heavens shall give sevenfold light.

And after that there will be many weeks without number for ever,
And all shall be in goodness and righteousness,
And sin shall be no more mentioned for ever.[1]

Once more:

Woe to you, ye rich, for ye have trusted in your riches,
And from your riches shall ye depart,
Because ye have not remembered the Most High in the days of your riches.

[1] Eth. Enoch xci. 14–17.

Ye have committed blasphemy and unrighteousness,
And have become ready for the day of slaughter,
And the day of darkness and the day of the great judgement.[1]

Or listen to this from the Sibylline Oracles :

Artemis' temple fixed at Ephesus . . .
By chasms and earthquakes shall come headlong down
Sometime into the dreadful sea, as storms
Overwhelm ships. And up-turned Ephesus
Shall wail aloud, lament beside her banks,
And for her temple search which is no more.
    And then incensed shall God the imperishable,
Who dwells on high, hurl thunderbolts from heaven
Down on the head of him that is impure.
And in the place of winter there shall be
In that day summer. And to mortal men
Shall then be great woe; for the Thunderer
Shall utterly destroy all shameless men
And with his thunders and lightning-flames
And blazing thunderbolts men of ill-will,
And thus shall he destroy the impious ones,
So that there shall remain upon the earth
Dead bodies more in number than the sand.[2]

Or recall the following passage from the Fourth Book of Ezra :

And the Most High shall be revealed upon the throne of judgement; (and then cometh the End) and compassion shall pass away, (and pity be far off,) and long-suffering withdrawn; But judgement alone shall remain, truth shall stand, and faithfulness triumph. And recompense shall follow, and the reward be made manifest; Deeds of righteousness shall awake, and deeds of iniquity shall not sleep. And then shall the pit of torment appear, and over against it the place of refreshment; The furnace of

---

[1] Eth. Enoch xciv. 8, 9.   [2] v. 293-305. Terry's translation.

Gehenna shall be made manifest, and over against it the Paradise of delight. And then shall the Most High say to the nations that have been raised (from the dead): Look, now, and consider whom ye have denied, whom ye have not served, whose commandments ye have despised! Look, now, before (you): here delight and refreshment, there fire and torments! Thus shall he speak unto them in the Day of Judgement. For thus shall the Day of Judgement be: (A day) whereon is neither sun, nor moon, nor stars, neither clouds, nor thunder, nor lightning; Neither wind, nor rainstorm, nor cloud-rack; neither darkness, nor evening, nor morning; neither summer, nor autumn, nor winter; neither heat, nor frost, nor cold; neither hail, nor rain, nor dew; neither noon, nor night, nor dawn; neither shining, nor brightness, nor light, save only the splendour of the brightness of the Most High, whereby all shall be destined to see what has been determined (for them). And its duration shall be as it were a week of years. Such is my Judgement and its prescribed order; to thee only have I showed these things.[1]

In these passages the Messiah is hardly mentioned, if at all. But in the following He takes an important part in the approaching change.

At that hour that Son of Man was named
In the presence of the Lord of Spirits,
And his name before the Head of Days.

Yea, before the sun and the signs were created,
Before the stars of the heaven were made,
His name was named before the Lord of Spirits.

He shall be a staff to the righteous whereon to stay themselves and not fall,
And he shall be the light of the Gentiles,
And the hope of those who are troubled of heart.

[1] vii. 33-44. Box's translation.

All who dwell on earth shall fall down and worship before him,
And will praise and bless and celebrate with song the Lord
    of Spirits.

    .   .   .   .

For in his name they are saved,
And according to his good pleasure hath it been in regard
    to their life.[1]

So also we find in the Sibylline Oracles :

For there came from the heavenly plains a man,
One blessed, with a sceptre in his hand,
Which God gave him, and he ruled all things well,
And unto all the good did he restore
The riches which the earlier men had seized.
And many cities with much fire he took
From their foundations, and he set on fire
The towns of mortals who before did evil,
And he did make that city, which God loved,
More radiant than stars and sun and moon,
And he set order, and a holy house
Incarnate made, pure, very fair, and formed
In many stades a great and boundless tower
Touching the clouds themselves and seen by all,
So that all holy and all righteous men
Might see the glory of the eternal God,
A sight that has been longed for. . . .

    .   .   .   .

It is the last time of the saints when God
Accomplisheth these things, high Thunderer,
Founder of temple most magnificent.[2]

In the Fourth Book of Ezra we read :

    'This is the Messiah whom the Most High hath kept unto the end [of the days, who shall spring from the seed of David, and shall come and speak] unto them ; He shall reprove them for their ungodliness, rebuke them for their

---

[1] Eth. Enoch xlviii. 2-7.
[2] v. 414-433. Terry's translation. *Cf.* also Lecture VII, pp. 253 *sq.*

unrighteousness, reproach them to their faces with their treacheries. For at the first He shall set them alive for judgement; and when he hath rebuked them he shall destroy them. But my people who survive he shall deliver with mercy, even those who have been saved throughout my borders, and he shall make them joyful until the End come, even the Day of Judgement, of which I have spoken unto thee from the beginning.[1]

The Syriac Apocalypse of Baruch is more precise:

After the signs have come, of which thou wast told before, when the nations become turbulent, and the time of My Messiah is come, he shall both summon all the nations, and some of them he shall spare, and some of them he shall slay. These things therefore shall come upon the nations which are to be spared by him. Every nation, which knows not Israel and has not trodden down the seed of Jacob, shall indeed be spared. And this because some out of every nation shall be subjected to thy people. But all those who have ruled over you, or have known you, shall be given up to the sword.

And it shall come to pass, when he has brought low everything that is in the world,
And has sat down in peace for the age on the throne of his kingdom,
That joy shall be revealed,
And rest shall appear.
And then healing shall descend in dew,
And disease shall withdraw,
And anxiety and anguish and lamentation pass from amongst men,
And gladness proceed through the whole earth.

. . . .

And it shall come to pass in those days that the reapers shall not grow weary,
Nor those that build be toilworn;

[1] xii. 32-34.

For the works shall of themselves speedily advance
Together with those who do them in much tranquillity.

. . . .

This is the bright lightning which came after the last dark waters.[1]

These few extracts from the Apocalyptic writings are sufficient to show the vividness of the hope that animated their authors. It is true that they are of different periods, Enoch and the Sibyllines belonging to the first century B.C., and Ezra and Baruch to the end of the first century A.D., but none of the passages quoted appears to have been influenced by Christian teaching, and thus they represent faithfully the current expectation of a large section of the Jewish people in the era when the doctrines of our faith were being formed. Those among the Jews who accepted the teaching of the Apocalyptic books were looking forward eagerly to the speedy consummation of the Divine promises, when the powers of the wicked should cease and the kingdom of God be manifested, in connexion with the coming of the Messiah, the Son of Man, and the Lord of Spirits. They believed that they were already in the last times, and that at any moment the revelation of the kingdom of heaven might be made.

II. What, then, was our Lord's attitude to this fundamental hope of the Apocalyptists, the immediate coming of the kingdom ? On His attitude to them in general Mr. Streeter rightly tells us : ' Jewish Apocalypse, albeit bizarre to modern eyes, was no ignoble thing. The eternal optimism, which is of the essence of true religion, expresses itself in different

[1] §§ 72–74.

forms in different epochs. To men appalled alike by the corruption and by the irresistible might of Roman civilisation, and inheriting the previous religious history of Israel and her prophets, it was an heroic confidence in the Divine intention to regenerate the world that found its most natural expression in terms of the Messianic hope apocalyptically conceived. On this side of triumphant and confident faith our Lord placed Himself definitely and unreservedly.'[1]

Yet while this is true generally, it is not at all easy to understand what was His attitude towards the hope of the *immediate* coming of the kingdom. Did He, or did He not, expect the kingdom to come in its fullness almost immediately after He spoke His various utterances on the subject? Nearly twenty centuries have rolled by since then. Did our Lord presuppose so long a lapse of time, or did He not?

We must examine His language before we can pretend to give an answer. And at this point it is necessary to recall the dominant theory of the sources used by the writer of this Gospel. These are, first, the source used both by him and St. Luke, generally called Q. Secondly, our present St. Mark, or a writing almost indistinguishable from it (Mk); and, thirdly, the material contributed by the writer himself (Mt).

Bearing these three sources in mind we may proceed to collect the more important evidence in answer to our question. The facts are simple enough, though rather dry to enumerate; the interpretation of them is not.

In some passages our Lord implies that His

---

[1] *Studies in the Synoptic Problem; Synoptic Criticism and Eschatology,* 1911, p. 434.

kingdom, the kingdom of God, *has already appeared.* To the question of John's disciples, ' Art thou he that cometh ? ' He replies : ' Go your way and tell John the things which ye do hear and see.' And, almost immediately after, He adds : ' From the days of John the Baptist until now the kingdom of heaven suffereth violence' (xi. 3, 4, 12, Q).[1] Again, 'If I by the Spirit of God cast out devils, then is the kingdom of God come upon you ' (xii. 28, Q). The same implication underlies the expression : ' Therefore every scribe who hath been made a disciple to the kingdom of heaven is like unto a man that is a householder, which bringeth forth out of his treasure things new and old ' (xiii. 52, Mt). Lastly, it is evident in the closing words of the Gospel : ' All authority hath been given unto me in heaven and on earth. Go ye, therefore, and make disciples of all the nations' (xxviii. 18, 19, Mt).[2]

In a second class of sayings the Lord plainly states that the kingdom is only *near at hand.* Among the better-known passages are : ' But when they persecute you in this city, flee into the next : for verily I say unto you, Ye shall not have gone through the cities of Israel, till the Son of man be come ' (x. 23, Q). ' There be some of them that stand here, which shall in no wise taste of death, till they see the Son of man coming in his kingdom ' (xvi. 28, Mk). ' Ye shall not see me henceforth, till ye shall say, Blessed is he that cometh in the name of the Lord ' (xxiii. 39, Q). ' This generation shall not pass away, till all these things be accomplished ' (xxiv. 34, Mk).

---

[1] Q or Mk or Mt *following* the references indicate the source, as stated above.

[2] We may add xvii. 11 (Mk); xxiii. 13 (Q).

x] COMING OF THE KINGDOM NOT IMMEDIATE

'I say unto you, I will not drink henceforth of this fruit of the vine, until that day when I drink it new with you in my Father's kingdom' (xxvi. 29, Mk). Observe in this class that although St. Matthew records these passages faithfully, not one of them belongs to the source which he alone used. They are all from Q and Mark.[1]

Besides these two classes, however, in which the Lord either speaks of the kingdom as present or as near at hand, there is a group of sayings in which He implies with differing degrees of clearness that *a long series of years will pass away* before the full manifestation of the kingdom. 'Can the sons of the bridechamber mourn, as long as the bridegroom is with them ? but the days will come, when the bridegroom shall be taken away from them, and then will they fast' (ix. 15, Mk). 'While men slept, his enemy came and sowed tares also among the wheat, and went away. . . . Let both grow together until the harvest : and in the time of the harvest I will say to the reapers, Gather up first the tares, and bind them in bundles to burn them : but gather the wheat into my barn' (xiii. 25, 30, see also 38–43, Mt). The parables of the Mustard Seed (xiii. 31, 32, Mk), and of the Leaven (xiii. 33, Q) also imply delay. So too : 'Again I say unto you, that if two of you shall agree on earth as touching anything that they shall ask, it shall be done for them of my Father which is in heaven. For where two or three are gathered together in my name, there am I in the midst of them' (xviii. 19, 20, Mt). 'Therefore say I unto you, The kingdom of God shall be taken away from you, and shall be given to a nation bringing

[1] We may add iv. 17 (Mk), x. 7 (Q) ; compare also xxiv. 27, 39, 44, 50 (Q).

forth the fruits thereof' (xxi. 43, Mt). 'This gospel of the kingdom shall be preached in the whole world for a testimony unto all the nations; and then shall the end come' (xxiv. 14, Mk). 'But if that evil servant shall say in his heart, My lord tarrieth; and shall begin to beat his fellow-servants, and shall eat and drink with the drunken; the lord of that servant shall come in a day when he expecteth not, and in an hour when he knoweth not' (xxiv. 48–50, Q). We may add the closing words of the Gospel: 'Lo, I am with you alway, even unto the end of the world' (xxviii. 20, Mt).[1]

Those are the facts, presented, as I trust, fairly and dispassionately. What are we to make of them? In the first place, this: that both Q and less certainly St. Matthew's private source of information (Mt) sometimes presuppose that the kingdom has already come; secondly, that Q and St. Mark (Mk) look forward rather to its immediate approach; thirdly, that St. Matthew's own source (Mt), while giving more Apocalyptic details about the Second Coming than either Q or Mk (for he seems to have been more in touch with Apocalyptic literature than either of them),[2] yet also brings out much more plainly than they the fact that *a long time will elapse* between the utterances of the Lord and the fulfilment of them.[3]

But here we cannot but ask: If Q and St. Mark

---

[1] We may add xviii. 23 (Mt); xx. 1–16 (Mt); xxii. 1–14 (? Mt or Q) xxiv. 3 (Mt).

[2] Dr. Burkitt even sees 'a real literary connexion' between Enoch lxii. and Matt. xxv., *op. cit.* pp. 23–25.

[3] Canon Streeter strangely ignores this, while rightly insisting on the greater wealth of catastrophic detail in Matthew (*op. cit.* p. 433). If the view of St. Matthew's account of the teaching of the Lord as given above is right,

give an accurate account of our Lord's sayings, when they make Him foretell the close approach of the kingdom, though it has not come in that fullness described, in spite of nearly twenty centuries having run their course, what can we say either of them or of Him? There is no reason to suppose that their reports of the sayings are erroneous, though, of course, they may be incomplete. Are we to infer, then, that our Lord was mistaken? Now we must remember that we have no right to answer this upon merely *a priori* grounds. Bishop Butler has warned us too plainly against applying such a method of reasoning to the way in which God deals with us. We dare not then rule the possibility of mistakes out of our Lord's life. For Him to have made mistakes may be exceedingly improbable, but we cannot say more. *Humanum est errare* may be true even of humanity that is sinless.

Yet it is not easy to combine the passages of the second class, namely, those which are to the effect that the final coming of the kingdom was at hand, with even ordinary intelligence. True, it is affirmed by some writers that our Lord was so carried away by the enthusiastic acceptance which He received in Galilee that He supposed the nation as a whole was about to acknowledge Him, and that therefore His Father in heaven would grant the full revelation of the kingdom at once.[1] But human foresight

there is no room for the supposition that His ethical teaching was intended to be merely temporary ('Interimsethik'), until His kingdom should come. On its true character see Lectures IV-VI. On Matt. xxiv. see Additional Note at the end of this Lecture.

[1] Dr. Charles writes : ' At the outset of His ministry he had, we can hardly doubt, hoped to witness the consummation of this kingdom without passing through the gates of death' (*Eschatology : A Critical History of the Doctrine of a Future Life*, 1913, p. 376).

of quite the conventional range was sufficient to see that Israel as a nation was not likely to accept Him. After all, it is unreasonable for us not to credit Jesus with more understanding of the times than that.[1] It is improbable, therefore, that our Lord expected that such prophecies of His were to be fulfilled within the few months that lay between the time of their utterance and the crucifixion.

For Him to have made a mistake of that kind is well-nigh incredible to a dispassionate thinker, whether he be orthodox or not.

Yet the possibility of a mistake of another kind is not to be dismissed so easily. Our Lord may have hoped that with the life-giving power which was to be poured out after His death by the coming of the Holy Ghost, the hour for the final release of the world from its sins and sufferings, its failures and its disappointments, would soon strike, and we are hardly in a position to say that such an expectation on His part was incompatible with His nature and character. For, as He Himself tells us, the day and hour were hidden from Him (Matt. xxiv. 36), and He might not unreasonably expect that the blessing of Whitsunday would prove irresistible. On this supposition we must say that to Him, like His predecessors in the prophetic office, the per-

[1] Albert Schweitzer's gruesome phantasy is to the effect that the prophecies of the Second Advent were the vapourings of an enthusiast, assured at first that He would come as the Son of man in glory, ere His disciples returned from their missionary tour (Matt. x. 23); and, when this proved to be mistaken, got Himself put to death by the authorities in Jerusalem that He might straightway return in the clouds of heaven, and bring earthly history to a close. But in vain, for the wheel of the world rolls onward, and Jesus is hanging on it, mangled and crushed (*The Quest of the Historical Jesus*, 1910, p. 369).

spective of age-long spiritual work was allowed to be foreshortened.[1]

We should, perhaps, be shut up to this interpretation of our Lord's mind if we had only some of the words recorded for us in St. Matthew which have been taken from Q and Mark. But in view of the further fact that many of His other sayings, which are found chiefly in St. Matthew alone, imply a long interval between the time when He uttered them and the day of His return in glory, it is possible that we misinterpret those former passages, and read into them more than He Himself intended to convey. The passages adduced chiefly by St. Matthew alone indicate that *Jesus was personally assured that a long period would elapse before* His return on the clouds of heaven. Yet at the very time He spoke thus He was also using strong, almost paradoxical, language of the immediateness of that return, in order apparently that He might deepen in His hearers the sense of their responsibility, and also lead them to see that events of infinitely less crucial importance than the last day were nevertheless practical examples of His coming in an inferior and partial sense. To His hearers, for instance, death was one such crisis; to the nation, or even to the whole civilised world of the time, the fall of Jerusalem and the destruction of the Temple were others. He appears to have referred to these events sometimes in terms that more strictly belonged to His return, and thus not to have been careful to distinguish between them and His final coming in glory, in order that thus He might impress upon

[1] *Cf.* von Dobschütz, *The Eschatology of the Gospels*, 1910, pp. 184-187.

His followers the assurance of His activity and the certainty of His Advent.

In any case St. Matthew takes pains to correct the false impression that might have been left by his extracts from Q and Mark, when taken alone, by insisting on the many occasions on which our Lord taught the existence of a long lapse of time between His two comings.

If, however, St. Matthew did this, why, it may be asked, did not the author of Q and St. Mark? Here we find the inconvenience of not knowing the chronological relation of these two. But if recent critics are right in holding the priority of Q, and in believing that it was composed within a very few years after the crucifixion, it may well be the case that its writer did not feel the difficulty of the lapse of time, and was himself so full of the eager expectation of the Lord's return, that his mind turned only, or almost only,[1] to those sayings of our Lord which lay stress upon it. This explanation in some degree applies to St. Mark also. He wrote, as it would seem, before the Fall of Jerusalem, and it was but natural that that catastrophe, minor though it seems to us, should almost entirely fill his vision. And in fact it was near, very near, at hand.

But St. Matthew, compiling his edificatory life of our Lord for the sadly tried Jewish-Christians after the Roman war, when city and temple had perished, and yet the Lord Jesus had not come and the kingdom not been consummated, felt himself constrained to bring out the true meaning of the Lord's teaching. He desired to show that the religious expectations of the Jews were not to be deceived, that the

[1] For he did not quite forget other sayings, see p. 361.

x] OUR LORD'S EXPECTATION OF SUFFERING

Apocalyptic Hope of the full establishment of the kingdom of God was not fallacious.[1] The kingdom had in truth been founded by the Lord Jesus; it was now being maintained and developed by agencies appointed by Him, and also by His own presence with them, and at last (though not necessarily, nor even probably, within a short time) it would be manifested in its completion and its glory; when Jesus the Messiah, the Son of Man, as well as Son of God, should return on the clouds of heaven, with His angels and His saints.

The Lord Jesus, then, looked forward to the future manifestation of the kingdom of heaven, when He Himself would return in glory.

And this expectation was not a *pis aller*, devised only in the latter part of His ministry, when He at last foresaw that He would fail to win the nation over to His cause, and that He would do well to invite death at the hands of His enemies in order that so His coming in power might be hastened.

For, as we have already seen in Lecture VIII, His identification of Himself with the Son of Man carried with it the expectation of suffering as well as of present power and future glory. And, as we shall see in the next Lecture, He was conscious even from His baptism of His call to suffering and death. He looked forward, therefore, even from the very first,

[1] 'The contents of the expectation of the future held by primitive Christianity did not grow out of the Gospel, but passed over to it almost entirely out of Judaism.' Brückner (*R.G.G.* ii. 612), who goes on to say that the separate thoughts of Jewish Apocalyptists acquire a different value, in as far as they are connected with the person and work of Jesus as the Messiah. 'Only one subject is never touched on in the Gospels, the judgment upon the external foes of Israel' (*ibid.* ii. 614). See also Sanday's remarkable article on the Apocalyptic Element in the Gospels in the *Hibbert Journa* for October 1911, pp. 83-109.

to the fire of extremest pain as a necessary prelude to His return in glory.

III. Lastly, it will not be out of place if we ask ourselves in a few words what is the real nature of the consummation predicted?

We may say at once that the form of our Lord's description of the end, whether it be symbolic or literal, seems to be inconsistent with a merely gradual change.[1] Unless we deprive words of their plain meaning, the end predicted by Him must be catastrophic.

But it is doubtful whether we can say much more. For we are very ignorant of the relation in which the various events connected in Scripture with that climax stand to each other. The Messiah will come visibly; Scripture seems to say that plainly enough; but will that coming usher in the resurrection of the saints and a reign of bliss, as our forefathers fondly thought, to be followed after a thousand years by the general resurrection and the Judgment? Or will the coming of Christ synchronise with that resurrection and judgment, and the destruction of the earth as we know it? On these and kindred questions Scripture speaks aloud, as with the blaring of a trumpet summons, that the Lord will come, but the notes are too deep for our untrained ears to distinguish, and the words, so far as we catch them, are so steeped in imagery and symbol that we cannot arrange in any order the details of the events bound up with that appearing. The instructed Christian shrinks from the attempt, though the fact of the Advent is certain.

The kingdom of God, our Evangelist would tell

[1] Matt. xxiv. 30; xxvi. 64. *Cf.* Acts i. 11; Rev. i. 7.

us, came when Christ was born at Bethlehem and was baptized in Jordan; it came in fresh power in His Resurrection and at Pentecost; its principles have since been spreading both within the Church and without; but we must wait for its final revelation at our Lord's return. Then will be the fulfilment of our cry for righteousness, of our desire for holiness, and of our sense of justice, when the veil now hiding the glory of Jesus Christ shall be rolled away, in the day of the LORD.

ADDITIONAL NOTE ON MATT. xxiv. (see p. 363)

This chapter, like so many of our Lord's addresses in the First Gospel, is composite, its basis being Mark xiii., which was also the basis of Luke xxi. 5–34, but containing other passages from Q. Such are verses 43–51 (Luke xii. 39–46); verses 26, 27 (Luke xvii. 23, 24), verse 28 (Luke xvii. 37), verses 37–41 (Luke xvii. 26, 27, 34–35). With the exception of verses 10–12, 30, there is nothing of importance peculiar to Matthew. We thus see that although the chapter is Matthean as it stands, its original sources are Mk and Q; *i.e.*, that even in its present form it belongs to a period earlier than the Fall of Jerusalem. This suggests either that the First Gospel as a whole was written before 70 A.D., or, and more probably, that this report of an address, dating as a whole not later than 60 A.D., has been faithfully preserved. May we not go further and say that it suggests also that the actual teaching of our Lord (whether given originally in one discourse or in more is of little importance) has been reproduced for us essentially free from error? The chapter then represents faithfully prophecies spoken by our Lord in which the Fall of Jerusalem [1] and His own Final Coming were not distinguished.

Neither is it possible for us to distinguish these two subjects

[1] Dr. Burkitt, however, does not think that Mark xiii. contains 'any prophecy of the siege of Jerusalem by Titus' (*op. cit.* p. 49).

save and in so far as we take history for our guide. But we cannot be far wrong in relegating those events foretold which did not take place at the Fall of Jerusalem to the Second Coming, though we cannot be quite sure that some of them ought not to be understood symbolically rather than literally.

Lecture Eleven

THE MESSIAH AND THE CROSS

'Jesus cried again with a loud voice, and yielded up his spirit.'—MATT. xxvii. 50.

Lecture Eleven

THE MESSIAH AND THE CROSS

THE narrative of the Passion of Christ, from the arrest to the burial, takes up nearly a twelfth of the whole Gospel according to St. Matthew, or, if we reckon it, as we should do, from the Last Supper, more than a ninth.

In the eyes of the Evangelist, therefore, the Passion of the Lord loomed very large indeed. And not in his eyes only, but also in those of the whole early Church. For both St. Matthew's account and St. Luke's are taken from St. Mark's, and there are very few critics who do not grant that this part of the Second Gospel was composed at least as early as 50 or 60 A.D. It is plain, therefore, that the death of Christ had so great an importance for the primitive Church that every detail of it, as compared with other parts of His history, was cherished and handed down for the edification of believers, and, we may suppose, for the instruction of catechumens.

It is our part now to consider the signification attached to it by St. Matthew, and the reasons that led him to give it so large a space in his presentation of the Messiah to his Christian fellow-countrymen.

I. But before entering upon this the question must be answered: On whom does St. Matthew lay the responsibility for the death of Christ? Who, in his opinion, are the parties guilty of that most signal of all examples of opposition to truth?

He certainly blames the Romans in the person of their representative, Pontius Pilate, Governor of Judæa, but whether he lays sufficient blame upon them is disputed. Dr. Emil Hirsch says : ' The facts show that the crucifixion of Jesus was an act of the Roman government. . . . Many of the Jews suspected of Messianic ambitions had been nailed to the cross by Rome. The Messiah, "king of the Jews," was a rebel in the estimation of Rome, and rebels were crucified (Suetonius, *Vespas.* 4 ; *Claudius*, xxv. ; Josephus, *Antt.* xx. v. 1, viii. 6 ; Acts v. 36, 37). The inscription on the cross of Jesus reveals the crime for which, according to Roman law, Jesus expired. He was a rebel. Tacitus (*Annals*, 54, 59) reports therefore without comment the fact that Jesus was crucified. For Romans no amplification was necessary.' [1]

Other writers put their case more attractively. Dr. Isaac Wise, who was a prominent leader of the Reformed Jews in the United States thirty years ago, wrote as follows : ' On the eve of the supper, Jesus announced to the apostles, not only his firm resolution to die for his disciples and friends, and to prevent the calamity which an insurrection in his favour was sure to bring on his people, but also that the end was nigh, and that the traitor would do his work quickly.' ' The plain fact is, that Jesus sacrificed himself to save his friends.' ' Unable to carry out the original plan—the restoration of the kingdom of heaven in

---

[1] *Jewish Encyclopedia*, iv. 374. *Cf.* M. Théodore Reinach: 'Le récit des Évangiles sur le procès de Jésus est d'une extrême confusion, qui tient au désir *politique* des rédacteurs d'innocenter le plus possible le gouverneur romain et de charger le sanhédrin juif.' . . .

'Jésus a été frappé par une loi inexorable, barbare si l'on veut, mais formelle, et pour un fait qu'il a tacitement avoué' (*Revue des Études juives*, xxxv., 1897, pp. 15, 17, 18).

XI] THE ROMANS RESPONSIBLE FOR HIS DEATH

Israel—and seeing his followers and admirers rushing heedlessly into a mad scheme of rebellion, he laid down his life heroically for his friends and countrymen.' [1]

According to this theory the Romans ought to bear the responsibility for the death of Jesus. If so, St. Matthew extenuated their crime that he might lay the blame for it upon the Jews. Yet he clearly indicts the Romans in the person of the Governor. For he informs us that Pilate's wife sent him a message warning him against having anything to do with that righteous man, and Pilate's own solemn protestation of innocence by washing his hands before the multitude can have had hardly any other object than that of showing that his own conscience accused him. St. Matthew certainly blames the Romans, and that severely.[2]

Does he also blame either or both of the two great parties in the Jewish State, the Sadducees and the Pharisees? Here we must be careful.

Throughout the whole account of the Passion until after the burial the words Sadducees and Pharisees are not mentioned by St. Matthew. He did not find the terms in St. Mark, the source he followed very closely, and he did not add them. But although he does not use those names he speaks

[1] *The Martyrdom of Jesus of Nazareth*, 1888, pp. 51, 126.

[2] M. Th. Reinach (*op. cit.*) complains that the Evangelist's description of Pilate as weak, playing 'le rôle d'un pacha debonnair,' is contrary to what we know from other writers of his cruelty, regardless of all consequences. But the New Testament suggests the contempt that the typical Roman felt for Jews, and normal savagery is not inconsistent with occasional weakness, especially when, as in this case, the personal influence of another is added. Dr. Isaac Wise has an extraordinary theory that it is not even certain that Jesus was crucified, 'He was given over to the Roman soldiers to be disposed of as fast as possible.... Some said he was crucified; others thought he was hung to a tree; and others again said he did not die at all' (*op. cit.* pp. 125 *sq.*). But this is to play fast and loose with evidence.

again and again of 'the High Priests,' with or without additions such as 'the elders,' 'the elders of the people,' 'the scribes and elders,' 'the whole Sanhedrin,'[1] as consulting how they might seize Jesus by craft and kill Him, avoiding if possible the days when the city would be thronged and disturbance be caused (xxvi. 3–5); as arranging for the betrayal (*vv.* 14–16), and sending men to take Him (*vv.* 47–50); as gathered in conclave, and straining every nerve to secure false witness against Him (*vv.* 57–61); and as condemning and ill-treating Him (*vv.* 66–68); meeting again in the early morning in order to give effect to their decision by handing Him over to Pilate (xxvii. 1, 2); rejecting Judas' blood-money, and afterwards using it for the purchase of a burial-ground (*vv.* 3–10); accusing Him before Pilate (*vv.* 12, 13); persuading the mob to ask for the release of Barabbas and the death of Jesus (*v.* 20); and, lastly, mocking at Him as He hangs on the cross (*vv.* 41–43).

Besides, the first meeting was held in the central court of the High Priest called Caiaphas (xxvi. 3), who afterwards conducted the first trial of our Lord, and did his utmost to secure His condemnation (xxvi. 57–65). Now we have already seen (Lecture II) that Caiaphas and his relations, the High Priests of the New Testament, were Sadducees, so that it is evident that St. Matthew blames at least Sadducees for the murder of Jesus. Nor does any one seriously deny this.[2]

---

[1] xxvi. 59.

[2] Even Dr. Isaac Wise grants this, though he says: 'Caiaphas and his conspirators did not act from the Jewish standpoint. They represented Rome, her principles, interests, and barbarous caprices' (*op. cit.* p. 30). Mr. Montefiore writes: 'The Gospel narratives are so far correct in that Jesus

We can understand the reasons for the bitterness with which ungodly Sadducees regarded our Lord. They feared the political issues of His appearance with His Galilean followers.[1] They belonged to the most worldly of all the movements in Judaism, and, further, as the guardians of the Temple they may well have been exasperated by His denunciation of their profanation of the house of God (xxi. 12-16).[2]

The Sadducees, it must be allowed, took a leading part in the death of Jesus. But if so we probably have the explanation of much of the disagreement that is often pointed out between the proceedings at the trial of Jesus and those enjoined in the treatise of the Mishna (Sanhedrin), which deals with the accusation and trial of criminals according to the precepts of the Jewish law. Nothing is more common than for Jews to assert that the Gospel narratives of the trial of our Lord are fictitious because they differ in so many particulars from the directions laid down in the written Oral Law. The trial, they say, can never have taken place as described in the New Testament.[3]

was really put to death by the Romans at the instance and instigation of the Jewish authorities, and more especially of the ruling priesthood' (*Synoptic Gospels*, p. 346). See also below, p. 380, note.

[1] *Cf.* Chwolson, *Das letzte Passamahl Christi*, 1908, pp. 86, 124.

[2] Dr. Kirsopp Lake thinks that 'financial interest rather than theological hatred was the real cause of the accusation of the priests' (*The Stewardship of the Faith*, 1915, p. 39).

[3] Mr. Montefiore, *Synoptic Gospels*, pp. 346 *sq.*, even objects: 'How could the full court be got together so rapidly in the middle of the night ? Jesus could hardly have arrived at the high priest's house much before midnight. . . . Did they at that hour of night send out messengers to summon the "Scribes and chief priests" together that a court might rapidly be constituted ? . . . We ask, how have the witnesses been obtained at this hour of night ?' But he forgets that Orientals are much less regular in their hours of sleep than we, and that at the crowded festivals the greater part of the

When, however, such opponents argue against the trustworthiness of the Gospel narratives because they differ from the Oral Law, they do not make allowance for three facts. First (as has been often pointed out in these Lectures), it is uncritical to assume that the Jewish law of later times was identical with the practice in vogue about 30 A.D. Secondly, it is not at all certain that the discussions of the Schools held at a date when the Jewish State had ceased, upon the legal procedure in cases of life and death, were not purely academic, and never literally carried out either then or at any other time earlier or later. Thirdly, the code in the Mishna is confessedly Pharisaic, and we have no right to suppose that it was the same as that of the Sadducees.[1]

St. Matthew, then, certainly lays much of the responsibility for our Lord's death on the Saducean leaders of the nation. But does this mean that he absolves the Pharisees from all participation in the crime?[2] The last chapter of the Gospel shows that he is very far from doing that, for he tells us that ' the High Priests and the Pharisees ' reminded Pilate of Jesus' prophecy that He would

population of a town is awake all night. Among more serious difficulties are the regulations in the Mishna that capital charges may not be tried at night, or completed in one day if the verdict of guilty is brought in, in order that leniency, not severity, should be the ruling principle. See in particular Chwolson, *op. cit.* p. 119. On the difficulty that a claim to be the Messiah was not considered blasphemy (xxvi. 65) see Lecture II, p. 68 note.

[1] It will be remembered (Lecture II, p. 74) that the Pharisees had no power until very near the Fall of Jerusalem. 'Zur Zeit Christi sassen wohl auch Pharisäer im Synhedrion, aber sie spielten damals in dieser Corporation noch eine untergeordnete Rolle. Die Vorsitzenden und die Hauptführer des Synhedrions waren damals die Sadducäer, und diese gaben in allen wichtigen Sachen den Ausschlag' (Chwolson, *op. cit.* p. 121). See also Büchler, *Das Synhedrion in Jerusalem*, 1902, *e.g.*, pp. 99, 240.

[2] As Chwolson would urge upon us, *op. cit.* pp. 118-125.

rise again, and they had a guard set over His tomb (xxviii. 62–66).[1] Besides, although for some reason the Pharisees are not mentioned by name in the two chapters of the Passion, their presence is implied almost as certainly as that of the Sadducees. After their hostility to Jesus personally had been brought out in earlier chapters (xii. 14; xxii. 15), and the opposition of their teaching to true religion had been shown by our Lord's invective (xxiii.), and as the Evangelist tells us that they carried on their hostility even after Christ's death, it is not probable that he held them guiltless in the proceedings of the Passion itself.

On the contrary, he almost certainly includes them, though under other expressions, just as he includes the Sadducees. Probably the reason why he does not use the terms Sadducees and Pharisees is the same in both cases. Those names referred primarily to religion, and therefore lent themselves readily to occasions when religious questions were under consideration, but other terms were more effective for the purpose of showing the part taken by the official and public representatives of the nation in compassing the Saviour's death.

We have seen that the titles 'the High Priest,' 'the High Priests,' refer to Sadducees, and it is probable that Pharisees are at least included in the phrases, 'the elders,' 'the elders of the people,' 'the scribes and elders,' 'the whole Sanhedrin.' The use of these terms in addition to that of High Priests suggests that the Evangelist desired to indicate the leaders of the nation generally, to whichever religious party the members severally belonged.

---

[1] See Lecture XII, pp. 398 *sqq.*

The form of legal procedure actually adopted may then well have been Sadducean, and yet the Pharisees have been one with the Sadducees in desiring His death, and in taking steps to secure it.

We may then conclude that St. Matthew deliberately intended his readers to understand that both of the great religious parties in Judaism, in their capacity as the nation's official leaders, concurred in their successful efforts to put Jesus the Messiah to death.[1]

The Evangelist, however, does not stop here. He shows more plainly than either of the other Synoptists that not only the leaders but the people themselves were guilty. For he alone records the incidents of Pilate washing his hands in the presence of the multitude, and saying : 'I am innocent of this blood: see ye to it.' And of the answer of 'all the people'—'His blood be on us, and on our children' (xxvii. 24 *sq.*, R.V. marg.). St. Matthew does not indeed labour the point, but if we are right in our supposition that his Gospel was written soon after 70 A.D. every reader of the time would have recalled the awful nemesis which the words had invoked in the butcheries of the city's siege and fall.

Thus the answer to the question : Upon whom does the Evangelist lay the blame for our Lord's death? appears to be : that he presents the Crucifixion as the result of the weakness and selfishness of Pilate, the Roman Governor; of the deliberate malice of

---

[1] To some extent this is admitted even by Mr. Montefiore: 'The precise proportion of responsibility which belongs to any section of the Jews of Jerusalem for the death of Jesus must always remain doubtful and uncertain. But the probability is that the Sadducean priesthood, perhaps backed up by some of the leading Rabbis, were responsible, together with the Romans, for his death' (*op. cit.* p. 382).

the Jewish leaders, Sadducees aided by Pharisees, and of the clamour of all the people—Gentiles not being innocent of it, and Jews being guilty.

In saying this, however, it is far from our desire to lay more blame on the Jewish than on other nations. No Gentile people would have treated Jesus any better. The judicial murder of Socrates is an example to the contrary. The shame is that the Jews, the most enlightened nation of the time, with a knowledge of God, theoretical and practical, far surpassing any other, acted as they did. They had made much more progress in true religion, and yet they crucified Jesus. The history of the Passion suggests, not that the Jews were sinners above all others, but that there was and is something radically wrong with the whole human race, when its best representatives act thus towards the embodiment of truth and holiness and love.

II. We turn now to consider the value and the effect of that death, in the light of the Evangelist's narrative.

Now it is very remarkable that at the two turning-points in our Lord's life, the Baptism and the Transfiguration, the commencement of His work and the decisive hour when He left Galilee and went towards Jerusalem, He should have heard addressed to Him from heaven words identifying Him with the Servant described in Isaiah xlii. to liii., the Beloved who was called to endure suffering and death.[1] God the Father would encourage Him in the day of His

---

[1] iii. 17, R.V. marg.; xvii. 5: 'This is my Son; my beloved in whom I am well pleased,' where 'beloved' (ἀγαπητός) answers to 'my chosen' in Isa. xlii. 1, as it does in chap. xii. 18; *cf.* p. 389, and Lecture I, pp. 40 *sq.*

consecration and in that of the manifestation of His glory, by reminding Him, first of His Divine Sonship, and secondly of what was involved in perfect service. He was not only the Son of God, but also the Servant; and the Servant must serve, however painful the form which the service would take.

He was thus aware of the issue of His call, and of the greatness of the cost. He accepted the summons, and went steadily forward, conscious of His end.[1]

Besides, there is other evidence than the divine words at the Baptism that Jesus was aware that He would have to die, long before the Transfiguration, with the events that immediately succeeded it. He knew His end during the earlier portion of His ministry. Recall His allusion to the marriage ceremony, the joy and shouts of the wedding guests, and then the sudden raid of a band of robbers, seizing the bridegroom and carrying him off, with the consequent mourning for his loss (ix. 15).[2] Or remember the simile of the cross, which each of Christ's followers must bear if he is to be worthy of His Master, and our Lord's insistence on the solemn fact that our earthly life may be preserved at too high a price, and that to lose it may be the best way of finding it (x. 38 *sq.*). This saying He repeats in an enlarged form (xvi. 24–26), immediately after He had said plainly that ' He must go unto Jerusalem, and suffer many things

---

[1] Observe that the identification of Himself as Messiah with the suffering Servant is expressly regarded by the Evangelist as a revelation made to Him from God, and not as the result of human teaching. This is in accordance with the Biblical knowledge of our Lord's contemporaries, for, so far as we are aware, no one had as yet seen the connexion between the Servant and the Messiah.

[2] From Mark ii. 20; see also Luke v. 35. *Cf.* 1 Macc. ix. 37–42, where Jonathan and Simon fall on a great marriage party, ' and the marriage was turned into mourning, and the voice of their minstrels into lamentation.'

XI] MESSIAH ACCEPTS THE CUP OF SUFFERING

of the elders and chief priests and scribes, and be killed' (xvi. 21). References to His death made after the Transfiguration are so frequent that they need not be quoted.[1]

St. Matthew, then, presented the Messiah to his fellow Hebrew-Christians, and through them to the Jews of the time, as One who was conscious, from the very first, of His call to suffering, and was firm in His resolve to go through His task in spite of all it would involve. Yet he depicts Him also as thoroughly human in shrinking from death, and indeed as fearing it, for some unstated reason, more than most men. 'Are ye able to drink the cup that I am about to drink?' He asked the sons of Zebedee, and they answered: 'We are able' (xx. 22); but when the cup came to Him Himself He was tempted to refuse it, gaining strength to drink it only by wrestling in extremest prayer to His Father against His natural abhorrence of what that cup contained. 'My soul is exceeding sorrowful, even unto death. ... O my Father, if it be possible, let this cup pass away from me: nevertheless, not as I will, but as thou wilt. ... O my Father, if this cannot pass away, except I drink it, thy will be done' (xxvi. 38, 39, 42).

What exactly that cup held the Evangelist does not tell us. For he desires to bring out the absolute victory of the spirit over the flesh, Messiah's complete acquiescence in His Father's will, His perfect obedience

---

[1] xvii. 12, 22 sq.; xx. 17–19, 28; xxi. 38; xxvi. 12, 28. The Evangelist, following Mark iii. 6, mentions the desire of the Pharisees to compass the death of Jesus as early as xii. 14, but it is possible that both writers are interpreting their action then by later events, and that St. Luke represents what took place the more exactly when he says: 'They were filled with madness; and communed one with another what they might do to Jesus' (Luke vi. 11).

as the Servant of God. Jesus knew that He could refuse the cup if He would. He was aware that He had only to pray, and twelve legions of angels would rescue Him (xxvi. 53). But He was content; He would drink it to its very dregs.

So far, then, all is clear. According to the Evangelist, the death of the Messiah was brought about by the leaders of the Jewish nation, and agreed to by the whole people, though actually carried out by Romans; it was regarded by the Messiah as the probable, not to say certain, issue of His ministry; and it was undergone by Him willingly, in so far that He could have avoided it if He had not known that it was the will of His Father in heaven that He should endure it. St. Matthew depicts the Messiah as consecrating Himself to the service of God, and obeying Him, even unto death.

But what does the Evangelist tell us of the reasons for that death, not, of course, the reasons which moved His enemies to compass it (these have already been shown), but those ideal, philosophical, religious causes, those which lie at the very heart of things, those which resemble in character the reasons for the creation and the preservation of the world, those which have to do with the eternal relation of God and man? For after all, these are the realities of realities; all else is the foam on the wave, or, at best the wave itself thrown up by the deep. What does our writer tell us of the underlying causes for Messiah's self-sacrifice?

Now it is hardly likely that any clear, decisive, logical, and comprehensive reason can be stated at all, if, as seems to be the case, it is to be on a par with that which brought about the creation and

WHY DID THE MESSIAH DIE

preservation of the world. The mysteries of God are beyond us; human terms fail, and must always fail, to express His relation to man. We can hope, at most, to receive hints, and to find terms used, of which the meaning may well be clear in transactions between one man and another, and very dim indeed when they deal with man and God.[1] Perhaps, too, we are less justified in expecting to see reasons recorded in a homiletical narrative of the life of Messiah such as the First Gospel, than in more directly hortatory and even theological writings such as the Epistles. In any case we find in this Gospel only three or four short statements, and must endeavour to deduce from them alone the reasons for the death of the Messiah which the Evangelist desired us to grasp.

For although it is true that the mind of those for whom he first wrote was no *tabula rasa*, ignorant of instruction in the character and meaning of the Gospel, and that therefore it would not be illegitimate for us, but quite the reverse, to interpret his hints by that teaching, yet this presupposes that we ourselves know precisely what that teaching was. But this is one of the chief of the subjects in dispute. No doubt, we personally may be confident that it is contained essentially in St. Paul's Epistles, all of which had probably been written before the First Gospel, yet many critics would not assent to this.

---

[1] 'The fact could not, as unintelligible to reason, be held or believed at all. But the fact, though never wholly compassed by our intelligence, is never unintelligible. Reason can—and must—understand it. . . . The fact itself is eternal and immutable. The fact itself is the very centre of the Gospel message to a world of suffering and sin. But the understanding of it must develop progressively; for it must seem to vary, while it grows in depth, with man's deepening capacity for intelligence of God, and of himself' (Moberly, *Atonement and Personality*, 1911, p. 412).

Hence we are compelled to exclude all external help, and to limit our enquiry to this Gospel only, gathering from it the doctrine of the value of the Cross, which is presupposed by the writer.

The first hint, and it is very far-reaching, lies in the forefront of his book, in the angel's charge to Joseph: ' She shall bring forth a son; and thou shalt call his name JESUS; for it is he that shall save his people from their sins ' (i. 21).

That, then, was the object of Christ's coming, which ended in His Death and Resurrection; His people were to be saved from their sins. The writer sweeps away with one stroke all lesser objects of the Messiah's advent. Whatever were the expectations concerning Him current in some circles, that He was to save Israel from earthly enemies, or that He was to rescue them from the power of evil angels, for the Evangelist and his fellow Hebrew-Christians He was ' to save His people from their sins.' A tenderness of conscience is presupposed, not only, it will be noticed, among the believers of the writer's age, but also among some at least of those devout souls who at the very beginning of the Christian era were waiting for the Messiah. They at least, whatever most of their contemporaries felt, were looking for Him as the Saviour from sins, from their own sins. This was to them, as to the Evangelist, the pre-eminent reason for His appearance. But the Evangelist knew, as they did not, the method and means by which this salvation from sin was accomplished, and he, having the end of Christ's life on earth in view, as they had not, deliberately chose to record the prediction that Jesus, and no other, would be the one who should save His people from their sins. To the Evangelist who laid so much stress upon the Passion, this, and nothing less, was the final aim of His coming, and herein lay the stress of his apologia for it.

The Messiah came to save His people from their sins, and He was to accomplish this by death. For His words reported in xx. 28, taken over from Mark x. 45, make this clear. Jesus is trying to persuade His disciples to a life of self-sacrifice for others, and He continues : ' Even as the Son of man came not to be ministered unto, but to minister, and to give his life a ransom for many.' His ministry, it will be observed, refers to the character of His daily life, but this was to culminate in His death, and His death was to be ' a ransom for many.'

The use of the simile of a ransom to describe the basis of a moral or spiritual transaction is very old. In Exod. xxi. 30 payment of a sum of money ' ransoms ' or ' redeems ' the life of the owner of an ox which has gored someone to death. In Num. xxxv. 31, 32, such a payment is expressly forbidden in the case of a wilful murderer. In Exod. xxx. 11–16 half a shekel is required from each Israelite to serve as ' a ransom for his soul unto the LORD.'[1] The metaphor would thus be intelligible at once in its broad meaning. The death of Jesus was to be the means whereby others were to be saved from death ; He in His death was to resemble the money-substitute still paid in the Temple ceremonies for lives actually due (xvii. 24). The idea of substitution, of vicariousness, in the death of the Messiah, is thus an important part of the doctrine of the Cross, according to St. Matthew. However strange the figure of speech may be to some,

---

[1] See also Job xxxiii. 24 ; xxxvi. 18 ; Ps. xlix. 7.

yet to the Evangelist and to Christ Himself it expressed solid truth, a part at least (we dare not say the whole) of the real facts ensuring peace between the believer and God.[1]

I say ' the believer '—for underlying the whole of this Gospel is the thought that apart from faith in Christ there is no benefit received from His life or death. Nothing was further from the Evangelist's mind than a mechanical change on the part of God towards man brought about by the mere advent and death of Christ, without personal faith upon Him exercised by the individual. Believers, and believers only, are benefited by the coming of the Messiah. Not indeed that we can read this into the word ' many,' found in our passage in St. Matthew, as contrasted with the ' all ' of St. Paul's Epistle (1 Tim. ii. 6), for it is probable that ' many ' serves here as in Rom. v. 15, 19, to indicate the contrast with the One who died. But it appears to be inherent in the validity and general effect of Christ's coming. The limitation of the word to believers does not lie in the word itself, but in the nature of the case.

Another valuation of our Lord's death is contained in His words at the Last Supper : ' This is my blood of the covenant, which is shed for many unto remission of sins ' (xxvi. 28), also taken over from Mark (xiv. 24), with the addition of ' unto remission of sins.' Here the Messiah regards His death not under the simile of a monetary or juridical transaction, but under that of a covenant or testament. His words recall, and probably were intended to recall, the

---

[1] The preposition in xx. 28 ($\mathit{\dot{a}\nu\tau\acute{\iota}}$) properly indicates correspondence, and so vicariousness (ii. 22 ; v. 38 ; xvii. 27), but even if this meaning cannot be pressed, in view of its occasional wider and freer use, the same idea lies in ' ransom ' and its associations.

covenant of blood made between the Jewish nation and God, whether that be circumcision (Gen. xvii. 10, 11 ; *cf.* Zech. ix. 11), or the solemn consecration of the nation recorded in Exod. xxiv. 5-8. With whichever reference He used the phrase, His death was to mark the entrance upon a new and consecrated life for those who received its benefits, a mingling of His life with theirs, a pledge of abiding union and incorporation with Him.[1]

His death, then, was no accident, nor was it unexpected by Him ; much less was it the frustration of His plans and hopes. It was a *causa causans* of His advent, to win for His followers a new, a happier, and a holier state with God. The death of the Messiah, in this fuller message of our Evangelist, was not only a ransom, but also the visible sign and means of the entry of believers into a fresh life, as members of a truly priestly nation, consecrated by blood, Messiah's blood of the covenant.

Yet as the thoughts of ransom, consecration, and incorporation are far from exhausting the interpretation of the death of Christ given to us in other books of the New Testament, so even in St. Matthew we may find a trace of something more. It is at least noticeable that he connects Christ with Isaiah's Servant of the LORD, not only in the words spoken at the Baptism and the Transfiguration (as we have seen), but also directly. In xii. 18-21 he quotes Isa. xlii. 1-4 of Him, a passage which lays stress on the absence of all self-consciousness and desire for

---

[1] In primitive times, and among savage races to-day, blood is drunk or imparted as the seat of life, or rather as life and vigour itself, and so as the pledge of fellowship and friendship. Wine became used as a representation of blood. See Trumbull, *The Blood Covenant*, 1887, *passim*, especially pp. 201, 289.

self-advancement on the part of the Servant, on His tenderness and thought for the crushed and the weak, and yet ends with a glorious promise of His final victory, and the recognition of Him by the world.

Another reference to the Messiah as the Servant is more mysterious. In viii. 16, 17, after describing the miracle of healing Peter's wife's mother, St. Matthew adds : 'And when even was come, they brought unto him many possessed with devils : and he cast out the spirits with a word, and healed all that were sick : that it might be fulfilled which was written by Isaiah the prophet, saying, Himself took our infirmities, and bare our diseases,' a quotation of Isa. liii. 4 : ' Surely he hath borne our griefs (Heb. ' sicknesses,' R.V. marg.), and carried our sorrows.'

What does the Evangelist mean ? Plainly not that the Lord Jesus endured the actual illnesses from which He cured others, for we never see in Him any trace of ill-health. Yet the terms ' take,' ' bear,' ' carry,' imply some kind of personal reception of the burdens named. What kind ? Partly, no doubt, the burden of the expenditure of that ' virtue,' that nervous force, that vital energy, physical, mental, and spiritual, to which He expressly refers at His miracle of healing the woman with the issue of blood.[1]

But this is hardly sufficient. The Evangelist appears to suggest a heavier burden. Can it be that he is thinking of our Lord as bearing upon Himself not the outer forms of disease, which, after all, are nothing more than the mere symptoms of ill, but their final cause, the origin of them all, the innate evil of sin ? It will be said that this is Pauline,[2] and that

---

[1] Mark v. 30 and Luke viii. 46 ; *cf.* also Luke vi. 19.
[2] 1 Cor. xi. 30 ; *cf.* also Rom. v. 12.

THE BEARING OF SIN

no hint of it seems to occur elsewhere in our Gospel, but if, as may well have been the case, it was a commonplace among the Hebrew-Christians for whom St. Matthew wrote,[1] he would be satisfied with referring, as he did, to the fifty-third chapter of Isaiah, knowing that his fellow-believers would at once grasp the intention of that reference, namely, to identify Jesus as the bearer of sin with the Sufferer there described, carrying it visibly, as we might almost say, in His removal of illnesses, and in fact and reality when He died upon the Cross. For there He took upon Himself the sin that belonged to all men, that so He might be able to annul the consequences of sin in particular men. He could remove men's illnesses because He was about to bear their sins.[2]

We must then add to those conceptions of the value of Christ's death which we have already found in the pages of our Gospel, namely, that it was to be a ransom and an inauguration of a new life; this also, that it was in some sense the bearing of sin, with the possibility of the final removal of evil in all its forms from those who come into personal contact with Him.

What St. Matthew would have understood that bearing of sin to mean, if he had worked the phrase out with any deep theological reasoning, we cannot say, and perhaps need not attempt to guess. To him as a Jew the figure of speech—for it cannot be more than a figure when we are dealing with eternal verities—suggested a victim such as the scapegoat, upon which, in symbolical fashion, the people's sins were laid,[3] or the lamb which was slain at Passover.[4]

---

[1] *Cf.* James i. 15.
[2] *Cf.* F. D. Maurice in Moberly, *Atonement and Personality*, 1911, p. 385.
[3] Lev. xvi. 21 *sq.*   [4] *Cf.* Isa. liii. 7, 12.

Jews, non-Christian Jews, might, and did, find the Cross of the Messiah a stumbling-block, but to the believer, the Christian, be he Jew or Gentile, it stood for the supremest act of self-sacrifice, the voluntary incurring of all that was involved in the presence of sin. Perhaps it was this that forced from the dying Christ the agonising cry: 'My God, my God, why hast thou forsaken me,' for with sin borne (however we may define the nature of the bearing) He could, for the moment, have no communion with His Father. Sin, unknown to Him before, must bring separation.

And then He died! Nay, not then. For although the Evangelist does not hint at any alteration in the experience of Jesus after that awful cry, he leaves room for such a change as is implied in other Gospels.[1] For after stating the anguish of separation (*v.* 46) he adds (*v.* 50): 'And Jesus cried again with a loud voice, and yielded up his spirit.' St. Matthew perhaps did not wish to tell us of Jesus' peaceful committal of Himself into His Father's hands; rather was he anxious to set before us the extremity of the Messiah's suffering, and its pathos.

But at this point the writer hastens on to show that though the Jews rejoiced at the consummation of the murder, and though Jesus drank of the cup of suffering to the very dregs, nature sympathised with Him, the saints arose, and the centurion himself, typical of the Gentile world, acknowledged the uprightness of Him whom he crucified.[2]

Thus even in that crucifixion of the Messiah, which to the Jewish mind of all ages has seemed to be nothing else than a crowning defeat and an irre-

---
[1] Luke xxiii. 46; John xix. 30. [2] *Cf.* Lecture IX, p. 317.

mediable disaster, there are rays of hope and of righteousness. For in spite of His crucifixion Jesus was still honoured.

But the Evangelist himself had far surer grounds of faith in Christ than this. For, as he will show in the few remaining verses of his Gospel, the trustworthiness of the Saviour was vindicated by His victory over death, His supremacy in creation, His claim to world-wide allegiance, and His everlasting presence with His people.

Lecture Twelve

THE MESSIAH—THE VICTOR

'Lo, I am with you alway, even unto the end of the world.'—MATT. xxviii. 20.

Lecture Twelve

THE MESSIAH—THE VICTOR

AT the close of the last Lecture we saw reason to believe that even in the death of Jesus there was encouragement, patent to one who recalled it as a believer in Him, and had eyes to see and ears to hear. But St. Matthew cannot end his Gospel thus. He will tell of the Resurrection and the Triumph.[1]

He was writing, we must remember, to Jewish-Christians, and it was not his business to tell all he knew about the Lord's resurrection, but only such incidents connected with it as were likely to strengthen his readers against the attacks made on their faith by the Jews, or to lay before them more of the meaning of it as taught by the Lord Himself. Perhaps we shall do well to consider, first, St. Matthew's reply to Jewish opponents; secondly, the true nature of the Lord's resurrection; thirdly, the Lord's final charge to His disciples.

I. St. Matthew's reply to Jewish opponents. The grave, he tells us, was empty: Jesus, says the angel, ' is not here; for he is risen, even as he said. Come, see the place where the Lord lay ' (xxviii. 6). The Jews have never denied that the tomb was

---

[1] Perhaps the fullest discussion of the whole subject is Dr. Sparrow Simpson's *The Resurrection and Modern Thought*, 1911. Dr. J. Orr's *The Resurrection of Jesus*, 1908, is also excellent, but rather more popular. Dr. Headlam's essay in his *Miracles of the New Testament*, 1914, pp. 244-268, was published after the following pages were written.

empty. They do deny that Jesus left it, save as a corpse carried out by human hands.

As they vilified the Birth of our Lord;[1] as they attacked Him for His miracles;[2] as they misquoted His words about the Law, and misinterpreted His attitude towards it;[3] so they spread a lie about His resurrection. Various forms of this are found in Jewish books, but the innuendo is essentially the same in all, that the body of Jesus was secretly removed.[4]

According to one form of the story, the disciples themselves were the violators of the tomb, in order that they might appeal to it in support of their assertion that Jesus had risen, and this is the tale known to the Evangelist. But he says that the facts of the case show its worthlessness.

For the Jewish authorities themselves had been afraid lest such an attempt should be made, and had obtained permission from the Roman Governor to affix a cord stamped with their seals to the stone door and the solid rock, and also to set a guard of soldiers until the third day, that thus all possibility of fraud might be excluded. The Evangelist tells us further that when the tomb was found empty, in spite of all these precautions, the chief priests bribed the soldiers to say that while they slept the disciples came and stole the body, adding that if the Governor should happen to hear anything of the

---

[1] See Lecture I.   [2] See Lecture III.   [3] See Lectures IV to VI.

[4] The *Toledoth Jeshu*, in some recensions, says that Judah the gardener (=Judas Iscariot) stole the body out of the tomb to prevent the disciples taking it away and saying He had risen. Judah buried it in his garden and turned a stream over it to prevent his garden being trodden. Krauss, *Das Leben Jesu nach jüdischen Quellen*, 1902, pp. 46, 80, 121, 129. *Cf.* also Tertullian, *De Spectac.*, § 30.

story, the soldiers need have no anxiety, for they would make it right with him.

Now, we can all see the difficulties that lie on the very surface of this statement, especially if we choose to strain it and make it say more than it does say.

For example, if St. Matthew's statement is true, why, it is asked, does St. Mark make no mention of the incident? For although much has been attributed to the missing conclusion of the Second Gospel, in deductions drawn from very slight evidence, there is no reason to suppose that this story ever formed part of it. But we may fairly retort: What reason is there to suppose that St. Mark would have cared to record it? He was not writing to Jewish-Christians but to Gentile, who were not likely to have heard the calumny. Besides, one cannot put everything into a twenty-paged tract.

Again, the question is raised: How should the Jewish leaders be 'quite well acquainted with the belief that Jesus would rise from the dead, whereas it is clear from the gospels generally that this belief was not common? Even if it be conceded that Christ prophesied His resurrection, it is at least plain that these prophecies were not understood by the disciples until after the event. It is therefore extremely unlikely that the Jews were so afraid of an attempt by the disciples to secure a false fulfilment, or that they understood Christ's prophecy before the disciples themselves.'[1]

Yet this way of putting the case overlooks one or two points in psychology. It was one thing for the disciples, when their minds were full of the coming

[1] Kirsopp Lake, *The Historical Evidence for the Resurrection of Jesus Christ*, 1907, p. 179.

glory of the Messianic kingdom and of the triumph of their King, to fail to attach any definite meaning to His predictions of death and resurrection, or, when they had seen Him die, to be unable at once to grasp that the second part of His announcement would be performed as literally as the first, and quite another for sharp-witted and unscrupulous enemies to remember the words, and to fear lest the disciples should presume upon them and use them as they chose.

Further, we know from the Gospels elsewhere that the idea that a person might rise from the dead, particularly a godly person, and more particularly perhaps one who had died a violent death,[1] was not unknown in Palestine.[2] If so, it is possible that the Jewish leaders may have feared the growth of such a belief about Jesus, without having actually known of His prediction. This would at least account for their action, though we should have to explain their words on the principle that St. Matthew put his own interpretation on what they did.[3]

Again, it is said that it is impossible that Roman soldiers would have escaped punishment if the grave was found empty, and would hardly have received bribes for saying that they were asleep when on military duty, a confession that would have brought them death.[4] Quite so, but this only shows that every early reader of the Gospel who lived when Romans ruled would have at once understood that the guards were not Roman. With a Jewish guard

---

[1] Baldensperger, *Urchristliche Apologie. Die älteste Auferstehungskontroverse*, 1909, pp. 14 sq.; J. Weiss, *Das Urchristentum*, 1914, p. 62.

[2] xiv. 2. See Mark vi. 14; Luke ix. 7.

[3] That they knew of the phrase 'the third day' is evident from xxvi. 61; xxvii. 40.

[4] Kirsopp Lake, *op. cit.* p. 178.

XII] THE NATURE OF HIS RESURRECTION

responsible, strictly speaking, to the High Priests alone, all difficulty ceases. For it is quite intelligible that it would still have been necessary to ask Pilate's leave to set a guard over the grave of a criminal put to death by his authority.

Although, then, we are not now able to test the truth of St. Matthew's statement, we can say that it contains nothing so improbable as to outweigh his evidence.[1]

His answer to His Jewish opponents is clear. Both the Jews and the Christians of St. Matthew's day agreed in this—that on the third day the tomb was empty. His arguments show that the tale of fraud was unfounded, and was disproved by the very action which the Jewish authorities had taken. Human hands had not carried the body of Jesus out of the tomb.[2]

II. What, then, was the true nature of our Lord's resurrection? In particular, is it right for us to-day to speak of the resurrection of His body, and if so what do we understand by this?

Now, it is said by many[3] that to the Jews of that time no other kind of resurrection than a bodily resurrection seemed possible, and that therefore

---

[1] There is no reason to suppose that there was not time to seal the stone before the commencement of the Sabbath, or, on the other hand, that even if the Sabbath had begun unscrupulous Sadducees would have hesitated to break the Sabbath laws, should they have thought it necessary to do so (against Kirsopp Lake, *ibid.*).

[2] Dr. Kirsopp Lake seriously suggested that the women made a mistake in their identification of the tomb in which our Lord was buried (*op. cit.* p. 250). But in his latest book he says: 'We may concede the fact that the tomb was empty' (*The Stewardship of Faith*, 1915, p. 51). Canon Streeter seems to think that the Romans removed the body, fearing a possible disturbance (*Foundations*, p. 134).

[3] Baldensperger, *op. cit.* p. 11, note 3; Kirsopp Lake, *Resurrection*, pp. 238, 241 *sq.*, 277.

when the Apostles saw Jesus they thought His body must necessarily have risen also, but that we, on the contrary, are able to imagine a resurrection of the Lord although His body was left to decay.

Jesus, it is alleged, passed unscathed in His essential nature through that separation of body and soul which we call death, and made His continued existence apart from His body known to His followers. Some writers, indeed, are of opinion that His appearance was only the projection of an image formed within the mind. He produced only a subjective impression of His personality.[1] But others [2] feel themselves obliged to grant that the impression was objective, caused by a real external revelation of Himself, living and moving outside the persons to whom He appeared.

If so, however, we may frankly ask wherein lay the speciality, the new and unique fact which appealed so strongly to the Apostles? All Jews of the time, except perhaps the Sadducees, believed that at least the righteous survived after death, and for the Apostles to be now convinced only to this extent that Jesus had so survived would put them in very little better position than they had been before. Even a

---

[1] Baldensperger, *op. cit.* p. 12, note 4; J. Weiss, *Das Urchristentum*, 1914, p. 20.

[2] Kirsopp Lake, *Resurr.*, pp. 266 *sq.*, 271, 275 ('not as the resurrection of a material body, but as the manifestation of a surviving personality'), 277. 'I certainly shall not complain of being misunderstood,' writes Canon Streeter, 'if . . . anyone . . . avers that I regard the question whether our Lord was "more risen" (whatever that may mean) on Easter Sunday than on the preceding day, as wholly unimportant. That is exactly what I do think; and I do not profess to know, or think it important to know, exactly what became of the material particles of the Body which was laid in the tomb' (*Guardian*, May 6, 1915). Canon Streeter, in fact, would be quite satisfied with the doctrine that our Lord's Body lay rotting in the tomb, though His personality survived.

NOT MERE SURVIVAL

Saul knew that Samuel survived death, and that the prophet took an interest in him, but he was not much benefited by this knowledge. It is incredible that the story of the resurrection of our Lord should mean in reality no more than that.[1]

For not only St. Peter and St. John, St. Matthew and St. Mark, but the whole body of primitive Christians, nay, the universal Church from the third day until now, imply that something took place which was much more remarkable than the assurance, however vivid and however convincing, that Jesus had survived His death. The Society for Psychical Research claims to have almost proved this much of ordinary individuals.[2] Was there nothing more in

[1] This theory is profoundly religious, but 'it reduces the appearances of our Lord simply to certificates of the satisfactory condition of Jesus of Nazareth in the other world' (Sparrow Simpson, *op. cit.* p. 119).

[2] See Kirsopp Lake (*Resurr.*, p. 245), who is still more ready to acknowledge the claim in his *Stewardship of Faith*, p. 140. Mr. F. W. H. Myers writes in a well-known passage: 'I venture now on a bold saying; for I predict that, in consequence of the new evidence, all reasonable men, a century hence, will believe the Resurrection of Christ, whereas, in default of the new evidence, no reasonable men, a century hence, would have believed it. . . . As a matter of fact—or, if you prefer the phrase, in my own personal opinion—our research has led us to results of a quite different type. They have not been negative only, but largely positive. We have shown that amid much deception and self-deception, fraud and illusion, veritable manifestations do reach us from beyond the grave. The central claim of Christianity is thus confirmed, as never before. If our own friends, men like ourselves, can sometimes return to tell us of love and hope, a mightier Spirit may well have used the eternal laws with a more commanding power' (*Human Personality*, ii. p. 288). Sir Oliver Lodge is reported as speaking even more strongly: 'I know that certain friends of mine still exist, because I have talked to them. Communication is possible. One must obey the laws, find out the conditions. I do not say it is easy, but I say it is possible, and I have conversed with them as I could converse with anyone in this audience now. Being scientific men they have given proof that it is real, not impersonation, not something emanating from myself. They have given definite proofs. Some of them are being published, many are being withheld for a time, but will be published later' (*The Times*, Nov. 23, 1914).

THE HEBREW-CHRISTIAN MESSIAH [LECT.

the case of Jesus ? Intrinsic probabilities require a real resurrection of His body, not a mere survival of His personality.

Yet it is alleged that even St. Paul implies the contrary, and, although the teaching of St. Paul falls outside the immediate subject of these Lectures, I trust that I shall be pardoned if I refer to him very briefly. For his words, as I believe, are misinterpreted in two contrary directions.

On the one hand, it is asserted that St. Paul did not accept the doctrine of the resurrection of the Lord's body because he abstained from mentioning the empty tomb, when he could have done so with great effect if he had known of it.[1] But the express reference to it was not necessary to his argument. It is at best only a negative proof, and St. Paul was concerned with enumerating the appearances of the Lord, that he might encourage his readers at Corinth in their hope of the glorious change that was to be theirs hereafter.

On the other hand, Dr. Kirsopp Lake thinks that St. Paul did believe in the empty tomb, but insists that he held that our Lord's body was at once changed into spirit. He deduces this from St. Paul's statement that ' flesh and blood cannot inherit the kingdom of God ' (1 Cor. xv. 50).[2] This is rather a subtle

---

[1] 1 Cor. xv. 3-8. See Baldensperger, *op. cit.* p. 17 : ' Er, unser älteste Zeuge für die Auferstehung, scheint von der Erzählung über das offene Grab, die erst die Evangelien bringen, nichts zu wissen.' Yet to the plain reader the connexion in *vv.* 3-5, 'Christ died . . . and was buried . . . and hath been raised . . . and appeared,' suggests *bodily* death, burial, resurrection, and appearance. See further Bishop Chase, *The Gospels in the Light of Historical Criticism,* 1914, pp. xx sq.

[2] ' The whole of St. Paul's argument that " flesh and blood cannot inherit the kingdom of heaven," and that " we shall be changed," would be meaningless if the special instance of Resurrection on which he based his reasoning had

distinction from the orthodox doctrine, and appears to be due to an unworthy fear of the grossness of matter as we commonly understand it, and a failure to appreciate the more philosophical view which is current to-day. After all, surely the natural interpretation of St. Paul's language is that flesh and blood *as we know them* cannot inherit the kingdom of heaven, and we shall all grant that this 'too solid flesh' of ours is unsuitable to be the perfect instrument of the soul, even in that quasi-heavenly state which Christ is depicted as enjoying between His resurrection and His ascension.

Yet in reality there is a wide difference between 'the transubstantiation of flesh and blood into spirit' and the common opinion. Dr. Kirsopp Lake's term 'spirit' here implies something other than matter; we mean, on the contrary, that His body remained matter, however glorified and transmuted. And St. Paul's sentence appears to be fully satisfied if we say that the elements composing Christ's body remained, but were glorified, and thus fitted for use in a higher sphere than earth. In fact, this is what the Apostle himself suggests in his succeeding verses : ' We shall not all sleep, but we shall all be changed, in a moment, in the twinkling of an eye, at the last trump : for the trumpet shall sound, and the dead shall be raised incorruptible, and we shall be changed' (*vv.* 51, 52). It is plain that at the trumpet summons we shall not slip out of our bodies, leaving them behind, and yet there is no reason to suppose that our bodies will be changed

been in reality a Resurrection of flesh and blood' (Kirsopp Lake, *Resurrection*, p. 220). Also : 'St. Paul's doctrine of the transubstantiation of flesh and blood into spirit implied a belief in an empty tomb' (*op. cit.* p. 192).

into spirit, in Dr. Kirsopp Lake's sense of the word. On the contrary, we must think of an immediate and glorious transmutation of body as well as of soul for those believers who are caught up in the air, when the Lord returns (1 Thess. iv. 17). And if this be true of the members can it not be true of the Head ? Will not the lightning-like process which will take place in ' us which are alive ' also have taken place in the Lord Jesus ? Is it not probable, then, that the material of His earthly body was permeated at once with spiritual power and heavenly capacities, though still His body, and not changed into ' spirit ' in any such sense that it ceased to be ' material ' ?

For it is not as though the resurrection of our Lord's body were an isolated fact, unconnected with His earlier life. We can see in this Gospel events preparatory for it, namely, the many examples of the influence of (shall we say ?) His mind, or rather His personality, over what we call matter.[1]

In particular, the nature miracles are examples of this, perhaps all of them, certainly the walking on the water,[2] and, in a different way, the Transfiguration.

The objectors, however, make short work with such premonitions of His supreme victory. They say that all these are fictitious stories, not facts at all, but only reflections from the legend of the resurrection.[3] His disciples believed that He rose again, and therefore regarded it as but fitting that during His earthly ministry He should have shown signs of superiority to the ordinary laws of Nature.

[1] See Lecture III.
[2] xiv. 25 ; *cf.* v. 29 ; *cf.* further Illingworth, *The Gospel Miracles*, 1915, pp. 135 *sqq.*
[3] Baldensperger, *op. cit.* pp. 26 *sqq.*

THE ENNOBLEMENT OF MATTER

But is criticism such as this more than arbitrary? Is it not, in the last resort, due to a disbelief in miracles? We have seen reasons in the third Lecture of this series to think that such unbelief is due to failure to consider both the circumstances in which our Lord's miracles were performed, and also the witness of secular history in all ages.

For we found reason to suppose that in the case of persons of remarkable holiness the so-called miraculous is not contrary to human experience, and that we are justified in regarding the miracles related of our Lord as events that really took place.

Further,[1] there is some reason for supposing that to-day even Science herself is making it easier to believe in the transformation and ennoblement of matter to such a degree that it can, under certain conditions, pass through solid objects such as stone and wood. Science at least hints to us that with an alteration in the rapidity of that internal motion which is indispensable to every kind of matter, its form visible, and, as we say, substantial, necessarily varies also, and that density and hardness (for example) may depend on the speed of the rotation of the molecules in each object. If so, it would seem to be not incredible that the physical Body of the Lord may have been changed, transmuted, transfigured, etherealised if you will, in its resurrection, without ceasing to be matter. One dare not indeed speak with any assurance on such a subject as the nature of the Lord's risen Body, but the fact that the tomb was empty forces upon us the question: What became of the matter of which that Body was composed? If any light at all is thrown upon this by

---

[1] I owe this paragraph to a suggestion made by a scientific friend.

the possibilities suggested by hints of Science we are compelled to take these into account.¹

III. We must pass on to our Lord's interpretation of His victory over death recorded in His final charge to His disciples.

They join Him in Galilee, as He had foretold (xxvi. 32). Why there ? Why not on the Mount of Olives, where indeed, according to St. Luke, they saw Him at the last ? It is difficult to say, but the reason is assuredly not to be found in the supposition that the disciples had fled to Galilee in unbelief and terror, and that it was there, there alone, that He really appeared to them, the appearances in Jerusalem being fictitious.²

But they meet Him there, the Eleven prostrating themselves in worship directly they see Him, while some of their companions doubted until He came nearer. Then these were sure it was He, and they too listened to His words in silence. And what words they are ! There is nothing that answers to them in the other Gospels, and nothing very like them in this. Yet they form the climax to St. Matthew's teaching, and focus his impressions of the Hebrew-Christian Messiah, his presentation of the Messiah to the Jews. We have already considered part of them in an earlier Lecture, but we must refer briefly to them now.

There are three chief thoughts in *vv.* 18–20, all

¹ *Cf.* C. H. Robinson, *Studies in the Resurrection of Christ*, 1911, p. 72 ; Orr, *op. cit.* p. 200 ; Sparrow Simpson, *op. cit.* pp. 412, 451 ; Dorner, *System of Christian Doctrine*, iv. 134 *sq.* ; R. O. P. Taylor, *The Athanasian Creed in the Twentieth Century*, 1911, pp. 139–144.

² Possibly the reasons for His choice of Galilee lay in His desire to free the minds of His disciples from too great a dependence on the narrower ideas current in the Jerusalem circle.

MATT. XXVIII. 18–20

satisfying the legitimate desires of Jews steeped in national hope based on scriptural promises. First, Messiah was to be supreme, and supremacy far beyond Jewish expectation is accorded to Him : 'All power is given to me in heaven and on earth.'[1] Jesus of Nazareth, poor in parentage, though not in descent ; unnoticed at birth by His own nation, though not by sages from afar ; persecuted by the rich and powerful, though followed by thousands of the poor ; executed as a felon, but victorious over death itself ; has now received the highest place of all in God's universe. Jews, therefore, may find their noblest aspirations for a Messiah (Ps. cx. 1) satisfied in Him.

Secondly, this supremacy is of such a kind that it embraces not Jews alone but Gentiles also. 'Go ye therefore, and make disciples of all the nations.' For although Hebrew-Christians were being taught to worship Jesus, as the Messiah who fulfilled the prophecies in general, and made the Law honourable, yet it was necessary that they should also learn to see in Him the one who was to accomplish the great and glorious promises of the ingathering of the Gentiles. The Hebrew-Christian Messiah was no narrow nationalist, holding them at arm's length, or admitting them to the full privileges of believers in Himself only when they had passed through the strait gate of Judaism. These last verses of St. Matthew's Gospel, on the contrary, fling the doors that lead into the palace of faith wide open for all the Gentile nations to enter in.

Nay, more than that. Not only are the Gentiles allowed to enter, but Jewish believers themselves

---

[1] It is perhaps worthy of notice that the wording of *vv.* 18, 19, suggests that of Dan. vii. 14 (LXX, not Theodotion).

are bid be active in admitting them.[1] And even if we do seem to hear echoes of a great controversy, and to distinguish the voice of St. Matthew taking part in it, yet we learn also the thoughts of the Master Himself, for we are taught His very words. Make disciples of all the nations, He says, requiring no ceremonial act for their admission save that of baptism into the Threefold Name,[2] but telling them their duties in accordance with My command—presumably, as we should say, telling them the inner meaning of the Law, with the spiritual duties that I set forth. Thus the Gospel message of salvation through Jesus is for the Gentile as well as for the Jew. Baptism is the rite of entrance for both; and ethics in the highest sense are required of the one as much as of the other. There is something strangely original in the nobility of this outlook, the limitation of the ritual, and the depth and width of the moral claim.

Lastly, there is the final promise of the continual presence of the Messiah with His people. For His ancient name, taken from the prophets, and suggested in the opening verses of the Gospel, ' Immanuel, which is, being interpreted, God with us ' (i. 23), is henceforth to take effect. He, very God as St. Matthew has portrayed Him, will be with us, without failure or intermission. Not one of His own shall ever be solitary, for, as He says, ' Lo, I am with you alway, even unto the end of the world.'

. . . .

We have thus come to the close of our enquiry

[1] That these believers of the Jewish race were addressed is evident, because when our Lord spoke there were no others.

[2] See Lecture IX, p. 322 *sq.*

SUMMARY OF THE LECTURES

into the character of the Messiah, as He was depicted by a Hebrew-Christian living in the end of the third quarter of the first century of our era. What have we learned from our study? In the first place, the thoroughly Jewish character of the document in which the presentation of Him is enshrined. It is Christian of course—but it is Jewish also, written for Jewish-Christians, and based throughout on Jewish modes of thought and of interpretation.

Secondly, when we endeavoured to understand the position and tenets of the Jewish parties, we saw that the Pharisees, accused of conscious deceit by some, and eulogised by others for their conscientiousness, lacked the one all-important quality of depth in spiritual religion.

Thirdly, when we consulted the miracles attributed to the Messiah, and remembered the wonders wrought by godly men in all ages, we perceived that although they do not afford direct witness to His divinity, they do supply evidence to the truth of the claim He made to be the Messiah sent by God.

Then, in the fourth, fifth, and sixth Lectures we touched on parts of the Evangelist's representation of the Messiah as a teacher, and we saw that although He used and assimilated what was best in the current ideas of His nation, yet no other man spake with so much originality of thought as He. The Lord's Prayer and His Commandment of Love were our illustrations. Further, we saw that He insisted on the permanence of the Law in its true meaning, and that He put forward ethical demands of so high and final a character as to meet all the desires and aspirations of those who are in touch with God, and are growing up into Him.

The seventh, eighth, and ninth Lectures dealt with three great phrases describing His personality, typical of the attitude of the Messiah to Jewish expectations. He fulfilled the title of the Son of David, but in a way far transcending the popular hope. He was the Son of man, for He answered to the twofold representation of manhood given in Ezekiel—man in his weakness and suffering, yet man akin to God, and therefore receptive of authority on earth, and to be made supreme hereafter. Yet He was also the Son of God. For the Evangelist, notwithstanding his monotheism, portrays Jesus as of superhuman origin, and even as divine in nature. Further, we ourselves, as we saw, could draw no other conclusion from the facts of His history.

Then came a Lecture, the tenth, on the relation of the Messiah to those obscure Jewish writers whom we call the Apocalyptists, for their hope of the early manifestation of divine power and righteousness, of God's judgment on a sinful world, and the establishment of His kingdom. Christ, as we saw, proclaimed the kingdom as at hand, yea, as already present, and yet as only to come in the future in all its fullness.

And so, in the eleventh Lecture, we passed by the Cross, and we gazed upon the sinless One hanging there; there by the will of the leaders of Judaism; there by the consent of the holy nation; there by the hands of Gentile tyrants; there, unable to save Himself, that thus He might save His people.

Last of all we have beheld Him, acknowledged even in dying by Nature, man, and Old Testament prophecy; victorious over death, seen of many, with the tomb empty not by human hands; claiming supreme authority, charging His own—Jews though they were—to go not to Jews only, but to all the nations of the world, and to admit these by baptism into union with the Triune God; and assuring His followers that He would be near them throughout all the days, whether dark or bright, till the completion, the consummation, of our age—'continua præsentia, eaque præsentissima.' [1]

The Christ of prophecy, the great Physician, the famous Teacher of the principles of the Law, the Davidic King, the perfect Man, Very God of Very God, the Inaugurator of the Divine rule, the willing Ransom, the Conqueror of the grave, who claims the obedience of the nations and is ever present with His people—such are the lineaments of the portrait of the Hebrew-Christian Messiah. 'This is my Beloved, and this is my Friend.'

[1] Bengel.

Index I

NAMES AND SUBJECTS

ABELSON, Dr. J., on the Kabbalah, 151
Abraham, son of, 15 *sq.*
Abrahams, I., on the legalism of Judaism, 196 *sq.*
Adam, The Second, 123 *sq.*; perhaps in our Lord's teaching, 306
Æsculapius, cures at his shrines, 103 *sq.*, 132 *sq.*
'*Almah*, 21 *sq.*
Amen, said to contain an oath, 226
American Episcopal Church accepts the principle of a Hebrew-Christian Church, 210
Angels as agents in healing, 105
Apocalyptists, The, the Messiah in relation to, Lect. X, 347-370; their teaching for the populace, 348 *sq.*; why their books were rejected by official Judaism, 350 *sq.*; their teaching a basis for Christianity, 351; their chief subject, 352-355; their doctrine of the Messiah, 355-358; our Lord's attitude to them, 358 *sq.*; apocalyptic teaching in Matt. threefold, 359-368; did our Lord teach a long lapse of time before His return? 359-368
Apollonius of Tyana, 121 *sq.*
Aramaic — Palestinian, of our Lord's time, not come down to us, 289
Asceticism, is it taught by our Lord? 224 *sq.*
Augustine, his doctrine of Grace has a legal tone, 203
Authority—External, insufficient for faith, 328-330

BACHER, W., on *Torah*, 195
Bacon, B. W., on *Haggadah*, 159

Baillie, J. B., on the ethics of institutions and individuals, 245
Baldensperger, W., on the Apocalyptic literature, 349; on our Lord's resurrection, 400-402, 404; on the nature miracles, 406
Baptism of Messiah, its reason, 38 *sq.*; the Voice, 40 *sq.*
'Bearing' sin, 390 *sq.*
Beer, G., on tradition, 158
Ben Pantera, 102
Ben Stada, 102
Bernard, Archbishop, on the miraculous in the Gospels, 98
Bernardino of Siena, S., on the *stigmata*, 139
Beth-lehem, 26-28
Betrothal and marriage, 20, 263
Bischoff, E., on the originality of our Lord, 162
Blasphemy, 68
Blood as the seat of life, 389
Body influenced by mind, 117 *sq.*, 139
Box, G. H., on Matt. i. 2-17, 16; on the Pharisees, 73, 82 *sq.*, 86
Bruce, A. B., on miracles, 97
Brückner, on Jewish eschatology, 367
Büchler, A., on the priests, 57, 84
Buddhism, its relation to Christianity, 144 *sq.*
Bushido and Christian ethics, 232
Buttenwieser, M., on the Messiah of Judaism, 257 *sq.*

CANCER, 118; miraculous cures of, 133 *sq.*
Catharine of Siena, St., miracles wrought by, 121, 135-138

INDEX I

Celibacy, commanded to Jeremiah, 224
Charity, Jewish teaching on, 220 sq., 226 sq.
Charles, Canon R. H., on our Lord's mistaken expectation, 363
Christian Science, how it differs from the Emmanuel Movement, 119
Christus Futurus, on evil powers, 107; on disease, 116
Church—Hebrew-Christian. *See* Hebrew-Christian Church
Chwolson, D., on Sadducean Scribes, 66; on the Pharisees, 81 sq., 84 sq.; on the intercourse of Jews with Jewish-Christians, 88, 151; on oaths, 220; on the responsibility for the Crucifixion, 377 sq.
Clouston, Sir T., on the brain, 117
Cohen, P., on a Hebrew-Christian Church, 211, 213
Covenant of Christ's death, 388 sq.
Crucifixion, The, Lect. XI, 373–393

Dalman, G. H., on 'the Son of man' in Aramaic, 289; on 'the Son of God,' 318, 320, 322
Dampier, Miss, on a Hebrew-Christian Church, 211
Dante, on hypocrites, 89; on nearness to the centre of light, 160 sq.
D'Arcy, Bishop, on miracles, 129 sq.
Dead restored to life, 119
Death, two stages in, 119
Death of Christ, the responsibility for, 373–381; He expected it from the first, 381–383; its value and effect, 381–393; the real reasons for it, 384–393; its effect not mechanical, 388; a 'covenant,' 388 sq.
Demons. *See* Evil spirits
Denney, J., on love to others, 241, cf. 243

Discourses of our Lord, how far in their original form, 156 sq.
Diseases, 'functional' and 'organic,' 113 sq., 114–118; punishment for sin, 125. *See* Miracles.
Divorce, 223–225
Doxology, The, why omitted in New Testament, 162

Edersheim on Matt. viii. 14, 101
Eighteen Benedictions, The. See Shemoneh Esreh
Elijah, his relation to Messiah, 35–37
Emmanuel Movement, The, 119
Enoch, Book of, probably known to many in our Lord's time, 285 sq., cf. 351
Esmun, 103
Essenes, no real connexion with the Baptist or our Lord, 51–53; and oaths, 226
Ethical demands made by the Messiah, Lect. VI, 217–246; much well known to Jewish teachers, 217–223
Ethics, essentially one, for individuals and society, 245 sq.
Evil spirits, dread of, to-day, 108; and the Messiah, 267 sq.

Facts as the basis of spiritual truths, 260
Faith-healing, 114–119
Feuerbach, A., on the treatment of an enemy, 173
Frederick the Great on the treatment of an enemy, 173 sq.
Friedlander, G., on the originality of the Lord's Prayer, 162 sq.; on Matt. v. 20, 200 sq.; on the impossibility of our Lord's requirements, 224; on our Lord's teaching about wealth, 227; on the Sermon on the Mount in general, 235, 236 sq., 244
Friedländer, M., on the influence of Greek-speaking Jews in Palestine, 7, cf. 349

INDEX I

GALILEE—why Messiah began His work there, 46 sq.; said to be the centre of Palestinian Demonology, 108; Gentile till c. 100 B.C., 262; why Christ there after the Resurrection, 408
Gaster, Dr., no Christians can be Jews, 213
Genealogy of Messiah, 14–20
Gentile Christians not considered in relation to the Law, 191 sq.
Gentiles to share the Gospel, 409
Gfrörer on ' David,' 16
Goodman, P., on the Sermon on the Mount, 229, 233, cf. 237
Gospel, The, not a new Law, 202–205
Greek, why chosen for the language of the First Gospel, 6 sq.
Greek thought, no direct influence on our Lord, 145 sq. See Hellenism
Gregory the Great regarded Christianity as Law, 203
Gressmann on ' the Son of man ' in the third person, 306
Guard at our Lord's tomb, Roman or Jewish? 400 sq.

HALDANE, Lord, on history, 330 sq.
Hamilton, M., on Incubation, Lect. III, *passim*
Harnack, on the cult of Æsculapius, 103 sq.
Hart, J. H. A., on the Pharisees, 73
Hebrew-Christians, their need of literature, 4 sq.
Hebrew-Christian Church, is it possible to-day? 193, 205–213
Heinrici on the Sermon on the Mount, 155, 157; on the Lord's Prayer, 163, 165
Heitmüller, W., on the historicity of the miracles, 99
Hellenism influenced our Lord through Apocalyptic thought, 146 sq.
Herford, R. T., on the Pharisees and our Lord, 84, cf. 91
Herods, The, and the title of king, 26

Hillel, on tradition, 158; on love to others, 171 sq.; forbade ostentation, 222
Hillelites, subordinate among Pharisees till 70 A.D., 75 sq.; sometimes treated Christians kindly, 88, 151; sometimes persecuted them, as shown in the case of St. Paul, 88
Holtzmann, H. J., on Matt. v. 20, 201
Humanity of our Lord not impersonal, 339–341
Humility before God, taught by Jews, 237 sq.; the essence of Christ's teaching, 238 sq.
Hypocrite, twofold use of the word by our Lord, 89–91

ILLINGWORTH, J. R., on miracles, 111; on matter and spirit, 334; on the Copernican astronomy, 336
Incarnation, in creation and in a Person, 335; this puny earth, 335 sq.; its object, 336 sq.; limitation of the activity of Divine attributes, 338
Incubation, 103 sq., 131–133, 139
Innocents, massacre of the, 31 sq.
' Interimsethik,' 363

JEHOVAH, the healer of disease, 105
Jehudah ha-Kadosh, kindly to Jewish-Christians, 88, 151, 209
Jeremias, A., on Isa. vii., 22 sq.
Jesus, Davidic origin of, 18, 261–272; Jewish arguments against His divinity, 43 sq.; both oral tradition and apocalyptic thought in His home, 148–150; to St. Matthew a teacher greater than the Rabbis, 152 sq.; as teacher, methods different from those of Rabbis, 158–162; the secret of His teaching, 160 sq., 176 sq.; suggestion that He was of Gentile origin, 261; Divinity of, growth of St. Matthew's

417   2 E

INDEX I

conviction of this, 326–328; why we believe it, 328–341; the irreducible minimum in the history of Him, 331 *sq.*; an acquired Godhead connotes idolatry, 332 *sq*; His Personality, 338–342; was He mistaken about the date of His return? 359–368; His return, the true nature of the consummation predicted, 368 *sq*. *See* Incarnation, Messiah

Jewish books, caution in using, 217 *sq.*

Jewish slanders rebutted, 19, 397–401

Jews, our present duty to, 8; the Jewish people blamed for the death of Christ, 380 *sq.*; the best representatives of the human race, yet crucified Jesus, 381

Jochanan ben Zakkai, R., his escape from Jerusalem, 3; his importance for Judaism, 153; a parable by him, 154

John the Baptist, 35–38

Joseph and Mary, 20, 263 *sq.*

KARAITES, have an oral Law, 212
King, the title as applied to Herods, 26
Kingdom of heaven, The, Lect. X, 347–370
Kirkpatrick, A. F., on 'fulfilment,' 188
Klausner, Jos., on the development of Messianic beliefs, 12 *sq.*
Knox, R A., on miracles, 123; on the authority of the Church, 329
Kohler, K., on the Pharisees, 80 *sq.*, 84; on *Torah*, 195

LAKE, Kirsopp, on our Lord's resurrection, 399–405
Languages, known by our Lord, 147
Law, The, if written requires oral interpretation, 63, 148, 186; permanent, but in what way? Lect. V, 181–205; Jewish teachers on its permanence or otherwise, 183–186; its literal observance not required by our Lord, 183 *sq.*; our Lord taught the permanence of its truths and principles in detail, 186–190; permanence of its principles taught by Jews, 190 *sq.*; are Gentile believers considered in relation to it? 191 *sq.*; are Jewish-Christians allowed to observe it literally? 193, 205–213; the meaning of the word, 194–198; St. Paul's language, 194–200; its fundamental difference from the Gospel, 201; the Gospel not a Law, 201-205; is it easy to be kept? 235

Law, The oral, not altogether rejected by Sadducees, 56; necessary, 63, 148, 186; nature of it in time of Christ uncertain, 149 *sq.*; indistinguishable from the written, in practice, 186, 211 *sq.*

Lectures, summary of these, 411–413

Leszynsky, his theory of the Sadducees, 58

Levi, Messiah to be of the stock of, 256

Lex, its meaning, 197

Liberal Judaism, Principles of, cited, 185

Lodge, Sir Oliver, on survival after death, 403

Loewe, H., on Demonology, 108

Lord's Prayer, The, 162–166; the test of true religion, 166; the antithesis to Pharisaism, 166

Lourdes, cures at, 104, 139

Love to enemies, 167–176; commended by Jewish teachers, 168–173; but never popular, 173; the centre of Christianity, 174–176; our Lord did not refer to treatment of Romans, 176; nor to parties among the Jews, or among the Pharisees, 176

Luzzatto, M., on ADaM, 123

INDEX I

McCabe, J., on telepathy, 125
Mackintosh, H. R., on Jesus becoming Son of God, 333; on Divine love, 338
Magi, The, 28 sq.
Mann, J. Dixon, on death, 119
Mansel, on miracles, 120
Mary, of Davidic stock, 264 sq.
Mason, A. J., on ' the Son of God,' 319
Masterman, E. W. G., on diseases in Palestine, 116
Matter, and spirit, 333–335; glorified at our Lord's resurrection, 405–408
Matthew, St., date of his Gospel, 3; used in these Lectures to = the unknown author of the First Gospel, 6; the object of his Gospel, 7; devotional character of his Gospel, 47 sq.; possible evidence for early date of its substance, 86 sq.; why he regards the Jewish leaders more harshly than St. Luke, 92; his character, 305; as a historian, 330 sq.
Medicine, Jewish knowledge of, 99–101
Meir, R., on man in Messianic times, 105
Messiah, representation current 25 A.D. difficult to learn, 11 sqq.; no reference to Him by a Palestinian Rabbi as early as 25 A.D., 12; representation of, modified by facts, 12 sq.; His originality, Lect. IV, 143–177; His preparation as a teacher, 143–152; a few said He was to be of the stock of Levi, 256; the Jewish, personally unattractive, 272 sq. See Jesus, Son of David
Messiah ben Joseph, 258
Miracles, Lect. III, 97–139; their place in evidence, 97, 107, 128–130; cannot be cut out of the Gospels, 98 sq.; their place in St. Matthew's presentation, 98–112; a subordinate reason for St. Matthew's relation of them, 112; attributed by Jews to our Lord, but as produced by Satan, 102 sq.; expected in Messianic times, 105; the Messiah's methods, 108–110; do not prove our Lord's divinity, 111 sq., 123; our Lord's, classified, 113 sq.; how were they wrought? 113–128; explanations of the classes of Christ's miracles, 114–120; ' Nature ' miracles, 120, 406 sq.; not wrought by our Lord as God, 123; human potentialities for, 124 sq., 126–128; non-Biblical, asserted monstrous cures, 118; wrought by what power? 121 sq.; heathen, 103 sq., 131–133; in early centuries of Christianity, 133 sq.; of the Middle Ages, 104; St. Thomas à Becket, 134 sq.; St. Catharine of Siena, 135–138; modern, 104, 138 sq.
Moberly, R. C., on miracles, 124; on impersonal humanity, 339; on the Atonement, 385, 391
Montefiore, C. G., on the Law, 195; on asceticism, 224 sq.; on our Lord's ' bias against the rich,' 228 sq.; on the impossibility of Jesus' demands, 233 sq.; praises the Sermon on the Mount, 240; on the Messiah as the Son of God, 315; on our Lord's Crucifixion, 376–378, 380
Mozley, J. B., on miracles, 120; on miracles and the Messiah, 129 sq.
Müller, Johannes, on the Good News, 236; on love to others, 241
Myers, F. W. H., on survival after death, 403

Nazarene, meaning of the appellation, 33
Neurotic theory of miracles, 115
Nomos, is it an accurate rendering of Torah? 194–199

INDEX I

OATHS, Jewish teaching concerning, 218-220, 225 sq.
Oesterley, W. O. E., on the Sadducees, 53, 57; on the Scribes, 64; on the Pharisees, 72 sq.
Oesterley and Box, on John the Baptist's invective, 62; on the Pharisees, 83, 85 bis, 86
Old Testament, Jesus uses Jewish methods of quotation, 157 sq.
Oral Law, The. See Law, the oral
Originality, its meaning, 164

PARABLES, Rabbinic, 154
Parseeism, no direct influence on our Lord, 145
Paul, St., a Hillelite, yet a persecutor, 88; his view of the Law, 194-200; not writing to theologians, 199 sq.; indicates a permanence in the Law, 200, 205; his occasional observance of Jewish customs, 209; and our Lord's resurrection, 404-406
Peile, J. H. F., on relieving distress, 241
Permanence of the Law, 183-191
Personality, what is it? 338 sq.
Pharisaic Christians perhaps sometimes in St. Matthew's mind, 93
Pharisees, 62-93 (esp. 72-93); connected with the Assidæans (Chasidim) of Maccabæan times, 72; meaning of word, 72 sq.; history of, 73-76; moulded nearly all Judaism after 70 A.D., 74; had no official power in the time of our Lord, 74, 378; their division into Hillelites and Shammaites, 74-76; our Lord's indictment of them, 76-80; praise of them by modern scholars, 80-83; explanations of our Lord's severity, 83-91; some had friendly relations with our Lord, 85 sq.; and some became Christians, 86; prayers composed by them, 91; St. Paul's verdict on, 91 sq.; blamed for the death of Christ, 378-380. See Hillelites, Shammaites
Prayer, ostentation in, 222
Purity, taught by Jews, 218. See Divorce

QUOTATIONS in the Gospel, after the Jewish methods, 24, 32, 33 sq., 157 sq.

RAMSAY, W. M., on restoration from death, 119
Ransom, Christ's death a, 387 sq.
Rawlinson, A. E. J., on miracles, 126
Reformed Jews, doctrines of, 185 sq.
Reinach, Théodore, on our Lord's Crucifixion, 374 sq.
Resurrection, especially of one who died a violent death, 400
Resurrection of Christ, The, Lect. XII, 397-413; Jewish attacks and St. Matthew's reply, 397-401; was it material? 401-408; wherein was it unique? 402 sq.; St. Paul on, 404-406
Richard, Dr. Timothy, on Buddhism, 145
Riches. See Wealth
Romans blamed for the death of Christ, 374 sq.
Ryle, R. J., on the Neurotic Theory of Miracles, 115

SADDUCEES, 53-62; the name from Zadok the High Priest, 53; but connoting opinions rather than lineal descent, 54 sq.; opposed to any Messianic movement, 55; the theology of, 56 sq.; portrayed in the *Assumption of Moses*, 57, and in the *Psalms of Solomon*, 61; literature attributed to them by some, 57; Leszynsky's theory, 58; their denial of the resurrection, 59

INDEX I

sq.; managed the temple till *c.* 63 A.D., 74; perished officially, 70 A.D., 74; blamed for the death of Christ, 375–378
Sanday, on the Sermon on the Mount, 244
Sanday and Headlam on Love, 175 *sq.*
Savage, H. E., on our Lord's doctrine of love, 176
Schechter, S., on the Torah, 190 *sq.*, 194 *sq.*
Schürer, on the preparation in Jewish thought for Christ's teaching, 144
Schweitzer, A., on mental delusions, being ascribed to our Lord, 230; his gruesome phantasy, 364
Science and the Resurrection of our Lord, 407 *sq.*
Scribes, 62–71; the professional students of the Law, 62; history of, 64–67; some perhaps reproved by Jeremiah, 64; in New Testament times chiefly laymen, 66; some perhaps Sadducees, 66; the progressive party, 67; some perhaps Christians, 67 *sq.*; the learned part of the Sanhedrin, 69 *sq.*; generally Pharisees and leaders of the Pharisaic party, 72
Sermon on the Mount, The, is it impracticable? 223–230; not a Code, 231; its supposed omissions, 231 *sq.*; compared with Lev. xix., 232 *sq.*; attacked by Jews, 232–4; for whom intended? 234–241; its precepts not to be obeyed blindly, 241–243; as regards society and the nation, 244–246
Servant, the, 302, 390 *sq.*; identification of Him with the Messiah revealed to Jesus, 381 *sq.*
Shammaites, supreme among Pharisees till 70 A.D., 75; their violence *c.* 44 A.D., 75; suggestion that these alone were the Pharisees attacked by our Lord, 86–89, *cf.* 176; differed from Hillelites in details, not principles, 87
Shemoneh Esreh (The Eighteen Benedictions), its connexion with the Lord's Prayer, 162–165; its inferiority, 164 *sq.*
Society for Psychical Research, its claims, 403
Son of David, The, Lect. VII, 249–273; in Old Testament, 251 *sq.*; in Apocrypha, 252; in Pseudepigrapha, 252–255; the earliest example of this title of Messiah, 253; in Talmudic and Rabbinic literature, 255–258; the typical Jewish idea of the Messiah, 41, 258 *sq.*; how applicable to Jesus? 259 *sq.*; Jesus such by birth, 260–266; Jesus addressed as such, 266–269; did our Lord reject the title? 270–272; Messiah in the Jewish conception is unattractive, 272 *sq.*
Son of God, The, Lect. IX, 311–343; exact phrase not in Old Testament, 312; Israel as God's sons, 312; Messiah as God's son in Old Testament, 313; in Apocalyptists, 313 *sq.*; Ps. ii. applied to Messiah, 314; Divine sonship attributed to Jesus in Matt., 315–325; growth of Evangelist's conviction of divinity of Jesus, 326–328; why we believe in the divinity of Jesus, 328–343
Son of man, The, Lect. VIII, 277–308; its connotation in Ezekiel, 278, 280, *cf.* 302 *sq.*; in Dan. vii., 279 *sq.*, *cf.* 303 *sq.*; in the Book of Enoch, 280–283; in 2 (4) Ezra, 283–285; in the New Testament, 285–301; why the title was not recognised as=Messiah, 285–287; not falsely attributed to our Lord by the Evangelists, 287 *sq.*; its meaning in the Aramaic used by our Lord, 288–290; three groups of passages, 291–301; the source of the phrase, 301–304; in Ezekiel, 302 *sq.*; in Apocalyptic writers, 303 *sq.*;

421

INDEX I

why it was our Lord's favourite title for Himself, 304 *sq.* ; why our Lord used the third person, 306 ; its anthropological teaching, 306 *sq.* ; its significance for ourselves, 307 *sq.*

Sources of Matthew, generally not important for these Lectures, 9 ; in his apocalyptic passages, 359–368

Streeter, B. H., on our Lord's temptation, 44 ; on Jewish Apocalypse, 358 *sq.* ; on our Lord's resurrection, 401 *sq.*

TACITUS, on the Jews, 168
Talmud, is it marked by love ? 172
Teaching of Christ had much in common with that of the Rabbis, 154–158
Telepathy, 125
Temptation of Messiah, its meaning, 41–45
Tertullian regarded the Gospel as Law, 202 *sq.*
Thomas à Becket, St., miracles connected with, 121, 134 *sq.*
Thompson, J. M., on Lazarus, 119 ; on the Nature-miracles, 120
Toledoth Jeshu, The, on the Birth of our Lord, 19 ; on the Resurrection of our Lord, 398
Tomb, the empty, 401–408. *See* The Resurrection of our Lord
Torah, the word discussed, 194–198 ; never means Law in the abstract, 197. *See* Law.
Transfiguration, The, 114, 406
Traub, G., on miracles, 120
Trench, Archbishop, on miracles, 97, 125
Trèves, the Holy Coat of, 104, 138
Trial of Jesus, difficulties in the narrative of, 377 *sq.*

UR-MENSCH, The, 280, 304

VIRGIN-BIRTH, The, 20–26 ; its value to St. Matthew, 24 *sq.*

Völter, D., on 'the Son of man' and Ezekiel, 279
Votaw on Matt. v. 18, 19 ; 181, 184

WARBURTON Lectures, trust-deed quoted, 9
Wealth, Jewish view of, 221 *sq.*, 227–229
Weinreich, O., on miracles and ancient thought, 113
Weiss, I. H., on the violence of the Shammaites, 76 ; on the differences between the Hillelites and the Shammaites, 87
Weiss, Joh., on the unlikeness of Jesus to the Jewish idea of Messiah, 41 ; on Jesus becoming Son of God, 333
Weitbrecht, H. U., on the loyalty of our Lord to the Old Testament, 222 *sq.*
Westcott, Bishop B. F., on our Lord's miracles 128
Weston, Bishop F., on the Personality of Christ, 340 *sq.*
Wine representing blood, 389
Winstanley, E. W., on Mark iii. 28 ; 295
Wise, Dr. Isaac, on our Lord's Crucifixion, 374–376
Worcester, E., on the Emmanuel Movement, 119
Worcester and McComb on the relation of man to God, 128
Works, the final test of character, 246
Wright, T. H., on the miraculous in the Gospels, 98 *sq.*

ZADOK, its form in the LXX and elsewhere, 53
Zadokite Fragments, The, provenance and date uncertain, 53, 57
Zahn, Th., on Matt. i. 2–17, 16 ; on history, 30 ; on 'the Son of God,' 319, 321 *sq.*

Index II

HOLY SCRIPTURE AND OTHER EARLY LITERATURE

(a) Old Testament

Lev. xix. ; 232
Deut. xxiv. 1-3 ; 188
2 Sam. vii. 8, 12, 13, 16 ; 251
Ps. ii. 7 ; 314
  cx. 1 ; 321 sq.
Isa. vii. 14 ; 21-24
  xlii. 1 ; 40 sq., 381
  liii. 4 ; 390 sq.
Jer. xxxi. (xxxviii.) 15 ; 31 sq.
Ezek. i. and ii. 1 ; 277 sq.
  xxxvi. 23-31 ; 163
Dan. vii. ; 279 sq.
Hosea xi. 1 ; 30
Micah v. 2 ; 27
  v. 3 ; 27 sq.
Zech. ix. 9 ; 268

(b) Apocrypha and Pseudepigrapha

2 (4) Esdras vi. 26 ; 35
  vii. 26-30 ; 255
  vii. 33-44 ; 354 sq.
  xii. 31-33 ; 254 sq.
  xii. 32-34 ; 356 sq.
  xiii. 1-13 ; 283 sq.
  xiii. 25 ; 284
Tobit iv. 15 ; 172
Ecclesiasticus xxxviii. 24, xxxix. 1, 2, 8, 9 ; 66
Psalms of Solomon xvii. xviii. ; 252 sq.
Enoch, Book of, i. 3-7, 9 ; 352
  xlvi. ; 280 sq.
  xlviii. ; 280 sq., 283
  xlviii. 2-7 ; 355 sq.
  lxii. ; 281 sq.
  xci. 14-17 ; 353
  xciv. 8, 9 ; 353 sq.
Enoch, Secrets of, xlix. 1 ; 220
  l. 3, 4 ; 171

Sibylline Oracles, iii. 46-50 ; 253
  iii. 652-657 ; 254
  v. 106-110 ; 254
  v. 293-305 ; 354
  v. 414-433 ; 356
Jubilees, Book of, x. 12, 13 ; 108
  xx. 4 ; 218
Testaments of the Twelve Patriarchs, 170 sq., 218, 221 sq.
Assumption of Moses, § vii., on the Sadducees, 57
Baruch, Syriac Apocalypse of, xl. 1-3 ; 254
  lxxii.-lxxiv. ; 357 sq.

(c) New Testament

Matt. i. 1 ; 14 sqq., 260
  i. 2-17 ; 16-20
  i. 18-25 ; 20-26
  i. 21 ; 386 sq.
  i. 23 ; 410
  ii. 1-12 ; 26-30
  ii. 13-15 ; 30
  ii. 15 ; 320
  ii. 16-18 ; 31 sq.
  ii. 19-23 ; 32-34
  iii. 1-15 ; 34-38
  iii. 7-12 ; 61 sq.
  iii. 16, 17 ; 39-41, 318 sq., 381 sq.
  iv. 1-11 ; 41-45
  iv. 12-16 ; 46 sq.
  v. 3 ; Lect. VI, 217-246
  v. 17-19 ; Lect. V., 181-205
  v. 20 ; 71, 200 sq.
  v. 27-32 ; 218, 223-225
  v. 32 ; 224
  v. 33-37 ; 219, 225 sq.
  v. 42 ; 220 sq., 226 sq.
  v. 43, 44 ; 167-176
  vi. 5 ; 222
  vi. 19-34 ; 221 sq., 227-230
  viii. 16, 17 ; 110, 125, 390 sq.

INDEX II

Matt. viii. 20 ; 291
  ix. 6 ; 293 sq.
  x. 23 ; 298
  xi. 25–27 ; 323–325
  xii. 8 ; 294 sq.
  xii. 14 ; 383
  xii. 27 ; 101
  xii. 32 ; 295 sq.
  xii. 21 ; 197
  xiii. 52 ; 67 sq.
  xv. 1–20 ; 86 sq.
  xvi. 1–4 ; 60
  xvi. 5–12 ; 61
  xvi. 13 ; 296 sq.
  xvi. 16 ; 317 sq.
  xvii. 5 ; 381 sq.
  xviii. 16 ; 188
  xix. 9 ; 224
  xix. 10–12 ; 223–225
  xix. 12 ; 230
  xix. 21 ; 189, 227
  xix. 28 ; 308
  xx. 23–33 ; 59 sq.
  xx. 28 ; 387 sq.
  xxi. 1–11 ; 268
  xxi. 12–16 ; 269
  xxi. 15 ; 70
  xxii. 32 ; 189
  xxii. 41–45 ; 270–272, 321 sq.
  xxiii. 16–22 ; 219, 225 sq.
  xxiii. 34 ; 67
  xxiv. ; 369 sq.
  xxiv. 36 ; 322
  xxvi. 28 ; 388 sq.
  xxvi. 63 ; 315
  xxvi. 64 ; 300 sq.
  xxvii. 46 ; 392
  xxvii. 51–53 ; 114
  xxvii. 62–66 ; 400 sq.
  xxviii. 11–15 ; 400 sq.
  xxviii. 16, 17 ; 408
  xxviii. 18–20 ; 408–410
  xxviii. 19 ; 322 sq.
Luke ii. 5 ; 263
1 Cor. xv. 3–8 ; 404. xv. 50 ; 404 sq.

(d) *Hellenistic and Patristic Literature*

Philo, *de Humanitate*, § 15 ; 171
  On the Ten Commandments, § 17 ; 219
  On the Special Laws, § 2 ; 219

Josephus, *War*, Preface, §§ 1, 2 ; 6
  II, viii. 6, 7, §§ 135, 139–142 ; 226
  II, viii. 14, § 166 ; 58
  Antt. X, xi. 7, §§ 277–281 ; 57
  XIII, x. 6, § 297 ; 56
  XVII. ii. 4 (§ 45) ; 106
Justin Martyr, *Dialogue*, § 67 ; 22
  § 68 ; 251
  § 69 ; 103
Chrysostom, *Matt. Hom.* xvi. 4 ; 182
  Act. Hom. v. 4 ; 202

(e) *Rabbinical Literature*

Mishna, *Berakoth*, v. 1 ; 238
  Sabbath, i. 4 ; 75
  Shebuoth, iv. 13 ; 219
  Pirqe Aboth, i. 3 ; 156
    i. 12 (13) ; 172
    ii. 19 ; 156
    iv. 19 ; 170
    v. 32 ; 149
    vi. 6 ; 159
Tosephta, *Berakoth*, i. 5 ; 238
  ii. 21 ; 222
  iii. 5 ; 238
  iii. 17 ; 237
  iii. 20 ; 222
  Sabbath, xi. (xii.) 15 ; 102
T.B. *Berakoth*, 43b ; 238
T.B. *Sabbath*, 31a ; 172
  67a ; 102
  104b ; 102
  116b ; 181
  153a ; 154
T.B. *Sukkah*, 52a ; 314
  52a, b ; 258
T.B. *Rosh ha-Shanah*, 7a, 19a ; 56
  25a ; 252
T.B. *Taanith*, 7b ; 168
T.B. *Megillah*, 15a ; 159
T.B. *Gittin*, 56a, b ; 3
T.B. *Baba Mezia*, 49a ; 220
T.B. *Sanhedrin*, 43a ; 33, 102
  67a ; 102
  90b ; 60
  98a ; 78 sq.
  97a ; 257
  98a ; 256
  98b ; 257

INDEX II

T.B. *Shebuoth*, 35a ; 219
  36a ; 220, 226
T.B. *Abodah Zarah*, 20a ; 218
  20b ; 238
T.B. *Chullin*, 87a ; 210
T.B. *Niddah*, 61b ; 183
T.J. *Berakoth*. ii. 4 (5a) ; 257
T.J. *Peah*, viii. 9 [8] (21b) ; 44
T.J. *Sabbath*, i. 4 (3c) ; 76
  xii. 4 (13d) ; 102
T.J. *Megillah*, i. 5 (7), 70d ; 183
Aboth d' R. Nathan, vi. ; 3
Megillath Taanith, iv. ; 58
Mekilta on Exod. xii. 26 ; 183
  on Exod. xix. 11 ; 105
Siphre on Deut. xi. 30 ; 65
Bereshith Rabba on Gen. xv. 18 ; 350
Shmoth Rabba on Exod. xiii. 2 ; 314
  § 28, on Exod. xx. 1 ; 64

Midrash Tehillim on Ps. cxlvi. 7 ; 183
Echa (Lam.) *Rabba*, i. 5 ; 3
Seder Olam, c. 3 ; 57
Pesikta Rabbathi, c. 15 ; 183
Yalqut Shimeoni on Ps. ii. 7 ; 314
Derek Erets Zuta, c. 10 ; 256 sq.

Berachya Ha Nakdan, *Masref*, § 13 ; 59
Maimonides, Introduction to *Sanhedrin*, x. ; 314
Rashi on T.B. *Sabb.*, 146a ; 105
Kimchi, D., on Isa. vii. 15 ; 22
  on Ezek. ii. 1 ; 278
Shulchan Arukh, Yore Dea, § 237. 6 ; 220
Isaac of Troki, R., *Chizzuk Emunah*, i. § 3 ; 259

www.ingramcontent.com/pod-product-compliance
Lightning Source LLC
Chambersburg PA
CBHW071138300426
44113CB00009B/1013